The Good Life Beyond Growth

Many countries have experienced a decline of economic growth for decades, an effect that was only aggravated by the recent global financial crisis. What if in the 21st century this is no longer an exception, but the general rule? Does an economy without growth necessarily bring hardship and crises, as is often assumed? Or could it be a chance for a better life? Authors have long argued that money added to an income that already secures basic needs no longer enhances well-being. Also, ecological constraints and a sinking global absorption capacity increasingly reduce the margin of profitability on investments. Efforts to restore growth politically, however, often lead to reduced levels of social protection, reduced ecological and health standards, unfair tax burdens and rising inequalities. Thus, it is time to dissolve the link between economic growth and the good life.

This book argues that a good life beyond growth is not only possible, but highly desirable. It conceptualises "the good life" as a fulfilled life that is embedded in social relations and at peace with nature, independent of a mounting availability of resources. In bringing together experts from different fields, this book opens an interdisciplinary discussion that has often been restricted to separate disciplines. Philosophers, sociologists, economists, and activists come together to discuss the political and social conditions of a good life in societies which no longer rely on economic growth and no longer call for an ever-expanding circle of extraction, consumption, pollution, waste, conflict, and psychological burnout. Read together, these essays will have a major impact on the debates about economic growth, economic and ecological justice, and the good life in times of crisis.

Hartmut Rosa is Professor of Sociology at the University of Jena, Co-director of the Kolleg Postwachstumsgesellschaften in Jena (with Klaus Dörre) and Director of the Max Weber Centre for Advanced Cultural and Social Studies at the University of Erfurt.

Christoph Henning is Junior Fellow for Philosophy at the Max Weber Centre for Advanced Cultural and Social Studies, University of Erfurt, Germany.

Routledge Studies in Ecological Economics

For a full list of titles in this series, please visit www.routledge.com/series/RSEE

The Good Life Beyond Growth

New Perspectives

**Edited by
Hartmut Rosa and
Christoph Henning**

LONDON AND NEW YORK

First published 2018 by Routledge

2 Park Square, Milton Park, Abingdon, Oxfordshire OX14 4RN
52 Vanderbilt Avenue, New York, NY 10017

Routledge is an imprint of the Taylor & Francis Group, an informa business

First issued in paperback 2019

British Library Cataloguing-in-Publication Data
A catalogue record for this book is available from the British Library

Library of Congress Cataloging-in-Publication Data
A catalog record for this book has been requested

ISBN: 978-1-138-68788-2 (hbk)
ISBN: 978-0-367-34044-5 (pbk)

Typeset in Times New Roman
by Apex CoVantage, LLC

Contents

Figures

Tables

Contributors

Alberto Acosta is an Ecuadorian economist. He is a professor and researcher at FLACSO-Ecuador, ex-minister of Energy and Mines, ex-President of the Constituent Assembly, ex-candidate for the Presidency of the Republic.

Klaus Dörre is Professor of Sociology at the Friedrich-Schiller-University Jena, Germany, and Co-director of the DFG research group on 'post-growth societies'. His latest works include (with B. Aulenbacher/M. Burawoy/J. Sittel, eds.): *Öffentliche Soziologie – Wissenschaft im Dialog mit der Gesellschaft.* Campus 2017; (with S. Lessenich/H. Rosa): *Sociology, Capitalism, Critique*, Verso 2015; and (with S. Lessenich/H. Rosa): Appropriation, Activation and Acceleration: The Escalatory Logics of Capitalist Modernity and the Crises of Dynamic Stabilization. In: *Theory, Culture & Society* 34.1 (2017), 53–73.

Dennis Eversberg is a post-doctoral researcher at the DFG research group on 'post-growth societies' at the Institute of Sociology, Friedrich-Schiller-University. His doctoral dissertation on dividualization in activating labor market policies appeared as Dividuell aktiviert. Wie Arbeitsmarktpolitik Subjektivitäten produziert (Campus) in 2014 and was awarded the German Sociological Association's dissertation prize the same year. His current research interests include the subjective limits to capitalist growth regimes, the sociology of growth critique and the Degrowth movement.

Martin Fritz is a post-doctoral researcher at the University of Bielefeld, Germany. He also works as a lecturer at the University of Osnabruck, Germany. He is interested in studying welfare regimes and eco-social policies. With Max Koch, he published several articles on these topics in journals such as *Ecological Economics* and the *Journal of Social Policy*.

Stefanie Graefe is a lecturer on Sociology, Friedrich-Schiller-Universität Jena. Her research interests include political sociology, subjectivity and social change, biopolitics and health studies, sociology of ageing, qualitative social research. Latest Publication: together with Ak Postwachstum (Eds.) 2016: *Wachstum – Krise und Kritik. Die Grenzen der kapitalistischen Lebensweise*, Frankfurt/New York (Campus).

Christoph Henning is Junior Fellow for Philosophy at the Max Weber Centre for Advanced Cultural and Social Studies, University of Erfurt, Germany. He worked in Switzerland for eight years; he also lived in Dresden, Leipzig, Berlin, Friedrichshafen, Greifswald and New York. His latest books include *Philosophy after Marx* (Brill 2014), a German introduction to theories of alienation (*Entfremdung zur Einführung*, Junius 2015), a book on political perfectionism (*Freiheit, Gleichheit, Entfaltung*, Campus 2015) and a volume on *happiness* (with D. Thomä/ O. Mitscherlich, eds.): *Glück: Ein interdisziplinäres Handbuch* (Metzler 2011).

Bettina Hollstein has been a research assistant to the Director of the Max Weber Centre for Advanced Cultural and Social Studies, at the University of Erfurt since 1998. She received her PhD in Mainz on Economic Ethics and Environment in Germany and France in 1994 and had positions in Cottbus and Bad Hersfeld. She is an editor of the *Journal for Business, Economics, and Ethics* (Zeitschrift für Wirtschafts- und Unternehmensethik). Her research interests are Economic Ethics, Action Theory, Pragmatism, Sustainability, Ecological and Feminist Ethics. Her last book is on volunteer work (*Ehrenamt verstehen: Eine handlungstheoretische Analyse*, Campus 2015).

Eva Illouz is a full professor of sociology at the Hebrew University in Jerusalem. Since October 2012 she has been President of Bezalel Academy of Art and Design. Since 2015, Illouz has been a professor at Paris' *École des hautes études en sciences sociales*. Her latest books include *Hard-Core Romance: 'Fifty Shades of Grey', Best-Sellers, and Society* (University of Chicago Press, 2014); *Why love hurts: A sociological explanation* (Wiley 2013); or *Cold Intimacies: The making of modern capitalism* (Polity 2007).

Max Koch is Professor of Social Policy in Lund, Sweden. His research has dealt with patterns of capitalist restructuring and their implications on social inequality, welfare and employment relations and the environment. His current work addresses climate change, 'sustainable welfare' and postgrowth societies. His recent books include *Capitalism and Climate Change. Theoretical Discussion, Historical Development and Policy Responses* (Palgrave 2012); *Non-Standard Employment in Europe: Paradigms, Prevalence and Policy Responses* (coedited with Martin Fritz; Palgrave 2013); *Sustainability and the Political Economy of Welfare* (coedited with Oksana Mont; Routledge 2016); and *Postgrowth and Wellbeing*: Challenges to Sustainable Welfare (with Milena Büchs; Palgrave 2017).

Ashish Kothari is a founding member of the Indian environmental group Kalpavriksh (www.kalpavriksh.org), taught at the Indian Institute of Public Administration, and has served in the guest faculty in several universities including as Mellon Fellow at Bowdoin College, USA. He coordinated India's National Biodiversity Strategy and Action Plan process, served on boards of Greenpeace International and India, Indian Society of Ecological Economics, World Commission on Protected Areas, IUCN Commission on Social, Economic and Environmental Policy, and Bombay Natural History Society. He helped to establish the IUCN Strategic Direction on Governance, Equity, Communities, and Livelihoods (TILCEPA) and the ICCA Consortium (www.

iccaconsortium.org). He is a founding member of Global Sustainability University. He is active in several peoples' movements, and a member of Indian government committees on National Wildlife Action Plan, Biological Diversity Act, Environmental Appraisal of River Valley Projects, and Implementation of Forest Rights Act. He initiated the Vikalp Sangam (Alternatives Confluence) process and website (www.vikalpsangam.org) to network development alternatives in India, and global dialogue process on Radical Ecological Democracy (http://radicalecologicaldemocracy.wordpress.com). He is the co-coordinator of the ACKNOWL-EJ project on transformative knowledge (www.worldsocialscience.org/activities/transformations/acknowl-ej). He has (co)authored or (co)edited over thirty books, including *Sharing Power* and *Churning the Earth*, two childrens' books, and over 300 articles (http://ashishkothari51.blogspot.in).

Serge Latouche is Professor Emeritus of Economics at the University of Orsay, France, and an 'objecteur de croissance'. He is a specialist in North-South economic and cultural relations and in the epistemology of the social sciences. He is one of the thinkers and most renowned partisans of the degrowth movement. His works include *Farewell to Growth* (Polity 2010), *Survivre au développement. De la décolonisation de l'imaginaire économique à la construction d'une société alternative* (Paris 2004).

Nicole Mayer-Ahuja is professor of sociology at University of Goettingen and Director of the SOFI (*Sociological Research Institute*). As a labour sociologist, her research has focused on the development of precarious work since 1973, on new forms of work organisation and control, and on transnational project work. Currently, she explores global perspectives on policies of precarisation and informalisation. Among her publications are: '*Everywhere is becoming the same'? Regulating IT-work between India and Germany*, Social Science Press 2014); *Wieder dienen lernen? Vom westdeutschen, Normalarbeitsverhältnis' zu prekärer Beschäftigung seit 1973*, Sigma 2003); Arbeit, Unsicherheit, Informalität. In: K.Dörre/D. Sauer/V. Wittke (eds.): *Kapitalismustheorie und Arbeit. Neue Ansätze soziologischer Kritik* (Labour Studies), Campus 2012, 289–301.

Manfred A. Max-Neef is Professor Emeritus of Ecological Economics at the Universidad Austral de Chile. He is a Chilean-German economist in the field of international development. His most important books are: *From the Outside Looking in: Experiences in Barefoot Economics* (Dag Hammarskjöld Foundation, 1982), *Human Scale Development* (Apex Press, 1991), and *Economics Unmasked* (with Philip B. Smith, Greenbooks, 2011). His books seek to counter the logic of economics with the ethics of well-being. He has worked for several UN agencies and between 1994 and 2002, he was Rector of the Universidad Austral de Chile in Valdivia. In 1983, he received the Right Livelihood Award (Alternative Nobel Prize). He holds honorary doctorates from Jordan, United States, Colombia (2) and Argentina (2), and has been the recipient of the University Award of Highest Honour from Japan.

John O'Neill is professor of political economy at the University of Manchester. He has written widely on philosophy, political economy and environmental policy. His books include *Markets, Deliberation and Environment* (Routledge, 2007), *The Market: Ethics, Knowledge and Politics* (Routledge, 1998) and *Ecology, Policy and Politics: Human Well-Being and the Natural World* (Routledge, 1993). He is co-author of *Environmental Values* (Routledge, 2008) with Alan Holland and Andrew Light. He has participated in a number of European and UK projects on environmental justice, climate change and biodiversity.

Felix Rauschmayer leads the research field of sustainability policy at the Department for Environmental Politics at the Helmholtz-Centre for Environmental Research, Leipzig. An Ecological Economist by training, his research interest lies in the construction of interdisciplinary models for transdisciplinary research in different fields of relevance to sustainability transitions. His latest works include (with Ortrud Lessmann): *The Capability Approach and Sustainability* (Routledge 2016); (with Ines Oman): *Sustainable Development: Capabilities, Needs, and Well-being* (Routledge 2012).

Hartmut Rosa is professor of sociology at the University of Jena, co-director of the DFG research group on 'post-growth societies' (with Klaus Dörre) and director of the Max Weber Centre for Advanced Cultural and Social Studies at the University of Erfurt. His latest works include *Resonanz: Eine Soziologie der Weltbeziehungen* (Suhrkamp 2016); *Social Acceleration: A New Theory of Modernity* (University Press 2015); (with K. Dörre/S. Lessenich, eds.): *Sociology, Capitalism, Critique* (Verso 2015); or *Alienation and Acceleration: Towards a Critical Theory of Late-Modern Temporality* (Arhus University Press 2012).

Andrew Sayer is professor of social theory and political economy at Lancaster University, UK, where he has worked for 23 years, following 21 years at Sussex University, UK. His main interests are inequality, normativity in everyday life, and the relation between philosophy and the social sciences. He has written eight books, the last two being *Why Things Matter to People: Social Science, Values and Ethical Life* (Cambridge University Press, 2011) and *Why We Can't Afford the Rich* (Policy Press, 2014).

Charles Taylor is a Canadian philosopher from Montreal, Quebec, and Professor Emeritus at McGill University. He is known for his contributions to political philosophy, the philosophy of social science, history of philosophy and intellectual history. This work has earned him the prestigious Kyoto Prize, the Templeton Prize, the Berggruen Prize for Philosophy, and the John W. Kluge Prize. His latest books include *The Language Animal: The Full Shape of the Human Linguistic Capacity*, Harvard (2016); (with H. Dreyfus): *Retrieving Realism* (Harvard UP 2011): *A Secular Age.* (Harvard UP 2007).

Michael J. Thompson is Associate Professor of Political Theory in the Dept. of Political Science at William Paterson University (USA). He is the author of *The Politics of Inequality* (Columbia University Press), *The Domestication of Critical Theory* (Rowman and Littlefield) and the forthcoming *The Republican*

Reinvention of Radicalism (Columbia University Press) as well as the editor of *The Palgrave Handbook for Critical Theory* (Palgrave Macmillan).

Philippe Van Parijs is a professor at the University of Louvain (Hoover Chair of Economic and Social Ethics) and a special guest professor at the University of Leuven. From 2004 to 2010 he was a visiting professor at Harvard University and from 2011 to 2015 at the University of Oxford. His books include *Real Freedom for All* (Oxford UP 1995), *Just Democracy* (ECPR 2011), *Linguistic Justice for Europe and for the World* (Oxford UP 2011, Suhrkamp 2014), *After the Storm. How to save democracy in Europe* (Lannoo 2015, with L. van Middelaar) and *Basic Income* (Harvard U.P. 2017, with Y. Vanderborght).

Yannick Vanderborght is professor of political science, Université Saint-Louis – Bruxelles and University of Louvain. His areas of interest are ethics, political sociology, comparative social policy and basic income. His latest works include: *Basic Income: An Anthology of Contemporary Research* (Wiley-Blackwell 2013, co-editor) and *Basic Income* (Harvard U.P. 2017, with Ph. Van Parijs).

Sarah C. White is Professor of International Development and Wellbeing at the University of Bath, UK. Her research concerns the ways that social identities, culture and relationships are engaged and represented in development processes. Since 2002, the main focus of her research has been well-being in developing countries, including an ESRC-DFID funded research project in Zambia and India, 2010–2014. In 2016–17 she holds a British Academy/ Leverhulme Senior Research Fellowship to work on relational well-being. Recent books are *Culture and Wellbeing: Method, Place, Policy* (Palgrave Macmillan, 2015), and *Wellbeing and Quality of Life Assessment. A Practical Guide* (Practical Action Publishing, 2014).

Good life beyond growth

An introduction

Hartmut Rosa & Christoph Henning

The criticism of economic growth has obtained acceptance in ever-wider circles recently. It is no longer evident that we need growth for modern societies to thrive. Social, cultural and political protests against the growth-dependence of contemporary societies, or against their growth-fetishisation, have become fairly widespread on a global level. Yet, a similar discussion was already prominent in the 1970s, mostly among leftist politicians and dissenting economists (from Mishan 1967 to Max-Neef 1982) or among alternative milieus which proposed alternative ways of life. These earlier debates were taking part in various regions of the globe, and they are worth reconsidering. Like its predecessor, the renewed criticism of growth coincides with a chronic and worldwide economic crisis. Many countries have experienced falling rates of economic growth for decades, an effect that was aggravated by the global financial and political crisis since 2008.[1] A detached observer could welcome this: the environmental crisis and its devastating effects on people especially in the south, as well as the widening inequality within and between nations, demand that humans share resources more equitably and use less energy and materials in order to reduce emissions and deforestation on a planetary scale. Endogenously falling growth rates could be used to implement some of the more demanding 'sustainable development goals' (UN 2016, see Kothari's comments in this volume). However, many governments, economic experts and industrial lobby groups are working towards the opposite end, thereby creating a 'consensus' in Western democracies that is passed on to the rest of the world. They try to *restore* economic growth politically, even if that translates into reduced levels of social security and social protection in general, reduced ecological and health standards, unfair tax burdens and a rising social inequality. It is dubious how these policies could contribute to a good life.

Now that the crisis has 'infected' politics as well, leading to the return of nationalism and a culture of hatred and xenophobia in many countries, it is the right time to call the dogma of growth into question. The function of the economy and of democratic politics should be to allow for a good life for people, to better, not to worsen their situation. If economic growth is no longer functional in this respect, we have to conceive of forms of a good life that no longer rely on an enforced regime of economic growth, and which oppose the belief in ever higher rates of production, consumption, waste and destruction, just for the sake of further enriching the material cosmos of the wealthy (Sayer 2014, Daly 2014).

Such a new perspective has to expect political resistance. Economic growth is not only a play with numbers over time, it is a concept deeply engrained in the social imaginaries and socio-economic structures of Western, post-1945 societies. We suggest that the social stability of dynamic growth societies rested on their capacity to increase economic and technical efficiency and material wealth. Economic growth played a major role in this dynamic stabilisation: it pacified social conflicts by providing employment and social security. By reducing social conflicts, the prospect of steady economic growth also justified the privatisation of the good life. The prospect of growth provided a justificatory basis for political decision-making, thus replacing a political debate about the good life as a goal for all citizens (for the depolitisation see Graefe and O'Neill in this volume). This is why the economic crises erode conventional theories of justice and corresponding political justifications. But it is also an impetus to rethink our conceptions of the good life. Why should these conceptions depend on growth? And is there any reason to further exclude alternative ideas from political debates?

The aim of this book is to demonstrate that a 'farewell to growth' (Latouche 2009) does not necessarily mean a decrease in the quality of life, as many economists and politicians still assume. To the contrary, there are many promising indicators suggesting that a 'good life beyond growth' is possible and even highly desirable (Muraca 2012). However, to achieve this we have to reconfigure some of modernity's central social imaginaries in order to decouple ideas of the good life from the logic of growth.[2] In this introduction we sketch why economic growth has become detrimental to core aspects of the good life today, and how it became such an inbuilt systemic mechanism in the western model of modernity that it still inspires politics in the 21st century, in spite of all its environmental and social costs. We will also introduce the papers in this volume which make headway in the direction of developing alternative visions.

The escalatory logic of growth in modernity: dynamic stabilisation

The defining feature of a modern society (or, in fact, a modern institution) seems to be that it can only stabilise itself dynamically.[3] More precisely, it can only reproduce its structure through an *increase* of some sort – quite regularly through economic growth, technological acceleration, and higher rates of cultural innovation. Hence, we suggest that a society is considered modern when it operates in a mode of 'dynamic stabilisation', i.e. when it systematically requires growth, innovation and acceleration for its structural reproduction and in order to maintain its socio-economic and institutional status quo (Rosa 2013).

At first glance, this definition appears to contain a contradiction: how can we talk of maintaining the status quo through innovation, acceleration and growth, i.e. through *change*? What is dynamic, and what is stable? Structural reproduction and reification of the status quo mean, firstly, the stabilisation of the basic institutional fabric of society, in particular the competitive market system, science, the educational and welfare institutions, the health system as well as the political and legal framework. Secondly, this refers to the basic structures of socio-economic stratification: the reproduction of class hierarchy and of what Bourdieu (1984) termed 'class fractions'. Thirdly, and perhaps most importantly, the status quo is defined by the operational logics of accumulation and distribution: the logic of capital accumulation and the very processes of growth, acceleration, activation and innovation themselves. Of course, many political, economic or educational institutions change their shape, form or composition over time, but what does not change are the systemic imperatives and requirements for augmentation, increase and escalation. This answer, however, raises other, serious questions: is modern society, then, equivalent to capitalist society? Does it simply mean 'capitalism' when we talk about the basic structures of modern society?

The capitalistic mode of production is a central motor, but dynamic stabilisation extends well beyond the economic sphere.[4] When we look at it historically, it turns out that the shift from an adaptive to a dynamic mode of stabilisation can be observed as a systematic transformation in *all* cardinal spheres of social life in Western countries which has been occurring, despite some historic predecessors, mainly from the 18th century onwards. Most obviously it can be found in the realm of the economy. The accounts of both Max Weber and Karl Marx vividly focus on this transformation. In a capitalist economy, virtually all economic activity depends on the expectation and promise of an *increase* in the sense of profit of one sort or another. Money – Commodity – Money' (m-c-m') is the short formula for this, where the prime signifies the increased return. It is realised through exploitation, innovation (of product or process) and acceleration, mostly in the form of increased productivity; the latter can be defined as an increase in output (or value production) per unit of time, i.e. as acceleration (for a critique of 'productivity' see Henning in this volume).

The need for innovation, acceleration and growth is intrinsic to the logic of capitalist production, to the logic of competition and the logic of the monetary and the credit systems (see Sayer in this volume). The net result of it is that without permanent growth, acceleration and innovation, at least under late-modern conditions of globalised economic and financial markets, capitalist economies can hardly maintain their institutional structures. Jobs are lost, companies close down and tax revenues decrease, while state-expenditure for welfare and infrastructural programs increases, which in turn tends to cause a severe budget-deficit at first and then a delegitimation of the political system. We saw this in the present crisis in Southern Europe, particularly in Greece, and in many other places worldwide. Thus, not just the economic system depends on the logic of escalation as a consequence of the dynamic stabilisation, but also the welfare-state and the system of democratic politics. As Niklas Luhmann (1990) has shown, the latter is based on dynamic stabilisation, too: not only has the rather static monarchical order – where monarchs rule for a lifetime and then are replaced by a dynastic succession that preserves order in an identical fashion – given way to a democratic system that requires dynamic stabilisation through repeated voting every few years, but, much more dramatically, elections can only be won on the basis of political programs that promise an *increase* – an increase in income, jobs, universities, high school diplomas or hospital beds.

Even if within one national economy a recession might persist for a few years or even decades, it could not persist for long on a world-wide scale in the given system. And even if the gross domestic product in a country does not increase for a couple of years, pressures for acceleration and innovation remain unaffected, and as a rule, non-growth or degrowth is coupled with elements of cannibalisation that increase social inequality and destabilise the institutional status quo and its social integration. Hence, the observable forms of long-term degrowth (e.g. as in Japan) support rather than contradict the definition that a modern society can only maintain a stable structure through steady escalation.

Yet, in addition to the logic of escalation of capitalist reproduction, the modern conception of science and knowledge displays a quite similar shift from an adaptive to a dynamic mode of stabilisation which transforms its institutional order. In non-modern social formations, knowledge is often considered and treated as a social good or treasure which carefully needs to be preserved and handed down from one generation to the next. This knowledge in many cultures is traced back to some ancient or sacred source, for example to 'holy scriptures', or 'the wisdom of the ancient', and there are often attempts to preserve this knowledge in a 'pure' form. It is practical knowledge about *how things are done*:[5] how one builds a home or produces clothing and food, for example, when to sow or to reap or how and when to hunt, and, not least, how to perform the sacred rituals. Knowledge is transferred from one generation to the next either as learning by doing and performing, or in some form of *schola*.

By contrast, modern societies shift from *Wissen* (knowledge) in this sense to Wissen*schaft* (science). As the second part in the German word indicates nicely, the central form of knowledge in modernity is not about preservation and schooling, it is no longer about treasuring, but about systematically pushing the borders, increasing the volume of the known, transgressing into the yet unknown. Science is about looking further into the universe than ever before, piercing deeper into the micro-structures and particles of matter, closer to the workings of life, etc. The sacred spaces of knowledge have moved from the *schola* to the laboratory: science is reproduced dynamically, through growth, increase and transgression. Just as the propelling dynamics of m-c-m' lies at the heart of modern economy, a similar process of knowledge – research – increased knowledge (k-r-k') provides the basis for modern science.[6] And in the times of intellectual property, the two accumulative processes are increasingly interdependent.

Finally, in the arts, the modus operandi resembles this very logic of increase and transgression, too. After millennia of a predominantly mimetic art, for which the goal of artistic creation was the emulation either of nature or of some traditional style or ancient mastery, there is a shift in literature and poetry as well as in painting, dancing and music that puts the onus on innovation and originality. As in science – and contrary to what Weber thought – to boldly go where no man has gone before, to do what no one ever did, becomes the central challenge in the arts as well (Groys 2014). In this way, the logic of dynamic stabilisation has become the hallmark of modern society in total. The circle of acceleration between technological acceleration, the acceleration of social change and the corresponding acceleration of the pace of life that results from dynamic stabilisation has become a self-propelling mechanism in modernity (Rosa 2013, 151–159). It maintains the socio-economic status quo as well as the institutional structure of the market system, of the welfare-state as well as of science, art and education, via a constant escalation of its productive power and substantive output. The stability achieved thereby has been robust enough to keep the machines going for now more than 250 years (from the industrial revolution until today – and even the World Wars rather accelerated change).

Nevertheless, this stability is becoming increasingly fragile. It can be undermined anytime either because of its externalities, e.g. in ecological costs; because of a failure of social integration despite growth and acceleration as, for example, in phenomena of 'jobless growth' and increased social precarisation (Dörre 2015), because the financialisation of the art market erodes the subversive and creative potential of the arts; or because of problems created by desynchronisation (Rosa 2015). Hence, dynamic stabilisation resembles a ride on a bicycle: the faster the bike goes, the more robust it is in its course (a slow bike can be brought to tumble at the slightest push from the side, not so a fast one), but the risk of severe accidents is higher.

Of course, no social formation could ever stabilise and reproduce itself in a merely static way. All societies occasionally need change and development. However, in non-modern social formations, the mode of stabilisation is instead *adaptive;* growth, acceleration and innovations can and do occur, but they are either accidental or adaptive, i.e. they are reactions to changes in the environment (e.g. climate change or natural disasters such as droughts, fires, earthquakes or the appearance of new diseases or new enemies, etc.). Dynamic stabilisation, by contrast, is defined by the systematic requirement for increase, augmentation and acceleration as an internal, endogenous requirement.

Loosening the ties between economic growth and the good life

Today this social 'assemblage' has become highly problematic because economic growth is eroding its own conditions, both socially and environmentally. The growth-oriented vision of society thus poses increasingly serious problems for people's efforts to lead a good life. Nevertheless, many still take it for granted that growth and the good life only come together. Only if we understand and dissolve this link can we try to spell out visions of the good life that no longer depend on this problematic assumption.

To begin with, we need to see that historically this link is not the rule, but rather an exception. The Aristotelian conception of the flourishing life was influential up until the 19th century. It did not know an intrinsic link between a good life and economic growth. According to Aristotle, happiness or *Eudaimonia* includes being an active political member of the community, having a family or household and being healthy, educated and wealthy enough to have free time and to develop our 'higher' human capabilities, such as aesthetic appreciation or cognitive contemplation. A focus on monetary gains or indulgence, however, is considered detrimental to happiness.[7] Similarly, for Plato the desire for growth simply was a symptom of *pleonexia*, a social disease and a form of injustice.

Historically, economic growth only took off with the industrial revolution of the 18th century (H.C. Binswanger 2012, Gordon 2017). Modern industrial and post-industrial societies with their strong focus on quantitative growth rely to a much lesser extent on qualitative ideas of the good life. There is a political reason for this: as growing societies allowed for more mobility, they were becoming less homogenous. 'Modern' states include all kinds of cultures or religions which have different ideas of a good life.[8] When 'comprehensive conceptions of the good' become pluralistic, attempts to derive a common understanding of the good run the risk of paternalism. Thus, liberal states reserve conceptions of the good for the private sphere. Growing economic means, however, seem to be 'value-neutral' and are thus considered essential for *any* private conception of the good – John Rawls (1971) speaks of 'social primary goods'. Freedom from a patronizing state that legislates morality is 'bought' at the cost of a wide-ranging monetisation, as Georg Simmel had already described. The outcome of this cultural-economic assemblage is clear: if the instrumental 'good' of money and wealth represents the good life *as such*, having less money (due to less growth) necessarily seems to reduce the quality of life.

So, modern societies strongly link theories of the good with economic growth. But there also is a strong link between economic growth and theories of *justice*. In order to justify our central institutions, we need a consensus concerning questions of the 'right'. Rawls' theory of justice suggests strong ties between growth and the concept of justice; first, by conceptualizing the theory of justice in terms of a 'fair cooperation' which originates in orthodox economic conceptions of the market that also celebrate growth (Henning 2014, ch. III.2). Second, because the 'differ-ence principle' allows for inequalities only as long as they benefit the worst off (Rawls 1971, § 12f). Yet concentrated wealth in the hands of some only benefits others if it is used to *accumulate even more wealth*, thus creating jobs, incomes and tax revenues for the state. In order to lift all proverbial boats, such a 'just' tide *needs* to rise constantly, or otherwise the justification of the difference principle will fail.

These ideas indicate why modern elites had a strong incentive to provide for ever more economic growth: it is the central justification for the persistent social inequalities. As such, growth clearly served as an ideology as well as a political strategy during the cold war and under the threat of a 'communist' alternative to capitalist society. If growth rates are shrinking, social inequality may no lon-ger be perceived as legitimate. Perhaps this is the reason why social inequality, which has been rising for decades already, is only scandalised in times of eco-nomic slump.[9] However, today there is mounting evidence that economic growth does not produce social equality; hence egalitarians no longer need to be growth-affirmative, as Rawls had suggested.

While growth has secured a steady improvement of well-being for recent gen-erations in the West, such a promise no longer holds. In modern societies both *subjective* (self-reported) well-being and *objective* quality of life (measured by indicators such as the 'genuine progress indicator', GPI) *decouple* from eco-nomic growth after a certain threshold.[10] For example, due to positional compe-tition ('keeping up with the Joneses'), the steady struggle for an improvement is 'trapped' on treadmills of happiness which foster constant dissatisfaction.[11] In addition to the tiring status competition and fundamental hedonic adaptations, we also perceive temporal rebound effects in technology; time-saving techniques intensify the workload and change the structures of interactional expectation, leading to even more time-pressure rather than saving time for other 'free' activities (Rosa 2010). In the global South, by contrast, movements in the official GDP (e.g. reflecting money flows from export processing zones or 'development' politics) are often disconnected from peoples' lives (see White and Kothari in this volume).

This indicates that a large part of the population no longer *needs* economic growth in order to achieve more happiness. There is also evidence that we cannot *have* growth much longer: ecological constraints in terms of resource scarcity and a sinking global absorption capacity increasingly reduce the margin of profitability on investments. Industrialised countries may have reached a threshold at which the feasible growth rates no longer secure employment, social mobility and welfare (Dörre 2013). If we nevertheless enforce growth politically, this may have dysfunctional social, political and cultural effects. Critics of growth have long warned that we are approaching a paradoxical inversion of the relation between growth and happiness. The attempt to cling to growth at any cost in times of crisis considerably limits the chances for a fulfilled and autonomous life. The enforced creation of additional economic value at the same time creates disvalues as a counterpart – for example more social inequality, isolation and new dependencies (Illich 1978; Paech 2013).

In a situation where economic growth is neither likely in objective terms, nor promising further increases in perceived happiness, we should rethink our conceptions of the good, as well as the structural conditions that make growth a necessity for the reproduction of the institutional status quo. What does the prospect of a post-growth society mean for theories of well-being and for a politics of the good life? On the one hand, as a consequence of the mode of dynamic stabilisation, the end of economic growth is often depicted in terms of recession, stagnation, and hardship. Keeping the economy growing further at any cost seems to be the only recipe to avoid a structural crisis. On the other hand, activists who welcome the vision of a post-growth society regard the current crisis as a chance to recover ideas of the good life and its social and economic conditions on a different footing.[12] Moving down this path, however, we should be aware of the danger of endorsing a merely adaptive mode that secures happiness beyond growth by a shift towards 'immaterial' values, coping strategies and compensatory imaginaries, which might mask anti-emancipatory discrimination ideologically (see O'Neill and Graefe in this volume). After all, the Aristotelian *Eudaimonia* relied upon an exploitation and exclusion of workers, women and foreigners, and it hardly allowed for Millian 'experiments in living'. We cannot simply go back to where we started. On our way toward a post-growth society, we therefore need a new debate about well-being and the good life. Can we conceive of criteria for and narratives of the good life that no longer measure it in the range of mere options and the availability of resources, without sliding into relativism or an arbitrary traditionalism? How do these ideas fit together with political liberalism and ethical pluralism, especially from a global perspective? And which practices and institutions are the most promising for realizing these forms of the good life?

Structure of the book

This volume documents a conference that took place in Jena, Germany, in May 2015. The conference celebrated the first four years (2011–2015) of the 'Kolleg Postwachstumsgesellschaften' at the University of Jena (DFG Research Group *Landnahme, Acceleration, Activation. Dynamics and (De)stabilisation of Modern Growth Societies*). It was funded by the German research foundation (DFG) in order to stimulate research on post-growth societies, and it has now been financed for four more years (2015–2019). In the first four years it was directed by Klaus Dörre, Stephan Lessenich, and Hartmut Rosa. It has produced considerable output and has been visited by fellows and scholars from all over the world. We are grateful to the DFG as well as to the Ernst Abbe Foundation in Jena for making this conference and the publication of this book possible.

The volume starts with a section on *Conceptions of the Good Life* (I), searching for alternatives to a quantitative measurement of economic means that systematically depreciates social, natural and psychological factors. Serge Latouche, a veteran of the degrowth movement and the French *revue du MAUSS*, delineates the history of the concept of happiness in the West, from Saint-Just to Herman Daly and Ivan Illich (text 1). He argues that the economisation of happiness, and especially the link to GDP, was a historical dead end that needs to be overcome. As an alternative, Latouche hints at conceptions both from the history of the West (Renaissance ideas of 'Civil Happiness', for example) and from the South, especially ideas of a 'Buen Vivir'. Alberto Acosta (2), formerly President of the Constituent Assembly of Ecuador, develops the notion of Buen Vivir in more detail, drawing from his own political experience and suggesting to extend it to the West. Hartmut Rosa (3), well-known for his book on *Acceleration* (2010), describes another alternative from a sociological perspective: for him, a good life is a life of 'resonance', a life of relating to the world in a non-instrumental manner. For Rosa, only in this way will the various regions of the world (social, natural, aesthetic or spiritual) 'answer' us. A life beyond the mindset of growth could thus be much more fulfilling than one with an instrumentalist focus on an everlasting expansion. The Canadian philosopher Charles Taylor, an expert on theories of the good life in the West (e.g., Taylor 1989), comments on Rosa's ideas (4). He argues that Rosa's ideas themselves 'resonate' with the Romantic tradition, whose sources Taylor traces as far back as the Middle Ages. Romanticism, however, is not an outdated concept for Taylor and Rosa. Rather, the Romantic longing for a reconciliation with nature, as well as the romantic reflection on the impact of language on our ways of relating to the world, may still guide our efforts to overcome the widespread attitudes of instrumentalism and extractivism. If we read these four papers together, it seems possible to develop a conception of the good life that is no longer coupled to notions of economic growth, and that bridges the gap between conceptions from the global North and South. Yet, in order to be successful, these ideas need a foundation beyond philosophy, so the next sections focus on economic and societal conditions for a good life.

In the second section on *Alternative conceptions of the economic* (II), Manfred A. Max-Neef, who like Latouche is a veteran of the tradition of dissenting economists, delineates alternative foundations for economic thinking (5). Like Taylor, he shows interest in Romanticism and cites Friedrich Schelling, the German philosopher of nature (who was based in Jena, where the conference took place). Schelling, Max-Neef argues, made one of the most profound statements in philosophy in arguing that human intelligence is not separated from nature, but is nature's consciousness itself. If an economic philosophy starts from this holistic insight, then adding nature's 'ecosystem services' to the old economic models (as the GPI does) cannot be enough; it is still dualistic. Max-Neef argues that if everything depends on life, including our economies, we can no longer juxtapose the two. It needs a new account which he calls 'Economics for Life'. Indeed, as the following papers show, because a belief in the economic orthodoxy's creed in economic growth has impaired current theories of justice and the good life, we need a substantial revision of our basic economic concepts as well.

In this line of thought, Christoph Henning launches a philosophical attack on the economic language of productivity in particular (from Locke to Hayek), uncovering a political and practical subtext that elicits and justifies violence (6). If growth justifies violence, then a good life beyond growth could also be more amicable, which is 'good' in a moral sense. Discussing recent theories of capitalism, Dennis Eversberg (7) argues that another economy is possible – but not within capitalism. He differentiates stages of capitalism and their regimes of subjectivation (liberal, organised and flexible), showing that corresponding ideas of the good life were embedded into the social settings of such regimes. Is resistance directed at achieving a good life thus destined to bring about ever new forms of capitalism? Eversberg's hope lies in the fact that this time social movements no longer believe in capitalism. This demonstrates again that a critique of political economy is needed in order to find paths to a good life beyond growth. UK-based Andrew Sayer expands on this hope in more detail (8). Adopting a moral economy approach, he uses J.A. Hobson's distinction between property and improperty to discuss how a fairer and more sustainable economy might be configured. Given capitalism's dependence on growth, Sayer argues that the challenge of building a carbon-neutral economy obliges us to go back to basics in order to reconsider what an economy is for and to rethink the nature of the social and environmental relations involved.

The third section on *The good society* (III) is opened by US-philosopher Michael J. Thompson, an expert on critical theory. He re-interprets the common interest as a structure of social relations that any good society maintains (9). These social relations should be organised for the benefit of both the relational-structure itself as well as those of its members. A better society must expand these social relations, instead of relying on what Thompson calls 'pleonexic goods' that only create oligarchic wealth. As social relations to a great extent are work relations, we need to ask what 'good work' is. From a sociological perspective, Nicole Mayer-Ahuja describes successful union campaigns in Germany that rediscovered the notion of good work (10). After the post-war consensus between capital, labour and the state eroded in the early 1970s, trade unions entered a severe crisis, as membership dropped and their notions of good work were ridiculed as being old-fashioned. Mayer-Ahuja argues for a 'flexibilisation from below' that might give new life to the rallying cry for 'bread and roses'. Struggles over the distribution of income could also be modified by a suggestion of Philippe Van Parijs and Yannik Vanderborght (11). They argue for an individual, universal and obligation-free basic income as a modest floor under the whole distribution of incomes. Such a scheme is a necessary – though no sufficient – condition for enabling all members of the present generation to lead a good life while preserving this possibility for the generations to come. Finally, John O'Neill argues against social relations of domination and inequality which could be the result of a post-growth society if applied from a politically problematic worldview (12). Interestingly, O'Neill attacks the Easterlin paradox and the 'gross domestic happiness' in Bhutan, both of which are often cited in favor of degrowth, for their blind eye on social relations. Instead, he suggests we focus on objective state accounts of well-being which are sensitive to political conflict and inequality.

The fourth section investigates *Changing practices* of individuals (IV). Bettina Hollstein demonstrates that happiness and the common good, although often juxtaposed in economic theory, are compatible in the practice of volunteerism (13). The paper concentrates on the experiences and practices of acting volunteers from a pragmatist perspective. Volunteers often state that volunteering makes them happy and is also crucial for the public wealth of a community. The example of voluntary action shows how societal institutions could improve happiness and the common good. Moving towards even more intimate regions, Eva Illouz asks whether romantic love is still a part of the good life (14). Historically, she describes romantic love as a liberation that affirmed the individual's right to their sentiments and to marry according to their will. However, as Illouz shows through examples from Flaubert, Houellebecq and John Williams, with the increasing demands of availability (also analyzed by Rosa), and with the sexualisation of love and commodification of beauty, romantic love is no longer a safe haven in which the intimacy of the couple 'anchors' the self in reality. It has become a conflict zone. This reminds us that the search for a good life is not automatically backwards-looking, but rather needs to develop new perspectives. Felix Rauschmayer spells out such a perspective for self-transformation (15). He asks psychologically how anyone may gain the freedom to live a post-growth good life in a society that is currently geared towards the imperative of economic growth. He uses a capability model enlarged by environmental psychology to explain current endeavours of transitions to a good life beyond growth. His examples are complementary currency initiatives aiming at more social inclusion, a lower environmental footprint and the establishment of local alternatives to globalised markets. Stefanie Graefe is sceptical when it comes to individuals' motivations (16). Whereas growth is an abstract category without immediate social or emotional experiences, and thus hard to politicise, enlarged consumer markets and an ever-increasing range of therapeutic discourses offer people the opportunity to work on their feelings in a concrete manner, which makes it highly attractive. Therefore, Graefe says, a good life beyond growth cannot be a mere 'lifestyle' amongst others, but needs to offer solutions to systemic problems. Hence, for her, apolitical notions like 'resilience' are not sufficient to repoliticise the growth issue. The private needs to be politicised again.

The last section describes *Alternative conceptions of the political* on a global scale (V). Martin Fritz and Max Koch compare the individual, social and ecological dimensions for the good life at national levels and empirically explore patterns of prosperity on a global scale (17). They analyze prosperity patterns in various parts of the world as well as country clusters which already manage to develop at least *some* elements of the good life within ecological limits. Likewise, Sarah C. White takes the perspective of villagers living with material scarcity and uncertainty in rural Zambia (18). How do they conceive a good life after growth? Villagers do state that the good life requires economic sufficiency, but also emphasise the relational context: it is crucial to be able to take care of others. Theoretically, the chapter suggests the need for a relational approach to well-being (see Rosa, Thompson and Sayer in this volume), which sees it as emerging through the interaction of personal, societal and environmental processes. Substantively, it suggests that local people do need to see *some* growth, but based on a new model of the good life, which is built on an ethic of mutual responsibility between people and the natural world, rather than on the enrichment of some at the expense of others.

Klaus Dörre examines the recent capitalist crisis dynamics (19). Starting from the causes of the economic-ecological double crisis in Europe, Dörre's concept of *Landnahme* describes the expansive nature of capitalism and the resulting destruction of its capacity to self-stabilise. Dörre suggests a framework for democratic alternatives. Finally, Ashish Kothari discusses the recent UN Sustainable Development Goals (20). For Kothari, this approach retains crucial flaws of the conventional development model, notably a central focus on economic growth as an engine of human well-being. He considers more radical alternatives to the (sustainable) development model. While taking many examples from India, this essay is relevant for many other parts of the world as well. The emerging concept and practice of 'radical ecological democracy' places the goals of direct democracy, local and bioregional economies, cultural diversity, human well-being, and ecological resilience at the core of its vision. The transition should be guided not only by hard-headed rationality but by a strong ethical and emotional foundation as well.

We think that together these twenty papers manage to outline ideas and practices of a good life which no longer relies on economic growth, but which rather focuses on social relations of equality and respect and on a renewed quality and fullness of life, including better relations to nature. This multifaceted idea has implications for economics, social theory, philosophy and psychology, and we hope that our volume may contribute to further research in this field.

Erfurt and Jena, March 2017

Notes

1 For the U.S., see www.tradingeconomics.com/united-states/gdp-growth-annual or Gordon 2017, for a global picture see http://data.worldbank.org/indicator/NY.GDP. MKTP.KD.ZG.
2 This is an inverted use of term 'decoupling': Whereas Easterlin 1974 proposed that more money no longer brings more happiness, we suggest that a better life no longer depends on more economic growth.

3   Hartmut Rosa has argued for this elsewhere (Rosa 2015, Rosa/Dörre/Lessenich 2017, see Rosa in this volume).
4   It als extends beyond *Capitalism*: Most socialist regimes also aspired growth (most notably the Soviet Union or China under Mao), but eventually they did not grow *enough* to keep people satisfied. Intellectuals (like Harich 1975) who desired communism as an instrument to put a *break* on growth (invoking Günther Anders) were a minority.
5   Gilbert Ryle (1946) called this knowing how, as opposed to knowing that.
6   Max Weber (1946, 138) has formulated this point quite forcefully: "In science, each of us knows that what he has accomplished will be antiquated in ten, twenty, fifty years. That is the fate to which science is subjected; it is the very meaning of scientific work, to which it is devoted [. . .] Every scientific 'fulfilment' raises new 'questions'; it asks to be 'surpassed' and outdated. Whoever wishes to serve science has to resign himself to this fact. Scientific works [. . .] will be surpassed scientifically – let that be repeated – for it is our common fate and, more, our common goal. We cannot work without hoping that others will advance further than we have. In principle, this progress goes on ad infinitum".
7   For modernized accounts see Kraut 2007, Hurka 2011 or Skidelsky 2012.
8   The literature on the "axis" argues that similar cultural modernizations occured much earlier already (see Bellah/Joas 2012).
9   Wilkinson/Pickett 2010; Stiglitz 2012; Piketty 2011.
10 See Easterlin et al. 2010; Max-Neef 1995; Lane 2001; Layard 2005 or the early studies by Scitovsky 1976 and Hirsch 1976. See Latouche and Hollstein in this volume.
11 Frank 1999; Binswanger 2006.
12 See Welzer/Wiegandt 2013; D'Alisa/Demaria/Kallis 2015, AK Postwachstum 2016, or Adler/Schachtschneider 2017.

References

Adler, F./U. Schachtschneider (eds., 2017). *Postwachstumspolitiken: Wege zur wachstumsunabhängigen Gesellschaft*. München: Oekom.

AK Postwachstum (2016). *Wachstum – Krise und Kritik: Die Grenzen der kapitalistisch-industriellen Lebensweise*. Frankfurt/New York: Campus.

Bellah, R./H. Joas (2012). *The Axial Age and Its Consequences*. Cambridge, MA: Harvard University Press.

Bellah, R. (1992). *The Good Society*. New York: Vintage.

Binswanger, H.C. (2012). *The Growth Spiral: Money, Energy, and Imagination in the Dynamics of the Market Process*. New York/Berlin: Springer.

Binswanger, M. (2006). Why Does Income Growth Fail to Make us Happier? Searching for the Treadmills Behind the Paradox of Happiness. In: *The Journal of Socio-Economics* 35, 366–381.

Bourdieu, P. (1984). *Distinction: A Social Critique of the Judgment of Taste*, transl. Richard Nice. London: Routledge.

D'Alisa, G./F. Demaria/G. Kallis (eds., 2015). *Degrowth: A Vocabulary for a New Era*. New York: Routledge.

Daly, H.E. (2014). *From uneconomic Growth to a Steady State Economy*. Cheltenman: Edward Elgar.

Dörre, K. (2013). Finance Capitalism, Landnahme and Discriminating Precariousness: Relevance for a New Social Critique. In: *Social Change Review* 10.2, 125–151.

Dörre, K. (2015). Social Capitalism and Crisis: From the Internal to the External Landnahme. In: K. Dörre/S. Lessenich/H. Rosa (eds.). *Sociology, Capitalism, Critique*. London/New York: Verso, 247–279.

Easterlin, R.A. (1974). Does Economic Growth Improve the Human Lot? In: P.A. David/ M.W. Reder (eds.). *Nations and Households in Economic Growth: Essays in Honor of Moses Abramovitz*. New York: Academic Press, 89–125.

Easterlin, R.A., L. Angelescu McVey, M. Switek, O. Sawangfa & J. Smith Zweig (2010). The Happiness-Income Paradox Revisited. In: *PNAS* 107, 22463–22468.

EK (Enquete Kommission). (2013). *Wachstum, Wohlstand, Lebensqualität. Schlussbericht*. Berlin: Bundestag Drucksache. Online at http://dip21.bundestag.de/dip21/ btd/17/133/1713300.pdf.

Frank, R.E. (1999). Luxury Fever: Why Money fails to satisfy in an Age of Excess. New York: Free Press.

Gordon, R.J. (2017). Rise and Fall of American Growth: The U.S. Standard of Living Since the Civil War (The Princeton Economic History of the Western World). Princeton: Princeton University Press.

Groys, B. (2014). *On the New*. London: Verso.

Harich, W. (1975). *Kommunismus ohne Wachstum? Babeuf und der Club of Rome*. Reinbek: Rowohlt.

Henning, C. (2014). *Philosophy After Marx: 100 Years of Misreadings and the Normative Turn in Political Philosophy*. Boston: Brill.

Hirsch, F. (1976). *Social Limits to Growth*. Cambridge, MA: Harvard University Press.

Hurka, T (2011). *The Best Things in Life: A Guide to What Really Matters*. Oxford: Oxford University Press.

Illich, I. (1978). *Toward a History of Needs*. New York: Pantheon Books.

Kraut, R. (2007). *What is Good, and Why? The Ethics of Well-Being*. Cambridge, MA: Harvard University Press.

Lane, R.E. (2001). *The Loss of Happiness in Market Democracies*. New Haven: Yale University Press.

Latouche, S. (2009). *Farewell to Growth*. New York: Polity Press.

Layard, R. (2005). *Happiness: Lessons from a New Science*. New York: Penguin.

Luhmann, N. (1990). *Political Theory in the Welfare State*. Berlin: Walter de Gruyter.

Max-Neef, M.A. (1995). Economic Growth and Quality of Life: A Threshold Hypothesis. In: *Ecological Economics* 15, 115–118.

Max-Neef, M.A. (1982). *From the Outside Looking in: Experiences in 'Barefoot-Economics'*. Uppsala: Dag Hammarskjöld Foundation.

Mishan, E.J. (1967). *The Costs of Economic Growth*. London: Staples.

Muraca, B. (2012). Towards a Fair Degrowth-Society: Justice and the Right to a 'Good Life' Beyond Growth. In: *Futures* 44, 535–545.

Paech, N. (2013). *Befreiung vom Überfluss: Auf dem Weg in die Postwachstumsökonomie*. München: Oekom.

Piketty, T. (2011). *Capital in the 21st Century*. Cambridge, MA: Belknap Press.

Rawls, J. (1971). *A Theory of Justice*. Cambridge, Mass.: Harvard University Press.

Rosa, H./K. Dörre/S. Lessenich (2017). Appropriation, Activation and Acceleration: The Escalatory Logics of Capitalist Modernity and the Crisis of Dynamic Stabilization. In: *Theory, Culture and Society* 34.1, 53–73.

Rosa, H. (2010). *Alienation and Accelaration: Towards a Critical Theory of Late-Modern Temporality*. Malmö: NSU Press.

Rosa, H. (2013). *Social Acceleration: A New Theory of Modernity*. New York: Columbia University Press.

Rosa, H. (2015). Escalation: The Crisis of Dynamic Stabilization and the Prospect of Resonance. In: K. Dörre/H. Rosa/S. Lessenich (eds.). *Sociology, Capitalism, Critique*. London/New York: Verso, 280–305.

Ryle, G. (1946). Knowing How and Knowing That: The Presidential Address. In: *Proceedings of the Aristotelian Society: New Series* 46, 1–16.

Sayer, A. (2014). *Why We Can't Afford the Rich*. Bristol: Policy Press.

Scitovsky, T. (1976). *The Joyless Economy: The Psychology of Human Satisfaction*. Oxford: Oxford University Press.

Skidelsky, R./E. Skidelsky (2012). *How Much Is Enough? Money and the Good Life*. New York: Other Press.

Stiglitz, J.E. (2012). *The Price of Inequality: How today's divided Society endangers our Future*. New York: Norton.

Taylor, C. (1989). *Sources of the Self: The Making of the Modern Identity*. Cambridge, MA: Harvard University Press.

UN (2016). *United Nations Sustainable Development Goals*. Online at www.un.org/sustainabledevelopment.

Weber, M. (1946). *From Max Weber: Essays in Sociology*, trans by H.H. Gerth/C. Wright Mills. New York: Oxford University Press.

Welzer, H./K. Wiegandt (eds., 2013). *Wege aus der Wachstumsgesellschaft*, Frankfurt am Main: Fischer.

Wilkinson, R.G./K. Pickett (2010). *The Spirit Level: Why Equality Is Better for Everyone*. London: Penguin.

Part I

Foundations

Alternative conceptions of the good life

1 The misadventures of the good life between modernity and degrowth

From happiness to GDP to Buen Vivir

Serge Latouche

Let us assume (certainly wrongly) that the expression "the good life" is a neutral term without connotations designating a universal and transhistorical aspiration reflected in various languages, cultures, and periods by means of different concepts such as, for example, *Glück, bonheur, felicità, happiness*, etc. but also *bamtaare* (Pular), *sumak kawsay* (Quechua), etc. We will consider all these expressions as what the Indo-Catalan philosopher and theologian Raimon Panikkar has called "homeomorphic equivalents of the good life". "Homeomorphic equivalents", he explains, "are not simple literal translations, any more than they simply translate the role that the original word claims to play; instead, they are aimed at an equivalent (analogous) function. We are not seeking the same function, but the function equivalent to the one performed by the original notion in the corresponding cosmovision" (Panikkar 1998, 104). "Bonheur" in its different European linguistic variants, but especially in the French sense of the term, certainly constituted the form of *eudaimonia*, of "the good life" of nascent modernity. Despite the interest of such an investigation, we will not be concerned here with how the good life was first embodied in the medieval *beatitudo*, but only with the twofold movement from the emergence of *bonheur* to its *economistic* reduction as the "gross domestic product per capita" and from the criticism of indicators of wealth to the birth of the recovered aspiration to *buen vivir*, to frugal abundance, to a happy sobriety in a context of "prosperity without growth", as Tim Jackson (2010) puts it.

From the emergence of bonheur to its economistic reduction

If, as the deputy to the Convention Louis Antoine de Saint-Just (1767–1794) thought, *bonheur* was a new idea in Europe on the eve of the French Revolution, that is because unlike heavenly *beatitude* and public *felicity*, it referred to a material and individual well-being, the antechamber of the economists' GDP per capita, whose ethical dimension is weak, if not null. This reflects the rupture brought about by the great European movement that agitated what was known at the time as "the Republic of Letters", before it overturned ordinary people's lives by galloping through Europe under the name of "the spirit of the times" and was incarnated in the form of Napoleon Bonaparte, the man whom Hegel was to meet in Jena. This cosmopolitan movement of the Enlightenment marked a radical break with the Christian *oecumene* (the Middle Ages being assumed to have been dark and obscure), whose ideal of the good life was expressed in the clerics' language by the Latin word *beatitudo* ("O beata solitudo, o sola beatitude"). Beatitude was primarily spiritual or even celestial, immaterial and collective (the Communion of the Saints repudiated by Luther).

The semantic field of each of the terms used in the various Indo-European languages to express "happiness" is significantly different, depending on the cultural and historical context. *Bonheur, happiness, felicità, jubilacion*, and *Glück* are not interchangeable. In Italian, *bonheur* is translated by "felicità", but French also has the term "félicité". Voltaire, assigned by Diderot and d'Alembert to write the article on "Heureux" for the *Encyclopédie* (vol. 15), notes the difference between *félicité* and *bonheur*. Félicité

> is the permanent state, at least for a time, of a content mind, and that state is very rare. *Bonheur* comes from outside, originally, it was a *bonne heure* (good hour). [. . .] One can have a *bonheur* without being happy. A man had the *bonheur* to escape a trap, and is sometimes only the more unhappy; it cannot be said of him that he has experienced *félicité*. There is a further difference between a *bonheur* and *bonheur* in general, a difference that the word *félicité* does not admit. A *bonheur* is a happy event. *Bonheur* in general signifies a series of such events.[1]

La *felicità*, on which Neapolitan *illuminismo* reflects, is primarily public; it is less an individual quest for *prosperity* than an objective of the Prince's "buon governo". It is, in a way, a terrestrial beatitude. One cannot save oneself by one's own efforts alone.

The greatest happiness for the greatest number with the greatest GDP per capita

It is not pointless to recall here the context in which Saint-Just uttered his famous formula. It was in his report on a new social policy on 13 Ventôse (March 3) 1794 – four months before Thermidor and his death at the age of 27, on the scaffold alongside Robespierre – that he wrote: "Let Europe learn that you want not a single unhappy man or oppressor on French territory, let this example bear fruit on the earth; let it propagate the love of virtues and happiness! Happiness is a new idea in Europe" (Saint-Just 1996, 61).

The great philosopher of technology, Jacques Ellul, comments on this statement:

> When Saint-Just proclaimed his famous formula according to which happiness is a new idea in Europe, he was wrong; for 2,500 years, the idea of happiness had been well-known and happiness had been consciously desired and wished for. But what was new, and there is no doubt that this is what Saint-Just had in mind, was a change in means: industrialization, the growth of the consumption of a wealth that should have benefited everyone, at the same time that the Republic was proclaiming Liberty and Equality, seemed

to him the means that would finally make the idea of happiness *possible* and *concrete*. What had changed is that people were emerging from the idea in order to enter into the possible realization.

(Ellul 2013, 183)

Even if for a disciple of Rousseau like Saint-Just, happiness is indissociable from virtue, the material and individual dimensions of the economists' GDP per capita are clearly present. With more cynicism, adumbrating the hedonism of the post-Thermidor period, Voltaire noted: "Around 1750, the nation, fed up with moral reflections and theological disputes about grace and convulsions, finally started thinking about grain".[2] Happiness, like material well-being, is thus directly a function of the wealth of nations. And in that sense, happiness is in fact a new idea that emerges almost everywhere in Europe, but mainly in England ("happiness") and in France (*bonheur*). The Declaration of Independence made on July 4, 1776 by the United States of America, a country where the ideal of the Enlightenment was to be realised on an allegedly virgin land, proclaims as its objective: "Life, liberty and the pursuit of happiness". The *Declaration of the Rights of Man* in the French constitution of 1793 is still more explicit: "The goal of society is the common happiness". Neither the promise of beatitude in the beyond nor the spectacle of the monarch's happiness (or even that of the nation) satisfied the members of a bourgeois society (*Gesellschaft* as opposed to *Gemeinschaft*, to use Tönnies' terms). In his critique of Kant, J. G. Herder is very explicit on this point (1971, 64):

Nothing is vaguer than this word *civilisation*, nothing more deceptive in its application to peoples and whole ages. How many civilized individuals are there in a civilized people? And what does this merit actually consist in? And to what extent does that contribute to their happiness? And, in fact, to what extent does it contribute to the happiness of individuals, because the notion that whole states can be said to be happy in the abstract, whereas their members suffer individually, is a contradiction or rather an imposture that is revealed as such at the first glance.

The program of modernity, which was to give rise to the society of growth, is nothing other than the greatest happiness for the greatest number. It was formulated almost simultaneously by a whole series of thinkers in the European Enlightenment, from Cesare Beccaria to Francis Hutcheson or Jeremy Bentham. The *wealth of nations* (the result of laws, updated in the eponymous book, which might "enrich the people and the sovereign", and of which Adam Smith made himself the propagandist) is the means for realizing this objective,[3] which, as utilitarian as it is, is not immoral. The goal is to realise the well-being of all thanks to the "trickle-down effect", and thus realise the good life and justice in the sense defined by John Rawls, since inequalities are reduced.

In the passage from happiness to the GDP per capita, a supplementary triple reduction is carried out: 1) earthly happiness is assimilated to material well-being, matter being conceived in the physical sense of the term; 2) material well-being is reduced to statistical well-having, that is, to the quantity of commercial goods and services produced and consumed; 3) the evaluation of the sum of the goods and services is calculated gross, that is, not taking into account the loss of the natural and artificial resources necessary for its production.

The first point is made explicit in the debate between Thomas Robert Malthus and Jean-Baptiste Say. Malthus begins by expressing his puzzlement: If the trouble we take to sing a song is productive labor, he writes, why would the efforts we make to make a conversation amusing and instructive and that assuredly provide a much more interesting result be excluded from the number of actual productions? Why would we not include the efforts that we need to make to regulate our passions and to become obedient to all divine and human laws, which are, certainly, the most precious of goods? Why, in a word, would we exclude any action whatever whose goal is to obtain pleasure or to avoid pain, either in the moment itself or in the future?

Then he himself observes that this leads directly to the self-destruction of economics as a specific field, remarking quite rightly that "It is true that in this way one might include all the human race's activities during all the instants of life". In the end, he adopts Say's reductive point of view:

> "If then we wish, with M. Say, to make political economy a positive science, founded on experience, and capable of making known its results, we must be particularly careful in defining its principal term, to embrace only those objects, the increase or decrease of which is capable of being estimated; and the line which it seems most natural and useful to draw, is that which separates material from immaterial objects"
>
> (Malthus 1836, 33)

Thus in agreement with Jean-Baptiste Say, who defines happiness by consumption, Ian Tinbergen (1972) once proposed to rename the GDP purely and simply "BNB" (*Bonheur national brut*, gross national happiness). This provocative claim by the Dutch economist is in fact only a return to the sources. Since happiness is materialised as well-being, a *euphemised* version of "good having", any attempt to find other indicators of wealth and felicity would be pointless. The GDP *is* happiness quantified.

But then, after two centuries of growth and a colossal increase in production, we should be swimming in happiness. And yet that is clearly not the case. By setting as the objective of modern societies not happiness but "the greatest happiness", the philosophers of the Enlightenment did include in addition the *illimitation* of which the economic was to be the medium. If it is no longer a matter of living well, but of living better, always better, quantification becomes indispensable for evaluating the realisation of this unattainable objective.[4]

The West's ethical turning point

The transgression erected into a system in *supermodernity* finds its source in the decisive ethical turning point of the Enlightenment. Western society is the only society in history that has set free what all the others have sought, with varying degrees of success, to curb, namely, Spinoza's "sad passions" (ambition, greed, envy, resentment, egoism) and Freud's aggressive passions which are close to them and, for him, responsible for "civilisation's discontents". In contemporary late modernity, it even goes so far as to make *transgression* a kind of paradoxical or even antinomic ethics. The great turning point occurs with Bernard de Mandeville and his famous *Fable of the Bees*. Mandeville's conclusion, namely that private vices produce the hive's prosperity, scandalised readers, but gradually became, through Adam Smith's invisible hand, the amoral or even immoral credo of Western societies. Modernity believed, and in fact continues to believe (or at least pretends to believe) more than ever, that private vices channeled by the economy, through self-interest, become public virtues and work, unbeknownst to the agents, for the common good. Consequently, they could be unleashed without danger. It was even obligatory to do so. That is why "Greed is good" is taught in business schools (and not only there). The wealth of nations is the equivalent of the public felicity of the Neapolitan School, which, while requiring action on the part of the legislator, nonetheless defends the liberal alchemy. Legislation, Giambattista Vico wrote in 1725,

> "modifies for this purpose the three vicious tendencies that lead the whole human race astray and which are: ferocity, greed, and ambition, and it causes them to produce the army, trade, and the court, that is, the power, wealth, and knowledge of republics. These three great vices, which would suffice to destroy all the generations of man on this earth, become the *source of civil felicity*"
>
> (quoted from Robin 2014, 34).

Thanks to the trickle-down effect, we are already on the way toward the greatest happiness for the greatest number that the consumer society has realised with Keynesianism-Fordism. It is remarkable and symptomatic that a philosopher influenced by Protestant pietism like Georg Christoph Lichtenberg wrote in his private notebooks in 1775/76: "If men suddenly became virtuous, several of them would die of hunger" (E 213). If in Saint-Just, a passionate admirer of Jean-Jacques Rousseau, the people's happiness results just as much from virtuous behaviour as it does from individual and collective material well-being, the same does not hold as the economy swallows up the social. In the consumer society of the 1960s, happiness was calculated by the accumulation of objects. Georges Perec's book *Things: A Story of the Sixties* (1965), which was contemporary with Jean Baudrillard's sociological study *The System of Objects* (1968), is a good testimony to this. The word *bonheur* occurs very often in the story of the heroes who are in search of it, and it would be difficult to find in it the slightest moral connotation, only consumerist bulimia. Baudrillard even speaks of the *terrorist conspiracy of happiness*.

Western economist imperialism made this conspiracy a worldwide phenomenon. Nevertheless, if the growth and development of the North were able to produce the illusion, especially during the *trente glorieuses* (the thirty years between 1945 and 1975), that a certain kind of justice was being realised through the statistical rise in the average standard of living, and thus of the good life, today we are witnessing the bankruptcy of this quantified happiness and thus the collapse of one of the imaginary pillars of Western society, which is now globalised. Other conceptions of happiness are sought here and there, but unless the foundations of the society of growth are challenged and a society of *frugal abundance* is invented, they have little chance of succeeding.

From the criticism of indicators of wealth to the rediscovery of "buen vivir"

The growth society, whose program corresponds to that of modernity, is failing to fulfill its promises. Consumption is limited to a small number of people and does not produce happiness, and on top of that, it ensures an ecological collapse. Once the bankruptcy of modern happiness as "the good life" has been recognised, and having taken into account the proposals of critical economists, don't we have to listen to the rising voice of native peoples and return to the age-old wisdom of limiting needs to rediscover abundance in frugality, with a view to constructing a sustainable future? That, in any case, is the path of degrowth.

From dream to nightmare: the bankruptcy of the greatest quantified happiness in the North

To conceive and construct a society of frugal abundance and a new form of happiness, we have to deconstruct modernity's ideology of quantified happiness. In other words, we have to decolonise the imagination of the GDP per capita; we have to understand how it was established.

It is easy to castigate the assimilation of happiness to the GDP per capita and to show that the GDP or GNP measure only commercial "wealth" and what can be assimilated to it. Transactions outside the market (domestic tasks, volunteer work, labor off the books) are excluded from the GDP, whereas the expenses for "repairing" the damage done by growth (insecurity, pollution, stress, illnesses, etc.) are counted as positive, and the damage done (negative externalities) is not deducted, any more than the loss of natural resources. Thus, Gadrey and Jany-Catrice note that "the GDP is, and this is essential, a flow of wealth that is purely commercial and monetary. As for growth, it is the growth of the GDP, that is, the growth of the volume of all the production of goods and services that are sold, or that cost monetarily, *produced by remunerated labor*" (Gadrey/Jany-Catrice 2005, 17). The GDP measures outputs, not outcomes. As Robert Kennedy put it in the famous speech given a few days before he was assassinated, it "measures everything [. . .], except that which makes life worthwhile".[5] The economic society of growth thus does not realize modernity's proclaimed objective, namely: the greatest happiness for the greatest number. That much is obvious.

Using the "genuine progress indicator", Herman Daly (Daly/Cobb 1989) has shown that beyond a certain threshold, the costs of growth (expenses for repairs and compensations) are on average greater than its benefits.[6] This reinforces Ivan Illich's intuition that "The rate of the growth of frustration greatly exceeds that of production". We are confronted by the sophistry of the provocative journalistic formula that echoes Herder's saying that the economy is doing fine, but the citizens aren't.[7] This is particularly relevant with globalisation, now that the famous trickle-down of development (that is, the diffusion of wealth) has been transformed into a trickle-up (an increase in inequalities).

If, taking another step, we try to move up from well-being to happiness, the gaps, so far as they can be measured, are pitiless. In a remarkable book Robert E. Lane (2000) reviews the possible theoretical angles of accounting in order to measure, in spite of everything, the evolution of subjective well-being in liberal societies. His conclusion is that progress in the material standard of life in the United States has been accompanied by an indisputable decrease in the real happiness of the majority of Americans. In his view, this decrease is essentially due to the actual deterioration of fundamental human relationships (what he calls "companionship", cf. Michea 2003, 162). This observation is confirmed by numerous opinion polls concerning subjective well-being as opposed to the having-a-lot statistic of the GDP. These polls allow us to form an idea on the subject. By comparing the results of polls on the sense of well-being, life expectancy, and the ecological footprint, a British NGO, the *New Economics Foundation*, has even established an index of felicity (the Happy Planet Index) that reverses both the classical order of the GDP per capita and that of the Human Development Index (HDI). In 2006, the countries with the highest scores were Vanuatu, Colombia, and Costa Rica, while France came in 131st, Germany 81st and the United States 150th. In 2009, the classification put Costa Rica in first place, followed by the Dominican Republic, Jamaica, and Guatemala, the United States being ranked 114th.[8] This apparent paradox is explained by the fact that the "developed" society is based on the massive production of decline, on a loss of value and a generalised deterioration, caused by merchandising that the acceleration of the "throw-away"-attitude quickly transforms into garbage, and by the exclusion or dismissal of people after they have been used, from the throw a way-attitude of CEOs and managers towards unemployed workers, homeless people, bums, and other human refuse. The assimilation of growth to a rise in well-being and *a fortiori* of happiness is, according to Jean Baudrillard (1970, 42), "an extraordinary collective deception [. . .], an operation of white magic".

The return of the repressed: the civil economy of felicity

To move beyond this collapse, various new indices are being sought that would re-establish the aspiration of the original concept of happiness. Thus, with a certain sense of humor, the king of Bhutan, picking up on Ian Tingbergen's proposal, but in an opposite way, has inscribed in the constitution the objective of increasing the GNH (gross national happiness). In the same vein, we have seen the flourishing of all sorts of projects for alternative indices to "reconsider wealth", often with a cooptation by politics and the media (Viveret 2003).

Especially the project of a "civil economy" or economy of felicity developed by a group of Italian economists (represented by Stefano Zamagni, Luigino Bruni, Benedetto Gui and Leonardo Becchetti) reconnects with the Aristotelian tradition that remained alive in Italy at least until the 18th century, and proceeds by a critique of individualism. With Stephano Bartolini (2010) and his "Happiness manifesto" we even encounter the *exit from the economy* advocated by the degrowth movement. The construction of such a civil economy seeks to reconnect with the "publica felicità" of Antonio Genovesi and the Neapolitan Enlightenment school that the triumph of Scottish political economy repressed. Terrestrial *felicity*, while awaiting the beatitude promised to the righteous in the beyond, and engendered by a just government (*buon governo*) pursuing the quest for the common good was, in fact, the object on which the Neapolitan economists reflected. At the same time that they included the market, competition, and the commercial subject's pursuit of his personal interest, these thinkers did not repudiate the Thomistic heritage. They were already aware of the "paradox of felicity" rediscovered by the American economist Richard Easterlin. Genovesi wrote: "It is a law of the universe that we cannot achieve our happiness without making that of others" (cited from Bruni/Zamagni 2007, 94). To rediscover these elementary truths, it took two centuries of frenetic destruction of the planet, thanks to the "good governance" of the invisible hand and individual self-interest erected into a divinity.[9]

Quite logically, the theoreticians of the economy of felicity ended up rehabilitating a certain form of sobriety close to the ideas of the movement for voluntary simplicity.[10] This civil economy of the *joie de vivre* resonates strongly with the vision of a society of degrowth. Nonetheless it conveys a twofold ambiguity. On the one hand, it allows the survival of the moribund body that it claims to abolish, the economy as a calculating rationality, and on the other hand, by abolishing the borderline between the economic and the non-economic, it keeps open, probably without knowing it, the path to a pan-economism still more invasive than the one it claims to be combatting. Trying to include the incalculable in the calculus obviously leads to a dead end. The philosopher Cornelius Castoriadis always said: "I prefer to acquire a new friend rather than a new car". Sure, but how much is a new friend worth?[11] Due to this ambiguity, the economists of the school of felicity (and all the advocates of an *alternative* economy) have a hard time being taken seriously by *true* economists, without however succeeding in representing a genuine alternative paradigm.

A path and a voice of hope from the South

Just as it is in the South that the imposture of the assimilation of the good life to well-being and the economisation of life has manifested itself most flagrantly, it is also from the South that the promise of a new path comes to us. "What the French call *development*", Thierno Ba, the head of a Senegalese NGO asks,

> "is that what the villagers want? No. What they want is what in Pular is called *bamtaare*. What does that mean? It is the search, on the part of a community strongly rooted in its solidarity, for a harmonious social well-being in which each member, from the richest to the poorest, can find a place and his personal self-realization".

(Cimade 1996, 43)

It is not without interest to note that we find here the aspiration to "living well" of the Amerindian peoples that recently led to resounding demands for alternatives to development. According to F. Huanacuni Mamani, "In Bolivia,the Aymara term *suma quamaña* is used, and in Ecuador the Quechua term *sumak kawsay*, both meaning 'live well', 'live in full', that is, live in harmony and balance with the cycles of the Earth-Mother of the cosmos, of life, and with all the forms of existence" (quoted by Morin 2013, 230). "Let us add", notes the anthropologist Françoise Morin,

> that the Aymara term implies a necessary conviviality in order to live in harmony with everyone, which asks us to share rather than compete with others. These two concepts are distinguished from the Western notion of "living better" which is synonymous with individualism, a lack of interest in others, and the quest for profit, whence a necessary exploitation of people and nature.
>
> (ibid., 230)

She goes on: "Living well must not be understood as a return to an Andean past but as a "concept under construction that results from the practices of autochthonous movements and the reflections of intellectuals" (231).[12] As for the Fula people's *bamtaare*, it would thus be nonsense to incorporate all that into the ideology of an *alternative* development or a new model of development, even an "Indigenizing Development", as some people call it, even if it were based on a biocentric conception. It is a matter of exiting the economic to rediscover the societal.

It certainly is a necessity to follow in the opposite direction to the path of economics, which has caused us to move from happiness, the terrestrial form of beatitude, to the GDP per capita through the reduction of experienced well-being to a statistical well-having that is ultimately measured by the quantity of commercial goods consumed individually, without being concerned with others and with nature. However, this *metanoia* (regression or regret) must not stop halfway and allow the myth of indefinite progress to continue. Isn't rediscovering the sense of measure first of all a matter of exiting the obsession with the measurable and saying farewell to the economic to rejoin the social? More consistent than the heterodox economists regarding what counts and cannot be counted, the Amerindians of Bolivia and Ecuador have more simply included *Sumak Kawsay*, a Quechua term meaning simply *buen vivir* or living well, as an objective in their new constitution, thus opening the path to a happiness rediscovered in convivial frugality.

Notes

1 In other words, "Pleasure is more fleeting than *bonheur*, and *bonheur* is more fleeting than *félicité*" (*Encyclopédie*, art. "Heureux, heureuse, heureusement »*, quoted by Salaün 2013, 77). For his part, Diderot wrote the article "Béatitude, bonheur, félicité", noting that "*Bonheur* marks a man rich in the goods of fortune; *félicité* [marks a man] content with what he has; *béatitude* awaits us in another life. The enjoyment of goods makes *félicité*; their possession makes *bonheur*; *béatitude* elicits an idea of ecstasy and delight that is felt neither in *bonheur* nor in the *félicité* of this world" (Ibid., 49).

2 Voltaire, *dictionnaire philosophique*, cited from Lasch/Castoriadis 2012, Postface by Jean-Claude Michéa, 69.
3 "No society can surely be flourishing and happy, of which the far greater part of the members are poor and miserable" (Smith 1902, 139).
4 By adding "for the greatest number", the prophets of modernity also set a paradoxical double objective, as has often been emphasized, because one cannot simultaneously maximize the number and happiness. A choice has to be made.
5 Robert Kennedy, Remarks at the University of Kansas, March 18 1968, cited from http://images2.americanprogress.org/campus/email/RobertFKennedyUniversity ofKansas.pdf (June 6 2017).
6 Here is the formula of the indicator: households' commercial consumption + services provided by domestic work + non-defense public expenditures – private defense expenditures = costs of damage to the environment – depreciation of natural resources + formation of productive capital.
7 Thus, *Le Monde* headlines on November 18, 2003: "Japan is better, the Japanese worse".
8 New Economics Foundation: "Happy Planet Index", Data from 2009, online at www.happyplanetindex.org (June 9, 2017), cf. Retico 2009.
9 Transformed into scientific language thanks to experimental tests, in 2004 this even won the Nobel Prize in economics for Daniel Kahneman. By demonstrating a treadmill effect, Kahneman showed that the increase in revenue required the continual search for new forms of consumption to maintain the same level of satisfaction.
10 Bruni writes: "I am in fact convinced that there is no felicity without a certain form of poverty (understood as self-liberation from merchandise, from power . . .) freely chosen: this poverty is one of the wounds to which a blessing is attached" (Bruni/ Zamagni 2007, retranslated from a French edition). However, to have an impact, this self-limitation must be not only an individual choice, it has to be a collective project.
11 "Let's put it still more clearly: the price to be paid for freedom is the destruction of the economic as the central, and in fact, the sole value. Is that such a high price? For me, it is certainly not: I infinitely prefer to have a new friend rather than a new car. A subjective preference, no doubt. But 'objectively'? I gladly leave to political philosophers the task of 'founding' (pseudo-) consumption as the supreme value" (Castoriadis 2010).
12 Morin (2013, 232) concludes: "We find this idea of 'living well' among other autochthonous peoples, such as the Guarani in Bolivia, with their expression *ñande reko*; but also among the Mapuche in Chile, who speak of *künme mongen*; among the Shuar in Ecuador, with the concept of *shir waras*, which describes a harmonious life that includes a state of balance with nature; among the Shipibo in Peru, with the notion of *jakona shati*, a sign of conviviality and sharing with others; among the Ashaninka of Rio Ene (Peru) with the expression *kametsa asaike*, which symbolzies a process of relating that unites people with one another and with their natural environment. In North America, we also find, among a certain number of Amerindian groups, this notion of 'living well', notably among the Crees".

References

Bartolini, S. (2010). *Manifesto per la félicita: Come passare dalla società del ben-avere a quella del ben-essere*. Rome: Donzelli.
Baudrillard, J. (1968). *Le système des objets: La consommation des signes*. Paris: Gallimard.
Baudrillard, J. (1970). *La société de consommation*. Paris: Denoël.
Bruni, L./S. Zamagni (eds., 2007). *Civil Economy: Efficiency, Equity, Public Happiness*. New York: Lang.
Castoriadis, C. (2010). *Démocratie et relativisme: Débat avec MAUSS*. Paris: Mille et une nuits.

Cimade Collectif (1996). Quand l'Afrique posera ses conditions, *Dossier pour un débat no. 67*, September 96, Fondation pour le progrès de l'homme.

Daly, H./J. Cobb. (1989). *For the Common Good*. Boston: Beacon Press.

Ellul, J. (2013). *Pour qui, pour quoi travaillons-nous?* Paris: La petite vermillon.

Gadrey, J./F. Jany-Catrice (2005). *Les nouveaux indicateurs de richesse*. Paris: La découverte.

Herder, J.G. (1971). *Idee per la filosofia della storia dell'umanità* [= Ideen zur Philosophie der Geschichte des Menschheit, 1784–91]. Bologna: Zanichelli.

Jackson, T. (2010). *Prospérité sans croissance*. Brussels: De Boeck/Etopia.

Lane, R.E. (2000). *The Loss of Happiness in Market Democracies*. New Haven: Yale University Press.

Lasch, C/C. Castoriadis (2012). *La culture de l'égoïsme*. Paris: Climats.

Malthus, T.R. (1836). *Principles of Political Economy*. London: Pickering.

Michea, J-C. (2003). *Orwell éducateur*. Paris: Climat.

Morin, F. (2013). Les droits de la Terre-Mère et le bien vivre, ou les apports des peuples autochtones face à la détérioration de la planète. In: *MAUSS revue no. 42: Que donne la nature ? L'écologie par le don*. La découverte.

Panikkar, R. (1998). Religion, philosophie et culture. In: *Interculture* 135, 101–124.

Perec, G. (1965). *Les choses: Une histoire des années soixante*. Paris: Julliard.

Retico, A. (2009). Felicità: I nuovi paradisi non conoscono il PIL. In: *La republica*, July 8.

Robin, C. (2014). *La gauche du capital. Libéralisme culturel et idéologie du marché*. Paris: Krisis.

Saint-Just (1996). *On ne peut pas régner innocemment*. Paris: Mille et une nuits.

Salaün, C. (2013). *L'art du bonheur selon les philosophes*. Paris: Mille et une nuits.

Smith, A. (1902). *The Wealth of Nations*. New York: Collier.

Tinbergen, J. (1972). *Politique économique et optimum social*. Paris: Economica.

Viveret, P. (2003). *Reconsidérer la richesse*. Paris: L'Aube.

2 Buen Vivir

A proposal with global potential

Alberto Acosta[1]

"First they ignore you, then they laugh at you, then they fight you, then you win".
—Mahatma Gandhi

With its postulation of harmony between man and nature, as well as between individuals and communities and as a concept based on experiences, the Good Living (Buen Vivir) allows for the formulation of alternative views of life – provided that it is exempt from prejudices and assumed as a permanent construction.[2] Before approaching its scope and its mobilizing potential, we should reflect on the usefulness of these ideas in a global context.

The concept of 'Good Living', which represents views of life and life practices that exist in various parts of the planet, offers multiple possibilities to rethink the logics of production, consumption, and distribution of goods and services, as well as the dominant social and political structures and experiences that are typical of capitalist civilisations. By challenging their concept of civilisation (which suffocates life and everything that has to do with it), the Good Living acquires the potential to multiply alternative experiences by taking as its reference points the axes that constitute the fundamental basis of those experiences. This will be discussed in more detail at a later point. I should say in advance that this task demands that we open up all possible lines of dialogue and exchange, without falling into the trap of useless romanticisms or vulgar and impossible copies.

But there is more. The Good Living, as long as its ancestral origins and communitarian potentials are neither forgotten nor manipulated, can provide a platform for discussion, agreement and reaction to the devastating effects of climate change and growing social marginalisation and violence in the world. This possibility arises amid a multifaceted crisis – social, economic, ecological, political, and even civilisational – that affects the planet.

From this multi-faceted perspective, visions of the Good Living allow us to break with the paradigm of progress and its stepson, development, that are sustained by economic growth and the permanent accumulation of material goods. The success of such a break will depend on our capacity to think, propose, develop, and even to be indignant, if that is the case, on a local level as well as on a global scale.

The bad living and its global projections

We should recognise from the start the global infeasibility of the dominant life-style, established on the premises of anthropocentric exploitation and exclusion. On a global scale, the conception of growth based on seemingly inexhaustible natural resources and a market, which absorbs everything produced, has not led (and never will lead) to the achievement of decent living standards for all inhabitants of the planet.

The growth of the economy does neither guarantee 'development', nor does it ensure happiness. Although this might come as a surprise, even 'developed' countries show increasing signs of what can be classified as *bad development* (see e.g. Tortosa 2011). Apart from being the main reason behind acute environmental problems (such as the ones resulting from climate change), the gaps that separate the rich from the poor in these countries continue to widen.

Even when there is growth, the latter ends up widening social rifts: the wealth of the few is usually based on the exploitation of large majorities (as seen with increasing frequency in recent years). Sometimes, even when poverty decreases – which is undoubtedly laudable – the structures of capitalist accumulation remain unaffected, the concentration of wealth increases, and inequalities grow. Its complex and painful consequences (both national and international) are evident. We can take as example the increasing migration from countries of the South to the United States and the European Union, which is caused by multiple factors. Iniquity, inequality, and injustice brought about by the increasing and outrageous demands of capitalist accumulation unleash more and more violence that ultimately results in the eviction of the population.

The demands of accumulation, which require a growing economy, are based on the exploitation of labor, as well as on oligopolistic and monopolistic practices to control markets, the increasing financialisation of the economy and, especially, the destruction of nature. Just consider the brutal wreckage caused – to varying degrees – by the expansion of activities inherent in capitalist modernity: industrialisation, urbanisation, extractivism, activities that have rapidly surpassed natural limits.

The challenge is set. It is urgent that we not only stop the whirlwind of economic growth, but also embark on a path of degrowth, especially in the global North.[3] A finite world cannot tolerate permanent economic growth. Following this path will lead to an environmental situation that is increasingly unsustainable and socially explosive. Attempts to overcome the almost religious pursuit of economic growth, which we can particularly observe in the global North, must go hand in hand with post-extractivism in the global South.[4]

It is not a matter of "living better" (better than others, indefinitely and in an unsustainable manner), but rather of building alternatives to the Bad Living that, although it is discernible across the planet, does not equally affect everyone. Due to the globalisation of capital and its multiple forms of accumulation, most of the world's population is far from material well-being and it is clear how this affects their security, freedom, and identity. If in the middle ages the majority of the population was structurally marginalised from progress, these conditions have by no means disappeared today. A large group of people finds itself unable to reap technological benefits; they are excluded from the arena of advantageous technological influence or merely receive crumbs. In many cases, without a job they do not even have the *privilege* of being exploited as they dream to achieve living standards that are unrepeatable on a global scale.

This is a very complex issue. The diffusion of certain patterns of consumption, in a spiral of absolute perversity, infiltrates the collective imaginary. Thus, vast groups of people who find themselves in economic conditions that will not allow access to that type of consumption are held captive by a permanent desire to achieve it. One should bear in mind that the contemporary media of communication – private, and even public and governmental – promote consumerism and individualism, amidst an informational turmoil in which everything dissolves into *programmed banality*. And similar to the inquisitorial practices of the Middle Ages and their logic of power, these media marginalise those messages that they consider to go against the grain of the dominant discourse, thus denying space for its publication.

In this context, institutions emerge which not only control information, but also convert individuals themselves (as mere consumers) into architects of their own alienation. Many people produce in order to consume but live in a state of permanent un-fulfillment of their needs at the same time, a state that is exacerbated by the demands of accumulation. Thus, production and consumption create a vicious circle with no future, irrationally depleting natural resources, polluting fields and cities, and intensifying social inequities. In addition, several technological advances accelerate this vicious circle of increasing production and unfulfilled desires.

This is a striking contradiction: the advancement of science and the development of its technological applications seems to open up an infinite field of possibilities, but in fact on many occasions it only further restricts our access to them. Without denying the importance of many technological advances, we must notice that it is not the entirety of mankind that benefits from those achievements. Moreover, technology is not neutral. It is often developed according to the demands of capital accumulation. Human beings have become mere tools for machines, when it should be the opposite. From that perspective, it is clear that in order to create another kind of technology, we must transform the conditions of its social production.

The good living: A realised utopia

In order to assess the contributions of the 'Good Living', one must understand that it comprises diverse forms of life present in several communities in various parts of the planet, as well as those practices of resistance to alienation and marginalisation caused by capitalist modernity and its aftermath. These visions emerge from ancestral cultures or, to be more precise, from "Indianness", in Aníbal Quijano's expression (Quijano 2014).

It is not a utopia to be built in the future. Its values, experiences, and civilisational practices, as alternatives to capitalism, make the Good Life a realised and realisable utopia. To the extent that it can become a means of deepening the critique of modern civilisation and offering concrete proposals for action, it could contribute to "a great transformation", in the terms proposed by Karl Polanyi (1944).

It is true that these experiences exist above all in communities that have not been fully absorbed by capitalist modernity or have remained at its margins. Yet, even in indigenous communities that have "succumbed" to modernity there are elements of what we could understand as Good Living. But even in other areas, not directly linked to the indigenous world, harmonious opportunities of communal life are built among its members and with nature. As a result of these discussions, significant bridges can be constructed for a joint reflection on what degrowth and post-development could represent, both of which find one of their major advocate in the Good Living.

We should assume that the Good Living, or good common life, does not represent a fully developed or indisputable proposal; it does not emerge from academic reflections or from party proposals. Similarly, it is not intended to become a single global imperative like the concept of 'development' became in the mid-20th century. So, when we speak of the Good Life we conceive of it in the plural, that is, as good ways of living together, and not as a single, homogeneous, and yet never-to-be-realised idea of Good Living. These good ways of living together (or Good Living, as presented in the rest of the text, but always thinking plural) can open up paths that must be imagined in order to be built, on the one hand, but that already are a reality, on the other. This is the great potential of these visions and experiences.

From the beginning, such a perspective takes into account that indigenous worlds, in a broad sense, have been victims of colonial conquest as a process of exploitation and repression, which is impactful until this day. The colonial and capitalist influence is present in those worlds in many forms, preventing any romantic approach to their realities. Growing segments of the indigenous population have been absorbed by the capitalist logic or are major players in the process of accumulation. There are also indigenous groups in situations of great precariousness, trapped in a mythical dream of progress that they – objectively speaking – will never reach. Furthermore, the intensification of migration processes from the countryside to the city aggravates situations of uprooting of urban Indians who gradually distance themselves from their traditional extended communities, but in some cases who are still somehow bearers of elements of Good Life.

Good Living consists, therefore, in a task of (re)construction that involves dismantling the universal goal for all societies: progress and its offshoot, development, as well as their many synonyms. Not only does it dismantle them, but ways of Good Living – in the plural – propose different visions, richer in content and certainly more complex. Thus, the Good Living presents an opportunity to build new forms of life together and to imagine other worlds. Ultimately, it is neither a mere sum of isolated practices, nor a mere catalogue of good wishes of those who interpret the Good Living in their own way.

It is worth noting that in Bolivia and Ecuador this proposal gained such momentum that it was enshrined in their respective constitutions, namely the Constitution of the Republic of Ecuador 2008 and the Constitution of the Plurinational State of Bolivia 2009. Unfortunately, in practice, the governments of these countries are inspired by the very logics of developmentalism in their administrations, notions that are very distant from the Good Living. The best known expressions of the Good Living, nonetheless, have grown out of the native languages of the afore-mentioned countries; in the first case the expression is literally 'Good Living' or *sumak kawsay* (in Kichwa), and in the second the idea of 'Living Well' or *qamaña sum* (in Aymara), *sumak kawsay* (in Quechua), *ñande reko* or *teko porã* (in Gua-rani).[5] There are similar concepts among other indigenous groups, such as among the Mapuches (Chile), the Guarani of Paraguay, the Kuna (Panama), the Shuar and Achuar (Ecuadorian Amazon), as well as in the Mayan tradition (Guatemala) and in Chiapas (Mexico).

Good Living, as a way of life that has different names and can be expressed in different varieties, has been, and continues to be, known and practiced dur-ing different periods and in different regions of our Mother Earth, not only in Latin America. Here we could include the *Ubuntu* in Africa or the *Swaraj* in India (Kothari/Demaria/Acosta 2014). Although it can be considered one of the pillars of the challenged Western civilisation, even some elements of Aristotle's "good life" can be retrieved in this collective effort to (re)construct a puzzle of elements supportive of new ways of organizing life.

This proposal is based on a principle of historical continuity, which equally resorts to the past and present history of indigenous peoples and nationalities. It draws on lessons and experiences of indigenous communities and their vari-ous ways of producing knowledge. It feeds on the different ways of seeing life and their relationship with Pacha Mama, or Mother Earth. It accepts the idea of relationality and complementarity between all living beings (whether human or not) as a unifying axiom. The proposal is forged out of the principles of multicul-turalism. It lives from the notions of solidarity and reciprocal economic practices. Moreover, by being immersed above all in the search for, and construction of, alternatives stemming from the popular and marginalised sectors, it will have to (re)construct itself mainly from below (and with Pacha Mama), from democratic and communitarian logics.

The remarkable and profound character of these alternative ideas lies in the fact that they emerge from traditionally marginalised, excluded, exploited, and even decimated groups. These are proposals which remained invisible for a long time and which now invite us to fundamentally break with several concepts assumed as indisputable. In short, they encompass post-developmentalist visions that go beyond the once valuable contributions of Latin American heterodox and "depen-dentist" currents, which focused on 'alternative developments'. Now, it is increas-ingly necessary to generate 'alternatives to development'. That is what the Good Living is about.

Good Living: Its fundamental axes

In some indigenous forms of knowledge there is no idea analogous to 'develop-ment', and in many cases the concept itself is rejected. There is no conception of a linear process of life based on a before and an after: e.g., underdevelopment and development, a dichotomy across which people and countries should move in order to achieve well-being, as it is usually interpreted in the West. Nor are there any concepts of wealth and poverty determined by the accumulation or lack of material goods. That is, a dignified life for the community must be secured now and not as a promise for tomorrow. In particular, there is no need for growth to ensure that all members of a community can live in dignity, as long as an adequate distribution of income and wealth redistribution to all members of a community is assured.

Good Living must be conceived as a dynamic category of permanent construction and reproduction. It is neither a static nor a retrograde concept. As a holistic approach, it must comprise multiple elements that determine human actions, which promote the Good Living: knowledge, codes of ethical conduct and spiritual attitudes in relation to the environment, human values, views regarding the future etc. In short, the Good Living is a central category of what could be understood as the philosophy of life of indigenous societies.[6]

From that perspective, conventional development (including progress) has been seen as an imposition handed down by Western thinking and is therefore colonial. Thus, many of the reactions against colonialism imply an attempt to distance oneself from developmentalism. Thus, Good Living implies a task of decolonisation (and also 'depatriarchalisation').[7] In order to achieve that, a process of intellectual, political, social, economic, and above all, cultural decolonisation is required. The challenge is to take control of knowledge and even of technologies – instead of the machines that control humans, as recommended by Ivan Illich.[8] Technologies, especially those capable of reducing work and physical effort, should create conditions to liberate human beings from work oriented towards capital accumulation. This must be pushed forward, liberating scientific knowledge and developing a respectful dialogue with ancestral forms of knowledge,[9] while also transforming structures of production and consumption.

Good Living, the emergence of non-capitalist communal roots, proposes a worldview different from the Western one. It breaks with the anthropocentric logic of capitalism as the dominant civilisational paradigm, as well as with the various actually existing forms of socialism, which need to be rethought from a biocentric perspective, rather than simply undergoing name changes. We should not forget that capitalists and 'socialists' of all kinds disputed which system best ensures development and progress, taking economic growth as a key instrument.

In contrast, the Good Living is part of a civilisational change that turns the prevailing anthropocentric civilisation on its head. That does not mean that we first have to completely exit the capitalist mode of living and can only then introduce the Good Living. In fact, many of the experiences intrinsic to the Good Living have persisted from colonial times until today. Now, as part of a profound emancipatory process, new proposals emerge that aim to develop those aspects of the Good Living that will allow us to overcome capitalist civilisation from within.

In other words, as a proposal with a prospective view, the Good Living does neither consist of a mere invitation to go back in time and reconnect with a previously idyllic world, a world that has in fact never existed. Nor can it become a type of religion with catechism, manuals, ministries, and political commissars. The Good Living does not deny the existence of conflicts and contradictions but also does not exacerbate them by fostering a society organised around the permanent and inequitable accumulation of material goods: a society that is driven by endless competition between people who appropriate nature in a destructive manner. Human beings cannot be seen as a threat, or as subjects to be overcome and defeated. And nature cannot be merely taken as a mass of objects to be exploited. Starting with these two remarks, we must promote the search for answers in various areas of strategic action.

In short, the Good Living is a civilizing proposal that reconfigures a horizon to allow us to exit the era of capitalism, the dominant civilisational paradigm of our times. However, this is not the only reason to promote the Good Living. Motivation for such a (re)construction of civilisational alternatives can also draw support from other philosophical principles: ecological, feminist, cooperative, Marxist, humanist etc, provided that these approaches overcome the dominant anthropocentric visions and accept that life either is dignified for all beings or is not dignified at all.

Good Living and its multi-scale implications

The Good Living, with its biocentric approach, projects itself as a platform to generate urgent answers to the current challenges facing humanity. It also provides powerful tools to face the devastating effects of climate change on a global scale and to address the growing social and economic inequalities that form the substrate of rampaging violence across the planet. Let us consider what it means to start the transition into a society centered on the Good Living, assuming the foundational principle that human beings must stand above capital and must live in harmony with nature to secure their own livelihood.

The search for such new forms of life involves revitalizing political discussions, obscured by the classic economist view on ends and means. As a consequence of the deification of the economy, and the market in particular, many non-economic tools indispensable to improve living standards were abandoned. For example, to believe that global environmental problems will be solved with market measures is a mistake that can cost us very much; it has been demonstrated that rules and regulations (however insufficient) have been more effective than the "laws" of supply and demand provided by the capitalist economy. However, this is not all. We cannot continue commodifying nature, a process that promotes unbridled exploitation. On the contrary, we must de-commodify it. We need to reconnect with nature ensuring its capacity to regenerate, based on respect, responsibility, and reciprocity.[10] In fact, the resolution of such problems requires a multidisciplinary approach, given that we live in a situation of multiple complexities that cannot be explained monocausally.

These proposals of the Good Living, as they are actively taken by societies, especially on the communitarian level, can be a strong argument in debates in various regions of the world and could even be a trigger to purposefully address the growing alienation of the vast majority of the planet. In other words, the discussion about the Good Living should go beyond the Andean and Amazonian realities, as well as beyond those constituencies in different parts of the planet where similar options are lived or built.

Although it is extremely difficult to take on the challenge of creating conditions for the Good Living in societies immersed in the turmoil of capitalism – especially in big cities – we are convinced that there are many options to start building this utopia in other parts of the world, including industrialised nations.

The starting point lies not in states nor governments, let alone in the market as a totalizing institution. A real democratisation of power requires participation and social control from the grassroots of society in the countryside and in cities, from neighborhoods and communities. A prominent role is played by social movements and newly formed political parties, deeply attuned to, and rooted in, their respective societies. Societies founded on the principle of horizontality of power demand democracy, direct action, and self-management. In turn, new forms of vertical imposition should be avoided, as well as individual and enlightened leadership. The resolution of the problems and demands of everyday life constitute the appropriate field for transformative political action from the grassroots.

Of course, this collective search for multiple alternatives, especially in communal spaces, should not ignore contemporary global challenges. For example, we should address the current international economic situation, which is intolerable in social, environmental, and also economic terms. Without delving further into this issue, I will only point out that it is widely accepted that we must dismantle the speculative structures of the international financial market, which holds ill-gotten capital, as well as money linked to war and terrorism, in so-called tax havens. Equally questionable is the existence of several financial institutions, which serve as political pressure tools, so that a large state or an institution controlled by a few powerful states can impose (typically unsustainable) conditions on weaker countries. This has happened, and still happens, with external borrowing, transformed into a tool of political domination.[11] It is also necessary to encourage solutions to achieve world peace. This means promoting a massive disarmament, allocating resources in such a manner as to meet the most pressing needs of humanity and, thus, disabling many violent processes. However, we must go further. If human beings do not restore a peaceful equilibrium with Mother Earth, there can and will be no peace for humanity. Therefore, a harmonious re-encounter with nature, as proposed by the essential logics of the Good Living, is urgent.

Thus, Good Living summons us to build a life of self-sufficiency and self-management for human beings living in communities and, hence, to ensure the self-healing power of nature. This is definitely a major challenge for humanity. All this strengthens the local. From local national and regional, decision-making spaces, democratic global spaces can be built, creating new territorial and conceptual maps.

Good Living and the recovery of utopias

Solving this puzzle will not be easy. To begin, we must rediscover 'the utopian dimension', as suggested in the 1980s by the Peruvian thinker Alberto Flores Galindo (1989). This involves reinforcing basic democratic values like freedom, equality, solidarity, and equity, as well as incorporating approaches and conceptual assessments of communal life into our political agenda. Such approaches include notions of reciprocity and relationality, in which real political, religious, sexual, and cultural tolerance prevail. As noted above, this involves a cultural-political encounter with nature.

In short, the Good Living presents an opportunity to create a new emancipatory project. This is a project that brings together many histories of resistance struggles and proposals for change. It draws on local experiences above all – to which contributions from various latitudes must be added – and can thus act as a starting point to build sustainable democratic societies in all areas. Therefore, issues such as the construction of a new economy or the rights of nature that would truly allow us to make human rights a reality also crystallise as matters of human concern and should be discussed and addressed as such.

There is no clear recipe to build different societies. However, not having a predetermined path is not a problem. In fact, the opposite may be the case. An unbeaten path frees us from dogmatic views, although it demands greater clarity vis-à-vis the destination at which we wish to arrive, namely initiating the transition to another civilisation as part of the Good Living itself. Not only does the destination count, but also the paths towards a dignified human life, so that we can guarantee a present and a future for all human beings and ensure the survival of humanity on the planet. As Flores Gallindo (1989) once said, "there is no recipe [to build a different society, A.A.]. Neither a traced path nor a definite alternative. It must be built".

Notes

1 The author thanks the Ecuadorian economist John Boxes Guijarro for reviewing this text; the editors thank Arthur Bueno for the translation.
2 The list of texts that address this issue is growing larger. One could mention, among many other contributions, Acosta 2013 (translated into French, German, and Portuguese).
3 The texts on this subject are becoming more numerous. Particularly interesting are contributions made by several authors in D'Alisa/Demaria/Kallis 2015.
4 On the issue of extractive activities I recommend Gudynas 2015.
5 It is important to note that the translations of these terms are not simple and are not exempt from controversy. At present one can find various and even contradictory descriptions and definitions.
6 In the indigenous world, there are usually few written texts. This is understandable, given that it consists of oral cultures. A text which contributed in Ecuador to spread these theses was Gualinga 2002.
7 We must recognize that in many indigenous communities patriarchal and chauvinistic traits are deeply rooted.
8 I suggest, from a long list of important contributions, Illich 1973 and Illich 1974.
9 On this topic one might consider Flok Society 2015.
10 Here it is worth noting the valuable reflections by Shiva 2010.
11 In this regard one can see the proposals by Acosta/Guijarro 2015.

References

Acosta, A. (2013 [2016]). *El Buen Vivir. Sumak Kawsay, una oportunidad para imaginar otros mundos*. Barcelona: ICARIA. Translated to French by Utopia 2014. In: German by Oekom Verlag 2015, and in Portuguese by Editorial Autonomia Literária and Editorial Elefante.

Acosta, A./J.C. Guijarro (2015). Instituciones transformadoras para la Economía Global – Pensando caminos para dejar atrás el capitalismo. In: *La osadía de lo nuevo – Alternativas de política económica*. Ed by Grupo de Trabajo Permanente de la Fundación Rosa Luxemburg. Abya-Yala: Quito, 133–192.

D'Alisa, G./F. Demaria/G. Kallis (eds., 2015). *Degrowth. A Vocabulary for a new Era*. New York/London: Routledge.

Flok Society (2015). *Buen Conocer, Modelos sostenibles y políticas públicas para una economía del conocimiento común y abierto en Ecuador*. Quito: Instituto de Altos Estudios Nacionales.

Galindo, A.F. (1989). *Reencontremos la dimensión utópica: Speech at the Instituto de Apoyo Agrario y El Caballo Rojo*. Lima. Online at https://marxismocritico.com/2016/01/08/reencontremos-la-dimension-utopica.

Gualinga, C.V. (2002). *Visión indígena del desarrollo en la Amazonía*. Quito: Polis.

Gudynas, E. (2015). *Extractivismos – Ecología, economía y política de un modo de entender el desarrollo y la Naturaleza*. La Paz: CLAES – CEDIB.

Illich, I. (1973). *Tools for Conviviality*. New York: Harper and Row.

Illich, I. (1974). *Energy and Equity*. London: Boder.

Kothari, A./F. Demaria/A. Acosta (2014). Buen Vivir, Degrowth and Ecological Swaraj: Alternatives to Sustainable Development and the Green Economy. In: *Development* 57.3/4, 362–375.

Polanyi, K. (2010 [1944]). *The Great Transformation: The political and economic origins of our time*. Boston: Beacon.

Quijano, A. (ed., 2014): *Descolonialidad y bien vivir – Un nuevo debate en América Latina*. Cátedra América Latina y la Colonialidad del Poder. Lima: Universidad Ricardo Palma.

Shiva, V. (2010). Resources. In: W. Sachs (ed.). *Development Dictionary: A Guide to Knowledge as Power*. Second Edition, London: Zed Books, 228–242.

Tortosa, J.M. (2011). *Mal desarrollo y mal vivir – Pobreza y violencia escala mundial*, ed. by A. Acosta/E. Martínez, series Debate Constituyente. Quito: Abya – Yala.

3   Available, accessible, attainable

The mindset of growth and the resonance conception of the good life

Hartmut Rosa

One very curious but consistent fact about late modern life is that almost irrespective of their values, status and moral commitments, subjects feel notoriously short on time and tirelessly pressed to hurry (Gershuny 2003; Robinson/Godbey 2008; Wajcman 2014). Individuals from Rio to New York, from Los Angeles to Moscow and Tokio feel caught in a rat-race of daily routines. No matter how fast they run, they close their day as *subjects of guilt*: they almost never succeed in working off their *to-do lists*. Thus, even and especially if they have enough money and wealth, they are indebted temporally. This is what perhaps characterizes the everyday predicament of the overwhelming majority of subjects in Westernised capitalist societies most aptly: amidst monetary and technological affluence, they are close to temporal insolvency. We need more time to do our work properly; we need more time to improve our skills and knowledge, to renew our hardware and software; we need more time to care for our kids and elderly parents, more time for our friends and relatives, for our house or flat and for our body, and finally, we need more time to come to terms with ourselves, our minds or souls or psyche. The problem, in fact, is that in all of these respects (and probably many more), there are legitimate expectations directed towards us by ourselves or by others – expectations turning into obligations which we feel we really should meet, and the neglect of which will be held against us in one context or another (Rosa 2017). *Of course, I should have done it long ago, but I just did not find the time yet*, has become something like the default-perspective with which we move from context to context. Thus, just as a person who is indebted financially permanently seeks to gain, save or earn a little money to pay back his or her debts here and there, the modern subject who is temporally indebted constantly seeks to gain or save a little time or find some postponement to meet his or her obligations. Yet, as with the monetary debts, once we are too deeply indebted, there is no way out of the trap. Now surely, the temporal predicament is of utmost significance for all our attempts to live a good life, for how we (want to) live our lives is equivalent to how we (want to) spend our time. Hence, the vexing question is this: How did we get here? How is this logic of escalatory acceleration tied up with our conceptions of the good life? And, first and foremost: How can we find a way out?

Given that modern societies are characterised by the fact that they can only reproduce their institutional structures dynamically, i.e. in an escalatory mode of growth, acceleration and innovation (cf. the introduction to this volume), I want to explore in this contribution the connection between this structural feature and the dominant conception of the good life that accompanies it. To this end, I will identify two corresponding cultural 'imperatives for growth' that provide the hamster-wheel of modern social life with motivational energy, or, put differently, that translate the structural requirement of growth, acceleration and innovation into a strategic necessity in our search for the good life. In a second step, I will show why this conception necessarily fails in a twofold way: It leads to the destruction rather than the control of nature – and to alienation rather than appropriation of the world. In the third and last step of this paper, I therefore want to present an alternative conception of the good life that might provide us with a cultural and motivational lever to counter those imperatives and collectively find a way out of the late-modern predicament.

Systemic requirements and ethical imperatives: the triple-A approach to the good life

If we accept that the escalatory logics of growth, acceleration and innovation implied in dynamic stabilisation are a systemic requirement and structural necessity of modern society, the core question that arises is how the resulting growth- and speed-imperatives are connected to, or translated into modern subjects' conceptions of the good life. For obviously, it would be highly implausible to suppose that individuals are merely the victims, or the passive receivers, of those requirements.

Surely, in the end, it is us humans who have to achieve growth, acceleration and innovation through incessant (self-) optimisation, and we play this escalatory game through the endless accumulation of economic, cultural, social and bodily capital. But in order to fully grasp the corresponding processes of translating the structural requirements into personal aspirations, we need to understand some peculiar features of the cultural predicament of modernity first.

The most important of these is ethical pluralism and what Alasair MacIntyre once called the *privatisation of the good* (MacIntyre 1990). For in parallel with the structural and institutional shift towards dynamic stabilisation, modern societies came to accept that they could not reach a binding consensus on the definition of the good life; that there is no way to rationally arbitrate between competing 'comprehensive conceptions of the good', as John Rawls termed it (Rawls 1993). Thus, ethical pluralism has become the basic cultural condition of modernity: whether one should abide by a religious belief, and if so, by which one; whether one should strive to develop political, artistic or intellectual capacities; whether one should marry and have kids or not, and all the other small and big questions about what kind of life one should lead, about leading a life as such – e.g. whether music should be important, whether literature should be a part of life, whether the town or the country is preferable, whether the local soccer team was important or not – were turned into strictly private questions. *You'll have to find out for yourself!* is the standard answer to all of them, and it is not just the proforma line taken in families and classrooms and even in the local pubs in order to ensure civility. In fact, that the question of the good should be an intimate, strictly private and individual matter is itself one of the founding and grounding ethical convictions of modernity. If a kid asks what to do with his or her life – questions such as: *Should I play soccer, or the flute? Should I be interested in politics? Should I believe in God? Whom should I marry? Where should I live?* – teachers, friends and family will be sure to offer their advice, but they will almost inevitably rush to add: *Just find out for yourself; listen to your heart; come to know your talents and your yearnings.* Thus, the good life has become the most intimately private matter of all things. It has become even more delicate by the fact that, by consequence of dynamic stabilisation, the background conditions of the life to be led are changing quickly: *You can never know what you will want, and what you will need, in the future. The world will change, and your own outlook on life will change, too.* Hence, the answer to 'what kind of life should I strive for'? has become very elusive, shrouded in uncertainty.

However, it is not that no ethical advice can be given at all. Quite to the contrary: modern society might not have an answer to what the good life is or what it consists in, but it has a very clear-cut answer to what the *preconditions* for living a good life are, and to what to do for meeting them: *Secure the resources you might need for living your dream (whatever that might be)!* has become the overruling rational imperative of modernity.

Harvard Philosopher John Rawls in his most remarkable *Theory of Justice* has outlined this predicament perhaps in the most straightforward way. There will be no agreement on the comprehensive doctrines of the good, he says, but there are a number of 'primary goods' of which to have *more* is clearly better than to have *less*, irrespective of what your conception of the good is. Such goods are, first and foremost, our freedoms and rights, but also our economic means, our cultural capacities and knowledge, our social networks, our social status and the recognition we earn, but also our health etc. (Rawls 1971). *No matter what the future might bring, it will help if you have money, rights, friends, health, knowledge.*

By consequence, the ethical imperative that guides modern subjects is not a particular or substantive definition of the good life, but is the aspiration to acquire the resources necessary or helpful for leading one. In a way, we moderns resemble a painter who is forever concerned about improving his materials – the colours and brushes, the air condition and lighting, the canvas and easel, etc. – but never really starts to paint.

Thus, when we consult the books in the self-help section of bookstores for happiness and the good life, we find that the increase in those 'primary goods' or resources more often than not is equated with an increase in the quality of life as such: the secrets to a good and happy life, we are assured, can be unraveled if we find out *how to get rich, how to be more healthy, or attractive, or have more friends*, or *how to acquire better skills, memory and knowledge etc.* In short, the aspirations and dreams, the strivings and yearnings, the fears and anxieties that have come to guide our actions and decisions are firmly fixed on our equipment with resources. Our libido is tied to the acquisition of economic and cultural, social and symbolic, and, increasingly, bodily capital (Bourdieu 1984).

This strategy, which seems thoroughly irrational at first glance, is made rational by the fact that the social allocation of resources is regulated through competition, while the allocation-game itself is increasingly dynamised, too.

Hence, the logic of competition installs the fear of losing out: as with Weber's capitalist entrepreneur (Weber 2001, 30), modern subjects find themselves unavoidably to be 'on their way down', like standing on a downward escalator or on a slipping slope, if they do not run uphill to improve their standings and keep track with the changes around them (Rosa 2016). Thus, we never simply 'have' the resources we need: if we do not increase, optimise and improve them, they are about to corrode, decay and dwindle. So, what is driving modern subjects to stay in the race, to a large extent, is their fear of virtual social death: sure, in most of the so-called developed countries, even if you lose too much ground, you will not starve, because the welfare systems provide you with the material necessities, but you will be excluded from the allocation-game, which is tied to employment. Without it, you cannot gain culturally legitimate resources, status, recognition or positions. You are given alms, but you do not have a legitimate, self-affirming place in the world that allows for a sense of self-efficacy.

As a result, the logic of incessant increase, the desire to grow, run and enhance is firmly anchored in the habitual structure of modern subjectivity. In fact, it is doubly entrenched in the modern character: as the *desire* to improve our resource base and as the *fear* of losing out, i.e. of losing the preconditions for a good life through erosion of this very base. Yet, the irresistible *desire* in this arrangement, the attractive cultural force of the escalatory logic, cannot fully be grasped by pointing to the resource aspect alone. (Economic) growth, (technological) acceleration and (sociocultural) innovation for modern subjects undeniably carry a genuine promise; they are tied to our conceptions of freedom and happiness.

Why is 'having more and moving faster' attractive for most modern subjects? It is, I want to argue, because the escalatory logic of dynamic stabilisation is tied to the promise of increasing our individual and collective scope and reach. This triggers what I want to call the 'Triple-A Approach' to the good life: the modern way of acting and being-in-the world is geared towards making more and more of its qualities and quantities available, accessible and attainable. This is what science does, and what science promises: peering farther into the universe through our telescopes, looking deeper into the micro-structure of matter and life through our microscopes, etc. Making the world knowable, calculable, disposable. It is what economic wealth is about: the richer we are (individually and/or collectively), the more the world is made available, attainable and accessible to us. We can build and buy castles and cathedrals, rockets and spaceships, yachts and hotels, etc. In fact, making the world available, accessible and attainable explains the lure of technology writ large: for a young kid, the first bike brings his or her friends on the other side of the village within the horizon of availability; the first moped enlarges this circle to the neighboring village, while the car expands the horizon of the world which is accessible on a regular basis to the larger cities around, and the airplane, finally, brings New York, Rio, Tokyo within reach. Similarly, the telephone and the radio make faraway places accessible acoustically, while the TV makes them visually available. The smartphone, finally, brings all of our friends, and all of the digitalised knowledge and images of the earth, straight into our pockets.

The power of the Triple-A Approach to the good life can be felt also in the attractivity of cities for modern subjects: almost universally across the modern world, the majority of people, and certainly of young people, want to live in large cities rather than in small villages. Ask them why: because in the city, you have the mall, the cinema, the theater, the zoo, the museum, the big stadiums, all within your everyday reach, within the horizon of availability. And it explains, in part, why knowledge and education are attractive even beyond their use as a resource base: *learn English, or Chinese, and you discover a whole new world of literature and art, culture and shopping*; the whole universe of that language becomes available for you, for example. In this way, the world is turned into a disposable place, with money, education and technology supplying the charms for incessantly increasing our reach and scope. Hence, culturally as well as structurally, modern society entrenches and even enforces a very particular stance and attitude towards the world, a stance that is defined by the logic of increase, control and augmentation.[1]

Alienation and pollution – or: what is wrong with the Triple-A Approach?

So far, I have tried to sketch out that we are driven by the desire to expand our horizon of the available, attainable and accessible. Our conception of the good life is rooted in the idea that we can 'gain' the world, that we can unlock it, make it 'legible' (Blumenberg 1979) and get its treasures and secrets to speak to us. Yet, most unfortunately, when we look at our current sociocultural predicament, this strategy seems to have failed thoroughly, and in a twofold way. First, of course, there is a widespread and growing sense across the world that we do not so much gain and dispose of the world than destroy and endanger it. This sense is most vivid in environmental concerns that in the mode of dynamic stabilisation, through incessant growth and acceleration, we damage and destroy, impoverish and reduce, pollute and poison our natural surroundings. In our late modern world, 'nature' has, quite paradoxically, become synonymous with the unattainable, non-available 'other' on the one hand, and with something we are guilty of destroying on the other. This, in turn, leads to the backlash of an unleashed nature striking out in tsunamis and typhoons, avalanches and droughts, viruses and bacteria resistant to antibiotics. The natural world, instead of being made available, attainable and accessible, in many respects appears to become endangered and dangerous instead. This relationship with what modern subjects still perceive to be their living and breathing, responsive, natural surrounding certainly does not correspond to the way of being-in-the-world that the strategy of increasing our reach and scope was aiming at.

Yet, when we look at the cultural history of modernity, there is a second, even more disturbing sense in which this very strategy turns out to be paradoxical. For ever since the 18th century, when the shift to the mode of dynamic stabilisation occurred, modernity has been haunted by the fear, and by the manifest experience, that the world seems to recede in parallel with the increase of our hold over it. In a phenomenological perspective, we appear to lose the world as we make it available. In cultural self-observations of modernity as well as in social theory and philosophy, this process has been observed from many different angles: Jean-Jacques

Rousseau, for example, experienced it when he disputed the gains allegedly made through progress and when he interpreted them as a genuine loss in the quality of our being-in-the-world, testified in the shift from *amour-de-soi* to *amour propre* (Rousseau 2012); Karl Marx identified it as a fivefold process of *alienation* from work, from the products of work, from nature, from our fellow human beings and, in the end, from ourselves, and he took it as the starting point for his philosophy (Marx/Engels 1988), which later on inspired the diagnoses of alienation and the corresponding forms of reification by Adorno, Fromm, or Marcuse, as well as by Georg Lukacs and, more recently, by Axel Honneth (2012) and Rahel Jaeggi (2014). In all of these conceptions, there looms the shadow of a world turned shallow and silent, mute and deaf through our very attempt to control and commodify it. Alienation has come to serve as the keyword for a world which has become cold and grey, harsh and non-responding, experienced by a subject that inwardly feels deaf, mute, cold, and empty, too. We find this sense of a serious loss of the world, of its slipping away from us, in other traditions of social philosophy, too: in Durkheim's conception of anomia (and his notions of anomic and egoistic forms of suicide; Durkheim 1997), in Georg Simmel's identification of a blasé attitude towards the things and events that surround us and a 'latent' aversion against our fellow human beings, which he deemed characteristic of the modern habitus (Simmel 1997), in Max Weber's notion of 'disenchantment' as the flipside of the longstanding process of 'rationalisation' (which he defines as the process which makes the world calculable and controllable), or in Albert Camus' definition of the 'absurd', which is born, he says, from the sense that we cannot but shout and yell at a world which never answers because it is, in its innermost core, cold and indifferent or even hostile to us (Camus 1991). Finally, for Hannah Arendt (1958), human subjects lose the world if they lose their capacity for joint, creative political action – irrespective of how successful they might be economically and technologically.

This failure of the triple-A strategy towards the good life is felt most vividly in the psychological state of 'burnout', which has become the iconic fear and disease of late-modernity (Ehrenberg 2010). People who suffer a thorough burnout – however problematic its exact medical definition may be – experience exactly that: a world which has turned hard and cold, grey or black, dead and deaf for them, while they inwardly feel empty and drained, too. *Burnout* thus is the most radical form of alienation in the sense of a complete loss or lack of a responsive, 'warm' connection with life and with the world. If my diagnosis of the receding of the world as the flipside of our making it available, accessible and attainable is correct, it is small wonder that 'burnout' has become the dominant cultural fear precisely in those social contexts where the triple-A strategy has been most successful and where there is an abundance of resources.

So the question arises: what has gone wrong? Why did modernity betray our hopes and fail to deliver its promise? In order to answer this, we have to go back one more time and ask: why was bringing the world within reach and scope so attractive for us moderns in the first place? What *was* the promise by which we were led in this strategy? To put it straightforwardly: I believe that at the heart of it, we are driven by the idea that through increasing scope and reach we can improve the quality of our relating to the world. The desire to increase our physical, material and social range is driven by the hope that we can find the *right* place for us, that we meet the people we *really* want to live with, the job that *actually* satisfies us, the religion or worldview which is *truly ours*, the books that actually *talk to us* and the music that *speaks to us*, etc. Thus, in the end, we hope, we will arrive at a form of life that turns the world into a living, breathing, speaking, responsive, 'enchanted' world. Alas, as I have tried to point out, instead of arriving there, we end up turning the business of increasing our scope and horizon of the available, attainable and accessible, and collecting resources into an end in itself, into an endless, escalatory cycle which permanently erodes its own basis and thus leads nowhere.

Let me try one small, idiosyncratic example: think of the way we relate to books and to music. For many modern subjects, literature and music have become central 'axes' or elements of a good life, crucial albeit somewhat luxurious indicators for the quality of life: a sphere in which they seek and find moments of happiness. For decades, it has become a cultural routine for many people (certainly not just academics and intellectuals) to gradually build up collections of records, or CDs, and a private library. As time has become an increasingly scarce commodity, while music and books have become more and more easily attainable and affordable, very often the books and CDs or records thus collected are never really or fully read or heard: they are stored away in shelves and cases for possible future use. They are acquired as mere potential, but they are not, or not fully, *appropriated* in the true sense of 'consumption'. For to consume a book or a record does not mean to *buy* them but to read or to listen to them. When we read a book or listen to a piece of music in the full sense of it, we have a chance of being drawn in, being touched and affected by it, and to some extent even of being *transformed* by it: very often, people refer to their most intense and rewarding experiences of reading or listening by claiming that the book or music in question actually 'changed their life'. Now, obviously, increasing the reach and scope of permanently available and accessible books and music through acquisition does not necessarily or directly translate into an increase in the quality and/or quantity of intense cultural experiences of this latter sort. In fact, there might even be a *negative* correlation that parallels the macro-story I just told in the section before: as we find less and less time to delve into a book or a piece of music, we seem to develop an increasing appetite to acquire more of them. This appears to be an almost 'natural' side-effect of dynamic stabilisation: literature and music as commodities become progressively cheaper, while the time taken to read a book or actually listen to an opera gets comparatively more 'expensive'.[2] Thus, instead of listening to the 170 CDs comprised in *The Complete Mozart* (or in the complete Pink Floyd recordings), which takes ages to do, acquiring the complete Beethoven (or Stones) collection as well for just 49 pounds, dollars or euros becomes an increasingly attractive alternative. Yet, the likelihood that none of those 170 CDs actually speaks to us increases as well.

Now, interestingly, as the reader certainly will have noticed a while ago, we have already taken the next step in the logic of increasing our range and scope of cultural accessibility: younger people tend to no longer buy books and CDs or DVDs – they buy mere *access* instead. For just a few bucks a month, they get *unlimited* access to millions of books, albums and/or movies! This seems like the ultimate realisation of modernity's dream. Yet, more often than not, we find ourselves sitting in face of this limitless horizon of availability and feel attracted to none of the options. A very similar story can be told about the history of private photography: for decades, many people used to take photographs in order to enable them to relate in an intense and intimate way to past experiences. The images were carefully selected when taken and then individually stored in physical albums. With the advent of fast and cheap digital imaging, pictures have become abundantly available and accessible: we can make, multiply and store hundreds and thousands of them, and we do so with the hope that they will release their true relational potential some time in the future. But in fact, more often than not, their time never comes. Increasing the scope of attainability appears to have significantly reduced the experiential and relational quality. This is precisely where cultural grey out or individual burnout actually loom large.

Thus, to sum up my argument so far, we have good reasons to assume that the good life in its essence is *not* a matter of scope (in money, wealth, options or capabilities), but a particular way of relating to the world – to places and people, to ideas and bodies, to time and to nature, to self and others. Increasing the scope is only a means and a strategy to enable or facilitate the latter – it becomes detrimental if it is structurally turned into an end in itself and thus culturally leads to alienation from the world (and to the destruction of nature on top of it).

The resonance conception of the good life

Now, if the two claims just formulated are plausible – i.e., that a) the good life is a matter of the way in which we are relating with and to the world, of our being in the world, and that b) dynamic stabilisation and the triple-A strategy lead to increasing alienation as a *failed* way of being and relating – then the question that remains to be answered is this: what is the opposite of alienation? What is a 'good' or fulfilling way of relating to places, people, time, things, and self? What is alienation's other? Let me start answering this question by defining alienation in a more precise way. Alienation, I want to claim, is a particular mode of relating to the world of things, of people and of one's self in which there is no *responsivity*, i.e. no meaningful inner connection. It is, to use Rahel Jaeggi's (2014) term, a relationship without (true) relation. As we have seen, in this mode, there certainly are causal and instrumental connections and interactions, but the world (in all its qualities) cannot be appropriated by the subject; it cannot be made to 'speak'; it appears to be without sound and colour. Alienation thus is a relationship which is marked by the absence of a true, vibrant exchange and connection: between a silent and grey world and a 'dry' subject there is no life; both appear to be either 'frozen' or genuinely chaotic and mutually aversive. Hence, in the state of alienation, self and world appear to be related in an utterly indifferent or even hostile way.[3]

But the true sense of alienation as I want to use it here only becomes comprehensible when we start to think of its alternative. Alienation's other is a mode of relating to the world in which the subject feels touched, moved or addressed by the people, places, objects, etc. he or she encounters. Phenomenologically speaking, we all know what it means to be touched by someone's glance or voice, by a piece of music we listen to, by a book we read, a place we visit, etc. Thus, the capacity to feel affected by something, and in turn to develop intrinsic interest in the part of the world which affects us, is a core element of any positive way of relating to the world. And as we know from psychologists and psychiatrists, its marked absence is a central element of most forms of depression and burnout (Fuchs 2008, Rosa 2016). Yet, it is not enough to overcome alienation. What is additionally required is the capacity to 'answer' the call: in fact, when we feel touched in the way described above, we often tend to give a physical response by developing goose bumps, an increased rate of heartbeat, a changed blood pressure or skin resistance (Massumi 2002). Resonance, as I want to call this dual movement of af←fection (something touches us from the outside) and e→motion (we answer by giving a response and thus by establishing a connection) thus always and inevitably has a bodily basis. But the response we give, of course, has a psychological, social and cognitive side to it, too: it is based on the experience that we can reach out and answer the call, that we can establish connection through our own inner or outer reaction. It is by this reaction that the process of appropriation is brought about. This kind of resonance we experience, for example, in relationships of love or friendship, but also in genuine dialogue, when we play a musical instrument or in sports, but also very often at the workplace. The receptive as well as active connection brings about a process of progressive self- and world transformation.

Thus, resonance is not just built on the experience of being touched or affected, but also on the perception of what we can call self-efficacy.[4] In the social dimension, self-efficacy is experienced when we realise that we are capable of actually reaching out to and affecting others, that they truly listen and connect to us and answer in turn. But self-efficacy, of course, can also be experienced when we play soccer or the piano, when we write a text we struggle with (and which inevitably speaks its own voice), and even when we stand at the shoreline of the ocean and 'connect' with the rolling waves, the water and the wind. Only in such a mode of receptive affection and responsive self-efficacy are self and world related in an appropriative way: the encounter transforms both sides, the subject and the world experienced.[5] That resonances of this sort are vital elements of any identity-formation can be read from the fact that claims such as *after reading that book*, or *after hearing that music* or *meeting that group* or *climbing that mountain, I was a different person*, are standard ingredients of almost all (auto-)biographical accounts given, for example, in interviews. It is important to notice here that the transformative effects of resonance are beyond the control of the subject: when something really touches us, we can never know or predict in advance what we will become as a result of this.

To sum up, resonance as alienation's other, then, is defined by four crucial elements: First, by af←fection in the sense of the experience of being truly touched or moved, second by e→motion as the experience of responsive (as opposed to purely instrumental) self-efficacy, third by its transformative quality, and fourth by an intrinsic moment of elusiveness, i.e. of non-controllability or non-disposability.

We can never simply establish resonance instrumentally or bring it about at will; it always remains elusive. Put differently: whether or not we 'hear the call' is beyond our will and control. This in part is due to the fact that resonance is not an *echo*: it does not mean to hear oneself amplified or to simply feel re-assured, but it involves encounter with some real 'other' that remains beyond our control, that speaks in its own voice or key different from ours and therefore remains 'alien' to us. Even more than this, this 'other' needs to be experienced as a source of 'strong evaluation' in the sense of Charles Taylor: only when we feel that this other (which can be a person, but also a piece of music, a mountain, or a histori-cal event, for example) has something important to tell or teach, irrespectively of whether we like to hear it or not, can we truly feel 'grasped' and touched (Taylor 1989, 3–109, see his paper in this book). Resonance, therefore, inevitably requires a moment of self-transcendence (Joas 2001). It does not require, however, that we have a clear cognitive concept or previous experience of this other. We can all of a sudden be touched and shaken by something that appears to be alien altogether. Therefore, resonance certainly is not just consonance or harmony; quite to the opposite: it *requires difference* and sometimes *opposition* and *contradiction* in order to enable real encounter. Thus, in a completely harmonious or consonant world, there would be no resonance at all, for we would be incapable of discern-ing the voice of an 'other' – and by consequence, to develop and discern our own voice. Yet, a world in which there is *only* dissonance and conflict would not allow for experiences of resonance either: such a world would be experienced as merely repulsive. In short, resonance requires difference that allows for the possibility of appropriation: of a responsive relationship that entails progressive, mutual trans-formation and adaptation. Resonance, then, is a condition between consonance and irrevocable dissonance. Because of this, I am convinced the concept can pro-vide a key to overcome the traditional stand-off between theories and philoso-phies based on identity and conceptions centered on difference. Resonance does not require identity, but the transformative appropriation of difference.

In light of this definition of resonance, it becomes clear that resonance cannot be stored or accumulated, and there cannot be a struggle for resonance either.[6] Therefore, resonance provides us with a conception of the good life that contra-dicts the logics of increase and the triple-A approach. We immediately understand this when we think of what happens when we try to play our favorite piece of music ten times in a row, or every day: we do not increase our experience of reso-nance, but we lose it. Similarly, the increase in our database of available music to millions of titles ready at hand does not, at least not necessarily, increase the likelihood of musical resonance.

But the elusiveness and moment-like character of resonance does not mean that it is completely random and contingent. For while the actual experience can never be completely controlled and predicted (in fact, just as we expect it to hap-pen most strongly, it is very likely that we will be disappointed – Christmas Eve in family life might be a good case in point), there are two elements involved here which depend on social conditions and which therefore turn resonance into a con-cept that can be used as a tool for social criticism. First, subjects individually and collectively experience resonance typically along particular 'axes' of resonance.

Thus, for some, music provides such an axis: Whenever they go to the concert hall, or to the opera, or the festival arena, they have a good chance of making that experience. For others, it will be the museum, the library, or the church, the forest or the shoreline. More than that, we also foster social relationships that provide something like a reliable axis of resonance: we can expect moments of resonance when we are with our lovers, with our kids or with our friends – even though we all know that very often, our respective encounters remain indifferent or even repulsive. And just as much, as we know from evidence provided by the sociology of labor (most instructive for this, Sennett 2009), most people, or at least very many people, develop intense relationships of resonance with their work, not just with their colleagues at the workplace, but also with the materials and tasks they are working and struggling with. Thus, the dough 'responds' to the baker as does the haircut to the barber, the wood to the carpenter, the plant to the gardener, the truck to the trucker, the body to the doctor or the text to the writer. In each of these cases, we find a true two-way relationship which involves experiences of self-efficacy, resistance or contradiction and appropriation as well as mutual transformation (Rosa 2016, 393–401).

When we scrutinise these axes more closely, we find that we can systematically distinguish three different dimensions of resonance. I want to call them the social, material and existential dimensions of resonance. *Social* axes are those that connect us with, and relate us to, other human beings. In modern, Western-type societies since the romantic period, love, friendship, but also democratic citizenship are conceptualised as 'resonant' relationships of this type. *Material* axes are those we establish with certain objects – natural or artefacts, pieces of art, or amulets or tools and materials we work with or we use for sports. Thus, the skis for the skier or the board for the surfer can very well become 'responsive' counterparts. Yet, I believe with philosophers like Karl Jaspers (2001), William James (1982), Martin Buber (1971) or Friedrich Schleiermacher (1988) that human subjects also seek and find 'axes of resonance' that connect them with and relate them to life, or existence, or the universe as such. As those authors tried to show quite convincingly, this is what brings about religious experiences, and what makes religion plausible in the first place. To me, the central element of the bible, or the Koran, is the idea that at the root of our existence, at the heart of our being, there is not a silent, indifferent or repulsive universe, dead matter or blind mechanisms, but a process of resonance and response: someone who hears us and sees us, and who finds ways and means to touch us and to respond, who breathes life into us in the first place. The very practice of prayer for the believer opens up such an 'axis' which connects his innermost core with outermost reality. The praying person turns inward and outward at the same time. However, of course, modernity has found other axes of existential resonance that do not depend on religious ideas. Nature, in particular, is experienced as an ultimate, comprehensive as well as responsive reality. To listen to the voice of nature has become a central idea not just in idealistic philosophy, but even more so in many everyday routines and practices. Thus, many people regularly claim that they need to take to the forest, or the mountains, or the oceans or deserts to find and feel themselves. They believe they can only 'hear themselves' when listening to the silence (or the music) 'out there'. Just as in the case of prayer, they experience something like a thread that connects their innermost nature to outer reality. In a strikingly similar way, music itself opens up an analogous axis for the listener: when we close our eyes to experience a piece of music, we turn inward and outward simultaneously. And something very similar happens in the case of other aesthetic experiences in the museum, the cinema or when reading a book, too. *Art*, therefore, alongside *nature* has evolved into a central existential axis of resonance for modern subjects. That resonance does not need to be a pleasant, harmonious experience, but can develop essentially disturbing aspects, can be learnt from experiences we might have with *history* as a powerful reality running through us, which connects us with those who came before and those who will come after us, a reality we cannot control or command but which nevertheless responds to our actions such that we can feel a certain sense of self-efficacy. Thus, it appears to be a not so infrequent experience that young people, when visiting a former Nazi concentration camp, feel existentially struck and addressed; they feel a 'call' to respond to the inhumanity of such a site which actually does change their lives (see Rosa 2016, 500–514).

Now, while I take it that such concrete axes of resonance are not anthropologically given but rather culturally and historically constructed, the establishment of some such axes is nevertheless indispensable for a good life, for they provide contexts in which subjects dispositionally open up to experiences of resonance. To shift into a mode of resonance requires that we take the risk to make ourselves vulnerable. It conceptually requires that we let ourselves be touched, and even transformed, in a non-predictable and non-controllable way. Thus, in contexts where we are full of fear, or in stress, or in a fight-mode, or concentrated on bringing about a certain result, we do not seek or allow for resonance; quite to the contrary, doing so would be dangerous and harmful. Given this, it becomes obvious that it would be foolish to require that we should always be in a mode of dispositional resonance. The capacity to leave this mode, to distance oneself from the world, to take a cold, instrumental, analytical stance towards it, very obviously is a cultural achievement that is indispensable not just for keeping up the business of modern science and technology, but to actually provide and safeguard a form of life that allows for human resonance in the three dimensions mentioned.

Towards a social critique of the conditions of resonance

With this conception in our toolkit, I believe that we can start to use resonance as a yardstick to do the job of social philosophy in the sense of a critique of the prevailing social conditions. Its starting point is the idea that a good life requires the existence of reliable and viable axes of resonance in all three dimensions. A subject will have a good life, I claim, if he or she finds and preserves social, material and existential axes of resonance which allow for iterative and periodic reassurance of 'existential resonance', i.e. of a resonant mode of being. The possibility of such a good life, then, is endangered if the conditions for these axes and for the dispositional mode of resonance on the side of the subjects are structurally or systematically undermined. The institutional mode of dynamic stabilisation, so my argument goes, does display the tendency and the potential for such a systematic undermining. For it forces subjects into a mode of 'dispositional alienation': they are forced into a reifying, instrumental mode of relating to objects and subjects in order to increase and secure their resources, to speed-up and to optimise their equipment. The pervasive logic of competition in particular undermines the possibility to get into a mode or resonance: if we have to outpace someone, we cannot resonate with him or her at the same time. We cannot compete and resonate simultaneously.[7] Furthermore, as we know from research on empathy and from neurological studies (Bauer 2006), time-pressure actually works as a sure preventer of resonance. If we are short on time, we try to be as goal-directed and focused as possible; we cannot afford being touched and transformed. The same is true, of course, if we are driven by *fear*. Fear forces us to erect barriers and to close down our minds, it shifts us to a mode in which we precisely try *not* to be touched by 'the world'. Therefore, the conditions of resonance are such that they require contexts of mutual *trust* and fearlessness; and these contexts in turn require time and stability as background conditions. Finally, the pervasive bureaucratic attempts to completely control processes and outcomes in order to ensure their efficiency and transparency, which define late-modern workplace conditions, are equally problematic for relationships of resonance, because they are incompatible with the latter's elusiveness and transformative potential.

I do not have the space to develop a fine-grained analysis of contemporary, late-modern conditions of resonance here (see Rosa 2016, Part IV), but I am confident that the reader will find it a plausible claim that the escalatory logics of dynamic stabilisation and the corresponding Triple-A Approach to the good life are rather detrimental to the establishment and preservation of the three-dimensional axes of resonance, and that a critique of the conditions of resonance, therefore, is a worthwhile undertaking.

Notes

1 Of course, this argument is strikingly similar to the conceptions of the first generation of critical theorists such as Adorno and Horkheimer's notion of instrumental reason (Horkheimer/Adorno 2002) or Marcuse's identification of the 'promethean' stance of modern man in *Eros and Civilization* (Marcuse 1974).
2 This argument was brilliantly developed by the Swedish economist Staffan B. Linder as far back as 1970.
3 I have developed this notion of alienation as well as the corresponding conception of resonance at great length and in a much more precise way in Rosa 2016.
4 On the notion of self-efficacy see Bandura 1993.
5 Of course, the notorious problem with this claim is that it immediately provokes the objection that while the *subject* might well be transformed by the interaction with the violin or the ocean, the latter hardly change. But while this argument in fact depends on a perhaps not-so-innocent epistemology in which the only things capable of responding are human beings, i.e. on an 'asymmetrical anthropology' (Latour 1993, cf Descola 2013), it cannot be disputed that the *experienced* world *is* affected by such encounters: What the violin and the ocean are *for us* changes progressively, and what they are as 'things-in-themselves' we will never know.
6 This is one of the reasons why resonance is different from recognition; for a systematic discussion of this, see Rosa 2016, 331–340.
7 The only exception to this rule is, of course, the context of game and play and thus of sports, where a sphere of resonance very often provides the grounds for competition.

References

Arendt, H. (1958). *The Human Condition*. Chicago: University of Chicago Press.

Bandura, A. (1993). Perceived Self-Efficacy in Cognitive Development and Functioning. In: *Educational Psychologist* 28, 117–148.

Bauer, J. (2006). *Warum ich fühle, was du fühlst: Intuitive Kommunikation und das Geheimnis der Spiegelneurone*. München: Heyne.

Blumenberg, H. (1979). *Die Lesbarkeit der Welt*. Frankfurt am Main: Suhrkamp.

Bourdieu, P. (1984). *Distinction: A Social Critique of the Judgment of Taste*, transl. by Richard Nice. London: Routledge Kegan & Paul.

Buber, M. (1971). *I and Thou*, transl. by Walter Kaufmann. New York: Touchstone.

Camus, A. (1991). *The Myth of Sisyphus and Other Essays*, transl. by Justin O'Brien. New York: Vintage Books.

Descola, Ph. (2013). *Beyond Nature and Culture*, transl. by Janet Lloyd. Chicago: University of Chicago Press.

Durkheim, E. (1997). *Suicide: A Study in Sociology*, New York: The Free Press.

Ehrenberg, A. (2010). *The Weariness of the Self: Diagnosing the History of Depression in the Contemporary Age*. Montreal: McGill-Queen's University Press.

Fuchs, T. (2008). *Das Gehirn – ein Beziehungsorgan: Eine phänomenologisch-ökologische Konzeption*. Stuttgart: Kohlhammer.

Gershuny, J. (2003). *Changing Times: Work and Leisure in Postindustrial Society*. Oxford: Oxford University Press.

Honneth, A. (2012). *Reification: A New Look at an Old Idea* (The Berkeley Tanner Lectures). Oxford/New York: Oxford University Press.

Horkheimer, M./ Th. W. Adorno. (2002). *Dialectic of Enlightenment*. Stanford: Stanford University Press.

Jaeggi, R. (2014). *Alienation*. New York: Columbia University Press.

James, W. (1982). *The Varieties of Religious Experience: A Study in Human Nature*. London/New York: Penguin.

Jaspers, K. (2001). *Von der Wahrheit*. München: Piper.

Joas, H. (2001). *The Genesis of Values*. Chicago: Chicago University Press.

Latour, B. (1993). *We Have Never Been Modern*, transl. by Catherine Porter. Cambridge, MA: Harvard University Press.

Linder, S.B. (1970). *The Harried Leisure Class*. New York: Columbia University Pess.

MacInytre, A. (1990). The Privatization of the Good: An Inaugural Lecture. In: *The Review of Politics* 52, 344–361.

Marcuse, H. (1974). *Eros and Civilization: A Philosophical Inquiry into Freud*. Boston: Beacon Press.

Marx, K./F. Engels (1988). *The Economic and Philosophic Manuscripts of 1844*, transl. by Martin Milligan. Amherst, NY: Prometheus Books.

Massumi, B. (2002). *Parables for the Virtual: Movement, Affect, Sensation*. Durham, London: Duke University Press.

Rawls, J. (1971). *A Theory of Justice*. Cambridge, MA: Harvard University Press.

Rawls, J. (1993). *Political Liberalism*. Cambridge, MA: Harvard University Press.

Robinson, J./G. Godbey (2008). *Time for Life: The Surprising Ways Americans Use Their Time*. University Park: Penn State University Press.

Rosa, H. (2016). *Resonanz: Eine Soziologie der Weltbeziehung*. Berlin: Suhrkamp.

Rosa, H. (2017). De-Synchronization, Dynamic Stabilization, Dispositional Squeeze: The Problem of Temporal Mismatch. In: J. Wajcman /N. Dodd (eds.). *The Sociology of*

Speed. Digital, Organizational, and Social Temporalities. Oxford: Oxford University Press, 25–41.

Rousseau, J-J. (2012). Discourse on the Sciences and the Arts. In: transl. by J. T. Scott (ed.). *The Major Political Writings of Jean- Jacques Rousseau*. Chicago: Chicago University Press, 1–37.

Schleiermacher, F. (1988). *On Religion: Speeches to Its Cultured Despisers*. Cambridge: Cambridge University Press.

Sennett, R. (2009). *The Craftsman*. London/New York: Penguin Books.

Simmel, G. (1997). The Metropolis and Mental Life. In: D. Frisby/M. Featherstone (eds.). *Selected Writings*. London/Thousand Oaks/New Delhi: Sage, 174–186.

Taylor, Ch. (1989). *Sources of the Self: The Making of the Modern Identity*. Cambridge: Cambridge University Press.

Wajcman, J. (2014). *Pressed for Time: The Acceleration of Life in Digital Capitalism*. Chicago: University of Chicago Press.

Weber, M. (2001). *The Protestant Ethics and the Spirit of Capitalism*, translated by Talcott Parsons. New York: Routledge.

4 Resonance and the romantic era

A comment on Rosa's conception of the good life

Charles Taylor

In this paper, I want to explore a facet of Hartmut Rosa's fertile idea, that the good life is impossible without a relation of resonance between self and world. Here is one characterisation of this relation:

> In this mode the subject experiences the world . . . as "answering", responding and carrying. The connection here is of an intrinsic nature and meaning, not causal and instrumental, but constitutive. In this mode, the subject is capable of "appropriating" the world in a manner that transforms the self's essence through "connection". Thus, the mode of resonance can be defined as a mode in which the self is moved, touched, "meant to be" or "addressed", but also feels capable of reaching out and touching or moving the external world.
>
> (Rosa 2013; see Rosa in this volume)

I think is it eminently worth exploring the relation of this concept to the Romantic era, because in the first place, this is the locus of its origin; and secondly, the thought of the Romantic era still has a lot to teach us about its nature and meaning.

Now this concept applies to human nature in many ways. There are, in other words, many facets of human life where we might speak of "resonance". We can give it meaning in relation to our jobs or professional life, in relation to our love life; but also in relation to Nature, Art, Religion. These constitute different "axes" of resonance in Rosa's terminology. In discussing the origin of the concept in the period, I shall be focussing on our relation to nature and to art; and moreover, the two relations will be shown to be closely connected and interwoven.

The Romantic era

But first of all, a word about what I mean by "the Romantic era". I am mainly here concentrating on German writers of the 1790s, because I think that this generation brought about a veritable revolution in our understanding of language, art, and our relation to nature. This is not to scant, or neglect other national literatures of the period: obviously, English, French, Italian, and other European writers contributed to the Romantic transformation in thought and sensibility. In addition, a fuller account would not confine itself to literature and poetry, but would also look at music, painting, and other arts. But I think that the German writers of this period, centring their attention mainly on poetry (*Dichtung*, understood in a broad sense), worked out some key ideas, which later spread to other nations and their literatures. The *locus classicus* of this spread is Coleridge's *Biographica Literaria*, which helped introduce the thinking of Kant and the Romantics to the English world, influencing both Carlyle and Emerson. The interesting point is that this came to be seen as articulating the theory that underlay the already existing practice of English writers of the Romantic period. So it might help at this point to articulate the thinking, one might say the ontology of the Romantic generation of the 1790s. I can set this out with perhaps unbearable terseness in seven inter-locking theses.

(1) The first is that, inspired by Goethe, they embraced a Spinoza-derived pan-theism. Literal readers of Spinoza might be horrified, because this vision com-pletely separated the 17th-century thinker from his Cartesian roots. Nature was not to be understood mechanistically. It was more like a living organism. In other words, the Romantics were rebelling against a dead mechanical view of nature. And they were also rebelling against mind-body dualism, and against a purely instrumental approach to nature. They rejected (a) the structures of discipline con-trolling impulses, particularly erotic; especially (b) discipline aimed at efficacy in the world; also (c) guilt over disturbing, especially erotic, impulses which upset (a) and (b). They longed for a unification of self, unity with our emotions, with nature in us, and with nature as a whole. In this regard, one of their primary sources of inspiration was Goethe (who was nevertheless uncomfortable with their more rebellious stances).

(2) Our soul communicates with this whole, nature. Nature resonates in us, and we intensify this through expression, art. But (3) our whole idea of nature has undergone a modern shift. It isn't just a static set, or ordered cosmos, of beauti-ful forms; rather it is striving, developing; nature is producing higher and higher forms. Spinoza's *natura naturans* is seen as in motion, unfolding, seeking its adequate form. Moreover (4), this is what we also are doing. We are striving to discover our true form through creative expression. Indeed, it is this new anthro-pology which lies behind the new view of nature (and perhaps vice versa).

(5) This notion of expression connects up to a new ideal of freedom; it is a facet of the new understanding of freedom as full autonomy, which was both an ethical and political ideal. Kant is the great articulator of this ideal, followed by Fichte, Schelling, then Hegel. (3) and (4) together with (5) suggest (6), the ideal of the perfect reconciling of freedom and unity with nature, within and without. The progress to this is then envisaged through a narrative of history, the so-called "spiral path" (ekzentrische Bahn), whereby we leave an initial state of harmoni-ous unity between freedom and nature, pass through a period of their opposition, to return to a higher unity. (This goal was often tersely defined as combining Fichte and Spinoza.) And finally (7), there is irony: the road to (6) may never be completed; we may always strive, suffer distance. Ironic expression, however, manifests the gap, shows what we strive for (cf. Richards 2002, Beiser 2003).

The Romantic attempt to recover an original language which figures its objects emerges from this ontology. We develop as nature develops, and indeed, our proper development matches that of nature, brings it to consciousness, and unites it with freedom. In fact, we partake in the development of nature, which requires conscious expression to realise its end. We are the locus where nature becomes aware of itself. Many of the writers of the 1790s shared the view, later articulated by Schelling (and in a more rationalist form in Hegel) that the full realisation of nature requires the conscious expression which only Spirit can give it. Art (or philosophy) and nature come into unison, because they come to fulfillment together.

We find our own goals in nature, which must thus be correctly read. But our spiral path has taken us away from our immediate unity with nature, and we can no longer read it easily. What Romantic poetry strives to do is recover an adequate reading, and this would of necessity mean the creation of a mode of symbolic access.

Sources of the Romantic philosophy of language

From the forgoing, we can already begin to see that the Romantic movement is the source (or at least one of the sources) of our contemporary idea of resonance. In a sense its view of history is that we lost an original resonant relation with nature, as a price for our understanding, and development, of rational freedom; and that we need to recover a new resonant relation on a higher level, which can incorporate this freedom. We can also see how for the Romantics, the resonance axes of art and nature are intertwined. But much more needs to be said in order (a) to explain this understanding of language, nature and art; and (b) to convince the reader that these theories are still relevant for us today. These two goals are in some tension, some might think they are even contradictory. From what has already been said, many readers may conclude that the Romantic outlook involves a metaphysic that they find unacceptable, including a notion of teleology in nature that runs against what we understand as modern natural science. So explaining this outlook won't help to convince these people to adopt it. We will have to return to this issue later.

But first (a) a fuller account of the Romantic view of language and nature. Language, the right language, that of Dichtung (poetry in an extended sense), is our means of recovering the contact with nature which we have lost. We recover this contact by revealing dimensions of nature which we have lost sight of, and the mode of revelation is the symbol. So the successful poetic creation always has two facets: it opens us to a reality we couldn't see before; and at the same time re-connects us with this reality.

Along with this, comes a view of language, which I want to call the "dual language thesis". Language can be simply an instrument to encode information, describing the reality which already lies open before us, and communicating the information to others. But there are levels of language which do something much more, where our expressions bring about the revelation-and-connection that we find with the symbol. This distinction between a higher, creative and a lower, merely instrumental language is one of the continuing legacies of the Romantic period.

In order to understand this higher role of language, we have to go back into the Medieval and Renaissance notions of the language implicit in reality, from which Romanticism derives via a number of crucial transpositions. This earlier understanding of the universe as the locus of "signs" was ridiculed and set aside by the views about language which grew up in the early modern theory, in the work of such thinkers as Hobbes, Locke and Condillac. (With these thinkers in mind, I often refer to this theory as the HLC.) For them, language was essentially an instrument by which we could control our imagination and build a responsible and reliable picture of the world which lies before us.

Words function here essentially as arbitrary signs, as Locke (1690, Book III) made clear; they are "unmotivated", to use the language of Saussure. That is to say, certain concepts (signifieds) are hammered out to fit a pre-disclosed reality, and vocables (signifiers) are attached to them. I say the signs are essentially arbitrary: while vocables can be found which in some way suggest or mirror the reality described (like 'cuckoo'), this plays no role in the process. The development of a descriptive language can quite well proceed (and has proceeded) without any attention to this. This reality of descriptive language contrasts with a long-standing set of beliefs or myths about an original language, or languages, which were not arbitrary, which were somehow motivated, where the vocables themselves somehow mirrored the reality, and offered insight into it.

This was a recurring idea in the medieval and early modern period: that of a language of insight. What would this be like? It would be a language in which the terms weren't just arbitrarily applied to what they designate, but would be somehow uniquely right or appropriate to the things they named. They would be appropriate because they would reveal something of the nature of the objects named.

The notion that the perfect language had already existed in Paradise was encouraged by a passage in *Genesis*: "So from the soil Yahweh God fashioned all the wild beasts of the field and all the birds of heaven. These he brought to the man to see what he would call them; each one was to bear the name the man would give it" (*Genesis* 2, 19). This seemed to suggest a superiority of the language Adam invented; the names he chose were those that things ought to bear. Or as the Archangel Gabriel was said to have remarked to John Dee, in the primal language of Adam, "every word signifieth the quiddity of the substance" (Eco 1995, 185).

Now this revelatory rightness could itself be understood in different ways. On the simplest level, we have the Cratylist hypothesis: the word, or phonetic element, qua sound mimics the object; which is plainly the case for words like "cuckoo", or "meow", referring to what cats do. But the revelation concerned could be understood on a deeper level, as showing something of the inherent nature of the object.

The notion of inherent nature owes a lot to the inheritance from Greek philosophy, in particular to the Forms of Plato and Aristotle. But this basic scheme comes to be applied in a host of different ways in the subsequent tradition, and surfaces in different forms in the Medieval and early modern periods. The basic feature of this scheme, which one already sees in Plato, is the notion of a self-realizing order. This is what Plato presents in the *Republic*: the things we see about us in the world are in each case striving to realise the Idea or archetype to which they belong; and the cosmic order in which these things have their place is itself given its shape by the architectonic Idea, that of the Good. Following Plato himself in the *Timaeus*, this was taken up by Christian theology, with the Ideas being the thoughts of God that he carries into effect in creating the world. In either variant, the cosmos and all it contains is to be understood as the realisation of a plan which presides over its unfolding. This basic scheme was carried forward into neo-Platonism, but here the unfolding plan was understood as a kind of emanation from the One, rather than a creation ex nihilo.

The nature of this plan will then be variously described, as for instance in the works of pseudo-Dionysios the Areopagite; and it finds application in such continuing schemes as the Great Chain of Being, described by Arthur Lovejoy (1960). The "principle of Plenitude", which Lovejoy identifies, follows from the premise that the plan is a perfect one, from which no possible degree of perfection can be omitted.

But the notion of a divine plan can be conceived in other ways. In the numerological Kabbalah, for instance, starting from the fact that in Hebrew numbers are indicated by letters, each word can be assigned a number by summing its letters. This allows us to uncover a mystic relation between words with different meanings but the same number. The serpent of Moses can be seen as a prefiguration of the Messiah, because both sum to the number 358 (Eco 1995, 28). In turn, the whole Creation can be understood as put together by God from certain foundation letters.

The basic notion of the cosmos as the realisation of a plan can allow for other links of affinity, as with the Renaissance theory of the Correspondences: the king in the kingdom corresponds to the lion among animals, the eagle among birds, the dolphin among fish, because in each domain we are dealing with the supreme, ruling being. An analogous set of links underlies the notion of the Creation as a Book containing signs.

Another influential source of ideas or order and affinity between things during the Renaissance was the Hermetic tradition, supposedly based on the thought of Hermes Trismegistus, an ancient Egyptian sage. Celestial bodies influence things on earth, and there exist relations of sympathy between the macrocosm and the human microcosm, and between heavenly and earthly beings. We can trace these links by recognizing the "signatures" in material things which are marks of the heavenly bodies, according to the theories of Paracelsus (Eco 1995, 118; cf. Yates 1964). The 17th-century mystic Jakob Böhme took over this term, and saw "signatures" in things as the key to reading the *Natursprache*, or the speech of nature, the language in which Adam had named the animals and other creatures at the beginning (Eco 1995, 182f.).

These links were considered of the greatest importance for Renaissance thinkers because they were not only theoretically relevant. Knowing the sympathies between higher and lower can enable us to harness these astral powers to change things, e.g., through alchemy. Hermetic and Kabbalistic research was at first interwoven with what later separated out as orthodox post-Galilean natural science. All this provides the background for a deeper understanding of what "revealing the nature" of an object can mean. On this view, the perfect language would somehow make plain the place of the things it named in the Plan, and their affinities. We are well beyond simple issues of acoustic mimicry. But this language can be occult, hidden, or almost irretrievably lost.

We can see from the above discussion why the very idea of a language which gives insight into things seemed weird and incomprehensible to the early modern theorists of the HLC. If we think of our lexicon as consisting of words introduced one by one to name the things we perceive, then it is hard to imagine how the sounds we coin can give an insight into their designata (apart perhaps from the exceptional but trivial case of onomatopoeia). But it is clear that the forms of perfect language envisaged in the Renaissance and before, based as they were on the idea that the cosmos was the realisation of a plan, claimed to offer insight not into individual items, but into the connections that linked them to each other and to the whole, whether through the correspondences, or Kabbalistic numerology, or through the signatures in things. And this also gives us insight into the crucial ethical importance of recovering this insight, which alone would show us how to live in tune with this order, and how to empower us to do so.

So it is unsurprising that the theories of this range were very popular with the Romantics. One of their ways of protesting against the reduced condition of language as purely instrumental was to invoke the Kabbala. The Schlegels and Novalis both mention it. Nor did it die with them, because in the last century, Benjamin, following them also invokes it. Novalis in turn invokes the 'signatura rerum'.

Just what is going on here? On one level, we might think that they are just underscoring the importance of symbolic access, and more generally of access to A through B, because this indeed involves figuring. In other words, symbols fit the specifications of the original Adamic language. They are the right terms, because they reveal (disclose) what they're about. To use them is to have insight, and if you put anything else in their place, you lose the insight. Some facet of our moral life shows up in the language of elevation: we talk of "higher" modes of life; and in some American dialects, inferior people are referred to as "low life". No other expressions have equivalent force.

Nor is this kind of indirect access confined to speech. We can see it in works of art more generally. A kind of courage and determination shines through Beethoven's Fifth Symphony as it does nowhere else. And we can see something similar in the enacted meanings of behaviour: the particular swagger which emerges in this gang which is evolving a new kind of machismo says it as nothing else can – because the expressive-enactive gesture is also far from the "arbitrarily imposed" sign; it also discloses its meaning. But clearly the Romantics had a stronger thesis than this. They wanted to claim that signs really do inhere in things, and that we have lost the capacity to read them.

Disenchantment and freedom

The Romantics belonged to two streams of Anthropocentrism, freedom, and the voice of nature within. Indeed, what they were striving to do was to bring them together, because contemporary versions were pulling them apart, while the Romantics were highly sensitive to the affinities between them. More, they saw their task as reconciling them in a new unity. Their protest was against the understandings of freedom and a life according to nature which were elaborated at their most extreme in the naturalist Enlightenment – say, with Helvétius, Holbach, Bentham – but which were also present in a milder form, in, say, Voltaire.

A certain conception of freedom emerges from Locke among others, in which we stress the right and competence of the individual to direct his own life, and to exercise control over the world around him. In its most debased form – with Helvétius, for instance – this seemed to be demanding freedom for desire, but had no place for freedom from desire. The human subject was elided with its desires. There were two ways of feeling unease at this. One focused on the fact that this view had no place for higher aspirations, even aspirations beyond life and human flourishing; the other was to attack the naturalist view for its 'heteronomy'. It made humans the servants of desire, incapable of judging or choosing their goals from a more radical standpoint. This critique develops into a notion of freedom as self-determination, giving the law to oneself, elaborated by Rousseau and then in its most imposing statement by Kant. It was then pushed to its most far-reaching and ambitious form by Fichte, for whom the self-determination of the subject was ontologically ultimate.

The Romantic generation were heirs to this critique, and were all deeply influenced by Fichte. But they were also critical of it, because the aspiration to be in tune with nature also was important for them. Here their critique of the standard Enlightenment view was that life according to nature was interpreted as the application of instrumental reason to fulfill human needs. It made us split reason from nature, and treat the latter, both within and around us, as a domain to be worked on and manipulated instrumentally. They yearned for re-union – within ourselves, between reason and desire, between ourselves and the larger world of nature, and between individuals in society. This criticism that reason divides us from nature, was directed also against Kant and the critics of Enlightenment naturalism, perhaps even more clearly against Kant, because the division was all the sharper in his philosophy. So Fichte couldn't satisfy them either. They wanted to marry his philosophy with a vision of humans and nature as united, which placed us not over against a refractory nature, trying to submit it to the dictates of reason, but rather as part of a larger stream of life. Spinoza, as somewhat idiosyncratically read by Goethe, was often taken as the philosophical exponent of this view. As I indicated above, one way of describing their goal was: to unite Fichte and Spinoza.

It was out of this search for unity with the current of nature that they turned back and drew on the earlier theories of ontic logos, of the world as the locus of living purpose, speaking to us in signs. But it was as heirs of modern anthropocentrism that they reconceived what it was to get back in tune with this current. We do not just register, we *recreate* the meaning of things, and in doing so draw on our own characteristic powers, those of symbolic disclosure (or Poetry). We don't simply receive the answer, but collaborate in defining it. Here we see the trace of the modern centrality of freedom. It is a variant different from that which defines autonomy in opposition to everything else, God and cosmos, but it is nevertheless a conception of freedom.

What distinguishes us from the animals, Hamann says, is freedom, which means the right to collaborate in defining ourselves. This is what underlies the new conception of what it means to grasp the signs of nature and bring ourselves into alignment with them, not simply as registering their meaning and conforming to them, but as collaborative re-expression. This is what is conveyed in the notion that our understanding them is a translation. It is in virtue of the same idea that, in both art and the elaboration of language, the Romantics rejected simple imitation as our model. When we imitate, we do so in a creative, transforming fashion; we are "selbsttätig" in our mimesis, as A.W. Schlegel says.

What is the significance of this for the Romantic theory of the symbolic? I want to mention three things. *First*: Symbolic disclosure involves a distance, a mediation, an acceding to A through B. Now we can see that this distance is not just to be understood negatively, a fruit of our incapacity, a look "through a glass darkly". It also has its positive meaning. Our translation is not just an imperfect approximation to the meaning; it is also our contribution to the collaborative work of re-establishing contact, communion between ourselves and the world.

Second: I used the word communion. 'Communication' often crops up in Romantic writings. The Romantics were indeed moving towards and finally embracing a dialogical view of language, which we see later fully developed in Humboldt. Hamann's peculiar position on the origin of language reflects this. Herder wrote his famous Ursprung essay critical of the "orthodox" theory of Süssmilch and others, that language was taught to humans by God. He presents it as a human potentiality, which we develop ourselves. Hamann, while unable to accept the rather simplistic picture offered by Süssmilch of God as a language instructor, nevertheless was uneasy with Herder's formulations. God didn't teach us language in the way we teach each other. But on the other hand, our language is a response to God's, the language of signs in the world. We don't develop language fully on our own, as the mainline Enlightenment theory had it, and as Herder seemed to be saying in his own way. Our language is already a reply to a message addressed to us, a reply which consists of a translation. Language is thus in its very origin dialogical, and continues to develop in exchange between human beings.

In a sense, the whole Romantic "take" on freedom is hospitable to a dialogical conception. Freedom is not deriving everything out of oneself, out of the Ego in Fichtean terms; it is a collaborative response, saying one's piece in a conversation. That's why Romantic eschatology points towards a universal communion.

Third: A new understanding of the nature of poetic language arises from this, which still shapes our outlook today. As Wasserman (1968) has argued, the Romantic period saw a profound shift away from a millennial outlook which saw the Chain of Being, and divine history, and ancient mythology, as treasuries of common reference points, on which poetry, and painting, could draw. This corresponded to a view of this order as reflecting a unitary set of meanings which could be publically registered and recorded.

The dissolution of this publicly accessible field of references brought us to an age in which each poet may struggle to create his *own* language, virtually his own mythology, if we take Blake as an example, or we refer to the aspirations that Friedrich Schlegel defined for his age. The poet may find himself struggling to create his own field of references, even as he is invoking them. Hölderlin's Gods, Rilke's angels, Yeats' Byzantium belong to no publicly recognised story or doctrine, although they draw on certain of the resonances that formerly established stories and doctrines have left behind. These are the "subtler languages" of Wasserman's title (1968).

The whole Romantic theory of the symbol has to be understood in this double perspective: on one hand, it is a response to disenchantment, flattening, a loss of vision. It is a work carried out in destitute times ("dürftiger Zeit", Hölderlin). The distance of the symbol is partly loss. But on the other side, it is an affirmation of our power, of our unelidable collaborative role in the recreation of meaning and communion. In both facets it is essentially modern: it starts from disenchantment, and gives an essential place to human freedom and creativity.

Two kinds of language

There was a Hegelian version of this story of separation/alienation and return, which was uncompromisingly rationalist, and saw the whole development of reality as aiming to provide the conditions for Spirit, which was destined to be both rationally self-conscious and free. We can take up the Schelling version, or the Schlegel; the understanding of reality comes in art, or in a philosophy which is highly dependent on art. Let us take account of the crucial change which Hamann made in our understanding of what it is to grasp, or to come in contact with, the Plan; that is, that we do it not through identifying the connections in the code (signatures, Kabbalistic numbers, correspondences), but through a kind of "translation". Human language, and thus artistic creation, is something very different from the language in things, that is, the universe as a manifestation of the Plan. But this language/creation can to some extent bridge the gap, can offer approximations of what the universe reveals. This is the best we can do. But it is crucial. We recall that recovering some contact with the Plan is of the first importance for human beings. This both reveals to us what it is to live up to our highest potential, and empowers us to do so. Offering our "translations" is now our only way of recovering this contact.

We can see that the two crucial amendments to the tradition of languages of reality (or insight into reality) which the Romantics made pull in the same direction: (1) The Plan is no longer seen on the Platonic model as laid out in Ideas of perfection existing in eternity, but is rather understood as a direction of growth, towards which reality is tending; and (2) our grasp of the plan is also incapable of matching it exactly, but rather constitutes a kind of translation in our terms of its thrust. This opens onto an era of subtler languages and the corresponding ontic indeterminacy. Our artistic (or philosophical) creations can be the locus of what I want to call "epiphanies", which both (partially) reveal the Plan/direction of things, and put us in empowering contact with it.

It took a while for the limitations of the subtler languages to be fully appreciated. F. Schlegel still hopes for a new common "mythology". But the legacy of the Romantic period is this understanding of epiphanies that involve something like a double approximation to a possible Plan or thrust of things (that is, both a revelation of this Plan and an empowering contact with it). Later the notion that our epiphanies can contribute to repairing the (damaged) order (Novalis) may be dropped or re-interpreted. Later again, it may seem less certain, even impossible that we could grasp the whole Plan or thrust of things; we can only hope for partial aperçus, a momentary grasp of something bigger, of a fuller context of whatever is the object of our attention. But, the notion of a revealing-empowering epiphany remains.

What also remains is a thesis about language. There are uses/forms of language which can serve to objectify and also on occasion manipulate the things around us. But this is the dead, uncreative side of language. Then there are the forms which are the sites of epiphanies. These constitute language as living, revivifying. Epiphanies in this sense don't just add to our knowledge, they inspire us; catching a glimpse of these connections powerfully moves us; the current between us and nature flows once more. We are in the domain of resonance.

So a crucial distinction comes to the fore, between ordinary, flat, instrumental language which designates different objects, and which combines these designata into accurate portraits of things and events, all of which serves the purpose of controlling and manipulating things (following the prescriptions of the HLC), on the one hand; and on the other, truly insightful speech, which reveals the very nature of things and restores contact with them. Epiphanic languages give us a sense that we are called; we receive a call. There is someone out there.

My claim is that this distinction between dead, "blind" uses of language, and truly revelatory, insightful ones which restore contact, continues after the Romantic period, and up to our time, even though many features of the Romantics' view of the world, of literature, of the current which passes between us and the world, have been abandoned or greatly modified.

The power of aesthetic experience

An important question remains: what underlies the power of these works, by which they seem to reveal and connect us with deeper realities? Without an answer to this underlying question, are we just left with the thought that the insight offered by a given work is merely in the eye of the beholder, that it's all simply "subjective"? Are we faced with the choice between a meaningless "ontology" and a subjectivist "psychology"?

There are purely psychological meanings: I like roses not peonies. This could easily change, you could even work on me to change it. And we all agree that there is no right and wrong here; you couldn't validly *convince* me to change my mind. Contrast life meanings: I need air, water, food. This not just a fact about me; all humans do. And it is not just a fact about humans; animals do. Moreover, even if I took it into my head to believe that I don't need these things, I would just be wrong, demonstrably wrong.

We might see this difference in kind of meaning as one of location. Liking roses is just in me, whereas these biological needs are facts about the interspace between animal and ecological niche. But there is also another difference. The

biological meanings are decidable through hard natural science; the likes and dis-
likes aren't; they are human meanings. Now the question: are there human meanings which are founded on facts about the interspace between human beings and
their ecological niche, comparably "objective" to the facts which found life meanings, but different from these? There seem to be: for instance, the joy we take in
spring, in life, in nature; our sense of being fed by the life around us. But can we
define the meaning here more fully? This is something we might try to do with
the terms "resonance": some movement of sympathy between us and our niche.

Of course, we might try to do this by making ontological claims about the
universe. God has created it as signs; there is a language here, which we have to
connect to. But the attempt to demonstrate something along this avenue, that of
the underlying story, seems blocked. Is there, however, another way to proceed,
which doesn't immediately involve such ontic claims, even though our ultimate
explanation of our experience might require some such claims?

Can we establish some claims to human meaning here, so that there would be a
right and wrong, founded and unfounded, without in the first instance making an
ontic claim about nature?

Let's look at certain Romantic poets; e.g., Hölderlin: Dichtung brings to light,
and connects us to, a movement in nature; which involves an intensification of
life; shows us a meaning of these movements in nature, and of our connection
with them, which makes a claim on us. There is a strong evaluation here: not to
see this is to be missing something true and important. Now this can't be shown
biologically as with life meaning. However, like life meaning it is situated in the
"interspace". This is the undistributed middle between the "ontological" and the
"psychological".

Are Wordsworth and Hölderlin bringing to light something in nature, and in
our relation to nature, which we should all recognise, some more intensely vivi-
fying meaning? Even though each of us may offer another interpretation of it,
or find something similar in somewhat different objects. This is indeed, a claim
which people make on behalf of certain forms of art, whether or not they evoke
resonance with nature; music, for instance, even though we differ about what
music we are moved by. We deal here with a human meaning which we consider founded, but couldn't ground biologically. (Or at least, not with our present
biology.)

Let's make a square with four boxes. On the horizontal, we have human vs
biological meanings, on the vertical, we have grounded (strong evaluation) vs.
ungrounded (weak evaluation):

Table 4.1 Types of evaluations

evaluations	human-related	biological
strong	*Beethoven*	*air, water*
weak	*roses vs. peonies*	*ice cream*

In the lower right quadrant, we have biological meanings which are just matters of individual psychology, like: I like strawberry ice cream, and you like vanilla. In the upper right, we have grounded biological meanings. In the lower left we have weak human meanings, the choice of roses vs. peonies. Is there anything in the upper left quadrant? Normally, we would concede that great music has a meaning which is in some way grounded. Also, some lives are very meaningful, like dedicating one's medical skills to helping people through *Médecins Sans Fontières* (MSF). But we have trouble saying what makes it the case that these are meaningful, something which doesn't arise with biological needs, like air and water. Should that bother us?

The question of this discussion is: is recognizing and connecting with a movement in nature, as with Wordsworth and Hölderlin, up there in the upper left, or does it fall into the lower left quadrant? This comes down to an issue of the good life, this central ethical notion. Is the connection that our two poets are pointing to and (claim to be) bringing about a crucial component of a full human life? The sense of heightened meaning we experience in reading Romantic poetry involves some notion of my realizing an important potential, which is a constituent of a full human life, of a meaningful life, worth living. So there is a strong evaluation underlying the experience here: not responding in this way is missing something important in the range of potentialities for a full life. It's similar to the experience of great art, hearing Beethoven late quartets, or seeing King Lear. But is this intuition valid?

Note that objectivity, groundedness, strong evaluation can go along with variation. To say Beethoven's last quartets are great music is not to say that people who are deeply moved by something else are misguided. The shape of meaning in music can be complex and varied. Something similar is true of meaningful lives: MSF is not the only such career.

But also in the upper left are moral judgments, like: all humans have a right to life. There we don't allow for variation of positions: we rightly reject the idea that only superior people deserve to live. Lots of people, even those who would abandon great art and meaningful lives from the upper left, want to plead for the groundedness of ethics.[1] But often one can question the arguments they offer to back this up: utilitarian and Kantian.

I said above that meaningfulness judgments can admit of variation, although not all do. There is another distinction which is orthogonal to the two mapped in this square; that is, meanings which are (with exceptions) invariably experienced, versus those which only some people have. Example: nausea. Not everybody likes ice cream, but all humans experience nausea before excrement (unless they have undergone special training). But still nausea belongs in the lower right quadrant. It is something generated by our biological make-up, and happens to be universal, but there are no grounds. You couldn't convince someone not to be nauseated.

So the issue is about the Wordsworth-Hölderlin idea, the alleged connectedness with the movement in nature: is it properly in the upper left quadrant? Or just the lower left? Is there some revivifying, intense meaning here, which is really there, but has no biological grounding (that is, grounding in biological science, as we presently understand it)?

When we ask our question of human meanings, we are clearly dealing with matters which are human-related. They exist only in the interspace defined by humans and their niche in the world. So if we read "ontological" as human-unrelated, then these meanings have to be "psychological". But this term often carries the implication: depending on the variations of individual psychology, i.e., belonging in the lower left quadrant. Combining the restrictive readings of the two terms entirely screens out the upper left quadrant. In order to ask the crucial question here, we have either to expand "ontological" to include this quadrant, or expand "psychological" to allow it to cover both left quadrants.

We can see how the question: ontological or psychological? still lacks precision. On a restrictive reading of each term, it prevents us asking the really important question about the status of meanings in the upper left quadrant. These are experienced as having validity independently of how we happen to feel; that is, they are lived as strong evaluations. Can we allow into our ontology a kind of objective validity which can't be backed up biologically, or more generally, in terms of natural science? Many thinkers, who take a reductive stance to explanation, want to say "no". But our actual human experience inescapably treats these meanings as objective. Moral right or wrong, great art, wonder at Nature, these don't come across to us as matters of shifting taste.

The unclarity around this dichotomy: ontological or psychological, also obscures the fact that there are two issues here. One is that of the account underlying our experience, which unquestionably involves human-unrelated realities; the other concerns the experiences themselves, their objective validity or lack thereof. The subtler languages of Romantic poetry make claims in this second domain. True, there will be references to a force "rolling through all things" (Wordsworth), or to "gods" (Hölderlin), or to "angels" (Rilke), but it is at most left uncertain what (human-unrelated) ontic commitments these images invoke, if indeed they are meant to affirm anything definite about underlying realities at all.

This of course, says nothing about what any given poet believed or would accept as an underlying story. In many cases, the poet might not even make a distinction between poetic force and underlying truth; but if pressed, might accept that the first should be taken as a first approximation, or manifestation, of the second (Wordsworth, Hopkins). In this they would not be followed by their more skeptical admirers, who would however enthusiastically recognise the revealing, even re-connecting power of their work.

The above discussion shows another possible blind spot. It's not just a matter of forgetting the upper left quadrant. It is also the fact that our convictions about matters in this quadrant can have two sources. We respond to the poetry of Hölderlin or Wordsworth with a conviction that there is a crucial human fulfillment or realisation in recognizing our relation to nature, and recovering it. But this conviction is different from beliefs we might have about a possible underlying story. It is grounded in the power of the experience, whereas the underlying story has to draw on beliefs about the universe, God, the Life Force, or human depth psychology, or whatever, which have other grounds, other sources, other bases. Subtler languages in the post-Romantic period usually bespeak their own limitations; the implicit metaphysic is either too sketchy and partial (Wordsworth's "force"), or too paradoxical (Hölderlin's "gods"), or is from the very beginning presented as tentative (Keats "Beauty"). That is why they can enjoy a certain independence from convictions about underlying realities, and why people of such different theological and anthropological persuasions could share a sense of the revealing power of Wordsworth's poetry.[2]

One might be tempted to say: the conviction this poetry commands is purely aesthetic, as against the intellectually grounded theories of theology or anthropology. But this isn't quite right, because intellectual reflection, in criticism for instance, can alter, refine, develop the actual experience. What is crucial is the grounding in this experience.

Conclusion: resonance between nature and poetry

The questions I've been dealing with concern one of the axes of resonance in Rosa's theory. This connection to nature would be one of the most important such axes. So how might we pursue this issue of what belongs in the upper left quadrant? Do the meanings of our relation to nature belong there, as Wordsworth and Hölderlin suggest?

Plainly, we need to define better the axes which relate us to nature, or more broadly, to our whole environment, natural and human-built. Let's imagine a nightmare science fiction scenario: we live in a concrete jungle, or an environment consisting entirely of airport lounges (non-lieux, in Augé's expression, no-places). We would find Shakespeare, Goethe, Keats, Hölderlin, not to speak of Pink Floyd recordings, all the more indispensable; we would cling to them like shipwrecked sailors to floating spars. But would that be enough, so we wouldn't need to ask for anything else? Certainly not. And of course, in these no-places, we might still have our relation to loved ones. Would we then have enough? Again not. We need a relation to the world, the universe, to things, forests, fields, mountains, seas, analogous to that we have to human beings we love, and works of art; where we feel ourselves addressed, and called upon to answer.

So how to explore this? There are two possible directions: the first would look at our behaviour, the way that people seek the countryside, the wilderness, gardens: to visit but also to plant; the way they want to return to the monuments of the past; and so on. There are deep hungers here. We could complement this with hermeneutic works, like Robert Pogue Harrison (1993) on forests, for instance, which try to lay out the meanings they have for human beings, to explain somewhat why people turn again and again to wilderness, for instance.

The second would be to follow the poetic discoveries/inventions of epiphanic languages, which have come in the wake of the Romantic period. The proposal which comes to mind, and which reading Rosa's work helped clarify, is to explore both these avenues, to take them as complementary perspectives on what we want to define and articulate. The complementary relation might be described in this way: the study of our desires and behaviour gives some idea of what in our world we seek to relate to, while the various forms of poetic response which we see emerging from the Romantic period offer definitions of what these relations mean to us.

Notes

1 But of course, there are subjectivists in morals as well; see the "error theory" in Mackie (1977).
2 This underlies the important difference between the mature Hegel and the rest of the Romantic generation of the 1790s, which he grew up with, and then repudiated. Hegel believed that he was offering a fully adequate underlying story, fully grounded in reason. He refused to be satisfied with a partly "symbolic" account through art, which even his close colleague Schelling thought unavoidable. Accounts in terms of art or "religion" has to be aufgehoben in a fully conceptual medium.

References

Beiser, F. (2003). The Romantic Imperative: The Concept of Early German Romanticism. Cambridge, MA: Harvard University Press.

Eco, U. (1995). *The Search for the Perfect Language*. Oxford: Blackwell.

Harrison, R.P. (1993). *Forests: The Shadow of Civilization*. Chicago: Chicago University Press.

Locke, J. (2004 [1690]). *An Essay concerning Human Understanding*. London: Penguin.

Lovejoy, A.O. (1960). *The Great Chain of Being*. New York: Harper Torchbook.

Mackie, J. (1977). *Ethics: Inventing Right and Wrong*. London: Penguin.

Richards, R. (2002). *The Romantic Conception of Life*. Chicago: University of Chicago Press.

Rosa, H. (2013). Resonance – Towards a New Conception of the Good Life. Unpublished Manuscript.

Wasserman, Earl R. (1968). A Subtler Language: A Critical Reading of Neoclassical and Romantic Poems. Baltimore: Johns Hopkins University Press.

Yates, F. (1964). Giordano Bruno and the Hermetic Tradition. London: Routledge.

Part II

Beyond the growth paradigm

Alternative conceptions of the economic

5 A philosophy of ecological economics

Manfred A. Max-Neef

The fact that we live in a world full of answers and very few questions has allowed for certain disciplines – particularly economics – to construct their arguments and theories based on an imaginary world. From quantum physics we now know that the world is not as we thought it was. The world is not mechanic and not Cartesian, but is organic and holistic. We are actually facing a perplexing reality. These fundamental messages have not reached the teaching of economics, which is still anchored in the mechanical worldview of the 19th century. In order to open the new space into which economics should adapt itself, the essay presents four visions that attempt to answer what are probably the most important questions: Why do we exist, and what is the purpose of life? The paper ends with considerations about "Economics and Life" and "Economics for Life". The conclusion is that drastic changes in the teaching and application of economics are fundamental for survival.

Four views of life

We live in a world full of answers and very few questions. What is especially sad is the absence of transcendental questions. I shall therefore start with what I consider to be probably the most profound of all questions: Why do we exist? What is the purpose of life?

As a first possibility I will suggest that life is probably the result of nature, which in order to achieve significance needs to discover itself. Without nature there would be no life, and without life the entire cosmos would be senseless. Today we have sufficient scientific evidences to support the assumption that such a mirror/image relation is not the product of chance.

1. In relation to life, we know that a living cell is composed of some twenty amino acids that form a sort of compact chain which, in turn, depends on a great amount of enzymes, plus the constituent parts of proteins, DNA and RNA. Considering such an enormous amount of components, the probability for a unique combination to occur for the formation of one living cell over an evolutionary process of millions of years, is in Prigogine's words, "vanishingly small".[1] An important question arises: How improbable does an event, sequence or system have to be before the chance hypothesis can be reasonably eliminated? I will try to answer with a very simple example.

Let us assume that one of these chains is composed of 1.000 elements. We know that there is just one combination of those elements that makes a living cell possible. Now, if the chain adopts a new combination every second, the more than 14 billion years of the Universe would not be enough to complete all the possibilities. Concretely all the possible combinations of a series with n elements will be equal to $n!$ (n factorial). So, if n is equal to 1.000, all possible combinations will be 1.000! which is an incommensurable number, beyond any computable capacity. And now, if we consider a complete living being, the magnitudes are simply unimaginable.[2]

The 14.500 million years of age of the universe are equivalent to 10 to the power of 19 (10^{19}) seconds, while the "vanishingly small" probability of just generating, at random, a functional sequence of amino acids in proteins is estimated to be one in 10 to the power of 65 (10^{65}). It should be noted that according to estimates, there are 10 to the power of 65 atoms in our galaxy (Dembski 1998).

Considering such incredible magnitudes, and remembering the law of chance of the great mathematician Emile Borel (1943), "The very improbable never occurs", we must reach an overwhelming conclusion. In fact, our being is the product of an absolute improbability. Or rephrasing the statement: *Despite the fact that it is impossible to be, nevertheless we are.*

I must clarify at this stage that I do not attempt to open doors to creationist or intelligent design interpretations of life. How life occurred is not my concern here. I am only interested in its infinite improbability. The how is an open discussion for others.

The fact that we have not apprehended the notion that, being a part of life, we are part of the only scientifically provable miracle – actually the greatest of all miracles – is something that should profoundly preoccupy us. Not only have we not grasped the idea, but we have taken life and all that goes along with it for granted; we act as if everything we destroy and everything we predate were mechanically reversible. Economics is in many aspects a perfect example of such an absurd behaviour. We can, no doubt, affirm that as a consequence of the presently dominant economic rationality, our capacity to destroy the infinitely improbable has become a certainty.

For this stage of our history, it is overwhelmingly evident that we require a new economic rationality. An ecological economics, as I like to call it, is a sensible alternative; because it puts economics at the service of life, and not, as has been the case so far, life at the service of economics.

2. An interesting debate took place in 1995, between the distinguished astrophysicist Carl Sagan and the great master of biology Ernst Mayr. The topic was the possibility of intelligent life on other planets (Sagan/Mayr 1995). Sagan pointed out that if many planets similar to ours exist, it is perfectly possible that intelligence may emerge in some of them.

Mayr pointed out that unlike physics based on laws, biology is based on concepts. Hence, if there are no laws in biology, the ground for its theories are concepts such as natural selection, fight for existence, competition, bio population, adaptation, reproductive success, selection of the female, male domination, etc. As a consequence, Mayr points out, a philosophy of physics based on natural laws is very different from a philosophy of biology based on concepts.

Mayr added that physicists tend to think that if life originated somewhere, it will also develop intelligence at some point. Biologists, on the other hand, are impressed by the improbability of such a development. One must be conscious that evolution never moves on a straight line towards an objective ("intelligence"), as is the case with a chemical process or a physical law. The lines of evolution are highly complex and are similar to the bifurcations of the branches of a tree.

After the origin of life, 3,800 million years ago, the earth showed solely *procariots*; that is, simple cells without an organised nucleus. Due to a unique event, up to this day only partially explained, some 1,800 million years ago a *eucariot* cell appeared for the first time. That is, a cell with an organised nucleus plus further characteristics that correspond to superior organisms. From the *eucariots* three multicellular types of organisms originated: fungi, plants and animals. However, of the billions of species of fungi and plants, not one was capable of producing intelligence. Mayr describes how the billions of branches of the tree of life generated lineages of species during 1,800 million years, pointing out that the brain of hominids was generated less than 3 million years ago, and the cortex of *Homo Sapiens* was generated only 300,000 years ago. Nothing demonstrates in a clearer manner the improbability of superior intelligence than the existence of billions of lineages that never managed to acquire it.

As mentioned, Mayr argued from the point of view of a biologist that it was highly improbable to find another case of superior intelligence. An additional argument was that intelligence is a lethal mutation. The most successful organisms are those who can mutate fast, like bacteria, or other species who have shown stability in a given ecological niche, like crabs. These species do very well and can survive environmental crises. Yet, going up the tree towards what we call intelligence, species are increasingly less successful. When we reach the stage of mammals we find a small number compared, for example, with insects. At the level of the first human beings (about 100,000 year ago) we see that the number is very small and very vulnerable.

Mayr's argument went further in the sense that to find intelligence elsewhere is as improbable as a much larger duration of ourselves as a species on this planet. In addition, he mentioned something that is quite disturbing. "The average life span of a species, of the billions that have existed, is about 100,000 years. This is more or less as long as we exist" (in Sagan/Mayr 1995). Could it happen, considering the increasing deterioration we are provoking on our planet, that the next generation may be the first one to decide whether it is going to be the last?

The reason to identify us as a lethal mutation is due to the fact that of all the billions of lineages and species that integrate the tree of life, from bacteria all the way up through plants, fungi and animals to humans, we are the only species with the capacity and the willingness to destroy the entire tree. This is certainly a mistake of nature; and nature – we suppose – never makes the same mistake twice. But I would add one additional aspect not considered by Mayr. The reason of our power and willingness to destroy is not the result of intelligence alone, but rather the result of intelligence plus manipulative capacity. Our hands and, in particular, the position of our thumb in relation to the other fingers (different from the hand of primates) makes fine manipulation possible. Without the type of hand that we have, all of our technological development would have been impossible. And why does this contribute to a lethal mutation? Because having the capacity to manipulate, we never adapt ourselves to an existing environment, but we transform it so that it adapts to our desires or purposes. Intelligence plus manipulative capacity is what makes us believe that we are above nature and not an inseparable part of it. Once again, improbability is a main actor.

3. In 1989, the Swedish scientist Karl-Henrik Robert wrote a paper about sustainability and distributed it among fifty of the most important scientists of his country, of different disciplines. The purpose was to organise a project to reach a consensus of the Swedish scientific community as to what the fundamental problems are that our life is provoking on us as a species and on our planet. The result gave origin to *The Natural Step*, which as an initiative has generated actions in over sixty countries. The essence of the consensus follows:

> Thousands of millions of years ago the earth consisted of a messed-up stew of toxic inorganic compounds. The transformation of such a stew into the wealth of mineral deposits, breathable air, water, soils, forests, fish and animal life that made possible a habitat for the human species and its civilisation to emerge; all that begun with the green cell of the plants. This admirable and formidable cell had the ability of capturing a surplus of solar energy (negative entropy) beyond its own needs for maintenance and growth. They utilized such ability over billions of years, to create all the complex compounds on which life and its activities depend.
>
> Humans remained in balance with the regenerative capacity of the green cells until about one hundred years ago. It was then that our technology allowed us to exercise control over concentrated forms of energy. That allowed us to expand our dominion over the ecological space with such velocity and force, that we begun to reverse the evolutionary process of the earth, transforming ordered matter into molecular trash at a much faster rate than what the remaining green cells were capable of reprocessing. It is an act of collective suicide. Ironically we have chosen to call it development.
>
> In recent years our technology has become so advanced that a great proportion of human wastes consists of toxic metals and non natural stable compounds that simply cannot in any way be processed by the green cells. The rubbish will remain here forever as a monument to our technological mastership and to our biological ignorance. That we also call development.[3]

As already mentioned above, this is an example of the fact that our capacity to destroy the infinitely improbable has become a certainty.

4. The opening statement of this essay was that life is probably the result of nature which, in order to achieve significance, needs to discover itself. Discovery is an act of consciousness. All that exists for us is the result of consciousness. We know from quantum physics that a given subatomic event occurs because of our observation. The observer and the observed are inseparable. Observation is an act of consciousness. Hence, consciousness creates reality. In this sense it has been my impression that Nature exists because we have consciousness of her. But

not long ago I realised, after rediscovering the *Philosophy of Nature* (1797) of Schelling (1775–1854), that my belief was inaccurate.

For humans, nature has always been around but, until 200 years ago, was never a main actor. If, for example, we go through the history of painting, we will realise that Nature was always the background of persons. It is only after the rise of Romanticism and Idealist Philosophy, which took place in the area of Weimar and Jena (former East Germany), that Nature becomes the main center of our attention. Landscape paintings are precisely the offspring of Romanticism (*Caspar David Friedrich* 1774–1840, *John Constable* 1776–1837). But not only painting. The same occurs with poetry and literature in general (*Goethe* 1749–1832, *Schiller* 1759–1805, *Hölderlin, Byron* 1788–1824, *Shelley* 1792–1822, *Keats* 1795–1821). Along similar lines my dear friend *Rafael Bernal* (1915–1972), a Mexican writer and historian, discovered something quite unbelievable in his historical research about the chroniclers of the American conquest. Not one of them ever makes a description of Nature or of a landscape. One must imagine people coming from a semi-desert like Castilla and Andalucía standing in front of the Chimborazo mountain or crossing the Amazon jungle without ever describing the landscape they are seeing. Their only topic is what they do and what they suffer, the people they encounter and with whom they fight, and what they achieve. Nature as such is irrelevant.[4]

I learned from Schelling that truth was one gigantic step ahead of what I had imagined. He poses that nature lacks consciousness, is unconscious, and hence has a metaphysical rank. The fact that Nature has no consciousness of herself, presupposes that where the Absolute Self manifests itself is not in human subjectivity but in nature. It is the objective processes of nature, as an unconscious expression of the absolute, that allows the overcoming of that unconsciousness through man. In fact, as well as I remember, he tells us in his *Philosophy of Nature* that man (humankind) *is* nature taking consciousness of herself. Hence, it is not that nature exists because I have consciousness of her, but she exists because I am her consciousness. This is in my view one of the most profound statements ever made. And if it is true (and I am certain that it is true) we must inevitably conclude that everything we destroy or depredate is an act of collective suicide. The forest I destroy is not a forest that was there while I was here. That forest is part of me and I am part of her. We are all inseparable partners of a whole.

The gigantic question now is: How should we behave in order to preserve the immense improbability of the miracle of life?

Economics and life

About ninety years have passed since quantum physics revealed that the world is not as we think it is. It is strange and disconcerting that such an important message has still not reached economics, which continues assuming an illusionary world as real.

Let us go through some revelations. For modern theories, the universe is no longer a machine full of components, but it is an indivisible dynamic whole. The world is not Cartesian. The behaviour of each part is determined by its relations with the whole. It is no longer the parts that determine the behaviour of the whole, but it is the whole that determines the behaviour of the parts. There are clear similarities between the structure of matter and the structure of the mind, because consciousness plays a crucial role in observation, and to a great degree determines the properties of the observed. The observer is not only necessary for the observation of the properties of an atomic phenomenon, but is necessary for those properties to arise. We can no longer talk about nature without talking simultaneously about ourselves.

Strangely enough very few have become aware of the truly revolutionary dimension of the new insights which have dramatically changed the world view. We are facing a perplexing new reality.

In this respect, I quote the distinguished German physicist Hans-Peter Dürr:

> This new reality is not based on matter anymore ('matter is not made of matter') but relates to a fundamental immaterial connectedness, obeying non-deterministic laws. 'Reality is not "reality but potentiality' which establishes an intimate, non-separable, non-reducible, holistic relationship between everything. [. . .] The future is essentially open, not strictly determined, allowing genuine creation. Predictability and knowledge and science (conditioned on determinism and reductionism) do not hold anymore in the strict scientific sense, but are basically limited (and not only due to our ignorance). Man is an integral and inseparable part of this more general, all-embracing immaterial reality.
>
> (Dürr 2001, Manuscript)

An essential aspect of the universe is consciousness, and as long as we continue to exclude it, we are severely limiting our possibilities of understanding natural and social phenomena. The great paradox may be that because we are intelligent (see Mayr's "lethal mutation" above), we tend to overshadow consciousness. In other words, while *ceasing to be conscious that we are conscious*, we have constructed the foundations of a possible collective suicide.

The preceding arguments imply, among other challenges, the urgent and inevitable need to substantially modify our economic visions and, above all, the teaching of traditional economics.

From an ontological perspective, neoclassical economics is anchored in a mechanic worldview in which systems are integrated by parts. Ecological economics, on the other hand, is anchored in an organic worldview, where systems are not composed by parts, but by participants, all interrelated and inseparable. The result is that epistemologically, ecological economics cannot be understood utilizing monodisciplinary perspectives like in neoclassical economics. In order to understand the interrelationship between economics, nature and society, we need transdisciplinary organic perspectives which, in addition, combine reason with intuition, the material with the spiritual, ethics with aesthetics, and beauty with truth.

The mechanical worldview supposes that physical matter is reality. Hence, mechanical explanations describe biological and social events as patterns of non-biological occurrence. We forget that the mechanical worldview of neoclassicism is an abstraction, and what is worse is that we believe that abstraction to be the concrete reality. When consciousness, emotions and values are absent, we overshadow the connectivity between economics, society and living nature. The organic worldview is characterised by non-linear interconnections between living entities, which means that the individual and the communal construct themselves and require each other at the same time.

According to the ontology of ecological economics, the organic world is based on a concept of nature and society as collective phenomena, and not as the sum of individual atoms. Nothing in nature can be what it is, except as an integral and integrated part of a dynamic whole.

In the mechanic world we pose problems and solutions as separated entities. In the organic world such entities don't exist. What we have instead is transformations and adaptations. Again, in the mechanic vision (still dominated by 19th-century thinking) we tend to believe that a natural law is that: "*the more likely will occur (in the future) more likely*" (Duerr 2001, 3). This fits the logic of the "realist". However, for the evolution of the living – which is the concern of this essay – we find on the contrary that, in the words of H. P. Dürr (2001, 3), "the less likely can occur (in the future) more likely". The best example, as has been expressed along this text is the evolution of the extremely improbable arrangements forming life in only 3.5 billion years time.

Again, in the mechanic world of conventional economics, the optimal chance for survival in the long run is achieved through fixed goals that select the best options and the highest efficiency to reach it. In the organic world, *the optimum is attained through "highest flexibility",* which means the possibility to adequately adapt to whatever conditions may arise in the future. In addition, to promote and respect the diversity of people and of cultures is fundamental for the quality of the whole.

As a conclusion, let me cite Ingebrigsteen/Jakobsen (2012), who claim that

> ecological economics requires a change from economic man to ecological man, from quantitative growth to qualitative development, from administration from the top down to initiatives from down to top, from competition to cooperation, from structures of globalised power to local power of circular networks.

Economics for life

Although neoliberalism is today the dominant economic model in the world, those who consider that an alternative is urgently required should not aim at the creation of another global model. What is required is diversity. That is, economic systems coherent with local and regional realities, with local and regional cultures, traditions, ways of living and worldviews. Diversity is good for strengthening living systems and for generating innovation and creativity, which are fundamental components of true development.

Assuming that a new world of diversity may emerge in the coming decades, each model should at least respect some basic principles. In coherence with the argumentation of this essay, I propose that all the diverse economies that may be designed should fulfill five fundamental postulates and one inalienable value principle, regardless of their final style.

The postulates are (from Max-Neef 2010): The economy is to serve the people and not the people to serve the economy. Development is about people, and not about objects. Growth is not the same as development, and development does not necessarily require growth. No economy is possible in the absence of ecosystem services. The economy is a sub-system of a larger finite system – the biosphere – hence, permanent growth is impossible.

The inalienable value principle is:

> "No economic interest, under any circumstance, can be above the reverence for life" (Max-Neef 2010, 10).

If we follow the list it becomes evident that, one after the other, what we have today is exactly the opposite. Just a few examples should clarity the statement:

1   Today there are more slaves in the world than before the abolition of slavery in the 19th century. Quite a service for the economy!
2   The production of colossal amounts of unnecessary consumer "bads", is a sign of progress. There appears the function of publicity: "induce you to buy what you don't need, with money that you don't have, in order to impress those who you don't know".[5] Great for the protection of natural resources!
3   All living systems grow up to a certain point where growth stops, but development continues. Growth is finite while development can go on forever. As Kenneth Boulding used to say: "those who believe that permanent growth is possible in a finite world are either mad or economists".
4   Just try to imagine what kind of economy could function without photosynthesis, without pollinisation, without the seasons, without the water, without thermodynamics, without all the other living species. None of which appears in any economics textbook!
5   The fact that something cannot be bigger than that of which it is a part, is only too obvious.
6   The life of people has no value if there is oil under their feet. If Iraq had been the world's greatest producer of radishes, and Libya had been the greatest producer of onions, Saddam Hussein and Muamar Gaddafi would still be there!

Coda

If from childhood on we were made aware of the true world in which we live, everything could dramatically change for the better. To understand, with all its implications of what it means to be part of an organic (non-mechanic) world, would promote diversity of people and cultures as important assets for the success of the whole. Life, instead of a program, would be an adventure where permanent discoveries would turn us into complete beings.

Notes

1 Personal conversation with Ilya Prigogine in Venice, May 1994.
2 For those who do not know the concept, a factorial number, for example 5! is $1 \times 2 \times 3 \times 4 \times 5 = 120$. It is not difficult to imagine the immensity of 1,000! In mathematics, the largest computable factorial number is 199! From 200! on, all are infinity.
3 The text was handed over to me personally by Karl-Henrik Robert in 1991 (see Robert 1990). See www.thenaturalstep.org/about-us.
4 Information obtained from conversations with Rafael Bernal in 1968 in Perú.
5 A comment of Pablo Calderón Salazar in a Seminar in Brussels a few years ago.

References

Borel, E. (1962 [1943]). *Probabilities and Life*. New York: Dover.
Dembski, W. (1998). Design Inference: Elimination Chance Through Small Probabilities. Cambridge: Cambridge University Press.
Dürr, H.P. (2001). *The Crisis and Challenge of Globalization: Insights From Physics*. Manuscript. Max Planck Institut für Physik, München. Online at www.gcn.de/download/eDuerr_crisis.pdf.
Ingebristen, S./O. Jakobsen (2012). Utopias and Realism in Ecological Economics – Knowledge, Understanding and Improvisation. In: *Ecological Economics* 84, 84–90.
Max-Neef, M.A. (2005). Foundations of Transdisciplinarity. In: *Ecological Economics* 53, 5–16.
Max-Neef, M.A. (2010). The World on a Collision Course and the Need for a New Economy. In: *Ambio* 39, 200–210.
Robert, K-H. (1990). *The Natural Step*. Unpublished Manuscript, Sweden. Distributed to 50 researchers in 1990, Leading to the Founding of *The Natural Step* (Online at www.thenaturalstep.org).
Sagan, C./E. Mayr (1995). Debate About the Probability of Intelligent Life in the Universe. In: *Bioastronomy News* 7.3/4, The Planetary Society. Online at http://daisy.astro.umass.edu/~mhanner/Lecture_Notes/Sagan-Mayr.pdf.
Schelling, Friedrich Wilhelm, "Ideen zu einer Philosophie der Natur" 1988 [1797]). There are many versions, for example this translation. In: *Ideas for a Philosophy of Nature as Introduction to the Study of This Science*, transl. by E.E. Harris. Cambridge: Cambridge University Press.

6 Productivity, property, and violence

A critique of liberal justifications of growth

Christoph Henning

> The law locks up the man or woman
> Who steals the goose from off the common,
> But lets the greater felon loose
> Who steals the common from off the goose.
>
> —The Goose and the Commons[1]

Economic growth, at least under capitalist conditions, brings wealth to some, but also entails growing social inequalities and ecological destruction. These short-comings form the basis for the main arguments in favor of the idea of degrowth: it promises more social equality and some "peace" with Mother Nature. Nevertheless, degrowth remains a contested concept, even within progressive thinking. One standard counter-argument is the falling *productivity* associated with a post-growth society. A less energy-intensive economy, burning fewer fossils and relying more on human reproductive labor, would be less productive in economic terms. In the common understanding, this lack of productivity will lead to less 'wealth'. Critics assume it would also be more unjust because the liberal conception of justice, as developed by John Rawls, is intrinsically linked to notions of economic productivity. Inequalities are justified, says Rawls, if richer people are more *productive* than poorer people, because the poor will benefit from the wealth of the rich. But is it true that without rising productivity we would also have less justice?

In this paper, I will decouple the concepts of productivity and justice to develop an argument in opposition to Rawls. In fact, our modern concept of productivity is both deeply entangled with historical *injustices* and inimical to ideas of the good life. Re-reading the history of economic thinking, I argue that the moral subtext of the notion of productivity is highly problematic. Arguments based on productivity can thus hardly justify the idea of growth, at least not in a moral sense. A closer historical look shows that the concept of productivity is not defined by a "neutral" economic theory. Rather, its interpretation in each historical period was the result of political struggles, and often served to justify political violence. Therefore, it is time to question the assumed link between the notion of "productivity" and issues of justice and the good life. I will demonstrate this via a re-reading of John Locke's manifesto of expropriative liberalism which shows that the moral problem with growth is not only its undesired external effects, but is also the inherent link between the notion of productivity and a corresponding license for political violence.

Productivity and violence: against the economic curriculum

The term *productivity* carries at least two different meanings. If we take an apple tree, then we could call it 'productive' in the literal sense: It produces apples. These apples weren't there before; they are brought to light by the tree (*producere* means 'to bring to the fore'). They exist as a result of the tree transforming sun, soil and water into fruit. Under normal circumstances this process is steady, more or less reliable and has a 'natural' ring to it. We may also call this process *re*production as the tree produced a similar number of apples the year before, and the apples are able to grow into new trees. (We may even have a feminine association here.)[2] However, this conception does not correspond to the contemporary economic meaning of 'productivity'. Two aspects are missing: novelty and growth.

This second meaning is normally associated with reason and technology (which may sound 'male' to some). Productive activity adds something *new* to the world. It increases the amount of goods available over and above the number of apples available the previous year, which easily connects with ideas of growth. The following analysis draws out the political implications of this ambivalence, exposing the striking amount of *violence* inherent in the classical notion of 'productivity'. This will allow us to question some standard assumptions taken for granted by most curricula for economics.

Growth is not an issue in Aristotle's early economic theory. Instead, one finds a critique of the limitless desire to make more and more money (Gronemeyer 2007). For Aristotle the kind of oikonomia that contributes to a good life is mainly reproductive. It is not by coincidence that 'flourishing' became the key word for the Aristotelian approach to the good life.[3] As most necessary work is done by others (which, of course, already includes domestic violence), the goal is to live a good life *outside of* work and to use resources wisely – not for luxury goods, but for things like education or inviting friends (applying the virtue of generosity, see Henning 2016). Notions of productivity and growth remained absent or even debased for a long time to come.[4]

The first time that a notion of growth enters economic thinking is in mercantilism. Here, however, it is the growth in national income (which translates into the king's 'treasure', hence the name 'cameralism') *without* increases in the productivity of labor (Mills 2002, 51ff). The message is simple: organise trade, especially 'international' trade, in such a way that you maximise gains and minimise expenses (buy cheap, sell dear). However, in the long run such profits from trade could only be made reliable by constructing oppressive structures to institutionalise an unequal exchange (Emmanuel 1972). In practice this motto translates into the maxim to 'grab as much as you can', which ultimately turned into the theoretical backbone of colonialism. In this sense, economics amounts to the art of *robbery* – taking from your colonies by imposing extraction on them; taking from your neighboring countries by influencing the terms of trade in your favor; and taking from your citizens by taxing them.[5]

It is important to see the violent *political* dimension in this – the extraction of a surplus by political means – because it explains why mercantilism's successor, Adam Smith's classical economics, was praised as the economics of 'liberty': It pledged to refrain from such a political imposition. However, the common emphasis on this obscures the dark sides of the liberal approach. Let us therefore turn to John Locke, in whose writings these more sinister aspects are more clearly visible than in Smith's work. Integrating an early labor theory of value with a theory of property, Locke came up with a contractualist theory of the state, according to which a state's key function is to preserve the property rights 'earned' by labor. This sounds peaceful, and it proved influential in North America (Isenberg 2016, ch. 2). But a closer examination of Locke's *Second Treatise on Government* from 1689 shows how the new economics of liberty itself turns into a justification of political violence, expulsion and dispossession.

To arrive at this, Locke juxtaposes the two understandings of productivity discussed above: The first is the natural one we started with (think of the apple tree). Marx later credited nature to be the author of this primary productivity.[6] Yet, according to Locke it is already labor to hunt, to fish, or to gather fruits. Therefore, he argued, people living on a piece of land do not only 'own' the products they reap, but also the land itself, because they 'mix' it with their own labor. However, he states, some people(s) are also productive in the second sense: they *increase* productivity. It is only here, in the struggle between two cultures of productivity that imply different conceptions of the good life that the labor theory of value takes off.[7]

The land that bears the fruit belongs to everybody. Nonetheless, for Locke, only the second group of people has a right to property. This second culture relies on acts of privatisation, which literally means 'robbing' the public (from Latin *"privare"*). This decision to award only *one* class of people the right to have rights (namely private property rights due to investments of private productive labor) is based on a particular conception of the good, which arbitrarily favors private over common conceptions of property. As the larger part of the argument is put in economic terms, this moral dimension is often glossed over, making it all the more important to bring this exclusion to light. It is only the beginning of a deep misrecognition.

What is the economic story, then? Locke asks: "Was it a robbery thus to assume to himself what belonged to all in common' (1689, V.28)? But instead of an answer, he only assumes a necessity: 'If such a consent as that was necessary, man had starved" (Locke 1689, V.28). However, such a necessity cannot claim moral weight in a state of common property, for the very meaning of sharing resources is to provide for everybody. Locke completely misrepresents this. Even in a Western social imaginary, taking from a common pool and thus risking the hunger of others is usually considered a crime. In order to avoid this accusation, Locke's labor theory of value reframes the term robbery (or enclosure) as something that is *not* stealing. Conversely, the people who live in the more sustainable culture of production appear as the ones who really steal and can be driven off their land. This narrative turns things upside down in a Nietzschean reversal of values: it declares robbers for heroes and the robbed for robbers.

How exactly can the labor theory of value justify this violent expulsion? First, Locke says that 90 percent of the value of the products produced by private property owners comes from labor, not from the land. So apparently, the wealth these people produce on the land they grabbed is *not* taken from the former occupants (be it peasants in England or Native Americans in the colonies), simply because what the private owners own *now* was not there before. However, this argument is not fully convincing. Covering only 90 percent of the value, it still leaves 10 percent that are expropriated – leading Locke to downplay the impact of land even more, to one or 0.1 percent (the higher the productivity of labor, the lower its moral entanglement). Nevertheless legally, robbery *remains* robbery, even when the booty is successfully re-invested afterwards. Moreover, at issue now are not only the products of the land, but the land itself. That is why Thomas Paine (1797) demanded that these 10 percent should be paid back to the population as an unconditional basic income.

Yet, we have to ask why the other, culturally 'inferior' classes are considered robbers now? From a numerical perspective a 'less productive' person takes wealth from the community: If private producer A could produce 1,000 units of value on soil C, whereas common ownership only produces 100 units, the common owners are responsible for a 'loss' (in the sense of opportunity costs) of 900 units. In Locke's view, they are stolen from the community. If common ownership is an obstacle to the common good, enclosing it is in the general interest.[8]

Therefore the more productive class has a right to redistribute existing assets, by virtue of the potential future assets it could create. Thus, property titles are unstable and call for a constant justification. Owning something without using it productively, or not as productively as another (with a lower output at a given input), invites others to snatch the property (whether private, common, or previously 'unowned'; see Goldstein 2013). This may happen in an economic process, when one capitalist 'decapitalises' another, or as a political process using direct force. Liberal economic and political theory justifies this violence. Hence, Marx's punch line both in the *Manifesto* and in *Capital* was that 'expropriation' is not a communist idea, but lies at the core of the capitalist ethos. It is not a prehistorical event (as the constitutive 'violence' before the law in Benjamin 1921), but a common practice of 'accumulation by dispossession' (Harvey 2004). Current movies like *Landgrabbing* (from Kurt Langbein, produced 2015) or *La buena vida* (from Jens Schanze, produced 2015) remind a Western public that this is not mere history, but a daily routine of global capitalism, both in its literal (geographical) and its metaphorical sense (concerning patents on living organisms or tissues, on intellectual or cultural commons, privatisations of public spaces or public goods etc; see Dörre in this volume). The liberal concept of 'productivity' justifies these seizures and unequal power structures as furthering the common good – a classically ideological argument that masks particular interests as universal norms.

Now, the Lockean narrative is not purely normative. It relies on the empirical assumption that everybody would benefit from the economic growth fueled by the violent introduction of private property. Both Locke and Smith were convinced of this when they favorably compared the British poor to the indigenous rich.[9] John Rawls' 'difference principle' still makes a similar point: inequalities are justified as long as the poorest benefit, too, at least in economic terms. Since the regime of private property seems to do this per se (the rising tide lifts all boats), there is no real need for redistribution in Rawls's *Theory of Justice*. However, this claim is erroneous, in Locke and Smith as well as in Rawls. There are at least two counter-arguments, concerning a) the assumed preconditions and b) the assumed consequences.

a) The story of the generally beneficial economic effects of private property assumes an initial 'poverty'. But as Marx claimed already, this story is an economic fairytale.[10] The situation *before* the enclosures is not adequately captured by claiming there was less wealth on a numeric scale. What existed was an altogether different mode of production, distribution and consumption that cannot be measured against the same yardstick (which means way more than the classical problem of comparing different 'utilities'). The question of the *status quo ante* must be asked empirically and in social terms. However, economic theory answers it *conceptually*. It is a dogma of economic theory to start with notions of scarcity. This dubious assumption is not a morally neutral statement: Once you assume that everything is scarce, that we never have enough, then the most productive person (or company) *automatically* is a 'virtuous' one, because they provide ever more of these scarce goods and services to everybody. Hence, increasing productivity appears as inherently 'good' and to be fostered at all costs, even if it entails inequality, waste and pollution. This is the usual picture in economics textbooks – common, but unfounded.

According to historians we do *not* find "scarcity" in earlier days. Instead, early civilisations feature an attitude of complacency. Poverty and scarcity had to be 'invented' and brought about by political means in order to make people act according to economic theory. Ranging from Thomas Paine to Karl Polanyi, dissenting authors have described the alternative picture.[11] Marshall Sahlins even turns the argument around to argue that early societies were ones of 'affluence'.[12] Not only did people have enough, he also demonstrates that they did not *want* more by indicating that they did not 'exploit' the given productivity level. They reaped less than they could. Instead of collecting a surplus, they preferred to enjoy a good day of sleep (Sahlins 1972, 15f.). However, if hunger and destitution as persistent social phenomena developed only after the enclosures – as partially unintentional and partly intentional results –, the *status quo ante* can neither juridically nor morally be 'translated' into a (Western) language of private property. There is an artificial void, another 'veil of ignorance'': the language of efficiency drives out any theory of the good, except the story of increasing material means (see the introduction to this volume).

If the guiding 'theory of the good' promoted by the previous stage is no longer visible in the new state, then social, ecological, cultural, traditional or even spiritual aspects do not 'count' any longer; 'good' for the poor is only what feeds and lodges them. The idea that earlier people did not *need* much in material terms earlier because they had plenty of wealth in other terms is conspicuously absent from liberal thought. This trait of Rawls's political liberalism is foreshadowed in Locke's legitimizing narrative.

b) Moreover, in terms of actual results the promise behind the primeval poverty narrative can only be kept if people really *are* 'better off' in the new regime.
Why, then, is there so much poverty and destitution in market economies and their
'peripheries' (Wallerstein)? Why does social inequality only decrease when the
market-regime of private property is *entrenched*?[13] A closer look at the economic
and political situation of the new poor exposes yet another entry of violence into
the picture. As the narrative does not allow for poverty (in theory, everybody
should be better off), even though in reality it appears to be rather extensive (especially in industrial towns where the new wealth is produced but also in the countryside), liberal thought faces a double problem: not only is the dire need of the
poor perceived as an issue, but the sheer fact that it *exists* at all undermines the
core assumptions of the liberal worldview – it is an insult.[14] No wonder, then,
that the poor met harsh resistance: to the bourgeois mind, they are remnants of
the (imagined) past in need of education to internalise the new rules – by force if
necessary. Thus the poor are also perceived as morally corrupt.[15] A bitter example
are the workhouses and poorhouses, in which even children were forced to work
in return for the bare minimum for survival.[16] Consequently, the reaction to the
erosion of the legitimizing narratives was not a retraction of the violence that was
now without proper justification (because the poor are still with us), but rather
its defiant *intensification*. As the laugh is on the loser, the moral contempt is, too.

One more paternalistic trait of liberal thought deserves attention. The alleged
'common good' is not only monetised, but it also has to pass through the bottle-
neck of the property-owner's ideas. *They* can decide what to do with their wealth –
they can hoard it or spend it on 'trinkets of frivolous utility' (Smith 1759, IV.I.6),
on servants, investments, or whatever they like. Counting all this as a 'common
good' only because it brings money (back) into the system distracts from the central fact that it confers tremendous *social power* to private property owners. There
is no automatism that guarantees that the private wealth of some benefits others
in any way (Sayer 2014).

A moral economy?

Nonetheless, let us try to be fair. Doesn't Locke also tie economics to "ethics"?[17]
Locke's text exemplifies the impact political struggles have on theory. He antici-
pates his readers' objections and preempts them beforehand. Knowing that the
enclosures were highly contested (see Winstanley 1652, e.g.), it seems that Locke
introduced a discourse of 'morality' in order to *limit* the power of productivity to
reap all the fruits of the social product. For a historical stage where the second
culture of productivity assumedly was already hegemonic, Locke invented three
moral limits to the effects of productivity. These appear to be the three imperatives of Locke's moral economy:

1   Do not appropriate more than you can produce with your own hands (1689,
    V.27).
2   Do not appropriate more than you can consume yourself; otherwise it will rot
    (V.31).
3   Always leave enough of the common property for others (V.27, V.33).

If these norms were binding in Locke's theory, then even for Locke, who was willing to expel people based on productivity differentials, productivity could not be the *only* norm. But what exactly is the status of these moral constraints? Is it a moral call to order, a symptom of a bad conscience even? Is it pragmatic caution, or mere political rhetoric? In my reading, the crucial motive for Locke's moral framework is itself based on concerns of efficiency, rendering these limits not moral, but ultimately economic ones. After all, they only refer to material goods. As soon as the economy becomes supposedly even more productive through the invention of *money*, the moral limits are promptly withdrawn (V.36). If they ever were valid, it was only in the imagined historical interim between the inventions of private property and money. Money neutralises this morality by its mere functionality (and not through a complex socio-psychological mechanism, as in Simmel or Marx). Unlike corn or wine, money can store the gained surplus-wealth *without* a danger of decay. It enables the accumulation of endless amounts of wealth without letting it rot, which for Locke means that it can be accumulated without taking it away from anybody (V.48, V. 50). Hence, in a monetary economy the moral limits to growth no longer hold, due to the supposedly superior productivity of money itself.

Yet Locke again jumps to conclusions too quickly. The mere fact that money does not rot (which is not true, exactly: gold wears out in circulation, and inflation is endemic to all sorts of money, see Caffentzis 1989) does not explain how it increases productivity. It *legitimises* the unequal distribution, says Locke. So, this increase in productivity depends on the lifting of the moral constraints on the acquisitive forces. The language of morals serves a rhetorical function to please readers but has no real effect on politics and practice.

Let us draw a conclusion. This kind of liberalism is violent in at least four dimensions: it accepts exclusion and expulsion as means to create private property; it produces wealth and social power only for some, not for others; it reduces the topics relevant for concerns of justice and the good life only to material and economic matters and, thus, systematically devaluates competing theories of the good and competing rights claims. Finally, it forces the poor (at home and abroad) into degrading jobs. All of this violence (which goes beyond mere symbolic violence) is accepted in the name of greater 'productivity'.

The politics of productivity

In conclusion, let us briefly turn to the adventures the concept of productivity underwent *after* Locke, who after all wrote in the 17th century. Subsequent economists took up his line of argument. The 'class struggle in theory' (Althusser) was waged between economic schools regarding the term 'productivity'. In these century-long debates, productivity was often related to economic growth, 'productive' types of labor or assets being those that contribute to the accumulation of the social product.[18] If growth is considered a good thing per se, it follows that the most productive class should also be in charge politically, as only they will be able to 'steer' the economy in the desired direction. As a current example recall the buzz about the 'creative classes' stirred up by city governments (Warwick report 2015) to justify urban restructuring and gentrification.

We saw how mercantilism guaranteed the constant flow of a surplus from one region of the world to the other by instituting unequal international exchanges. Such exploitation through institutionalised plundering marked the cornerstone of colonialism. It assigned legitimate power to *merchants*, as those who provided the wealth of the nation. We then saw how in Locke's writings, private property owners legitimised 'enclosures' both in the colonies and at home by claiming that higher productivity resulted from their new ownership. An accompanying 'moralisation' of the poverty created by these enclosures punished the poor once more by imposing forced labor and applying direct force on anybody 'unwilling' to work under the new regime.

A competing class was that of *landowners*. The corresponding 'physiocratic' theory reserved the term 'productive labor' for the agrarian classes. Arguing that the nobility spends a lot of wealth without reproducing any of it, François Quesnay's *tableau économique* counted their expenses as losses. Other classes fare little better: for Quesnay's merchants, technicians and manual workers produce something, but they also spend a lot, so in the end their total *input* to society is zero. They are only reproductive ("neutral"). The task of covering the losses incurred by society by being 'productive' in the *creative* sense is now assigned to land owners who know best how to *increase* the productivity of the soil. Real productivity, then, is the surplus in this year's total output as compared to last year's.[19] Again the political dimension of the term is clear: only if these productive classes are given enough leeway (low taxes, the bulk of the resources produced, and the *political* power to appropriate more and more land), can they further increase productivity. Thus, even the seemingly descriptive approach of the 'tableau économique' (the grandfather of the GDP) is a normative-political one: productivity requires that economic and political power are handed over to these classes.

For Adam Smith, the division of labor accomplishes this task. But it needs to be permanently instated: once initiated, you need to continue, at peril of being outcompeted. Unfortunately, the labor power that capitalists "command" (note the military undertones) remains more or less at the same productivity level all the time; at least to capitalists' minds. How can it be made ever *more* productive? The answer is: by dividing and mechanizing the labor process, and thus increasing the unit output per hour worked. This requires capital – machinery to divide the labor process, and money to pay for the machines. Thus, for Smith, industrial capitalist drive growth and deserve the most power in society.

Even the 20th-century Keynesian welfare state was legitimated in productivity terms. Keynes claimed that the economic system, being intrinsically unstable, does not automatically supply enough profitability, opportunities for investments, or jobs and income for everybody. Therefore, he shifted the responsibility for 'productivity' further, from capital to the government. It can bring the system back to its growth path by investing in a time of crisis and providing the jobs the system no longer delivers. The idea of the 'multiplier' promises a 'magic' productivity: if you invest one million (not necessarily financed by debts) as a stimulus and administer it correctly, the beneficial effects in the system will account for, say, 4 million. With the government as the most productive factor, Keynesianism clearly expresses the worldview of state bureaucrats.

Monetarism reacted with the injunction that governments are doomed to be economically unproductive, as they could only make ineffective investments (crowding out business, or investing in unproductive areas where the market does *not* invest). The state will invest in childcare and health institutions, free education, social insurance and the like. None of these produce a profit. Neoliberalism thus aimed to restore the profitability of money capital against the interests of the rest of society. This time, financial capitalists benefited tremendously.[20]

The lesson from this quick rundown seems obvious: The standard argument that we 'need' growing productivity rates to sustain justice and a good life is not waterproof. So far, the notion of 'productivity' has always been tied to systems of injustice and class domination, and it has silenced questions about the good life by translating them into mere numbers. A defense of the growth imperative in terms of "productivity" can hardly rely on justice or the good life, for there is no analytical link between them. They are mediated by ideologies that also justify political violence.

The fact that the idea of growth is increasingly questioned by dissenting economists, ecological scholars and global social movements should cue efforts to unpack the black box of central ideas in western economic philosophy that used to pass as self-evident. The idea of 'productivity' is a good example: the problems it highlights are not limited to the external effects of a political restoration of economic growth at all costs. Rather, the inherent problem is the license for violence that seems to be built into the very idea of 'productivity' itself – from its Lockean origins to this very day. Forgoing this violence should not count as a loss. It would be a gain.

Notes

1 From an anonymous poem of the 17th century, cited from http://wealthandwant.com/docs/Goose_commons.htm.
2 For the gender-subtext see Federici 2004.
3 For a renewed concept of "plenitude" see Schor 2010 or Jackson 2009, 143 ff.
4 Greed (pleonexia) was considered a deadly sin in catholic thinking, and Grimm's fairy tale of the Fisherman and his wife still shows that.
5 Adam Smith looked down on this doctrine with contempt (large parts of the *Wealth of Nations* criticize it). Even in current day visualizations, it is still pictured as morally bad (think of the Sheriff of Nottingham in the tales of *Robin Hood*, or the gold-loving Dragon „Smaug" in *The Hobbit*).
6 "As William Petty says, Labour is the father of material wealth, the earth is its mother" (Marx, *Capital*, quoted from www.marxists.org/archive/marx/works/1867-c1/ch01.htm).
7 Tully 1993 emphasized Locke's colonial subtext already; for his 'classism' (in his constitution for the Carolinas, e.g.) see Isenberg 2016, ch.2.
8 He "that encloses land, and has a greater plenty of the conveniencies of life from ten acres, than he could have from an hundred left to nature, may truly be said to give ninety acres to mankind" (Locke 1689 V.37; cf Ince 2011).
9 "There cannot be a clearer demonstration of any thing, than several nations of the Americans are of this, who are rich in land, and poor in all the comforts of life; . . . a king of a large and fruitful territory there, feeds, lodges, and is clad worse than a day-labourer in England" (Locke 1689, V.41); "the accommodation of an European prince does not always so much exceed that of an industrious and frugal peasant, as the

accommodation of the latter exceeds that of many an African king, the absolute master of the lives and liberties of ten thousand naked savages" (Smith 1776, I.2).

10   "In times long gone by there were two sorts of people; one, the diligent, intelligent, and, above all, frugal elite; the other, lazy rascals, spending their substance, and more, in riotous living" (Marx, *Capital*, www.marxists.org/archive/marx/works/1867-c1/ch26.htm).

11   "There is not, in that state, any of those spectacles of human misery which poverty and want present to our eyes in all the towns and streets in Europe. Poverty, therefore, is a thing created by that which is called civilized life. It exists not in the natural state" (Paine 1797, 331). "It is the absence of the threat of individual starvation which makes a primitive society, in a sense, more human than a market society, and at the same time, less economic. Ironically, the white man's initial contribution to the black man's world mainly consisted in introducing him to the uses of the scourge of hunger. Thus the colonist may decide to cut the breadfruit trees in order to create an artificial food scarcity" (Polanyi 1944, 164).

12   "Almost universally committed to the proposition that life was hard in the paleolithic, our textbooks compete to convey a sense of impending doom, leaving one to wonder not only how hunters managed to live, but whether, after all, this was living? The specter of starvation stalks the stalker through these pages. [. . .] The traditional wisdom is always refractory. One is forced to oppose it polemically, to phrase the necessary revisions dialectically: in fact, this was, when you come to examine it, the original affluent society" (Sahlins 1972, 1).

13   Rousseau's point was that the social contract could be revoked if it did not deliver the desired result, here: a better economic situation for everybody.

14   "The growth of the poor must therefore have some other cause; and it can be nothing else but the relaxation of discipline, and corruption of manners: virtue and industry being as constant companions on the one side as vice and idleness are on the other" (Locke 1697, 447).

15   "God gave the world to men in common; but . . . it cannot be supposed he meant it should always remain common and uncultivated. He gave it to the use of the industrious and rational, . . . not to the fancy or covetousness of the quarrelsome and contentious" (Locke 1689, V.34).

16   Locke demands „that all men begging . . . shall be sent to the next house of correction, there to be kept at hard labour for three years" (Locke 1697, 449, cf Katz 1994). This element also resurfaces in Rawls: As Rawls counts „leisure" as a basic goods, this implies that the poor can be *forced* to work (Howard 2005).

17   See Waldron 2002, 151ff; Ince 2011, also Caffentzis 1989.

18   "There is one sort of labour which adds to the value of the subject upon which it is bestowed; there is another which has no such effect. The former, as it produces a value, may be called productive; the latter, unproductive labour. Thus the labour of a manufacturer adds, generally, to the value of the materials which he works upon, that of his own maintenance, and of his master's profit. The labour of a menial servant, on the contrary, adds to the value of nothing" (Smith 1776, II.3).

19   This third class produces *surplus value*: more output than input in terms of value.

20   "Neoliberalism is the expression of the desire of a class of capitalist owners and the institutions in which their power is concentrated, which we collectively call 'finance,' to restore . . . the class's revenues and power" (Dumenil/Levy 2005, 17).

References

Benjamin, W. (1986 [1921]). Critique of Violence. In: *Reflections: Essays, Aphorism, Autobiographical Writings*, ed. by P. Demetz, transl. E. Jephcot. New York: Schocken, 277–300.

Caffentzis, G. (1989). *Clipped Coins, Abused Words, and Civil Government: John Locke's Philosophy of Money*. New York: Automedia.

Dumenil, G./D. Levy (2005). Costs and Benefits of Neoliberalism: A Class Analysis. In: G. A. Epstein (ed.). *Financialization and the World Economy*. Cheltenham, UK: Edward Elgar, 17–41.

Emmanuel, A. (1972). *Unequal Exchange: A Study of the Imperialism of Trade*. New York: Monthly Review Press.

Federici, S. (2004). *Caliban and the Witch: Women, the Body and Primitive Accumulation*. New York: Automedia.

Goldstein, J. (2013). Terra Economica: Waste and the production of nature. In: *Antipode* 45.2, 357–375.

Gronemeyer, M. (2007). *Profitstreben als Tugend? Zur politischen Ökonomie bei Aristoteles*. Marburg: Metropolis.

Harvey, D. (2004). The 'New' Imperialism: Accumulation by Dispossession. In: *Socialist Register* 40, 63–87.

Henning, C. (2016). Formen der Muße zwischen Faulheit und Fest. In: Deutscher Hochschulverband (ed.). *Glanzlichter der Wissenschaft – ein Almanach 2016*. Heidelberg: Winter 2016, 89–96.

Howard, M.W. (2005). Basic Income, Liberal Neutrality, Socialism, and Work. In: *Review of Social Economy* 63.4, 613–631.

Ince, O.U. (2011). Enclosing in God's Name, Accumulation for Mankind: Money, Morality, and Accumulation in John Locke's Theory of Property. In: *Review of Politics* 73, 29–54.

Isenberg, N. (2016). *White Trash: The 400-Year Untold Story of Class in America*. New York: Viking.

Jackson, T. (2009). *Prosperity Without Growth: Economics for a Finite Planet*. Abingdon: Routledge.

Katz, M.B. (1994). *In the Shadow of the Poorhouse: A Social History of Welfare in America*. New York: Basic Books.

Locke, J. (1988 [1689]). Second Treatise of Government. In: *Two Treatises of Government*. Ed. Peter Laslett. Cambridge: Cambridge University Press.

Locke, J. (1993 [1697]). Report respecting the relief and employment of the poor. In: *Political Writings*. New York: Mentor, 446–461.

Mills, J. (2002). *A Critical History of Economics*. Basingstoke: Palgrave.

Paine, T. (1797). *Agrarian Justice* (Pamphlet). Online at http://piketty.pse.ens.fr/files/Paine1795.pdf.

Polanyi, K. (2010 [1944]). *The Great Transformation: The Political and Economic Origins of Our Time*. Boston: Beacon Press.

Sahlins, M.D. (1972). *Stone Age Economics*. New York: DeGruyter.

Sayer, A. (2014). *Why We Can't Aafford the Rich*. Bristol: Polity Press.

Schor, J.B. (2010). *Plenitude: The New Economics of True Wealth*. New York: Penguin.

Smith, A. (1759). *The Theory of Moral Sentiments*. Online at www.econlib.org/library/Smith/smMS.html.

Smith, A. (1776). *The Wealth of Nations*. Online at www.econlib.org/library/Smith/smWN.html.

Tully, J. (1993). Rediscovering America: The Two Treatises and Aboriginal Rights. In: Q. Skinner (ed.). *An Approach to Political Philosophy: Locke in Contexts*. Cambridge: Cambridge University Press, 137–176.

Waldron, J. (2002). *God, Locke and Equality: Christian Foundations in Locke's Political Thought*. Cambridge: Cambridge University Press.

Warwick Commission (2015). Enriching Britain: Culture, Creativity and Growth. *The 2015 Report*. Online at www2.warwick.ac.uk/research/warwickcommission/futureculture/finalreport.

Winstanley, G. (1652). *The Law of Freedom in a Platform*. Online at www.marxists.org/reference/archive/winstanley/1652/law-freedom.

7   Growth regimes and visions of the good life

Why capitalism will not deliver

Dennis Eversberg

Is a good life possible under capitalism? In this contribution, I want to suggest both a non-answer and an ultimate answer to this question. The non-answer is that it is impossible to answer this question at such a general level, since capitalist societies, including the opportunities for and the barriers against a better life inherent to them, are much too diverse to make any such general statement. Still, the ultimate answer I want to offer in conclusion is: No.

But first things first: As an initial approach, it is possible to say a few things about the fundamental logic of capitalist societies and the problems they pose to pursuing a good life. The specificity of *capitalist* social orders is that, since profits are never high enough and social stability requires economic growth (Dörre/ Lessenich/Rosa 2016), there is necessarily always *something* that is *not enough*, and people – be it in their capacities as producers, consumers or citizens – must be exhorted to constantly intensify their contributions to bringing about *more* of that something. In this respect, living under capitalism always implies an impediment to a good life: whatever you do, you never do it good enough, and you must never be content with the state of things. Now, this is a structural property of capitalist social formations that puts them fundamentally at odds with any idea of a good life – at least as long as you assume, of course, that a good life in some way implies being content with what you've got (more on that in a moment). However, it's impossible to make any general statement about *what* social exhortations actually constitute the object of people's discontents, because in their daily lives, people never deal with "capitalism" as an abstract entity, but always with specific types of social relations and institutional arrangements that form a historically and geographically variable capitalist formation or, in the terminology I will use here, *growth regime*.[1] What the proper functioning of these regimes demands from people is historically and geographically variable to a large extent, and this variation implies that there will (almost?) always be some other variant of capitalism that will (at least seemingly) offer a *better* life in terms of the specific discontents of people living under any one variant – and as we will see later on, people's expressed discontents are indeed a key driving force in the emergence of new growth regimes.

But from the perspective I'm suggesting here, the same also holds the other way around: People's subjectivity (in terms of their specific discontents) is a force that shapes capitalist regimes, but that same subjectivity is itself (in terms of these discontents, but also of their preferences, desires, attitudes and capabilities) shaped by the specific capitalist formation they grew up under. A growth regime is therefore never 'only' a mode of organizing production, consumption and political regulation, but also a *subjectivation regime* that produces specific types of producers, consumers and citizens. Against this backdrop, the structural problem identified above may be rephrased as follows: Since they make permanent escalation a basic principle of subjectivation – i.e. 'striving for more' is built into growth subjectivity – capitalist growth societies inevitably create *mental infrastructures of discontent*, meaning that growth subjects are invariably *dissatisfied* subjects (cf. Kallis 2011, 877). This makes it all the more complicated to say anything substantial about 'the good life'. Not only is it unlikely that anyone will perceive their own life as 'good' just because it happens to conform to the normative criteria or minimum standards enumerated by some philosophers or sociologists (e.g. freedom, equality, justice, democracy, or resonance): What people will actually *want*, what *visions* of a better life they will be willing to fight for in any specific historical situation, is an altogether different question. And more than that, we cannot even assume that everyone living within the geographical purview of a specific growth regime will experience the same sense of loss or deficit and thus share a broadly similar vision of what a good life would look like: Since capitalist societies are class societies that expose people to very different demands depending on their position relative to the means of production and power, these visions are themselves invariably particular to certain social groups. And of course, any such class specific vision of a subjectively better life – i.e., a life without the escalatory pressures of the respective current growth regime on the lives of people in that particular class position – would not, when generalised, guarantee a better life for all. This is for two reasons: First, because people in different social or class positions, making different everyday experiences of lack or discontent, will not necessarily deem the same vision desirable. And second, from a normative standpoint, a way of life that some may subjectively desire – say, one in which one is surrounded by sports cars, yachts and other luxury goods – cannot be seen as 'good' simply because it can never be equally available to everyone on the planet. Therefore, the question for the good life can never be answered by exclusive recourse to either the subjective ('a good life for all is when everyone gets what they desire') or the normative dimension ('a good life for all is when everyone has equal access to a globally sustainable mode of living'). Instead, a valid answer can only arise from a reflexive engagement between both ways of posing the question.

Based on these preliminary considerations I would like to make the following proposition, to be further substantiated in the remainder of this contribution: In any specific capitalist social formation, the visions of a better life that dominate the collective imaginary will be ones that promise relief from the most pressing, restricting demands that the current mode of organizing production, consumption and citizenship subjects people to. Both these demands and the visions of a life beyond them will always be class specific, and the struggles for that better life will be *class struggles*. These struggles have historically been a driving force of capitalist development, overthrowing outdated growth regimes and replacing them with new ones – which then, in turn, have gone on to subject people to other demands, creating different dominant visions of the good life and leading to new struggles.

I will illustrate this historical cycle of events by giving a highly stylised account of the history of Western European capitalism as a succession of three growth regimes – *liberal capitalism, organised capitalism* and *flexible capitalism* – along with the restrictions they have forced on people, the visions of a better life put forward against them and the battles waged to make these visions a reality, ending up, in each case so far, in a new capitalist growth regime. As a conclusion, I will pose the question whether any resistance directed at achieving a good life is destined to bring about new forms of capitalism, or whether a post-capitalist prospect may eventually be in sight.

Growth regimes and struggles for the good life: a brief historical account

In French regulation theory, the notion of 'growth regime' has been used to describe temporarily stable constellations of institutional arrangements that stabilise a social setting conducive to a specific mode of economic activity that will ensure rising profits to capital (Boyer 1988; Aglietta 2000). The advantage of this notion is that it allows us to distinguish between different modes of operation of capitalist economies, while maintaining that all of them are manifestations of the same mode of production. The theoretical punch line of this idea is that growth regimes have *inherent economic limits:* Any social-institutional constellation capable of securing growth for a prolonged period will gradually chip away at the foundations it rests on, ending up in a crisis out of which a new formation can emerge (Aglietta 2000; Lordon 2002). Now, if we assume that any growth regime is also a subjectivation regime, such endogenous economic crises may equally well be understood as *subjective crises*, setting in when a one-sided way of shaping people and drawing on their subjective capacities is no longer bearable or acceptable for them. The regime reaches its *subjective limits* once the ensuing forms of widespread and growing unrest become an ineluctable political factor, contributing to its destabilisation and eventual demise. In other words: As a mode of subjectivation, any growth regime produces subjects whose inner constitution and desires will sooner or later transcend it.

Following these minimal definitions, let me sketch out what such a view amounts to by giving a brief account of the subjective history of Western European capitalism since the 19th century.

Liberal capitalism: collectivizing individuation

The latter half of the 19th century was a phase of rapid industrialisation, bringing high growth rates and quickly rising numbers of waged employment. In Germany, the number of workers in industry rose from one million in 1850 to 6 million in 1895 (Alber 1986, 5). Most of these 'free' wage workers' families had only recently been separated from the land as their means of subsistence, and were still strongly enmeshed in dense networks of collective relations shaped by rural family structures. They were used to living in mutual dependency and viewing themselves as a collective with a common fate. Their integration into wage labour, however, subjected them to the labour contract as an *individuating* social technology (Meyer 2010): By obliging her to fulfil her work duties regardless of all other social obligations, suppressing non-compliance by force and penalties, and simultaneously integrating her socially as an individual market subject by virtue of the money paid as a wage, the worker was both *addressed* as an individual and *forced* to act as one. This initial individuation did not bring her the freedoms enjoyed by bourgeois individuals, while subordinating her to the *unifying* structural forces of the economic field and their subjectivating effects (Bourdieu 2003; Eversberg 2014, 100).

Factory organisation in this period primarily relied on technologies designed to *discipline* workers, make them work swiftly and constantly and render them permanently observable (Foucault 1979, 216). These were no less individuating, serving to separate workers from each other and subject each of them to the same coercive force. In this period, industrially produced goods were not intended for workers' consumption; their consumption was not a relevant factor of demand for industrial products, and labour was abundant. Therefore, capitalists had no reason to pay more than a minimum or organise production in a way that would preserve workers' health and motivation. Growth did not require their loyalty, and wages appeared as a cost factor only. The result for workers was poverty, bad working conditions and a largely disenfranchised status – in short: *proletarianisation*.

Consequently, the ideas of a better life that workers and their supporters came up with aimed at overcoming this collective suffering: They struggled for higher wages, labour rights and better conditions. The key resource they posited against the de-collectivizing logic of the labour contract and its adverse effects was the collective ethic of mutual dependency inherited from their rural and agrarian mental traditions. It provided fertile ground for the 'making of the working class' as a 'learning process' leading to the emergence of social, cultural and political organisations and, eventually, powerful labour movements (Thompson 1963; Vester 1970).

By the end of the 19th century, the *individuating* logic of liberal capitalism had, in a dialectical historical movement, sparked the *collective* formation and political mobilisation of the working class, and the demands for a better life in terms of wages, rights and working conditions that labour movements forcefully articulated marked the liberal-capitalist growth regime's subjective limit. Over the following decades, in a process full of setbacks, even crushing defeats, and through long periods of political and social instability, workers' collective struggles became one of the key forces in the erection of the organised capitalist growth regime that finally came to fruition after World War II.

Organised capitalism: individualizing collectivisation

Organised capitalism's crucial feat was that it granted the working class full citizenship in capitalist society through the establishment of what Robert Castel (2002) has termed 'social property': Institutionalised, individually guaranteed entitlements to social benefits and support that could compensate for the lack of personal wealth as a protection against the risks of life and that could contribute to a more even distribution of 'life chances' (Weber). The key technologies that provided social property exerted a *collectivizing* force on workers' subjectivities: *Social insurances* against sickness, accidents and for pensions provision were based on the discovery of *risk* as a genuinely *social* concept that could only be calculated statistically and managed collectively at the level of populations (Ewald 1986). In Germany, even before World War I, social insurance had expanded to cover large segments of society, including white-collar workers, widows and orphans. The Weimar Republic saw further elements of organised capitalism's collective social order appear: the eight-hour workday, public labour exchanges, autonomous wage bargaining, rules for labour conflict arbitration and workplace co-determination. Social assistance was extended, further groups covered by social insurance, and unemployment insurance was introduced as a wholly new element (Alber 1986, 9).

In Germany and some other European countries, this collectivised mode of subjectivation was further entrenched by the institution of the *occupation*, itself deriving from the medieval self-organisation of crafts. In pushing for the canonisation of industrial labour in terms of occupations – standardised bundles of skills and aptitudes acquired during a multi-year apprenticeship and certified to the worker – and making occupational groups the structuring category of collective agreements, the labour movement had effectively used a pre-capitalist institution to strengthen workers' labour market power and to protect each of them from the negative effects of fragmented workplace organisation. These rights were not, in principle, to be thought of as the individual worker's 'property', but they in fact accrued to her as a member of the occupational collective.

But organised capitalism also, and primarily, meant a high degree of integration and interconnectedness of large firm conglomerates (Lash/Urry 1988; Aglietta 2000). These, crucially, also had something to gain from workers' social integration. Through the *Fordist* link between standardised mass production and standardised mass consumption, the collectivizing logic of organised capitalism became the catalyst of a temporarily stable high-growth regime lasting for about two decades after World War II. Linking commodity production to the production of everyday life through the regulation of wages enabled a historically unique synergy between workers' interest in collective agreements and high wages and capital's interest in high and stable demand. Highly integrated firms and an expanding public sector drew a majority of the economically active population into this nexus, turning them all into wage earners and effecting a far-reaching homogenisation of the social fabric as that of a *wage society* (Aglietta 2000; Castel 2002). This, of course, was not the full story: The necessary counterpart to the Fordist factory was the (nuclear) family, in which the production and maintenance of workers' labour power was to be equally effectively organised – a task unquestioningly imposed upon women. As a result, the task profile and social identity of 'housewife and mother' was, though less formalised, subject to a similar degree of standardisation as the occupationally defined identity patterns of the (predominantly) male workers.

Again, all these structurally collectivizing sociotechnical arrangements did not seamlessly turn people into collectively thinking and acting subjects, but sowed the seed of their own antithesis: The rising standard of living that the growth model afforded them provided people with expanding opportunities to develop *de*-standardised lifestyles and individualised social practices *outside* the formal economic and political structures. In another dialectical turn of events, the most thorough institutionalisation of working people as a collective that history had known simultaneously allowed them to actively de-collectivise themselves and to become more individual than ever. Ordinary working people now had at their disposal, to a constantly increasing degree, the means to engage in all sorts of lei-surely and voluntary social and personal activities. The secure and rising 'family wage' of the male worker could cover steadily more than the basic necessities of life, and the parallel shortening of working hours (as well as technical innova-tions reducing the time needed for household work) freed up time for things like sports, tourism, 'hobbies' and such: practices that were not directly tied to the production of the family's material conditions of living (as, for instance, the once predominant 'pastime' of gardening had been for many), but enabling a gradual differentiation of tastes, through which the sense of collectivity in people's every-day self-understandings was gradually weakened and that of being a singular, non-standard, unique person took – at first in the realm of the 'lifeworld', outside the institutions of work and state – more and more hold.

A renewed subjective crisis began to dawn when the degree of differentiation of people's demand for commodities reached a point beyond which the Fordist mode of organizing production proved dysfunctional, being too rigid and inflex-ible to cater to the diversified tastes: "By way of simplification, one could say: What mass series production has to offer in terms of market diversification is sufficient for a *group* differentiation among consumers, but not for individualiza-tion" (Lüscher 1990, 171, my translation). True, economic factors like the end of the gold standard and the Bretton Woods system as well as the subsequent 'oil shocks' certainly did theirs to end the Fordist constellation. However, parallel to the erosion of the regime's economic infrastructure ran the gradual crumbling of its *mental infastructure* (Welzer 2013). In other words: Organised capitalism could not deliver on visions of a 'good life' that was to be freely designed by the individual – and its rigid social norms and institutional hierarchies kept directly contradicting such desires. The late 1960s marked the becoming apparent of a world of unrest that had been gestating in different sectors of Fordist society. The common underlying experience was that of a growing discrepancy between a multiplication of opportunities in the private sphere and the strict standardisation of roles and biographical patterns on the institutional side of society. The greater the opportunities for an autonomous life conduct outside the roles of employee or 'housewife and mother', the greater became the discontent at a kind of future that was *secured*, but also turned into the prospect of a permanent *fate* by the institutions of organised capitalism: The outlook of being, for all of one's 'active' life, bound either to children and the household or to a highly fragmented kind of labour offering little chances for personal satisfaction. At the end of the 1960s, this escalating discrepancy between growing desires for *autonomy* and a prescribed monotonous life sparked a broad popular insurgency against the future Fordism held in store. Individually, a growing share of the youth took the tension between their aspirations and the prospects offered as a "challenge to learn" (Vester et al. 2001, 261f.), seeking to flee their prescribed future through higher education or, in the case of quickly growing numbers of women, through entering the labour market. And collectively, groups of apprentices, students and women, as well as the discontented youth in general, started to organise, express their demands and experiment with alternative lifestyles in the numerous social movements springing up across Europe and North America. Series of wildcat strikes, often initiated by migrant workers, indicated similar discontent among the lower ranks of those already integrated into Fordist working life. "It was not moral principles or a 'tacit' value change that motivated the new social movements, but the practical experience of a contradiction of growing, yet denied potentials for freedom, which could not be legitimized" (ibid.: 256). Years before the 'oil shock', these forms of practical revolt signaled the subjective limits of Fordist growth society.

Flexible capitalism: dividualisation

Organised capitalism is certainly dead and gone. Despite heated debates on whether there is such a thing as a 'post-Fordist growth regime', there is in any case no new 'canonical model'. Still, I would hold that there is indeed a common logic to the restructuring of modes of subjectivation in the most advanced capitalist societies. Since the late 1960s, people's struggles for individuality and personal freedom and the long-term effects of anti-Fordist revolt have helped pave the way for a regime of structural *dividualisation* (Eversberg 2016a), in which the de-collectivisation that people fought for out of individualist intentions turns on them as a dynamic that fragments the individual herself, subordinating life to the demands of work, and delegating the responsibility for being an individual to subjects themselves. Dividualisation has at least three dimensions, each of which is enabled by specific social technologies. It correlates to the rise of a *flexible capitalist* growth regime, in which the main method of further optimizing the relation between *inputs* and *outputs* is to constantly break down all inputs to production into ever smaller units in order to eliminate all forms of deadweight and drag in the productive process.

The first dimension of dividualisation is the *dimension of competence*: the *occupation*, as a subjectivation model that increasingly appears as too cumbersome and laden with inappropriate expectations, is gradually superseded by the model of *competence*. The abilities, aptitudes and attitudes that had formerly been tied together in a standardised and relatively stable occupational profile which, when acquired for once, guaranteed collectively backed claims for decades, have since been unbundled. For the differentiated and highly volatile labour demand of flexible production, firms increasingly seek to buy only highly specific sets of competences for narrowly defined periods at the lowest price possible. The occupational 'wholesale' in labour power is thus gradually being supplanted by a competence-based 'specialist trade', making it crucial for owners of labour power to be able to navigate unstable market environments with constantly changing requirements by constantly updating the *assets* in one's 'competence portfolio'. This shift was effected through social technologies such as modular apprenticeships and courses of study, calls for and offers of 'lifelong learning', and 'neosocial' policies of 'activation' and responsibilisation intended to render individuals responsible for the constant improvement and active marketing of their labour power (Lessenich 2011). The pioneers of dividual self-marketing were fractions of the cultural and artistic elites, whose models of living and working had long been in line with the demands for autonomy and difference articulated by the anti-Fordist movements. In their specific labour markets, highly specific skills and references had always been more important than staple degrees – and in a situation of rising unemployment, this specific experience could be converted into new 'portfolio'-based strategies of competitive self-marketing. These have since 'trickled down' into other, broader segments of the labour market and, in a general climate of harsher competition for fewer and more precarious jobs, mutated from an initially freely chosen lifestyle into an external imposition enforced through modified personnel management techniques and labour market policies (Eversberg 2016b).

The second dimension is the *spatio-temporal*: flexibilised, project-based and competition-oriented modes of firm organisation and the destandardisation of employment have weakened the ties between firms and workers, while mobile communications and network technologies have enabled a whole new level of short-term demand-oriented reorganisation and coordination of work processes. Thus, working subjects can now also be disassembled in space and time: "When we move into the sphere of info-labor there is no longer a need to have bought a person for eight hours a day indefinitely. Capital no longer recruits people, but buys packets of time, separated from their interchangeable and occasional bearers" (Berardi 2009, 32). In effect, it is no longer the (normed) individual that constitutes the basic unit of trade in labour power, but it becomes possible to buy and sell only specific *parts* of the person for the exact *time* and only according to the exact *demands* they are needed for, thus reducing friction and 'unnecessary' costs.

And thirdly, dividualisation has a *functional* dimension, reflecting the contradictory multiple positioning of working subjects in the economic field with respect to their several 'partial identities'. Resulting from the process of financialisation – featuring the broad distribution of firm ownership through investment trusts and capitalised pensions as well as credit-driven consumption to compensate for declining real wages – the post-Fordist wage earner has undergone a series of *inner divisions*. In several superficially separate, yet structurally connected spheres, she appears in partial identities as producer, consumer, investor, real estate speculator or taxpayer. All these identity segments relate to the economic field, and in financialised capitalism, they can no longer coexist without contradiction, but constitute interests diametrically opposed to each other.

Across all three dimensions, these changes mark a decisive rupture with the collectivizing logic of Fordism, but not with the escalatory imperatives of capitalism. It is the transition to a *society of control*: Technological change has created the conditions for a mode of integrating workers into production that is neither primarily *disciplinary* (as in liberal capitalism) nor built on the logic of *insurance* (as in organised capitalism). Instead, drawing on 'digital doubles' of their abilities, knowledges and personal risks that circulate as packages of information within digital networks, people's inner potentials can now be precisely allocated in space and time in the matrix of open *environments of control* constructed across the previous spaces of disciplinary enclosure, and permanently surveyed in their optimal use (Deleuze 1992).

Conclusion

Evidently, this last account must remain fragmentary for the time being, as it's too early to say with certainty what forms of oppositional life-worldly subjectivation may eventually topple the dividualizing regime of flexible capitalism. Then again, we are not completely clueless. Rising incidences of depression, burnout and other exhaustion-related illnesses, increasing consumption of psychiatric drugs and related phenomena suggest that the extremely high cognitive and social demands of remaining functional under the current regime, as well as the stress caused by permanent insecurity, are already hitting tangible limits of what people can cope with both mentally and physically (Neckel/Wagner 2014). If this is correct – and it remains to be shown whether it is –, the question is whether these forms of suffering can turn into a political factor that eventually enforces change. If it can, it is somewhat hard to see how these desires could be turned into the basis of a renewed regime of 'ever more'. Indeed, it might turn out that capitalism itself, having 'categorially exhausted' (Offe 1972, 24) the possibilities of further rationalizing the exploitation of human labour power, has eventually reached an *absolute limit*, marked by mass psycho-physical exhaustion.

Corresponding to the 'mass exhaustion' diagnosis, most of the visions of a better life currently being put forward express desires for a slower, calmer, less fragmented and more communal way of life – whether they are being expressed by retreating into the harmonious micro-environment of home and family, by consuming idealised depictions of the 'simple rural life' or by an identitarian separatism of subcultural communities. At present, however, these visions of the good life are highly fragmentary, socially particular and torn by contradictions. The degree of coherence and broad social appeal needed for them to actually become a political factor does not seem at hand.

Indeed, achieving this would require the sublation of the social particularisms inherent to all of them and an effort to come up with a potentially global vision. Remembering our two criteria from the introduction, such a vision would need to be both subjectively desirable for everyone *and* normatively feasible, i.e. capable of being universalised. This, however, will require that a growing number of social groups enter into a reflexive process in which they *integrate* the normative demand that the good life be possible for everyone on a global scale into their socially particular visions of a better life. Challenging as this may be, social actors that do this arguably exist, ranging from Latin American indigenous debates about *buen vivir*, Indian activists calling for *radical ecological democracy* or global networks struggling for *environmental* and *climate justice* to the European *Degrowth* movement. The task is certainly daunting, and the reflexive effort is anything but guaranteed to succeed – but as can already be seen from the character of these

104   *Dennis Eversberg*

movements, they share an awareness that the good life they envision cannot be arrived at within capitalism – it lies beyond it.

Note

1 Let 'growth regime', for the purposes of this chapter, be any formation that is *in principle* geared to rationalizing and accelerating certain kinds of economic process and maximizing certain types of output, regardless of whether there actually *is* such growth or not. What counts here is the way in which the overarching capitalist imperative of escalation translates into specific demands that successful social integration poses to people. Just as 'growth society' doesn't refer to a society in which the economy is growing, but to one that is, in its material, institutional and mental infrastructures, *geared to* generating permanent growth, 'growth regime' denotes the specific way in which these infrastructures are *arranged* to allow for a specific mode of growth.

References

Aglietta, M. (2000). *A Theory of Capitalist Regulation: The US Experience*. London: Verso.
Alber, J. (1986). Germany. In: P. Flora (ed.). *Growth to Limits: The Western European Welfare States Since World War II*, Vol. II: Germany, UK, Ireland, Italy. Berlin: De Gruyter, 1–154.
Berardi, F. 'Bifo' (2009). *Precarious Rhapsody: Semiocapitalism and the Pathologies of the Post-Alpha Generation*. London: Minor Compositions.
Bourdieu, P. (2003). Vereinheitliche und herrsche. In J. Jurt (ed.). *Absolute Pierre Bourdieu*. Freiburg: Orange Press, 200–210.
Boyer, R. (1988). Formalizing Growth Regimes Within a Regulation Approach: A Method for Assessing the Economic Consequences of Technological Change. In G. Dosi/C. Freeman (eds.). *Technical Change and Economic Theory: The Global Process of Development*, vol. 2. London: Frances Pinter, 608–630.
Castel, R. (2002). *From Manual Workers to Wage Labourers: Transformation of the Social Question*. Piscataway, NJ: Transaction Publishers.
Deleuze, G. (1992). Postscript on the Societies of Control. In: *October* 59, 3–7.
Dörre, K./S. Lessenich/H. Rosa (2016). *Sociology, Capitalism, Critique*. London: Verso.
Eversberg, D. (2014). *Dividuell aktiviert: Wie Arbeitsmarktpolitik Subjektivitäten produziert*. Frankfurt am Main: Campus.
Eversberg, D. (2016a). Beyond Individualisation: The German "Activation Toolbox". In: *Critical Social Policy* 36 2, 167–186.
Eversberg, D. (2016b). Destabilisierte Zukunft. Veränderungen im sozialen Feld des Arbeitsmarkts seit 1970 und ihre Auswirkungen auf die Erwartungshorizonte der jungen Generation. In: A. Doering-Manteuffel/L. Raphael/T. Schlemmer (eds.). *Vorgeschichte der Gegenwart: Dimensionen des Strukturbruchs nach dem Boom*. Göttingen: Vandenhoeck & Ruprecht, 451–474.
Ewald, F. (1986). *L'État providence*. Paris: Grasset.
Foucault, M. (1979). *Discipline and Punish: The Birth of the Prison*. New York: Vintage Books.
Kallis, G. (2011). In Defence of Degrowth. In: *Ecological Economics* 70 5, 873–880.
Lash, S./J. Urry (1988). *The End of Organized Capitalism*. Madison: University of Wisconsin Press.
Lessenich, S. (2011). Constructing the Socialized Self: Mobilization and Control in the "Active Society". In: U. Bröckling/S. Krasmann/T. Lemke (eds.). *Governmentality: Current Issues and Future Challenges*. New York: Routledge, 304–319.

Lordon, F. (2002) Formalising Regulationist Dynamics and Crises. In: R. Boyer/Y. Saillard (eds.). *Régulation Theory: The State of the Art*. London: Routledge, 174–180.

Lüscher, R. (1990). *Henry und die Krümelmonster: Versuch über den fordistischen Sozialcharakter*. Tübingen: Konkursbuch Verlag.

Meyer, L. (2010). Das Recht des Kapitalismus: Überlegungen zu den monetären Implikationen der Entstehung des modernen Rechts. In: H. Pahl/L. Meyer (eds.). *Gesellschaftstheorie der Geldwirtschaft: Soziologische Beiträge*. Marburg: Metropolis, 127–164.

Neckel, S./G. Wagner (2014). *Leistung und Erschöpfung: Burnout in der Wettbewerbsgesellschaft*. Berlin: Suhrkamp.

Offe, C. (1972). *Strukturprobleme des kapitalistischen Staates: Aufsätze zur politischen Soziologie*. Frankfurt am Main: Suhrkamp.

Thompson, E.P. (1963). *The Making of the English Working Class*. London: Gollancz.

Vester, M. (1970). *Die Entstehung des Proletariats als Lernprozeß: Die Entstehung antikapitalistischer Theorie und Praxis in England 1792–1848*. Frankfurt am Main: EVA.

Vester, M./P. v. Oertzen/H. Geiling/T. Hermann/D. Müller (2001). *Soziale Milieus im gesellschaftlichen Strukturwandel: Zwischen Integration und Ausgrenzung*. Frankfurt am Main: Suhrkamp.

Welzer, H. (2013). *Mental Infrastructures: How Growth Entered the World and Our Souls*. Berlin: Heinrich-Böll-Stiftung.

8 Political economic conditions of a good life beyond growth

Andrew Sayer

For over two centuries, it has been widely assumed that economic growth is not just necessary for a good life, but is a part of it. One reason for our reluctance to accept that it is neither inevitable nor desirable, at least in the rich countries, is that zero growth in capitalism comes with crises and hardship, and it is hard to imagine a feasible alternative political economic system that could support a good life beyond growth. In this contribution I suggest what kind of economy might be environmentally sustainable and fair and conducive to well-being. Our current economy performs badly on the first and second of these criteria, and unevenly on the third. Although there are some obvious regulatory changes to protect the environment and social welfare that might help to meet these criteria, it is argued here that particularly given capitalism's evident dependence on economic growth, and the need to drastically cut emissions of greenhouse gases, deeper changes in economic institutions are also needed.

And since our economy is not simply a technical system but a *political economy* – a vast network of social relations in which a highly unequal distribution of power inheres – we need to make the political challenges clear. As we shall see, in many ways, there is a convergence between traditional left critiques of our dominant economic system – capitalism – and environmental critiques.

The challenge of building a carbon-neutral economy obliges us to go back to basics and reconsider what an economy is for, and consider the nature of the social and material, environmental relations involved. So before discussing some alternative political economic institutions, I will begin with some of these basic issues and argue for a moral economic approach.

Back to basics

The point of economic activity is simply to enable us to live well. Wealth is not money but whatever supports flourishing. Economies are systems of provisioning – ways of providing us with the wherewithal to live a decent life – and of course some systems of provisioning are much better than others. In capitalism, provisioning is not the prime goal, but a common, though not universal, by-product of the pursuit of profit.

Provisioning involves two kinds of relations:

- relations between people, whether as buyers and sellers, employers and employees, lenders and borrowers, landlords and tenants, citizens and governments, or as providers and beneficiaries of unpaid work.
- our relations to the environment: All material wealth ultimately depends on this, so looking after the environment should make economic sense: degrading it does not.

No one ever became rich or poor outside these two sets of relations. 'Moral economy' focuses on these and examines whether they are fair or unfair, functional for provisioning or not, and sustainable or unsustainable (Sayer 2007; 2014). Particularly at this time of economic and environmental crisis, it can provide us with signposts to a different way of doing things. I shall introduce features of a moral economic approach that deal primarily with the social relations of the economy, before moving on to environmental issues.

Mainstream economics ignores or misunderstands these relations: *homo oeconomicus* is assumed to be a free-standing, adult man, self-interested and entering only into contractual relations with others where he wishes. But a society comprised wholly of such individuals is an impossibility. We are social beings. This means not merely that we happen to live in groups, but that we are *inherently* dependent on others: entering into social relations is not only necessary but unavoidable. Most fundamentally this is because we all start off as helpless babies, utterly dependent on our carers. This is a universal. And particularly in old age or illness we again become dependent on others. Dependency can be good (having good parents), or it can be bad, a source of exploitation and domination. It's important to know the difference, but mainstream economic thought ignores the first and largely conceals the second. Both are of primary interest to moral economy,

To recognise the difference we need to notice that there are three ways you can get an income:

> *First,* you can produce some goods or services that others want and can pay for. (Something-for-something.) This *earned income* can come either from selling the goods, or in the case of the public sector, from taxes. This is not to say that the pay reflects the value of what is contributed, merely that getting paid is conditional on making some kind of contribution to the production of goods and services.
>
> *Second*, if you're not able to produce goods or services or provide for yourself – because you're too young, old or infirm to work, or because there are not enough jobs to go around – others may agree to meet your needs, whether privately or through democratically agreed *transfers* via the state. The criterion for transfers is generally one of need: the recipients are unable to contribute to provisioning (or do but without getting paid for it), and hence depend on transfers to meet their needs.

Third, you can get money from others by controlling existing assets like property or money that they need but lack, and can therefore be made to pay for. If the assets already exist and have been paid for, then the income is unearned – something-for-nothing. And since the money the owners get only has any value if there are goods and services they can buy with it, then those who produce them must be producing more than they themselves can buy with their pay in order to support this free-riding. This is unearned income based on power, through control of assets.

These three sources are to be found in any modern economy; outside the cash economy their equivalents involve payments received in kind. Whereas the first two are clearly needed in some form, the third is not: as something-for-nothing, it is both unjust and dysfunctional. Earned income is conditional on contributions to wealth creation, where wealth can include non-monetised goods, like education. Asset-based unearned income is based on wealth extraction, on free-riding or exploitation. An alternative economy that is both feasible and fair must be one that blocks or taxes away most of this, and that provides transfers and supports earned income, whether funded via markets or taxes.

In thinking about alternative economies as well as already existing ones it's vital to note that what is commonly called 'investment' can involve wealth creation and/or wealth extraction. In the former case, it involves funding and creating things that enhance our possibilities for flourishing – new technologies, infrastructure, training and education, or replacing worn out stuff in order to prevent deterioration. It may yield the investor a return, or it may not. The second sense of 'investment' focuses on the investor and their return, regardless of whether the money they put forward funds the creation of anything new. Returns on savings, rent, capital gains, dividends on shares, and speculative gains need not have any connection to wealth creation; they are forms of wealth extraction. The use of the same word for these two different activities allows the latter to be passed off as the former. The elision contributes to the mystification of contemporary economic life, and legitimises the activities of rich 'investors', most of whose income has little to do with wealth creation.

We can also think about property in more critical ways that complement the above points. Nearly one hundred years ago, J.A. Hobson highlighted the difference between property and 'improperty' (Hobson 1937).[1] Property includes objects individuals use themselves or with other co-owners, like a home, the equipment and materials they use to make things with, such as cooking equipment, and other possessions. In other words, their point is their use-value to the owner(s). By contrast, where such objects are held not for the owner's own use, but as a means of getting others who lack them to work for the owner for them or pay them rent, they are improperty, and an investment only in the second sense. If you are a self-employed plumber, your equipment is property; you use it to produce useful goods and services. But the owner(s) of a plumbing firm can make it merely a means for getting money by delegating management and still extracting profit without contributing anything themselves in terms of work (or they can get a combination of earned and unearned income by working too). It is not only unjust but dysfunctional since the unearned income provided for the owner is a deadweight cost on the system. Whereas property is limited to what the owner can use or work with, the lack of restriction on how much improperty individuals or institutions may hold and on what they may do with it, means its scope for growth is larger than for property, though ultimately the value of money gained thereby depends on the production of goods and services by others which it can buy. Further, since receipts of rent and other forms of unearned income tend to concentrate at the top of the income distribution, they support wasteful and shockingly unsustainable consumption by the rich and super-rich, while revenue they don't consume is recycled into further rent-seeking activities (Sayer 2014).

Wherever, as under capitalism, market competition is coupled with the rule of improperty, and unrestrained by legislation and organised labour, it rides roughshod over the interests of workers and over environmental concerns. Those who produce the goods that provide the owners with profit have little or no say in their organisations' running, and particularly on the disposal of its revenues, so instead of inter-firm competition being regulated by the players or producers, it is dominated by the interests of owners. Under capitalist rules, while one can work for a firm for decades and never have any influence over its running, anyone with enough money to buy the company can step in and do what they like with it, and extract as much income as they wish without any responsibility to others, with fateful consequences. Here the basic social relations are problematic, and constitute a form of ill-being.

Rent, interest, capital gains, and dividends are all forms of unearned income deriving from improperty. The traditional term for recipients of this income is *rentier*, though of course it's possible for individuals to get both earned and unearned income, and so be part-rentiers. Given that organisations can function as rentiers, those who work for them may get a salary and appear to have earned income, but actually be rentiers at one remove. Capitalist-owned means of production is also improperty, though for capitalists,[2] unlike rentiers, their profit is at least dependent on its use for producing commodities. A viable alternative, advanced economy will need both private and social property (local and national), but it does not need improperty.

A sustainable economy

Never-ending growth – at least in the rich countries – in a finite world is an absurdity. And yet the growth imperative is a near-universal assumption of mainstream politics and popular thinking on the economy. No wonder then, that the dream of 'green growth' – in which carbon emissions are decoupled from economic growth – should be so appealing. But as Tim Jackson has demonstrated, this is, to say the least, improbable.[3] Even though the energy and carbon intensities per unit of output have declined, so that the 'energy intensity' of each unit of output is 33 percent lower now than in 1970 globally, this has been more than offset by economic and population growth, such that CO_2 from fossil fuels increased by 80 percent from 1970 to 2007 and by 40 percent from 1990, growing at 3 percent per year between 2000 and 2007 (Jackson 2009). Since that time, the situation has become still more urgent. Even during the most serious economic recession since the Great Crash of the interwar period, emissions have continued to grow.

As the Pope argued in his encyclical in 2015, inequality and climate change are inextricably linked. If we are to stand a chance of reducing carbon emissions to a sustainable level, then the biggest emitters – the rich countries and especially the rich and well-off within them – need rapidly to cut their emissions. The most straightforward model for this is 'contraction and convergence'. This is based on a simple calculation in which one takes an estimate of the world's capacity for reabsorbing carbon sustainably, and divides it by the world's population to give an individual emissions allowance. There might be qualifications needed to such a policy, but its moral force is clear: those individuals or countries which exceed this and hence are damaging the planet for everyone need to cut back their emissions to this level, while those individuals or countries which emit less than the allowance should be allowed to grow up to it. Of course, this idea horrifies the governments of rich countries, though it lets them off lightly because it is based only on current, not historical emissions, even though greenhouse gases take many decades to be reabsorbed.

Climate scientist Kevin Anderson and colleagues argue that given the long lead-times involved in substituting low carbon energy sources for fossil fuels, the only way we can avoid 'extremely dangerous climate change' now is by cutting consumption itself in the rich countries. Carbon emissions per head correlate positively with income, and globally, 49 percent of consumption-related emissions derive from the richest 10 percent of the world's population,[4] so according to the polluter pays principle, it is here that the biggest responsibilities lie. Anderson estimates that a "30 percent reduction in global emissions could be delivered in under a year, simply by constraining the emissions of that 10 percent responsible for half of all global $CO2$ to the level of a typical European" (Anderson 2015). Given the seriousness of the situation, the need to consider zero growth and actually reduce some activities is inescapable.

Could there be zero-growth capitalism?[5] Empirically, the association of capitalism with growth is very strong, indeed in a broader historical perspective it's spectacular. Further, in periods when growth has stalled, capitalism has gone into crisis, causing widespread unemployment. Capitalism is not only growth-oriented but tends to over-accumulation as each enterprise seeks a dominant position, so productive capacity tends to grow faster than demand, leading to recurrent crises in which surplus capital is destroyed. There can be no equilibrium or steady-state in which owners merely use profits to cover replacement investment, and consume what's left themselves, abstaining from any innovation or change that might increase their profits. As long as capitalist investors (in either sense) see opportunities for increasing their returns, they are likely to pursue them, compelling competitors to do so too, or go bankrupt (Blauwhof 2012).

On the face of it, increases in labour productivity are the essence of economic development, enabling us to do far more in a given time than our ancestors could. They offer us the chance to reduce working time and enjoy more leisure. But for capitalist firms this is not an option. Labour productivity gains are pursued in order to increase or defend profits in the face of competition, and that means producing more per worker without reducing working hours. This may drive down prices and increase demand and drive growth, but if not, increased labour productivity can lead to the downsizing of the work force and forced leisure without pay – i.e. unemployment. Not surprisingly, labour interests within capitalism tend to be pro-growth.

In a steady-state economy, it is therefore important to legislate to reduce labour hours, to inhibit growth while avoiding unemployment, and to improve our work-life balance. At the same time, unless there are restraints on competition from firms in other countries that have longer working hours, such a policy may fail. However, as we shall see, competition is likely to reduce anyway in such an economy. In addition, economies can shift resources to lower productivity sectors such as social care. From a capitalist perspective these are unattractive because their low labour productivity makes them unprofitable, but from the point of view of well-being and zero growth, they make perfect sense (Jackson/Victor 2011).

Labour productivity improvements can also be problematic insofar as saving labour time is prioritised over conserving resources. In many cases reductions in the labour intensity of production have been bought at the expense of increased energy and materials throughput. Thus disposable plastic spoons save us the labour of washing-up, but depend on continued extraction of oil, and the use of more fossil fuel to convert it into plastic and mould it. In a sustainable economy, some sectors will need to be *more* labour intensive – as we find with organic farming. Undoubtedly, environmentally destructive practices have to be blocked by regulation.

It might seem that the most straightforward way to get a green economy would be not just to regulate it comprehensively plan it centrally, to ensure that this goal was met. But the history of such systems is of course damning. As Frederik Hayek and Alec Nove explained in different ways, the complexity of modern economies, their millions of different products, the intractability of their divisions of labour and the impossibility of centralising the knowledge that is needed for their myriad economic activities, make comprehensive central planning technically infeasible Hayek 1988; Nove 1983; Sayer 1995).[6] Moreover, the hierarchical organisation of the economy required by central planning suppresses local initiative and democratic voice, and supports authoritarian political regimes. So while state ownership and central planning may be best for a few sectors, such as large-scale energy production and distribution, markets – with appropriate regulation to protect labour, health and the environment – would be preferable for coordinating much of the remainder.

But if markets can provide an effective and politically acceptable way of coordinating much of the division of labour, does this not entail capitalism and competition? Not necessarily. Capitalism combines markets with improperty, but markets can also be combined with property, if enterprises are run by those who work for them. In the case of worker-owned co-operatives producing for markets, there would still be competition, though it is likely to take a milder form than under capitalism. Such enterprises are unlikely to accept continually intensified work, or to make themselves redundant in order to transfer production to cheaper, more exploitable labour, or to take a short-term view of strategy. And faced with opportunities for increased labour productivity, cooperatives would have less incentive to pursue growth rather than reduced work time, particularly if they didn't have to compete with *capitalist* enterprises, and if maximum working hours were regulated nationally, and perhaps internationally (as they are already in many EU countries). Finally, as any shares in them could not be sold and would normally be redeemable only at their original value, their value would not increase if the co-operatives grew, thus making growth less attractive (Johanisova/Padilla/Parry 2015).

While some competition would remain we might also expect it to be reduced and localised as a consequence of the high cost of transport, which would follow from drastic reductions in the supply of fossil fuels on which road, air and sea-transport currently rely. The resulting processes of 'de-globalisation' would also reduce the reliance of the global north on cheap labour in the global south. Environmentally, this would also mean that carbon emissions would be harder to export to other countries through offshore manufacturing.

All this may mean that some goods and services will be more expensive than they would under a system of unrestrained capitalist competition, but then this will be necessary for protecting workers and the environment. The rate of innovation might slow down too, but it would mean greater economic security and less stressful work, and in any case, we must learn to make things that last instead of continually replacing them with newer models.

Particularly in light of its rise to dominance under neoliberalism, we need also to consider the financial sector and its role in a post-growth society. In the last 35 years the financial sector has shifted from servant to master within the economy, so that it now mainly serves itself. Most of its lending is against existing property and improperty, producing asset inflation and a succession of bubbles, transferring income from the asset poor to the asset rich, and with little real investment as a result. Its reckless expansion of debt has been underwritten by the public, allowing it to continue much as before the crash, retaining gains and socialising its costs. These debts can only be paid off by continued growth in the so-called real economy. As it stands, then, the sector could scarcely be more dysfunctional for a green economy. Here it will be necessary to regulate all financial products to determine whether they are socially beneficial, in much the same way as new drugs have to be approved before being released onto the market. But it will also be necessary to create publicly-accountable regional, national and sectoral investment banks that undertake real investment in projects that benefit the environment and society. Further, as Mary Mellor argues, the power to create money is of central importance in any economy and society. At present most money – 97 percent in the UK – is digital money created as debt by private banks. Democratic control over money creation is vital if we are to shift to a sustainable economy (Mellor 2015).

A universal basic income has been proposed by some advocates of degrowth (D'Alisa/ Demaria/Kallis 2015). While this might have many benefits, there are two kinds of objection to it. First, as regards principle, as an *unconditional* transfer of income from those who worked for money and paid tax, to everyone else (including themselves), it differs from transfers as we have defined them above in that even those perfectly capable of working are freed from any responsibility to do so. Of course, they might do unpaid work such as childcare and eldercare, but then there are arguments for making specific payments via the state for such socially-beneficial activities. But otherwise, it licenses free-riding on others' work, and is therefore questionable from the point of view of economic justice. (Contrary to a common view in both liberal and socialist circles, economic justice is about contribution as well as distribution.) Nevertheless, if it were democratically approved, then that objection would be overruled.[7] Second, as regards practicality, for democratic decisions on a universal basic income to be adequately informed, realistic estimates would be needed of the amount of paid work that would need to be performed to provide enough to meet the demand it created, and of the level of taxation of workers necessary to fund it. Too often its feasibility is simply assumed. In view of these objections, I suggest that an extension of conditional transfers and full employment policies would be preferable.

While markets are likely to work differently with worker-controlled competition, there would still need to be strong regulation of markets, and a raft of other policies including maximum as well as minimum pay limits, protection and enlargement of carbon sinks. Some products and services could still be decommodified, as called for by many supporters of degrowth (D'Alisa/Demaria/Kallis 2015), and increased support for those currently providing important services – particularly care work – unpaid.

These proposals would redistribute income and power to the lower half of the income distribution, at the expense of those with incomes above the well-being threshold. In a world where the richest eight people have as much wealth as the poorer half of the world's population, all 3.6 billion of them (Oxfam 2017), it would be naïve to think this concentration of economic power was not coupled with an extraordinary concentration of political power. At base, this power derives simply from big corporations' control of the commanding heights of the economy and of much of the media, but it is heavily backed up by political funding, lobbying, and influence over political change and the rules of economic engagement (for example, as in trade treaties like the Transatlantic Trade and Investment Partnership). It is clear that a good life beyond growth will only be attainable through counter forces strong enough to challenge and remove their political power. Legislation will be needed to change capitalist property relations, and to block or tax away unearned income deriving from control of improperty. In the case of our current fossil-fuel dependent energy companies, their size and political clout is such that the only way to wean them off fossil-fuel sources quickly enough to stop runaway global warming is to nationalise them and force them to change.

Conclusion

"Green is the new red", warned Nigel Lawson, former UK Conservative Chancellor and prominent climate change sceptic. He was partly right. At both international and intranational scales there are synergies between movements for social and economic justice and for a sustainable economy, though much of the left has still to face up to the implications of runaway global warming.

There are some obvious preconditions for a good life beyond growth, most obviously massive investment in renewable energy and low-carbon production. But the idea that capitalism can be steered in a zero-growth direction simply by appropriate policy carrots and sticks – such as carbon taxes and clean energy subsidies – overlooks its most destructive features: its growth imperative, and its associated concentration of economic and political power. In evaluating possible alternatives, a moral economic approach that assesses the fairness of basic economic relations and our unequal impact on the environment, has much to offer.

Notes

1 R.H. Tawney's view that property should be "an aid to work, not an alternative to it" complements this (Tawney 1920, 54).
2 Here I am referring to capitalists in the classic Marxist sense i.e. directly involved in the circuit of capital M – C … P … C' – M', excluding those who make money from money M-M'. See Rosa in this volume.
3 However, Jackson considers zero-growth capitalism a possibility under certain circumstances (e.g. Jackson/Victor 2011).
4 Source Oxfam 2015.
5 For discussions of this issue, see the debate in *Ecological Economics* (2012), particularly Griethuysen's contribution (2012), and also Jackson/Victor (2011) and Kallis (2015).
6 There is a danger that some degrowth supporters, like many socialists before them, underestimate the inevitable complexity of the division of labour required for an advanced economy, and hence underestimate the problems of coordinating provisioning activities without markets.
7 As regards well-being, being able to work and contribute to society is an important component of flourishing; again, the work might be voluntary rather than paid, but in either case it is something which should be encouraged, not devalued.

References

Anderson, K. (2015). *Duality in Climate Science*. Online at http://kevinanderson.info/blog/category/quick-comment.
Blauwhof, F.B. (2012). Overcoming Accumulation: Is a Capitalist Steady-State Economy Possible? In: *Ecological Economics* 84, 254–261.
D'Alisa, G./F. Demaria/G. Kallis (eds., 2015). *Degrowth: A Vocabulary for a New Era*. London: Routledge.
Griethuysen, P. van (2012). Bona Diagnosis, Bona Curatio: How Property Economics Clarifies the Degrowth Debate. In: *Ecological Economics* 84, 262–269.
Hayek, F.A. (1988). *The Fatal Conceit: The Errors of Socialism*. London: Routledge.
Hobson, J.A. (1937). *Property and Impropery*. London: Gollancz.
Jackson, T. (2009). *Prosperity Without Growth: Economics for a Finite Planet*. London: Earthscan.
Jackson, T./P. Victor (2011). Productivity and Work in the 'Green Economy': Some Theoretical Reflections and Empirical Tests. In: *Environmental Innovation and Societal Transitions* 1, 101–108.

116   *Andrew Sayer*

Johanisova, N./R.S. Padilla/P. Parry (2015). Co-operatives. In: D'Alisa, G./F. Demaria/G. Kallis (eds., 2015). *Degrowth: A Vocabulary for a New Era*. London: Routledge. 152–155.

Kallis, G. (2015). *Is There a Growth Imperative in Capitalism?* 'Online at http://enti tleblog.org/2015/10/27/is-there-a-growth-imperative-in-capitalism-a-response-to-john-bellamy-foster-part-i/.

Mellor, M. (2015). *Debt or Democracy*. Chicago: Chicago University Press.

Nove, A. (1983). *The Economics of Feasible Socialism*. London: Allen and Unwin.

OXFAM (2015). *Extreme Carbon Inequality*. OXFAM Media Briefing. Online at www. oxfam.org/sites/www.oxfam.org/files/file_attachments/mb-extreme-carbon-inequality-021215-en.pdf.

OXFAM (2017). *An Economy for the 99%*. OXFAM Briefing Paper. Online at https:// www.oxfam.org/sites/www.oxfam.org/files/file_attachments/bp-economy-for-99-per cent-160117-en.pdf.

Pope Francis (2015). *Encyclical Letter Laudato Si' of the Holy Father Francis on Care for Our Common Home*. Online at http://liberationtheology.org/pope-francissencyclical-on-ecology-june-2015.

Sayer, A. (1995). *Radical Political Economy: A Critique*. Oxford: Blackwell.

Sayer, A. (2007). Moral Economy as Critique. In: *New Political Economy* 12 2, 261–270.

Sayer, A. (2014). *Why We Can't Afford the Rich*. Bristol: Policy Press.

Tawney, R.H. (1920 [2004]). *The Acquisitive Society*. Mineoloa, NY: Harcourt, Brace and Howe.

Part III

The good society

Alternative conceptions of social justice and well-being

9   The common good as a principle of social justice

Michael J. Thompson

Every society is essentially a cooperative enterprise. Each consists, at any given moment, of a series of nested forms of cooperation and interaction, some small, some large, but all for the purpose of producing some end, some purpose. This cooperative enterprise that is society should not be seen, however, simply as the result of some social contract or as the deliberate choice of each member of the community. It is, rather, the very ontological feature that circumscribes the social itself; it is what society is and also defines and constitutes, reciprocally, what each individual is and can be. Society cannot be understood merely as the aggregation of persons, it is also, and more correctly, an entity with relations, processes, and structure. We all share, therefore, basic commonness with others within society. Within these relations, processes, and structures, individuals are shaped and thus, the relation between the individual and the community is dialectical in nature. Hence, the purposes toward which we orient these relations, these processes and structures tell us much about the kinds of lives and goods that each of us as individuals can enjoy. The idea of a good life that I will advocate here is one that sees society in these terms and which uses this ontological view of the social as not only a descriptive but also an inherently normative claim. Since cooperation and interaction can be oriented toward very different ends and purposes, we can ask ourselves what the best, or ethical ends of such cooperation might be. What kinds of goods and purposes are worthy of our commitments as rational members of any form of sociation and society therefore constitutes the basic question I want to investigate here. My intention is to show that a common interest is a specific kind of end or purposes that describes the status of the best end or purpose of social life and to suggest this as a basic conceptual groundwork for a theory of social justice.

The relation of this discussion to the question of growth comes into play when we consider the way that the capitalist paradigm of growth is premised not on orienting cooperative relations toward common ends and purposes, but toward *particular* ends and purposes. This kind of growth is produced through the expansion and intensification of social relations that are extractive and exploitive, i.e., those that generate surplus through unequal forms of social cooperation. The good life, by contrast, which I identify with the common good and with a condition of social justice, is organised not according to competitive, extractive and exploitive relations, but through relations oriented toward those ends and goods that are beneficial for the association as a whole. My starting point is the ancient thesis by Plato in his *Republic* that the essence of justice is to be found in the ways that social relations are structured; that justice and the common good are synonymous terms. To live in a *good* society is to live in a *just* society; and to live in a just society must mean that our economic life and institutions are oriented to maximise those goods that are beneficial to society as a whole. This is because, since our individual lives are each interdependently related to others, society constitutes for us a kind of ontological structure of relations and interdependencies that make a good life possible. Justice is a matter of maximizing those goods that fortify and expand the structures of social interdependencies and the specific kinds of powers that those social interdependencies make possible. In deep contrast to the liberal theories of the good society, we should not see equality of opportunity as the end of a just community since this tells us nothing about the kind of society of which individuals are members.

One reason I think that this argument serves as a more compelling theory of justice is that it forces us to look not only at the "basic structure" of any society, but, more importantly, at the ends and purposes that any society is oriented toward. If we equate justice with an equality of opportunity, basic liberties, and a "difference principle", we are not able to judge the ends of that society. A society whose collective efforts and purposes undermine its own social foundations – whether through the production of environmentally destructive ends, a facile consumerist culture, or whatever – cannot be considered just, on this view, even if it were to meet the basic Rawlsian criteria of "fairness". This is because these ends can be seen to violate a common interest and it is this common good, rather than merely "fairness", that should be a criterion of judgment when evaluating a just society. I would like to explore what this entails and what kind of ideas we can glean from it. Given these preliminaries, my thesis here is that the common interest does not lie in a particular norm or set of values, but rather in the *nature and structure of social relations themselves*. The idea here is that the common good must refer to the kind of social relations to which any individual belongs: the common good is a product of the structure of social relations to which I belong which promotes the highest possible enhancement of the goods shared by all.

A common good therefore is something to which I belong and which is *both* individual-enhancing and public-enhancing. This means seeing the wealth of society, its productive energies and resources, as a property and a capacity of the community as a whole; that the social resources of the community should be oriented to mutual needs of its members. By far, though, the view of contemporary moral and political philosophy has been to negate the existence of any kind of common interest or good. Indeed, although late-19th- and early-20th century liberal theory restricted liberal thought through the positing of a common interest, contemporary liberal theorists have renovated the conception of liberalism toward anti-perfectionist premises. According to this view, we can establish a foundation for rights and a "basic structure" to regulate the capacity of social arrangements to construct an equal opportunity for individuals to pursue their personal conceptions of a good life. This turn in liberal theory makes the pursuit of a common good not only illogical but also undesirable. The common good cannot be simply understood as an emergent property of atomic individuals pursuing their self-interests. Rather, it needs to be seen as a property descriptive of the socially interdependent relations that constitute social reality. In this sense, the common good can be discerned only by inquiring what goods, ends and purposes enhance the shared social-relational structures and processes that constitute the community and to judge these purposes and ends according to what enhances the social goods that can lead to enhanced collective and personal goods.

In modern republicanism, the question of the common good was a central concern for thinkers such as Machiavelli, Rousseau, Hegel and Marx, something that has been marginalised in contemporary neo-republican theory which has placed emphasis on more liberal concepts of individual liberty as "non-domination". Emphasis on a common interest and common good was displaced over time in political philosophy by the growth and development of political liberalism. Thinkers such as Benjamin Constant were adamant in their separation of the modern from the ancient ideas of society; the former concerned with the liberty of the individual and the latter with the community over the individual. This thesis still plagues and limits our moral and political imagination. Liberalism has absorbed this individualist ideal into its basic foundation. According to this latter view, modernity was to be conceived not as a synthesis of the individual and collective good, but rather with a political and cultural order where a plurality of conception of the good would be allowed. If we were to prioritise the good over the right, so this argument goes, we would find ourselves in a state of accepting the good of others rather than freedom to choose our own conception of the good. Hence, the central tenet of political modernity has been to discard the notion of a common good and instead accept a pluralist conception of privatist ideas of the good. Ever since Kant, the basis of this liberal view has been that we should privilege the "right" over that of the "good". This means that, according to Charles Larmore, that liberalism "has also taken to heart one of the cardinal experiences of modernity. It is the increasing awareness that reasonable people tend naturally to differ and disagree about the nature of the good life" (Larmore 1996, 122).

But Larmore's remarks, often repeated by liberals, is too simple. A common good can be understood in objective, rational terms once we understand that certain kinds of cooperative activity (i.e., any basic social action) are interdependent and the ends of that activity are best when they are *general*, i.e., when they satisfy the needs of the association as a distinct entity since members of that association will therefore be enhanced as a result. As I see it, the common interest is any end or relation that provides goods that are equally beneficial to all members of the community and not simply to a portion of that community. This means that economic institutions and activities must be subject to principles that serve social ends and purposes. Given the kind of embeddedness of society in market relations described by Karl Polanyi, modern capitalist societies operate under the conception that that which benefits the market must also benefit society. Employment, consumption, education, and so on, are all circumscribed by the narrow logics of economic growth – a kind of growth that is itself defined by its own expansion and its own interests.

But if we reverse this idea and instead see economic activity as re-embedded within society, a new set of principles can be seen to emerge. One of them I will seek to develop in this chapter, and that is that a society has a common interest in any end or good that all will be able to consume or from which they will be able to benefit. Although this can be seen to rely on certain ontological ideas about the nature of social life, I will not dwell on this and instead inquire into the nature of common goods, which must be seen as those goods that enhance the interdependent nature of the relational structure to which each member of the community belongs as well as be, in some basic sense, enhancing or beneficial to each member in a non-extractive, non-exploitive sense.

Two kinds of social goods

We can begin this analysis by defining two basic kinds of social goods. In its broadest sense, a good, as I will define it for my purposes here, *is any end sought or desired.* There can be personal or private goods, as when I simply seek or desire to listen to music or read a book, or take a walk, or whatever. In this case, a personal or private good is something I desire on my own, for my own reasons, and which requires no effort from anyone else to fulfill it. However, a good is a *social good* whenever it is something that requires another agent for it to be produced or obtained. Hence, a social good is distinct from a private or personal good to the extent that any private good is one that neither effects another agent nor requires another agent for it to be obtained (whether in terms of production or consumption). *Any good that requires or affects another agent or group of agents therefore is a social good.* This means that social goods entail certain kinds of relations insofar as they require some degree of social cooperation to achieve and/ or to produce them. It does not mean that this good is necessarily a good for those others; it simply means that it requires some degree of social cooperation for it to be produced and obtained.

Two basic kinds of relations can be understood to be subclasses of social goods. On the one hand, a social good can be produced through an equal, cooperative relation. I can ask someone to help me fix my car, I can pay a doctor to help cure my illness, and a group of individuals can come together to produce some other good that all may need, such as food, shelter, and so on. These goods are *common goods* in the sense that all members of the community do or potentially can benefit from them and that they are produced for the general interest of the association itself. But there is another way that goods can be produced and obtained. I can use cooperation to produce goods that are not for the benefit of all; I can in fact utilise and shape social relations in order to achieve a good that is for my particular or arbitrary benefit. In this sense, I can *extract* benefit from another or others, as when I organise labor to produce goods that are not of common benefit, but for my own profit. These goods I will call *pleonexic goods* in the sense that they serve to produce some kind of surplus benefit for the person seeking the good.[1] The basic idea of power as the capacity to extract benefit from some other person or group of persons *for one's own arbitrary or particular ends* therefore is the essential background for the negation of the common good and of any conception of social justice. These are examples of pleonexic goods in that they are goods produced and obtained for the surplus benefit of one or a small sub-group of the community.

Pleonexic goods have the feature that they create and sustain unequal relations between social members or classes.

To formalise this a bit more, we can say that what I am calling *pleonexic goods* are those that are obtained by (i) extracting benefit from another person or group; (ii) redirecting or re-orienting the capacities and resources of individuals or the community as a whole toward one's personal or partial benefit; and/or (iii) invading group or collective resources for particular benefits that could otherwise be beneficial to that group as a whole. A pleonexic good therefore means that the benefit of A is obtained by detracting from the benefit of some other agent or group, B. We can therefore see that growth can be cast in either common or pleonexic terms. The former would be a kind of growth that would satisfy the conditions of common needs and interests; it would be able to expand social goods and to nourish the social-relational structures that form the contexts for individual actions and needs. Pleonexic growth would expand economic activity and wealth, but would violate a significant number of those common needs. In capitalist society, growth is of a kind that creates but for the benefits of those that control resources. Social wealth is not only mal-distributed; the content of much of this wealth – i.e., the ends that are produced – are constantly mediated by capital and private interest or ownership. This is not a simplistic problem of a zero-sum where some benefit at the sole expense of others. Rather it is a problem where the ends of production are to meet the needs of surplus first and social goods second, if at all. A pleonexic good and relation therefore are not strictly zero-sum, but must be extractive from one agent to another. The kind of goods and growth that pleonexic relations produce can be seen to violate the principle of the common interest since that growth is generated at the expense of many for the benefit of some. Surely, being employed at a McDonalds is better than being unemployed; but, this does not take into account the very ends and purposes of this work and this kind of enterprise. The question is not simply whether or not the worker should get "fair" wages; it is more importantly about the capacity of members of the community to organise the labor of others, to sell unhealthy food, to sustain chains of meaningless, alienated labor, and so on. The owner has clearly created some new economic value where none has existed before; but the more important question is whether or not this is a value that enhances common, public ends and goods or pleonexic ends and goods.

In this sense, pleonexic goods are defined in opposition to common goods insofar as the former are not pursued for the benefit of the community, but only the arbitrary interests of the person seeking them. *Pleonexic* goods are therefore those that can only be attained by extracting some benefit or resource or capacity from another, whether these be other people, individuals or groups, or from nature itself. A *public* or *common good*, on the other hand, is a kind of good that is (i) attained without extraction from any other agent (individual or group); (ii) has beneficial consequences, either *actually* or *potentially*, for anyone within the community; (iii) where there are no barriers to access those goods; and (iv) the use of that good does not deprive anyone else of that same good.

A consequence is *actual* when the benefit is immediate for all (such as clean air, clean water, and so on) and it is *potential* when it is a good to which I might, at some time, need to have access (such as quality health care, good school systems, and so on). The common interest must therefore embrace both the diminishment of pleonexic goods as well as the protection and expansion of public goods. These two attributes taken together can be seen to constitute a basic conception of the common interest. In other words, a society that prevents pleonexic relations and goods and promotes common goods and relations is also one which promotes the benefits of individuals themselves because individuals are constituted by their relations and are a function of the kinds of common goods to which they have access. As T.H. Green puts the matter: "it is only in the intercourse of men, each recognised by each as an end, not merely a means, and thus as having reciprocal claims, that the capacity is actualised and that we really live as persons . . . . society then is the condition of all development of our personality" (Green 1969, 192; cf. Simhony 2001). Given the discussion thus far, we can say that:

1   Common goods are goods procured by a group for the good or interest of that group; group members are not only conceived as members of the group, but also as individuals who instantiate that group itself. Goods of the group must also be goods for each member.
2   Pleonexic goods are procured by a group for a sub-group and its arbitrary ends and/or interests.

Pleonexic goods diminish the common interest because they orient the activities and capacities of individuals toward the partial interests of the community. Social extraction is a central mechanism for this kind of power enhancement because *it consists of reorienting the ensemble of capacities and resources that belong to individuals and the community as a whole toward elite interests and benefits.* Whenever I extract a surplus benefit from someone, I detract not only from their own good, but from the potential good that could have been shared by the community as a whole and that I instead consume or accumulate it for my own, private ends and control. Indeed, Rousseau saw this as the genesis of inequality for which the general will was a solution: "as soon as one man needed the help of another, as soon as one man realised that it was useful for a single individual to have provisions for two, equality disappeared, property was introduced, labor became necessary. Vast forests were transformed into smiling fields which had to be watered with men's sweat, and in which slavery and misery were soon seen to germinate and grow with the crops" (Rousseau 1964, 171). Rousseau's thesis is that the origin of inequality is simultaneously the decline of any capacity to realise the common interest since each person sees that they can gain more benefit by seeking to have others work for them, or to extract some benefit from them for their own ends or purposes. Extraction is therefore at the basis of detracting from those goods that which could be better realised for all if they were diverted away from public ends by extractive means.

The common good therefore has to proceed along the lines of understanding benefits and ends that are utilised by the community as a whole; they are not utilised for a subgroup of the community *at the expense* of any other member. In this respect, the common good is something that cannot simply be understood in individual terms, but must be understood in terms of the relational structure of social cooperation. Each individual receives benefit from the corporate, interdependent entity which is society.

The common good or common interest consists in the orienting of these capacities and resources toward goods and purposes that are best for the community as a whole because such goods and purposes *constitute a developed individual existence as well*. This is no communitarian argument; it is a thesis that uses the common interest as a metric to understand when the social practices and structures of the community are being oriented toward the good of all or the good of the few. It does not seek to place communitarian limits on the ideas and opinions of each individual; it seeks to undermine the ideological complexes, the constellation of *moeurs*, as Rousseau would refer to them, that distract citizens from this insight, this very fiber of what they saw as civic-mindedness, civic virtue itself. Radical republicans are therefore primarily concerned with the common interest, but from the perspective of social power, or material forms of power. In this sense, the continued relevance of this tradition retains its salience in an age of corporate, administered capitalism.

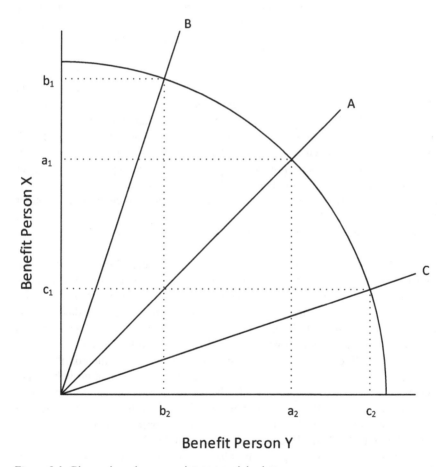

Figure 9.1   Pleonexic and common interest social schemes

If we consider Figure 9.1, we see that different social schemes can lead to different kinds of benefit schemes. Suppose that the convex line represent the possibility frontier of social production between agents X and Y (these can be individuals, classes, or groups). Further suppose that each ray bisecting the convex possibility frontier represents the distribution of possible benefit that can be shared by X and Y cooperating in some basic way. When pleonexic goods are pursued, there is some degree of extraction taking place and the distribution of benefits is asymmetric. The rays B and C represent social schemes that are pleonexic. If we consider line B which shows an extractive relation of X from Y, then we see that the amount of benefit derived by X is proportional to the amount of benefit diminished for Y. Hence, if we take the ray a, which represents a scheme which pursues common interests and goods, we see that the benefits for a and b are such that they are not only equal but that they reveal the relevant extent to which where the benefit derived by b is greater than that derived by a. In any relation where a_1 and a_2 are the result, then we can see that X and Y both are able to utilise the same amount of benefit. It is not the purpose of any socially-cooperative activity to benefit one member at the expense of any others. For this would establish the view that some are to benefit from others, and would transform the very purpose of social membership from achieving general ends toward achieving only particular ends.

If we consider that A represents a scheme where both X and Y receive the requisite amount of benefit from any social relation or social scheme, then we can also see that $\{b_1 - b_2\}$ is a surplus benefit gained by Y from the extraction of benefit from X and that $\{a_2 - b_2\}$ gives us the relative amount extracted from X in order to provide for the surplus of Y. In this sense, pleonexic schemes are such that the relation or scheme of relations that exist allow for the extractive power of one agent or group over another. The pleonexic scheme represented by B, for example, implies that Y would benefit at the expense of X according to $\{b_1 - c_1\}$, and so on. Similarly, the area of the square $\{a_1, a_2\}$ is larger than the areas of either the rectangles $\{b_1, b_2\}$ or $\{c_1, c_2\}$ which would imply that the general amount of benefit produced is larger than in schemes which are organised for extractive purposes.

Of course, this discussion is highly abstract and ideal. But it lays a certain logical foundation for the discussion of certain kinds of social schemes and social relations and their properties. One thing we can take from it is that pleonexic forms of social relations are such that they generate growth of individual benefits at the expense of others. Indeed, there can be social schemes where inequality and exploitation exist without growth. But the key here is to find a scheme that can satisfy the conditions of justice that I am describing as well as the possibility for the growth of social resources. There is no reason to assume that growth cannot occur within the confines of a social scheme that serves common ends, goods and purposes, does not undermine members of the community for the benefit of others, does not destroy the natural and social environment, and allows for the expansion of technological, scientific, and cultural development.

One way of understanding this problem is to see it as *social waste*: i.e., as the ways that we conceive the congealed efforts of socially organised labor and production.[2] As I have been arguing, common interests and goods are those that result from certain social relations; that the social relations themselves are always of a kind that they are pursuing some kind of good or end. The central question is therefore how to judge those goods and ends?

If we view the matter of justice through the lens of the common interest, then it becomes clear that desert is not the criterion for judging a just social scheme. One reason for this is that desert is defined internally by the ends of the system already in place – e.g., profit. Hence, desert is subjective defined by the purposes of profit expansion rather than by social ends and purposes. Rather than desert, the criterion that has warrant is the extent to which essentially cooperative activities satisfy the self-enhancing and group-enhancing ends of social life. This is because, unlike the basic social ontology that undergirds liberalism and utilitarianism that view society as aggregates of individuals, a more accurate social ontology would conceive individuals as integrally-related and mutually-constitutive members of an essentially associative and cooperative body. This does not dissolve the individual into the community, but shows the socially-interdependent dimensions of a true conception of developed individuality, but one that is also a function of the shapes of social-interdependent and cooperative activities that any society puts into place. When we see that self-enhancing and group-enhancing variables are mutually constitutive of one another, when we see that social forms of cooperation and interdependence are ontological features of sociality, we are moving in a different space of reasons. Assessing a just social scheme now becomes premised on the extent to which it can be said to satisfy the ends and needs of the community in which it is embedded. This should not be taken to mean that questions concerning proportionality and distribution are irrelevant. It only means that they need to be considered within a new moral context that places the question of common goods and its core. It is not simply the case that pleonexic relations and goods are unjust because of any sense of desert; rather, they are unjust because they violate the basic purposes for which all human association is constituted: the self- and group-enhancing potentiality of cooperative group membership itself.[3] The common good as a category of social goods is therefore the optimal category for judging the ends and purposes of any social scheme.

Purposes and ends

One of the consequences of a society that is dominated by pleonexic interests and goods is that the efforts of human social labor are wasted. What this means is that social waste becomes more prevalent. Social waste comes into play whenever some thing, or some person, or some group, or aspect of nature is unable to bring forth into the world the maximum of its abilities and potentialities, either because of *non-use, under-use or misuse*. We are concerned here about how social resources (labor, education, skills, etc.) as well as natural resources are organised, deployed, utilised and toward what ends they are invested and oriented.

For an activity not to be wasteful, it needs to be able to satisfy the greatest amount of potential needs that any specific resource possesses and it also has to be able to employ resources for the benefit of the society as a whole, and not merely for an exclusive part of it, or at the expense of it. In this sense, waste comes into play when society is deprived of the powers of certain human or natural resources; when those resources are under-used, mis-directed or mis-used, or when they are not used at all. Waste therefore occurs when the use of any resource (human or natural) is (un-, mis-, or under-) used in such a way that it fails to have maximum benefit for social needs. In effect, as Locke suggests when he says of the individual who has allowed spoilage that "he has invaded his neighbor's share" (Locke 1689, II.37), waste is a kind of theft from others; and the larger the degree of waste, the more it becomes a kind of theft from society as a whole, often for the benefit of a minority share of that society. The simple fact that a given resource is employed for some *productive* use (as the classi-cal economists theorised) is not sufficient, on my account, to guard against the charge of waste, because this fails to account for the *ends, purposes, or projects toward which that production is directed*, which could, in fact, be wasteful. It is also not enough that there is efficiency in the process of production since that, too, would fail to consider the ends to which that activity of production was being put to use.

If this basic thesis is accepted, then it can also be argued that waste relates directly to issues of power and domination. The reason for this is that the capac-ity to generate and to direct social surplus and social production according to elite ends and interests entails that social life exists for the sake of those elite interests. This may seem intuitive on some level, but to formalise it, we need to see that waste *is that amount of effort or resources used or unused in such a way that their potential benefit for others has been taken away*. That potential benefit is the complex part, for it implies that we can discern a superior good than that toward which the owners of those resources have decided to put it. This higher good can be understood by asking whether or not the production decisions of such owners of those resources satisfy common needs and ends, and not needs and ends that are arbitrary. We can classify social forms of production and con-sumption as either being socially valid or wasteful. In the former, activities of production and consumption are performed for the benefit of as many individuals within the community as possible. Wasteful forms of activity (production and consumption) are those that benefit some rather than others and thereby misuse the resources within society that could otherwise have gone to meeting the needs of those in common. A common need, or *socially valid purpose*, should not be seen as the result of the aggregation of the preferences of individuals. Rather, it is a normative criterion that asks for the extent to which human and natural resources are utilised for the interests of a minority's benefits or for the benefits of the community as a whole.

Oligarchic and democratic social wealth

Once we see that there is distinction between the kinds of social goods that we can produce, we are in a position to understand the nature of social wealth as a whole, i.e., of the results of the ensemble of productive activities in which any society engages. If we choose to see any society as a whole as organised to produce different kinds of surplus, or wealth, then the question is: what kind of wealth is produced by a society made up of largely pleonexic versus common social relations? As I see it, this results in two different ways of understanding social wealth. Any society dominated by pleonexic relations and goods, we can say, produces oligarchic social wealth which is *defined as the relative extent to which any individual within the community is able to control the labor and resources of other members of the community* as well as direct that labor and those resources toward their own arbitrary ends and not toward public or common ends. A highly *oligarchic* form of social utilisation would therefore be when one individual receives the total benefit from the labor of everyone else, or from the social product as a whole; or when that one individual's interests are the sole direction of social and resource utilisation. The more *democratic* the social utilisation, by contrast, the more each individual within the society benefits from the collective resources available to them, or from the collective efforts and labor of others as well as the employment of resources (natural and human).

A just social arrangement will seek to enhance democratic forms of wealth over oligarchic forms because only the former are able to satisfy the mutual needs of the members of the association. Since society is not an aggregate of individuals, but is an entity with a distinct ontological status, it has certain causal powers over its members. Different shapes of sociality therefore have the ability to either enhance or degrade its members. Democratic forms of wealth seek to maximise the general interests of the members of the community for enhancement whereas oligarchic forms seek particular gains at the expense of the society as a whole.

Growth and justice

In this respect, the question of growth needs to be posed in a different way: any form of socio-economic growth that replies on pleonexic ends and relations will produce oligarchic forms of social wealth, whereas those that rely on and promote common goods and relations will enhance democratic forms of wealth. If we utilise the basic concepts I have elaborated above to understand the nature of just and unjust social schemes, relations and goods, then I think it can be extended to illuminate a conception of growth that can conform to the common good, or a just form of growth. As I see it, this would entail the expansion of the powers of the community through the growth of democratic wealth. We can see a path toward a just form of social organisation that can also provide the expansion of social and technological progress – a kind of progress that is premised on collective ends and needs and not on the particular ends and interests of the part over that of the whole. A key idea here is to include not only social resources and goods, but ecological and natural ends as well. Productive growth that damages or in any way unsustainably destroys the natural world cannot count as a common good or interest since human communities are situated within the natural world. Undermining the natural world therefore is against the common interest and good. Although this argument I have developed here is not an exhaustive account of the good life, it nevertheless contributes to a basic social framework that can make the good life more realisable for each and for all.

Notes

1 The term "pleonexic" comes from the Greek πλεονεξία which means to have more than what one needs, and to want still more.
2 I have explored this concept of social waste directly in Thompson 2015.
3 Cf. the important discussion by Hurka 1993, 176ff.

References

Green, T.H. (1969). *Prolegomena to Ethics*. New York: Thomas Y. Crowell.

Hurka, T. (1993). *Perfectionism*. New York: Oxford University Press.

Larmore, C. (1996). *The Morals of Modernity*. New York: Cambridge University Press.

Locke, J. (1988 [1689]). Second Treatise of Government. In: *Two Treatises of Government*. Ed. Peter Laslett. Cambridge: Cambridge University Press.

Rousseau, J-J. (1964). *Discours sur l'origine et les fondements de l'inégalité*. Paris: Bibliotheque de la Pleiade.

Simhony, A. (2001). T. H. Green's Complex Common Good: Between Liberalism and Communitarianism. In: A. Simhony/D. Weinstein (eds.). *The New Liberalism: Reconciling Liberty and Community*. New York: Cambridge University Press, 69–91.

Thompson, M.J. (2015). On the Ethical Dimensions of Waste. In: *Archiv für Rechts- und Sozialphilosophie* 101.2, 252–269.

10 Bread and Roses

"Good work" from a union perspective

Nicole Mayer-Ahuja

> Our days shall not be sweated from birth until life closes,
> Hearts starve as well as bodies, give us bread, but give us roses.

These lines stem from a poem by James Oppenheim (1911/12). They are inspired by the slogans displayed and speeches held in the context of a strike of (mainly female) textile workers in Lawrence, Massachusetts for better wages, decent working conditions, and a right to collective action (Eisenstein 1983, 32). From the 1970s onwards, the lyrics were set in music by several artists, and "Bread and Roses" turned into a hymn of women unionists all over the world. It was this tradition Ken Loach invoked when he chose this phrase as a title for his movie about the "Justice for Janitors" campaign of the US-service workers' union (SEIU) in 2000. For the purpose of this article, the song constitutes an ideal starting point, since it addresses notions of "good work", in the context of the international workers'[1] movement. Moreover, it indicates that it has never been common practice among unions to restrict the quest for "good work" to a demand for "more money", as some of their critics argue. Obviously, the fight for "bread" (i.e. for living wages and social security) constitutes an important part of union activity; after all, power relations between capital and labour are structurally unequal, and poverty tips the scales even further. Still, the demand for "roses" has been an integral part of workers' struggles since the early days of trade unionism as well.

Thus many labour conflicts have unfolded around issues of social emancipation, of working and living in safety and dignity, and of reproducing labour-power. In many ways, such conflicts transcend purely "material" concerns, but at the same time, bread and roses are closely intertwined. On the one hand, even simple wage questions reflect (a lack of) social recognition (Honneth 1996), which is why an expansion of low-wage jobs, for instance, poses not only financial problems, but also a threat to the self-esteem and social integration of those forced into this kind of employment. On the other hand, a long-term reproduction of labour power (whether in the sense of self-care and daily recreation, or of social reproduction, by way of having a family) implies a safe workplace, a fair treatment by superiors, and practices of work organisation supporting the development of one's personality and skills at the shop-floor and beyond – but at the same time, these aspects have direct implications for workers' chances to earn a living and to secure their material existence over time.

In order to approach notions of "good work", with regard to bread as well as roses, and to discuss them from a union perspective, it is crucial to consider several conceptual issues, however: Notions of "good work" change over time; they vary across space; even unionists in one specific spatio-temporal context may not necessarily share a common sense of what constitutes "good work"; and such notions transcend trade union circles. After all, unions are part of the society they operate in: they influence standards of utilizing labour power in negotiations or struggles with employers at the site of production, take part in the political regulation of labour, and develop their policies in close interaction with their (actual, but also potential) members. For this reason, it is impossible to draw a clear-cut, and generalising picture of "good work" from a union perspective. Instead, the following passages will focus on notions of "good work", which have proved more or less controversial, in the context of changing political tides and power relations, discussing their implications for trade union positions and politics, in (West) Germany as one of the centres of capitalist development, since the mid-1970s, when the prosperous post-war years came to a close.

"Good work" in times of economic growth

When Ulrich Mückenberger published his famous article about the erosion of (West) German "standard employment" (Normalarbeitsverhältnis) in 1985, he implicitly commented on notions of "good work" that had emerged since the late 1950s, under conditions of unprecedented economic growth, and had come under pressure in the aftermath of the world-wide economic crisis, initiated by the "oil price shock" of 1973. The term "standard employment" was not coined before the 1980s, when the phenomenon it referred to had already started to lose momentum. Still, contemporary observers shared a remarkably clear perception of what constituted a "normal job" in West Germany (for an overview see: Mayer-Ahuja 2003, 34). According to several authors, "standard employment" implied a full-time job with an open-ended contract, full coverage by social insurance and labour law, a long-term perspective ("from apprenticeship to retirement") within one company, regular working hours, the representation by works council and trade union, collective wage agreements, and, of course, a wage sufficient to support a family (as a matter of fact, a growing part of the working population in West Germany had experienced regular and substantial pay rises since the late 1950s).

As Mückenberger has rightly pointed out, "standard employment" was considered "normal" in a double sense: On the one hand, it had become "normal" in *statistical* terms, given that wage-earners had long turned into the largest group within the working population of West Germany, and their share continued to grow throughout the 20th century.[2] Moreover, the differences between blue collar and white collar workers had gradually been abolished, and an ever-larger share of those in dependent employment met the criteria of "Normalarbeit" as outlined above; resulting was the emergence of what Castel (2002, 305) has called a "wage earning society". On the other hand, "standard employment" had come to be equated with "normal work" or "good work", since it was very much in line with *normative* perceptions of a decent job.

During the post-war decades, these notions seem to have been shared by representatives of capital and the state, as well as by society at large, which is regarded as one reason for the stability of the "Fordist" regime of accumulation by representatives of regulation theory (Hirsch/Roth 1986). In any case, many employers (and especially big industrial firms) opted for "standard employment" from the late 1950s, because these were times of severe labour scarcity. Companies were desperate to establish long-term stable employment relationships, by way of creating internal labour markets, with in-house career ladders, promotion schemes, and collectively agreed pay increases, that would prevent employees from changing jobs for financial reasons (Lutz 1989). These corporate strategies were supported by state policies turning permanent full-time jobs into a prerequisite for comprehensive social insurance provisions and legal protection – whoever abstained from "standard employment" and worked part-time or displayed a sketchy employment biography, instead, thus faced insufficient old age pensions, for instance. Finally, the working population of West Germany seems to have regarded "standard employment" as the embodiment of a "normal job", "decent employment" or "good work", which parents wished for and expected of their children – and which functioned as a cornerstone of the collective negotiations pursued by trade unions.

Even in these "Golden Years" (Hobsbawm 1994) of mass production and mass consumption, however, "good work" was not only about "bread" (i.e. about income and social security), but also about "roses": about the chance to earn one's living in safety and dignity. After all, one result of the "liberal consensus" between capital, labour, and the state during the decades of the economic boom (Döring-Manteuffel/Raphael 2008) was the implementation of substantial research programs targeting a "humanisation of work"; funded by the Federal Government, they mainly aimed at a coordinated improvement of working conditions. Unions played an important role in these activities, within the tripartite reform coalition, not least because their (actual and potential) members formulated demands with regard to "good work", which clearly reached beyond material concerns.

Despite academic discussions indicating that workers' "subjective" engagement with their tasks was a rather recent phenomenon, and a distinguishing feature of high skill labour (for debates on a "subjectivisation of work", see: Voß/Pongratz 1998; Kratzer/Sauer 2005), empirical evidence suggests that even industrial workers in the mid-1970s were not only concerned about wages and employment security, but also about the quality of work on the shop-floor. As Birke (2014) and Bluhm (2014) have pointed out, based on the secondary analysis of a sociological study on shipbuilding in a period of sectorial crisis and intensive rationalisation (Schumann et al. 1982), that most workers did not formulate an elaborated concept of "good work" in the interviews, but had no doubt about what impeded the latter. Thus pipe fitters (as skilled workers) and welders (as semiskilled workers) both criticised that they had no say in the overall organisation of work and the distribution of work tasks, that the labour process was rationalised in a way which put their health at risk and left little scope for the maintenance and improvement of technical skills, and that neither management nor works council cared about everyday problems on the shop-floor (like the lack of warm water in the changing room, which motivated workers to organise a wild-cat "shower strike").

Obviously, such conflicts have financial implications – rationalisation, for instance, threatens not only workers' skills, and their influence on work organisation, but also their very jobs, as the closing down of many shipyards in Germany has demonstrated. Again, bread and roses are closely intertwined. For our discussion, it is thus important to keep in mind that notions of "good work" refer to employment relationships, but also to issues of work organisation and social recognition at the workplace and beyond; and that they hint at statistical "normality", but also at normative ideals, political goals, and visions of a better future.

"Good work" after the boom

As economic growth slowed down and labour scarcity gave way to mass unemployment from the mid-1970s, the "short dream of eternal prosperity" (Lutz 1989) was over, and the "liberal consensus" that "standard employment" and humane working conditions were in the common interest of capital, labour, and the state, gradually lost momentum. Under these conditions, mainly three lines of argument challenged earlier notions of "good work".

"Good work" as historical exception and impediment to economic growth

During the last years, it has become common to argue that the "trente glorieuses" (Castel 2002, 359) were not only a rather short, but also a historically exceptional period. In fact, notions of "good work" as outlined above had emerged under conditions of unprecedented economic growth after World War II, commonly referred to as the "economic miracle" in West Germany. During these years, real wages were rising in line with economic productivity, and sometimes even surpassing profits (Busch/Land 2010). Trade unions could negotiate attractive wages and working conditions, given the scarcity of (skilled) labour and the "liberal consensus" with regard to "good work". After the recession of 1973/4, however, growth slowed down, and the dynamics of economic redistribution lost impetus. Wage earners' share in economic surplus decreased, since real wages lagged behind corporate profits for many years; and while large parts of the working population had experienced social advancement before 1975 (in terms of income and consumption, but also in terms of access to higher education, for instance), social polarisationand even poverty returned.

This development indicates that the post-war community of interests between capital, labour, and the state had come to an end – from the perspective of employers and state authorities, what had earlier been considered "good work" was now perceived as an impediment to economic recovery. Employers, especially in the most influential industries, now increasingly opted for an export strategy, rendering them independent from purchasing power within Germany. Moreover, many companies in the manufacturing as well as in the expanding service sector started to restrict "standard employment" to their core workforces, while establishing and expanding flexible fringes (of part-timers, agency workers, or employees on time contracts).

The state supported such corporate strategies in several ways, in order to support economic growth and job creation: On the one hand, social security contributions (that used to be paid by employer and employee in equal shares) were reduced, in an attempt to decrease labour costs, and to strengthen Germany as an investment location. As a result, insurance benefits were cut, and wage-earners were subject to stricter sanctions in case of unemployment (Hartz-reforms) or were prompted to invest in costly private (old age) insurances (Riester-Rente). On the other hand, labour laws were modified, widening the legal scope for precarious jobs that undermined earlier standards of material, legal, and social integration as associated with "Normalarbeit" (Mayer-Ahuja 2003). On the part of labour, instead, most wage-earners as well as trade unions still subscribed to earlier notions of "good work", but were not strong enough to prevent the expansion of "bad work" in West Germany. Thus an increasing part of the working population suffered severe cuts, with regard to income, to the level of security provided by an employment contract (given the increase of low-wage jobs, time contracts, agency work, or the infamous "mini jobs", below the threshold of social insurance coverage) and to their access to "social property", whether in the shape of social insurance or public services (Castel 2002).

Under these conditions, unions faced a serious crisis. High unemployment and the expansion of precarious jobs made their membership decline. At the same time, their notions of "good work" were ridiculed by neoliberal "reformers" as being utterly old-fashioned, and incompatible with the flexibility and innovation that was so urgently needed in the face of persistently high unemployment. Despite the apparent necessity to promote "good work" as an alternative political concept in the course of the 1990s, trade unions grudgingly accepted the argument that "(almost) every job is better than none" (Streeck/Heinze 1999).

"Standard employment" entails discrimination and enforces discipline

According to a second line of argument, "standard employment" as advocated by unions, but also by capital and the state, during the prosperous post-war decades was not "good work" after all. From the 1980s, as the focus of attention shifted from the quality of work to "jobs, jobs, jobs" (as an election poster of the social-democratic party read), "standard employment" was increasingly presented as a highly problematic phenomenon, by neoliberals as well as by "alternative" circles, assembled in new social movements. On the one hand, it was argued, permanent full-time jobs in the core workforces were a preserve of elderly white men, equipped with certified skills ("Facharbeiter"), who fought off women, young people, migrants, low-skill workers, and the unemployed, with support by their backward and chauvinist trade unions. In short: "standard employment" was discriminating, and the labour regulation on which it rested had to be abolished, from this perspective, in order to facilitate the access of "outsiders" to the labour market. On the other hand, "standard employment" was criticised for subjecting the workers concerned to a harsh regime of discipline. While "alternative" circles propagated "ways to paradise" (Gorz 1985) beyond wage-labour and considered a life-sentence of nine-to-five work in one and the same company as a veritable nightmare, neoliberals would typically claim that "rigid" labour regulation posed undue restrictions on the freedom of employers and employees to negotiate conditions flexibly, and in their best interest.

Given trade unions' self-perception as agents of social emancipation and working peoples' solidarity, this combined criticism of neoliberal and alternative forces was difficult to counter. Defamed either as "dinosaurs" at the edge of extinction (Ebbinghaus 2002) or as lobby of a saturated labour aristocracy, they remained in the defensive. This applied even when it became obvious that corporate and state policies of "flexibilising" labour markets and work contracts in fact aggravated both discrimination (as former "outsiders" were the first to be stuck in precarious jobs) and work discipline (since even core workforces bowed to management, in fear of precarisation and unemployment; Bourdieu 1998, 96ff). As a result, the quality of work turned into a non-topic for many years – after all, workers in precarious jobs were busy struggling to enter the core workforces, while those in stable jobs mainly focussed on employment protection (Dörre 2005). "Good work" as a political project was thus impeded by a lack of proponents among workers, but also by the crisis of legitimacy as experienced by trade unions during the 1990s.

Standardised labour regulation cannot do justice to variegated human needs

Finally, and much in line with the "artistic critique" described by Boltanski/Chiapello (2005), it has become common to argue that the needs and expectations of the myriad individuals who populate the colourful world of work have become so manifold that the formulation of standardised criteria for "good work" is no longer possible. Viewed from this perspective, the "flexibilisation" of work contracts and working hours, of work organisation and of work biographies serves, first of all, the working individual. "Good work" is thus re-interpreted to entail "flexible work" – and to be utterly incompatible with the regulatory standards that have shaped (and continue to shape) "Normalarbeit", with their reference to the collective rather than the individual. Accordingly, regular working hours, for instance, are perceived to collide with a widespread wish to organise "work and life" according to personal priorities. Hence works councils and trade unions acquire a bad reputation as inflexible bureaucrats, when fighting excessive overtime work (for the IT-industry see Boes/Baukrowitz 2002).

In fact, an individualisation of interests must pose problems for unions, since their strength has traditionally been based on the capacity to set and defend collective standards with regard to wages and working conditions, and it is difficult (though not impossible) to integrate individualised solutions into collective agreements. Despite all common-sensical reference to individualisation, however, workers still seem to face strikingly similar issues, for instance, with regard to flexible working hours. Hence empirical evidence suggests that "trust based working time" (Vertrauensarbeitszeit), which has long been promoted as a perfect means for reconciling work and private life, has in fact paved the way for an enormous expansion of working hours, both paid and unpaid (Hacket 2010), in accordance with the requirements of production, rather than reproduction. After all, "trust-based working time" is typically accompanied by a shift to indirect forms of controlling the labour process: employees are free to organise their work independently, as long as they meet deadlines. However, since material resources, staffing, the nature of the task, or the deadline itself remain beyond the influence of workers, the likely result of indirect control is "more pressure through more freedom" (Glißmann/Peters 2001).

Trade unions are thus confronted with a situation in which an increasing number of workers face the same set of problems, which should be an obvious case for collective interest representation – but these problems are perceived as individual issues, arising from an individual, and very specific work situation (for this effect also see Graefe in this volume). Under these conditions, any attempt of trade unions to establish standards for the regulation of working times, for instance, must appear as unjustified external interference, which increases the pressure it aims to reduce.

"Good work" as challenge for union strategies in the 21st century

Against this background, it is all the more remarkable that trade unions in Germany have re-discovered the notion of "good work" as a cornerstone of their policies and campaigns in the early 2000s.[3] In many ways, invoking "good work" implies to identify normative criteria, which may function as reference points for the future regulation of labour, whether with regard to the labour market or to work organisation on the shop-floor. Given that the earlier consensus between capital, labour, and the state with regard to "good work" has ceased to exist, trade unions need to – and are free to – set their own agenda today, drawing upon the experiences, fears, and hopes of their (potential) members, in order to set up a political project, apt to mobilise broad support in and beyond union circles. This is certainly not an easy task, but it is facilitated by the fact that notions of "good work" are considerably less individualised than one might think, after more than 30 years of discussion about the increasing differentiation of the world of work (for a starting point see: Habermas 1985; for a critique see: Mayer-Ahuja 2011).

Just like a century ago, these notions revolve around "bread" and "roses". "Bread" still refers to subsistence wages and social protection in the early 21st century: wage labour must prevent poverty, which is by no means self-evident given that Germany has the fastest growing low-wage sector in Europe, with grave consequences for the social protection of the working poor, in a welfare system based on social insurance. In order to secure "bread", however, it is not enough to put pressure on employers; state policies have to change as well. Instead of subsidizing low wages with public funds by way of providing the working poor with complementary benefits ("Arbeitslosengeld II für Aufstocker") and tolerating a semi-legal "grey labour market" (as constituted by virtually unregulated "mini jobs", for instance), state authorities have to effectively abolish sub-standard work and to invest in public employment, with adequate remuneration.

Under conditions of the early 21st century, then, the innocent union demand for "good work" acquires almost revolutionary qualities, since it implies putting an end to privatisation policies pursued since the 1970s as well as to the austerity programss invoked after the world economic crisis of 2008/09, as manifested in the "brake on public debts" (Schuldenbremse) in Germany. At the same time, however, trade unions continue their quest for "roses" even today, since "good work" in terms of working in safety and dignity has still not been achieved for many workers. In fact, health hazards and physical strain persist; psychic strain and incidents of burnout increase; many jobs do not allow for professional or personal advancement (Fuchs 2010); and the chances of many workers to influence tasks or work organisation are limited, especially for those in time contracts, agency work, or "minijobs". Finally, "good work" implies the formal right and actual chance to organise collectively, and again, trade unions seem to face similar challenges as the striking textile workers of 1912 who first demanded "bread and roses". After all, workers in large parts of the service sector, for instance, remain un-unionised, even though several organizing campaigns have targeted new parts of the working population during the last years (Dörre 2008).

Is there nothing new under the sun, then? In many ways, the essence of "good work" as advocated by trade unions has remained unaltered over the last decades, but the capacity to turn concepts into politics was subject to considerable change, with regard to political tides and power relations. Under conditions of the early 21st century, trade unions face mainly three challenges with regard to an effective promotion of "good work":

First, they need to win back their organisational strength, reaching beyond their classical member-base. Secondly, they will have to call into question political decisions, generally presented as "objective" economic restraints (Sachzwang), with regard to austerity policies, for instance, and struggle for a renewal of economic redistribution, in order to secure "bread" for the working population. Thirdly, the provision of "roses" does require the adjustment of the very notion of "good work", in reaction to some of the debates outlined above. Despite all neoliberal critique, binding regulatory standards are indispensable, for instance, with regard to subsistence wages, to legal as well as social protection, and to labour contracts that provide workers with some basis for planning the future.

The regulation of working-times, instead, constitutes a useful example for a field in which "good work" may well imply a wide range of practices. In fact, trade unions have started to change their policies accordingly, as indicated by recent initiatives of the German metal workers' union, aiming at "time sovereignty" (Zeitsouveränität). As argued above, however, even with regard to working-time, "flexibilisation" is likely to turn into a "flexibilisation from above", in the sole interest of employers, if workers lack a reliable set of material and legal rights, enabling them to make choices at all, and to confront corporate strategies, thus effecting a "flexibilisation from below", in accordance with their own needs. If trade unions reformulate their quest for "bread and roses" accordingly, the demand for "good work" might once again turn into a powerful vision for grassroot mobilisation and collective protest, and into a rallying cry for the 21st century.

Notes

1 The term "worker" refers, in this article, to wage-earners in general, whether in blue collar or white collar occupations.
2 In 1950, 69.4 per cent of the working population were performing wage-labour; in 1985, their share had already increased to 88.2 percent (Klammer et al. 2000, Tab. 2.A.19a, based on German Mikrozensus, FS 1, Reihe 4.1.1.).
3 The German Trade Union Confederation (Deutscher Gewerkschaftsbund, DGB) publishes a journal called *Gute Arbeit: Gesundheitsschutz und Arbeitsgestaltung* since 1988 and has started the "Index Gute Arbeit" in 2006. The metal workers' union (Industriegewerkschaft Metall, IGM) was the first to develop a campaign on "Good Work", starting with a conference in 2002 (*Good Work – Humane work organisation as future task of trade unions*). The service sector trade union (Vereinte Dienstleistungsgewerkschaft, ver.di) has formulated a codex on "Good Work" (*Kodex Gute Arbeit*) in 2013, and publishes a yearbook, jointly with IGM, under the same title (*Jahrbuch Gute Arbeit*) since 2009.

References

Birke, P. (2014). From "Autonomy" to "Subjectivation of Work". Paper presented in the session *New contours in Industrial relations. Secondary analysis of case studies conducted since the 1960s*. European Social Science History Conference, Vienna, 23–27 April. Unpublished Manuscript.

Bluhm, F. (2014). Lack of Self-Confidence and Wildcat Strikes – Secondary Analysis of a Shipyard Study of the late 1970s. Paper presented in the session *New contours in Industrial relations. Secondary analysis of case studies conducted since the 1960s*. European Social Science History Conference, Vienna, 23–27 April. Unpublished Manuscript.

Boes, A./A. Baukrowitz (2002). Arbeitsbeziehungen in der IT-Industrie: Erosion oder Innovation der Mitbestimmung? Berlin: Edition Sigma.

Boltansky, L./E. Chiapello (2005). *The New Spirit of Capitalism*. London: Verso.

Bourdieu, P. (1998). *Gegenfeuer: Wortmeldungen im Dienste des Widerstands gegen die neoliberale Invasion*. Konstanz: UVK.

Busch, U./R. Land (2010). Teilhabekapitalismus – fordistische Wirtschaftsentwicklung und Umbruch in Deutschland: 1950 bis 2009. In: Forschungsverbund Sozioökonomische Berichterstattung (ed.). *Berichterstattung zur sozioökonomischen Entwicklung in Deutschland: Teilhabe im Umbruch*. Zweiter Bericht, Kapitel 4, Wiesbaden: VS, 111–151.

Castel, R. (2002). *From Manual Workers to Wage Laborers: Transformation of the Social Question*. New Brunswick, NJ: Transaction Publishers.

Dörre, K. (2005). Prekarität als arbeitspolitische Herausforderung. In: *WSI-Mitteilungen* 5, 250–258.

Dörre, K. (2008). Die strategische Wahl der Gewerkschaften: Erneuerung durch Organizing? In: *WSI-Mitteilungen* 1, 3–10.

Ebbinghaus, B. (2002). Dinosaurier der Dienstleistungsgesellschaft? Der Mitgliederschwund deutscher Gewerkschaften im historischen und internationalen Vergleich. *MPIfG Working Paper* 03, Köln.

Eisenstein, S. (1983). *Give us Bread But Give us Roses: Working Women's Consciousness in the United States, 1890 to the First World War*. London: Routledge.

Fuchs, T. (2010). Qualität der Arbeit. In: Forschungsverbund Sozioökonomische Berichterstattung (Hg.). *Berichterstattung zur sozioökonomischen Entwicklung in Deutschland: Teilhabe im Umbruch*. Zweiter Bericht, Kapitel 14, Wiesbaden: VS, 417–447.

Glißmann, W./K. Peters (2001). *Mehr Druck durch mehr Freiheit: Die neue Autonomie in der Arbeit und ihre paradoxen Folgen*. Hamburg: VSA.

Gorz, A. (1985). *Paths to Paradise: On the Liberation from Work.* London: Pluto.

Habermas, J. (1985). *Die Neue Unuebersichtlichkeit.* Frankfurt am Main: Suhrkamp.

Hacket, A. (2010). Arbeitszeit und Lebenszeit. In: Forschungsverbund Sozioökonomische Berichterstattung (Hg.). *Berichterstattung zur sozioökonomischen Entwicklung in Deutschland: Teilhabe im Umbruch.* Zweiter Bericht, Kapitel 22, Wiesbaden: VS, 507–532.

Hirsch, J./R. Roth (1986). *Das neue Gesicht des Kapitalismus: Vom Fordismus zum Postfordismus.* Hamburg: VSA.

Hobsbawm, E. (1994). *Age of Extremes: The Short Twentieth Century 1914–1991.* London: Joseph.

Honneth, A. (1996). *The Struggle for Recognition: The Moral Grammar of Social Conflicts.* Cambridge, MA: MIT Press.

Klammer, U./C. Klenner/C. Ochs/P. Klenner/A. Ziegler (2000). *WSI-FrauenDatenReport.* Berlin: Sigma.

Kratzer, N./D. Sauer (2005). Flexibilisierung und Subjektivierung von Arbeit. In: SOFI/ IAB/ISF/INIFES (eds.). *Berichterstattung zur sozio-ökonomischen Entwicklung in Deutschland: Arbeit und Lebensweisen.* Wiesbaden: VS, 225–249.

Lutz, B. (1989). *Der kurze Traum immerwährender Prosperität.* Frankfurt am Main/New York: Campus.

Mayer-Ahuja, N. (2003). *Wieder dienen lernen? Vom westdeutschen "Normalarbeitsverhältnis" zu prekärer Beschäftigung seit 1973.* Berlin: Sigma.

Mayer-Ahuja, N. (2011). Jenseits der "neuen Unübersichtlichkeit". Annäherung an Konturen der gegenwärtigen Arbeitswelt. *SOFI-Working Paper* 2011–6.

Mückenberger, U. (1985). Die Krise des Normalarbeitsverhältnisses: Hat das Arbeitsrecht noch Zukunft? In: *Zeitschrift für Sozialreform* 7, 415–434 & 457–475.

Oppenheim, J. (1911). Bread and Roses. In: *The American Magazine*, December.

Raphael, L./A. Döring-Manteuffel (2008). *Nach dem Boom? Perspektiven auf die Zeitgeschichte seit 1970.* Göttingen: Vandenhoeck & Ruprecht.

Schumann, M. et al. (1982). *Rationalisierung, Krise, Arbeiter: Eine empirische Untersuchung der Industrialisierung auf der Werft.* Frankfurt am Main: EVA.

Streeck, W./R. Heinze (1999). An Arbeit fehlt es nicht. In: *Der Spiegel* 19/1999, 38–45. Online at www.spiegel.de/spiegel/print/d-13220370.html.

Voß, G.G./H. Pongratz (1998). Der Arbeitskraftunternehmer: eine neue Grundform der Ware Arbeitskraft? In: *Kölner Zeitschrift für Soziologie und Sozialpsychologie* 50.1, 131–158.

11 How not to argue against growth

Happiness, austerity and inequality

John O'Neill

One of the central claims made by critics of growth is a claim about well-being: the ending of continuous economic growth is consistent with or, more strongly, a condition of the maintenance or improvement of well-being. There are good arguments for this claim (O'Neill 2006, 2008a & b). Here, however, I will be principally concerned with versions of the argument for the claim that critics of growth should avoid. Two arguments for the claim that have been particularly popular amongst critics of growth have serious weaknesses. The first is the appeal to subjective well-being and the Easterlin paradox – that economic growth has not been correlated with a rise in subjective well-being. The second is the appeal to the concept of gross national happiness and its use in Bhutan as an exemplar of how well-being should be measured. I will argue that both have serious problems. Problems of adaptation mean that arguments that appeal to subjective well-being fail to address problems of inequality both within and across generations. The absence of a change in subjective well-being in conditions of austerity is indicative of the problems. A robust defence of the well-being claim needs to appeal to objective state accounts of well-being. The appeal to gross national happiness highlights problems of treating debates about well-being in a depoliticised fashion, ignoring the politics that underpin some concepts of well-being and the ways that they can support forms of oppression and inequality. It also illustrates a failing of much radical politics of the past 100 years which might be called the politics of radical tourism – the belief in a utopia that is always somewhere else.

To criticise these arguments is not to claim there is no case against growth. There are stronger arguments from limits, justice and freedom, as well as sounder arguments from well-being. Since most of this paper is an exercise in how not to argue for degrowth, the first section will briefly review some of the stronger of the arguments against growth.

How to argue against growth

Climate change

A central argument for degrowth concerns what is physically possible given the impacts of climate change on the physical conditions for human life and livelihood. In making this argument a distinction has to be made between two senses of growth: growth in the physical sense – the increase in the energy and physical throughput of the economy; growth in the sense of rising GDP – the increase in the total monetary value of the goods and services in an economy. The two concepts are logically distinct. It is logically possible to have increasing GDP and a decreasing physical and energy throughput in an economy. However, it is a fallacy to move from claims about what is logically possible to claims about what is physically possible and another from what is physically possible to what is empirically actual.

When one turns from logical possibilities to physical possibilities and empirical actualities, there is a relationship between increasing GDP and increasing greenhouse gas emissions. GDP measures consumption for goods and services over which there are market transactions or over which market prices can be imputed. Some of these goods and services may have no direct associated emissions – say buying a tip for a horse race – and some may even contribute to a reduction in emissions – say buying a seedling for a tree one intends to grow. However, empirically most goods and services which people pay for have a carbon footprint. So it is unsurprising that there has been a close correlation between increasing consumption in marketed goods and services and increasing emissions. Given a static or rising population and growth in per capita consumption, all other things being equal, there will be a growth in physical and energy throughput and a corresponding growth in greenhouse gas emissions.

Proponents of green growth claim that all other things are not equal. Falls in the carbon intensity of consumption can lead to not just a relative but absolute decoupling of growth in GDP and rising emissions. Technological change and a shift in consumption from things to services will lead to a combination of continuing growth and declining rates of emissions. The problem with this argument is that it is empirically weak. While there has been some relative decoupling and a flattening of the rate of increase in emissions, there is little evidence to support the claim that the absolute decoupling at levels required to avoid dangerous climate change is likely or possible (Jackson 2009). Since emissions are cumulative – emissions from CO2 and some other greenhouse gases will remain in the atmosphere for long periods of time – peak emissions need to happen sooner rather than later. (Anderson/Bows 2012; Anderson/Bows 2008 and 2011; Bows/Barrett 2010). There is no good empirical evidence for the belief that the level of decoupling of increasing emissions and growth in GDP is likely within the time frames required to avoid dangerous climate change.

Arguments from justice

A second group of arguments appeal to considerations of global justice and inequality. One is an argument from justice in the use of common or collective resources. It is unjust, as Goodin puts it, to "allow some co-owners of a common property resource to use it in certain ways, without allowing all co-owners to use it similarly" (Goodin 1994, 585). The atmosphere is a common resource. It is unjust that some consume in ways that cause emissions that could not be generalised to all without causing serious climate change. Hence the patterns of consumption of those responsible for luxury emissions are unjust. A second argument appeals to the needs of the worst off. Large parts of the population of the globe live at levels of consumption that fail to meet basic needs. It is a duty of justice that those levels of need are met. If it is a condition of meeting those needs and keeping emissions within dangerous levels that those on luxury emissions emit less, then justice demands a fall in luxury emissions (Shue 1993). A third argument appeals to the condition of those on the commodity frontier: the continuous expansion of the economy requires the extraction of resources and disposal of waste which disproportionately harms the lives and livelihoods of marginalised and poor communities (Martinez-Alier et. al 2010).

Arguments from freedom

A third set of arguments in the Marxian tradition appeal to human freedom. A distinguishing feature of modern capitalist societies that is responsible for continuing growth is the reinvestment of surplus value into productive processes that allow for not just the reproduction but the expansion of the productive capacity of an economy. It contrasts with the use of surplus in earlier societies, where it was employed to reproduce the social power and standing of those who lived off surplus labour and to maintain their time free of labour. For Marx, this shift in the use of surplus labour is both a source of human liberation and a source of unfreedom. It is a source of liberation:

> [T]he old view, in which the human being appears as the aim of production . . . seems to be very lofty when contrasted to the modern world, where production appears as the aim of mankind and wealth as the aim of production. In fact, however, what is wealth other than the universality of human needs, capacities, pleasures and productive capacities etc., created through universal exchange.
>
> (Marx 1973, 487–488)

Universal market exchange also releases producers from relations of dependency on particular persons (Marx 1973, 163). However, at the same time the shift also creates a form of unfreedom – 'objective dependency'. The forces that drive growth in modern capitalist societies are systemic. Capitalists as capitalists are forced to recycle the surplus into expanding production as a condition of their existence (Marx 1970, ch.4). Declining growth within the context of a capitalist economy is a sign of an economy in crisis. All actors are "the plaything of alien powers" (Marx 1974, 220). On this Marxian line of argument, a post-growth society is one in which production again is not for production's sake, but subordinated to human needs. As such, it is one in which production comes under human conscious control. Growth no longer has a life of its own to which the lives of human beings are subordinated.

Arguments from decommodification

A fourth set of arguments against growth are de-commodification arguments. The growth in GDP is a consequence not just of increasing consumption of goods and services as such, but also of their increasing marketisation. Only those goods and services that are the subject of market exchanges or are imputed a monetary value contribute to growth in GDP. Selling blood or bodily parts contributes to GDP. Donating blood or bodily parts does not. Knowledge that is commodified through intellectual property rights contributes to GDP. Knowledge that is freely available does not contribute directly to GDP. Paid care work adds to GDP. Care within family, friendship and community networks does not. There are independent normative arguments against the growing marketisation of goods in capitalist society (Anderson 1993; O'Neill 1998; Satz 2010; Sandel 2013; Walzer 1983). These include: injustices in the outcome of market transactions in conditions of inequality of wealth and power; the incompatibility of market relations with social practices and relationships that are conditions of human well-being; failures of respect for human dignity and vulnerability; forms of environmental degradation associated with market modes of governance, and the absence of market solutions to those failures (O'Neill 2007; 2016). Recapturing and expanding the domains of activity outside of the market place constitute a form of degrowth.

Arguments from well-being

Finally, there are arguments from well-being. Any plausible criticism of growth relies upon a distinction between increasing economic growth and improving human well-being, knowledge and culture. As Mill put it, a stationary state economy "implies no stationary state of human improvement" (Mill 1848, IV.6.9). The claim that the absence of growth is consistent with the maintenance or improvement of human well-being returns discussion of well-being to a classical question: Are there bounds to the goods required for a happy or flourishing life? The classical answer in Aristotelian and Epicurean traditions was that bounds do exist to the goods required for a happy life (O'Neill 2006; 2008a & b). That answer survives into some central texts of modern economics. Consider for example the paper on saving by Ramsey in which he introduces the formula that still forms the starting point for debates about discounting. A claim that Ramsey defends in that paper that has disappeared from contemporary discussion is that there is a "maximum obtainable rate of enjoyment or utility" which he terms 'Bliss' (Ramsey 1928, 545). The point of saving for a community is to have that level of goods at which they reach or approximate to Bliss. Beyond that point saving is no longer required. Ramsey assumes that there are limits to the goods required for a good life.

That assumption has disappeared from modern economic textbooks. Rather the opposite is assumed, that more is better. The rational economic agent prefers more goods to less. As Gauthier puts it: "Appropriation has no natural upper bound. Economic man seeks more". (Gauthier 1986, 318). Given the preference satisfaction theory of well-being that lies at the basis of neo-classical welfare economics – that well-being consists in the satisfaction of preferences – then it follows that there are no limits to the goods required for well-being.

The assumption that more is always better is one that has been open to criticism from two different directions that have their origins in classical Epicurean and Aristotelian perspectives on well-being. Both have been influential on discussions of degrowth. However, both can take problematic forms. In following I outline how not to argue from well-being to degrowth.

How not to argue for degrowth

Subjective well-being

One standard line of argument for degrowth is an appeal to the finding of Easterlin and others that above a certain level, growth in GDP is no longer correlated with a growth in subjective well-being as measured by self-reported life-satisfaction (Petridis/Muraca/Kallis 2015, 179; Porrit 2003). The graph for the UK is fairly typical (figure 11.1).While relative income within a society at any point in time is positively correlated with life-satisfaction – the wealthier express higher life satisfaction – absolute increases in GDP over time are not. There are two standard grounds offered for this lack of correlation. One is the positional nature of many goods in market society – that they are goods, like status goods, whose value to the individual is affected by their availability and possession by others. Insofar as goods and income are valued comparatively by reference to the goods and incomes possessed by others, increasing overall consumption will not increase reported well-being (Hirsch 1977). The second is 'hedonic adaptation' (Frederick/Loewenstein 1999), that is the tendency for individuals to adjust to changes in their life situation and to return to previous levels of self-reported experienced well-being. While changes in circumstances can result in a short-term shift in subjective well-being, over a period, individuals adjust and shift to a prior reference point.

Both positional goods and adaptation result in a hedonic treadmill: beyond a certain level of consumption and income, as absolute, as opposed to relative, levels of income increase there is no corresponding increase in subjective well-being. Overall life-satisfaction remains stable: "Even though rising income means people can have more goods, the favourable effect of this on welfare is erased by the fact that people want more as they progress" (Easterlin 2001, 481).

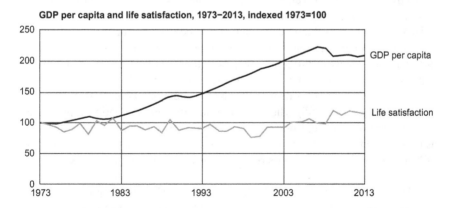

Figure 11.1 Well-being: measuring 'what matters'
Source: from McKinnon 2014

This treadmill effect appears to make the hedonic approach to well-being particularly promising for critics of growth. Well-being can be improved if individuals are taken off the hedonic treadmill to which material consumption is subject and our collective choices as a society are refocused on other goods that are positively correlated with life-satisfaction and which do not require ever increasing GDP as a condition of their existence: familial and social relationships, secure and intrinsically worthwhile work, health, personal and political freedoms. It might indeed be thought that findings of hedonic psychology confirm the claim of the classic founders of hedonism, in particular of Epicurus, that the desire for wealth without limits is founded upon error – the wealth required for hedonic happiness is limited: "Natural wealth is both limited and easy to acquire. But wealth [as defined by] groundless opinions extends without limits" (Epicurus 1988, XV).

The environmental story around subjective well-being is understandably influential. However, while some of the underlying arguments that are independent of a subjective theory of well-being are important, in particular those concerning positional goods, the appeal to subjective well-being is one that should be resisted as an argument for showing that well-being and growth can be decoupled. An initial point to notice is that the concept of subjective well-being is ambiguous: it can refer to the content of well-being – well-being consists in being in the appropriate subjective states, e.g. in classical hedonism, pleasure and the absence of pain; it can refer to the evaluation of well-being – the use of individual self-reports to estimate levels of well-being (O'Neill 1998, ch.3). Life satisfaction surveys are subjective in the evaluation of well-being. It does not follow that they are surveys of subjective states. They are neutral as to the content of well-being. If you ask someone how satisfied they are with their lives, you are not necessarily asking them about their recent subjective states rather than other constituents of their lives that matter to them. This may include their psychological states but also directly other objective dimensions of their lives, such as family, friendships and work. A life-satisfaction survey is about subjective well-being understood as a subjective evaluation of well-being. It is not directly an assessment of the content of well-being understood as subjective states.

Both subjective evaluation and subjective content are open to problems of adaptation. A central problem with subjective assessments of well-being is that different individuals in different contexts will appeal to different standards and expectations of what counts as a good life. It raises problems of adaptive preferences – that one way to deal with adverse situations is to shift expectations downwards (Sen 1992, 55). The problem is apparent in the relationships between austerity and well-being. Look again at Figure 11.1. A point to note is that as far as life-satisfaction is concerned austerity has had little impact at all. As the Office of National Statistics notes in its report on the quality of life in the UK:

> The recession has led to a higher proportion who are unemployed, with a particular impact on the young, and in 2009/10 more than 1 in 8 (12.3%) of us were finding it quite or very difficult to manage financially. Life satisfaction

presents a more resilient picture, having remained broadly stable throughout the last decade.

(Self/Thomas/Randall 2012, 2)

While the young and those on low incomes are particularly badly affected by austerity, including on objective measures of psychological well-being such as rates of anxiety and depression, this has not led to decreased life-satisfaction. There is good evidence that the lack of relationship between reported life satisfaction and austerity is a matter of adaptive preferences. They are a result of a shift in the aspirations of those most affected:

> [H]ard economic times did enter into people's practical reasoning about what constitutes a good life: during hard times there was widespread re-specification of ends in accordance with subsistence goals such as security, stability and certainty, with effects concentrated among those living in low-income households, and the formative generation. This adaptation represents a move away from higher human potential goals, and a diminishment of internal capability. The combination of constrained external circumstances and diminished internal capability amounts to a double setback for the combined capabilities of these groups.
>
> (Austin 2016, 240)

In this context subjective well-being measures are simply not picking up the losses in well-being. Indeed one might say that the real social problem in this context is the absence of appropriate dissatisfaction which can drive social change.

The problem of adaptation also raises problems for intergenerational justice. Given adaptation, those in the future who suffer the adverse consequences of current decisions and practices may not experience them as adverse. A biologically impoverished world may lack many species of flora and fauna that we experience today, but their loss may no longer be experienced as a loss but simply as a background condition of life. A world geo-engineered through the release of sulphur particles into the upper atmosphere may lack blue skies, but for generations brought up in their absence, this absence they may not be experienced as such. A subjective well-being metric will fail to capture the wrongs done to future generations. An adequate account of the harms done to future generations requires reference to an objective state account of well-being (Gough 2015).

If the argument from well-being for degrowth is to avoid problems of adaptive preferences it needs to appeal to more objective metrics of human well-being. The concept of 'objective well-being' like 'subjective well-being' is ambiguous. It can refer to either objectivity in the content of well-being or objectivity in the evaluation of well-being (O'Neill 1998, ch.3). Approaches that are objective in content include those that appeal to needs (Wiggins 1998, 2006; Doyal/Gough 1991; O'Neill 2010) and those that appeal to capabilities and functionings (Sen 1993, 1995; Nussbaum 2000; Jackson 2009; Muraca 2012). Both needs and capabilities are open to both subjective evaluation, for example through self-reported health, and objective evaluation, for example through morbidity and life expectancy measures. On objective content theories what matters to well-being are not just psychological states, but what people can do or be in their lives. Such accounts will be multi-dimensional, given the variety of different constituents of a good life. To live well is to have or realise a variety of states – particular forms of social relations, physical health, autonomy, knowledge of the world, aesthetic experience, accomplishment and achievement, pleasures, a well-constituted relation with the non-human world and so on.

The claim that there are limits required for a good life understood in this objective sense is also an old one: the number of goods which "suffices for a good life is not unlimited" (Aristotle 1948, book 1, ch.8). Just as the Epicurean case for the existence of limits to the good life has seen a revival, so also has the Aristotelian case. However, making it good requires a detailed analysis of the different constituents of the good life – material, social and cultural – and of what is required for their realisation. Critics of growth are required to move away from the simple appeal to the Easterlin paradox – there is no simple Easterlin paradox for objective evaluations of well-being – and onto much more difficult territory of objective measures and indicators of well-being. This includes standard indicators of poverty reduction, life expectancy, morbidity rates, literacy rates (Steinberger/Roberts 2010) and consideration of the social conditions in which relationships of community and social practices that are constitutive condition of the good life can thrive.

Gross national happiness: capabilities, needs and the politics of well-being

Specifying the goods that are constitutive of a good life brings its own politics. The problems are evident in the multidimensional approach to measuring well-being that has been particularly popular amongst environmentalists, gross national happiness (GNH) of Bhutan. In critical discussions of growth the metric of gross national happiness (GNH) of Bhutan is often cited as an alternative metric to GDP (Daly/Farley 2010, 274; Costanza et.al. 2014). The measure takes a multi-dimensional approach to well-being that is "not focused only on subjective well-being to the exclusion of other dimensions" (Ura et al. 2012, 7). It includes both objective and subjective measures of well-being and both subjective and objective dimensions of the content of well-being. It is also explicitly social: "it internalises responsibility and other-regarding motivations explicitly" (Ura et al. 2012, 7). The gross national happiness index covers nine domains each with weighted indicators:

1   Psychological well-being (Life-satisfaction 33%, Positive emotions 17%, Negative emotions 17% Spirituality 33%);
2   Health (Self-reported health 10%, Healthy days 30%, Disability 30%, Mental health 30%);
3   Time use (Work 50%, Sleep 50%);
4   Education (Literacy 30%, Schooling 30%, Knowledge 20%, Value 20%);

5   Cultural diversity and resilience (*Zorig chusum* skills (artistic skills) 30%, Cultural participation 30%, Speak native language 20%, *Driglam Namzha* (the Way of Harmony) 20%);
6   Good governance (Political participation 40%, Services 40%, Governance performance 10%, Fundamental rights 10%);
7   Community vitality (Donation of time & money 30%, Safety 30%, Community relationship 20%, Family 20%);
8   Ecological diversity and resilience (Wildlife damage 40%, Urban issues 40%, Responsibility towards environment 10%, Ecological issues 10%);
9   Living standards (Per capita income 33%, Assets 33%, Housing 33%) (Ura et al. 2012, 26).

With the explicit inclusion of cultural diversity, ecological diversity and community relationships, GNH has been taken as a model for measuring human well-being by many environmental critics of growth.

While this multi-dimensional approach to well-being is one that has real virtues, what is absent from the idealisation of GNH is an appreciation of the politics that underpins some of the goods that appear on the list. GNH puts great emphasis on the cultural dimensions of well-being and in particular its appeal to 'cultural diversity' and the maintenance of Bhutan's distinctive culture:

> The distinctive culture of Bhutan facilitates sovereignty of the country and provides identity to the people. Hence the preservation and promotion of culture has been accorded a high priority both by the government and the people . . . The diversity of the culture is manifested in forms of language, traditional arts and crafts, festivals, events, ceremonies, drama, music, dress and etiquette and more importantly the spiritual values that people share . . . To assess the strength of various aspects of culture, four indicators have been considered: language, artisan skills, cultural participation and *Driglam Namzha* (the Way of Harmony)
>
> (Ura et al. 2012, 144).

The maintenance of a distinctive culture is taken to be important in the context of Bhutan's being surrounded by larger more populous countries. The concept of Driglam Namzha is particularly prominent: "*Driglam Namzha* (the Way of Harmony) is expected behaviour (of consuming, clothing, moving) especially in formal occasions and in formal spaces"(Ura et al. 2012, 148).

The centrality of this cultural dimension has a strong political dimension. It has to be understood against the background of the Bhutanisation policy pursued by the government in relation to the Nepalese Lhotshampa population in southern Bhutan (Hutt 2003, ch.11). The 1985 Citizenship Act denied citizenship rights to those who could not show residence in Bhutan prior to 1958 (Hutt 2003, ch.10; Sharma/Sharma 1998, 251–252). Following this law and a 1988 census, a large portion of the ethnic Nepalis in Bhutan were reclassified as illegal immigrants. A 'one nation, one people policy' introduced in the sixth

Five-Year Plan (1987–92) enforced the cultural practice of Driglam Namzha as a way of preserving Bhutanese national culture (Hutt 2003, 164–173). Nepalese was discontinued as a language in schools in 1989. Following political repression, by 1992, more than 80,000 Nepalese Lhotshampas had left Bhutan and ended up in refugee camps in eastern Nepal (Amnesty International 1992; Human Rights Watch 2007a). It is against this background that the commitment to 'cultural diversity' and priority accorded to 'the preservation and promotion of culture' need to be understood. In this context the demand for happiness can take a particularly ironic turn:

> The army sent us the form issued by the government [voluntary migration form]. They said that we had to go out. They said if you go now you will get some money. Some people got a little money. On the way [as we left Bhutan] there were many police. We were forced to sign the document. They snapped our photos. The man told me to smile, to show my teeth. He wanted to show that I was leaving my country willingly, happily, that I was not forced to leave
> (Refugee testimony Human Rights Watch 2007b, 16.
> See also the testimonies in Sharma/Sharma 1998, 257–267)

The cultural dimensions of policy of gross national happiness have a particular political content.

To make these observations is not to reject the importance of multi-dimensional approaches to well-being. However, it is to insist that any such exercises need to be understood in their wider political context. In particular, there is a recurrent danger in radical politics to see utopias in exotic places elsewhere, a kind of radical tourist perspective, in this context in an imaginary Shangri La which is very different from the actual place of conflicts and suffering it disguises (Hutt 2003; Pellegrini/Tasciotti 2014).

There are, as I noted in the first half of this paper, good grounds for criticism of limitless economic growth. However, critics need to avoid easy but problematic arguments against growth. Simple appeals to subjective theories of well-being and the Easterlin paradox fail to provide a robust case against growth. Arguments need rather to focus on the conditions for meeting human needs and functionings. However, those arguments in turn need to be placed in the context of the larger social and political context in which deliberation on the constituents of the good life take place.

References

Amnesty International (1992). *Bhutan: Human Rights Violations against the Nepali-speaking Population in the South.* Online at https://www.amnesty.org/en/documents/asa14/004/1992/en (June 30 2017).

Anderson, E. (1993). *Value in Ethics and Economics.* Cambridge Mass: Harvard University Press.

Anderson, K./A. Bows (2008). Reframing the Climate Change Challenge in Light of Post-2000 Emission Trends. In: *Philosophical Transactions of the Royal Society A* 366, 3863–3882.

Anderson, K./A. Bows (2011). Beyond 'Dangerous' Climate Change: Emission Scenarios for a New World. In: *Philosophical Transactions of the Royal Society A* 369, 20–44.

Anderson, K./A. Bows (2012). A New Paradigm for Climate Change. In: *Nature Climate Change*, 639–640.

Aristotle (1948). *Politics*, transl by E. Barker. Oxford: Clarendon Press.

Austin, A. (2016). Practical Reason in Hard Times: The Effects of Economic Crisis on the Kinds of Lives People in the UK have Reason to Value. In: *Journal of Human Development and Capabilities* 17, 225–244.

Bows, A./J. Barrett (2010). Cumulative Emission Scenarios Using a Consumption-Based Approach: A Glimmer of Hope? In: *Carbon Management* 1.1, 161–175.

Costanza, R. I. Kubiszewski/E. Giovannini/H. Lovins/J. McGlade/K. Pickett/K. Ragnarsdóttir/D. Roberts/R. Vogli/R. Wilkinson R. (2014). Time to Leave GDP Behind. In: *Nature* 505, 283–285.

Daly, H. E./J. Farley (2010). *Ecological Economics: Principles and Applications*, Second edition. Washington, DC: Island Press.

Doyal, L./I. Gough, I. (1991). *A Theory of Human Need*. New York: Palgrave Macmillan.

Easterlin, R. (2001). Income and Happiness: Towards a Unified Theory. *The Economic Journal* 111, 465–484.

Epicurus (1988). Principal Doctrines. In: B. Inwood/ L. Gerson (eds.). *Hellenistic Philosophy*. Indianapolis: Hackett, 32–36.

Frederick, S./G. Loewenstein (1999). Hedonic Adaptation. In: D. Kahneman/E. Diener/N. Schwartz (eds.). *Scientific Perspectives on Enjoyment, Suffering, and Well-Being*. New York: Russell Sage Foundation, 302–329.

Gauthier, D. (1986). *Morals by Agreement* Oxford: Oxford University Press.

Goodin, R. (1994). Selling Environmental Indulgences. In: *Kyklos* 47.4, 573–596.

Gough, I. (2015). Climate Change and Sustainable Welfare: The Centrality of Human Needs. In: *Cambridge Journal of Economics* 39, 1191–1214.

Hirsch, F. (1977). *Social Limits to Growth*. London: Routledge/Kegan Paul.

Human Rights Watch (2007a). *Discrimination against Ethnic Nepali Children in Bhutan*. Online at www.hrw.org/legacy/backgrounder/crd/2007/bhutan1007.

Human Rights Watch (2007b). Last Hope: The Need for Durable Solutions for Bhutanese Refugees in Nepal and India. Online at www.hrw.org/reports/2007/bhutan0507.

Hutt, M. (2003). *Unbecoming Citizens: Culture, Nationhood, and the Flight of Refugees From Bhutan*. Oxford: Oxford University Press.

Jackson, T. (2009). *Prosperity Without Growth: Economics for a Finite Planet*. London: Earthscan.

Martinez-Alier, J. /G. Kallis/S. Veuthey/M. Walter/L. Temper. (2010). Social Metabolism, Ecological Distribution Conflicts and Valuation Languages. In: *Ecological Economics* 70, 153–158.

Marx, K. (1970). *Capital I*. London: Lawrence and Wishart.

Marx, K. (1973). *Grundrisse*. Harmondsworth: London.

Marx, K. (1974). On the Jewish Question. In: L. Colletti (ed.). *Early Writing*. Harmondsworth: Penguin, 211–241.

McKinnon, E. (2014). *Wellbeing – Measuring What Matters (Gov.UK)*. Online at https://coanalysis.blog.gov.uk/2014/08/06/wellbeing-measuring-what-matters.

Mill, J.S. (1848). *Principles of Political Economy with some of their Applications to Social Philosophy*. 7th edition, 1909, London: Longmans, Green and Co.

Muraca, B. (2012). Towards a Fair Degrowth-Society: Justice and the Right to a 'Good Life' Beyond Growth. In: *Futures* 44, 535–545.

Nussbaum, M. (2000). *Women and Human Development: The Capabilities Approach*. Cambridge: Cambridge University Press.

O'Neill, J. (1998). *The Market: Ethics, Knowledge and Politics*. London: Routledge.

O'Neill, J. (2006). Citizenship, Well-Being and Sustainability: Epicurus or Aristotle? In: *Analyse & Kritik* 28, 158–172.

O'Neill, J. (2007). *Markets, Deliberation and Environment*. London: Routledge.

O'Neill, J. (2008a). *Living Well Within Limits: Well-Being, Time and Sustainability*. London: Sustainable Development Commission. Online at www.sd-commission.org.uk/publications/downloads/John_ONeil_thinkpiecel.pdf.

O'Neill, J. (2008b). Happiness and the Good Life. In: *Environmental Values* 17, 125–144.

O'Neill, J. (2010). The Overshadowing of Need. In: F. Rauschmayer/I. Omann/J. Frühmann (eds.). *Sustainable Development: Capabilities, Needs, and Well-Being*. London: Routledge, 25–42.

O'Neill, J. (2016). Markets, Ethics and Environment. In: S. Gardiner/A. Thompson (eds.). *Oxford Handbook of Environmental Ethics*. Oxford: Oxford University Press, 40–50.

Pellegrini, L./L. Tasciotti (2014). Bhutan: Between Happiness and Horror. In: *Capitalism Nature Socialism* 25, 103–109.

Petridis, P./B. Muraca/G. Kallis (2015). Degrowth Between a Scientific Concept and a Slogan for a Social Movement. In: *Handbook of Ecological Economics*. Cheltenham: Edward Elgar, 176–200.

Porritt, J. (2003). *Redefining Sustainability*. London: Sustainable Development Commission.

Ramsey, F.P. (1928). A Mathematical Theory of Saving. In: *Economic Journal* 38, 543–559.

Sandel, M. (2013). *What Money Can't Buy: The Moral Limits of Markets*. London: Penguin.

Satz, D. (2010). *Why Some Things Should Not Be for Sale*. Oxford: Oxford University Press.

Self, A./J. Thomas/C. Randall (2012). *Measuring National Well-Being: Life in the UK*. London: Office for National Statistics.

Sen, A. (1992). *Inequality Reexamined*. Oxford: Clarendon Press.

Sen, A. (1993). Capability and Well Being. In: M. Nussbaum/A. Sen (eds.). *The Quality of Life*. Oxford: Clarendon Press, 30–53.

Sen, A. (1995). *Development as Freedom*. Oxford: Oxford University Press.

Sharma, S./U. Sharma (eds., 1998). *Documents on Sikkim and Bhutan*. New Delhi: Anmol Publications.

Shue, H. (1993). Subsistence Emissions and Luxury Emissions. In: *Law and Policy* 15.1, 39–59.

Steinberger, J./J. Roberts (2010). From Constraint to Sufficiency: The Decoupling of Energy and Carbon From Human Needs, 1975–2005. In: *Ecological Economics* 70, 425–433.

Ura, K. S. Alkire/T. Zangmo/K. Wangdi. (2012). *An Extensive Analysis of GNH Index*. Thimphu: The Centre for Bhutan Studies.

Walzer, M. (1983). *Spheres of Justice*. Oxford: Blackwell.

Wiggins, D. (1998). The Claims of Need. In: *Needs, Values, Truth*. Third edition. Oxford: Clarendon Press, 1–57.

Wiggins, D. (2006). An Idea We Cannot Do Without. In: S. Reader (ed.). *The Philosophy of Need*. Cambridge: Cambridge University Press, 25–50.

12 Basic income and the freedom to lead a good life

Philippe Van Parijs & Yannick Vanderborght

How can poverty and unemployment best be addressed?[1] The 20th century's received wisdom was clear: through growth. The growth of production will generate jobs and thereby provide directly a decent income to the bulk of the population. It will provide indirectly an income to the others through social insurance benefits to which these are entitled thanks to their past employment. The strong positive correlation between poverty and unemployment and the strong negative correlation between unemployment and growth were sufficient to make this strategy self-evident to many.

However three facts have been shattering this confidence. Firstly, despite GDP per capita having doubled or trebled since the golden sixties, we are now struggling in many countries with greater joblessness and job insecurity than then. Might it only be the shortsighted who still believe that growth could do the trick? Secondly, given the ecological limits, including those derived from the impact of human activities on the climate worldwide, does it really make sense to try to reduce the current level of unemployment through a growth of output that would outpace the expected increase in productivity? Assuming growth could secure an income through employment to all our contemporaries, would it be a fair thing to do if it means making the economic machine work at such a pace that it destroys the planet for our followers? Thirdly, even among economists who do not question the desirability of growth or its ability to tackle unemployment, some now have doubts about the very possibility of sustained growth. In Europe and North America, they believe that we are doomed to "secular stagnation".

Three models of social protection

Such doubts about the effectiveness, desirability and possibility of growth have fed interest in other ways of securing an adequate income to everyone. For people committed to freedom for all, the proper way of addressing today's unprecedented challenges and of mobilizing today's unprecedented opportunities is to introduce a new model of social protection that is unconditional in a number of ways in which existing minimum income schemes are not. Unlike social insurance schemes, social assistance schemes can be called unconditional in the sense that they are not restricted to people who paid enough social contributions to qualify for social insurance benefits. What we shall call an *unconditional basic income* or, for short, *basic income* is, in addition, unconditional in the sense that (1) it is a strictly *individual* entitlement, rather than one linked to the household situation, (2) it is *universal* rather than subjected to an income or means test, and (3) it is *duty-free* rather than tied to an obligation to work or to be willing to work.[2] In this contribution, we spell out these three distinctive features and explain why they are of key importance for addressing poverty and unemployment in a post-growth era.

When discussing basic income as an immediate policy proposal within the context of a particular country, it may be useful to think of a monthly amount pitched, say, at one fourth of that country's current GDP per capita.[3] This amount could be modulated according to age, with the children receiving less and possibly the elderly receiving more. Such a basic income is of course not meant as a cash substitute for the public funding of quality education and quality health care. Nor must it be conceived as a substitute for all existing social transfers. It provides a full substitute only in the case of individuals receiving benefits lower than the basic income and a partial substitute in the case of individuals receiving more. In the latter case, it constitutes an unconditional floor that must be topped up by conditional supplements. These supplements can be earnings-related social insurance benefits but also can be public assistance benefits to people in specific circumstances, with the existing conditionalities maintained and the post-tax levels adjusted downward so as to maintain the total incomes of the beneficiaries undiminished.

There is a profound difference between social assistance and basic income. Both can be viewed as ways of addressing income poverty, but only the latter can claim to get to the root of the new challenges we face. It does not operate at the margin of society but affects power relations at its very core. It is not just there to soothe misery but to liberate us all. It is not a way of making life on earth tolerable for the destitute. It is a key ingredient of a society and a world in which each human being is given the real freedom to pursue, as much as is sustainable, the realisation of her or his conception of the good life. To see this, let us consider one by one the three unconditionalities that distinguish basic income from social assistance.

An individual income

Firstly, a basic income is unconditional in the sense that it is strictly individual. "Strictly individual" refers to both of two logically independent features: paid to each individual and at a level independent of that individual's household situation. Let us consider each in turn.

A basic income is not paid to one person, the "head of the household", on behalf of all the latter's members. It is given individually to each adult member of the household. In the case of minors, it will need to be given to one of these adult members. Essential is that each of these adults has an individual entitlement. Such direct payments to each individual make a big difference. For a woman with low or no earnings, control over the household's expenditures will tend to be greater, and exit options will tend to be less forbidding if she receives a regular income as an individual entitlement for herself (and, possibly, her children) than if her existence and that of her children entails a higher net income for her partner.

A basic income is also strictly individual in a second and more controversial sense. Existing social assistance schemes are household-based in the sense that how much a person is entitled to depends on the composition of the household. Typically, adults are entitled to significantly higher benefits if they live alone than if they live in a household with one or more other adults. The argument is straightforward: when addressing poverty, one needs to pay attention to economies of scale in consumption. Single people need more to be lifted out of poverty, and it makes sense to differentiate entitlement according to household composition.

And yet we should go for a basic income that is strictly individual in this second, logically independent sense too: how much individuals are entitled to should be independent of the size of the household they belong to. Why? For two reasons. Firstly, there used to be a time where marriage and cohabitation could, for most administrative purposes, be regarded as synonymous. Checking whether two people are married is an easy job. Today, unregistered cohabitation tends to become far more frequent than marriage. Given that it is cohabitation, and not marriage, that justifies differentiation, preserving this differentiation now requires more invasive ways of checking the satisfaction of the relevant criterion. The more general the trend towards informality and volatility in the formation, decomposition and recomposition of households, the more authorities are stuck in a dilemma between arbitrariness and unfairness on one side and intrusiveness and high monitoring costs on the other.

Secondly, differentiation according to household composition amounts to discouraging people from living together. Paradoxically, the strictly individual character of a tax or benefit scheme makes it community-friendly. A household-based scheme amounts to creating a loneliness trap: people who decide to live together are penalised through a reduction in benefits. As a result, the mutual support and sharing of information and networks stemming from co-habitation is weakened, scarce material resources are being wasted, and the number of housing units for a given population increases. The sustainable pursuit of freedom for all in a post-growth era demands that co-habitation should be encouraged, not penalised.

A basic income is unconditional in two further senses. It is unconditional in the sense of being *universal*, not subjected to a means test: the rich are entitled to it just as much as the poor. And it is unconditional in the sense of being *obligation-free*, of not being subjected to a (willingness to) work test: the voluntarily unemployed are entitled to it just as much as the employed and the involuntarily unemployed. The combination of these two unconditionalities is absolutely crucial. The former frees people from the unemployment trap, the latter from the employment trap. The former facilitates saying yes to a job offer, while the latter facilitates facilitates saying no. The former creates possibilities, while the latter lifts obligations and thereby enhances those possibilities. It is the joint operation of these two features that turns basic income into a paramount instrument of freedom. Let us now consider them each in turn.

A universal income

Social assistance schemes all involve some kind of means test. The benefit received typically amounts to the difference between the household's total income from other sources and the stipulated minimum income for that particular category of household. Consequently, its level is at its highest when income from other sources is zero, and it falls as income from other sources increases. Any such scheme needs to operate *ex post*, i.e. on the basis of some prior assessment, reliable or not, of the beneficiaries' material resources.

A basic income, by contrast, operates *ex ante*, with no means test involved. It is paid at the same level to rich and poor alike, regardless of the income they derive from other sources. The benefit is paid in full to those whose income exceeds the minimum that a basic income scheme guarantees to all, as well as to those whose income falls short of it. Consequently, if it is funded through the taxation of income or consumption within the population concerned rather than from an outside source, it is clear that high earners and big spenders will fund their own benefit (and more). The key difference between a basic income and an income-tested scheme is therefore not that a basic income would make everyone richer, and even less that it is better for the rich. Paradoxically, the key difference is instead that it is better for the poor.

How can one make sense of this counter-intuitive claim? If the aim is the eradication of poverty, the universal character of basic income, added to its individual nature, easily looks like a pathetic waste of resources. A social assistance scheme that strictly targets the poorest by making up the difference between their income and the poverty line looks hugely superior to a basic income. Yet, a basic income is to be preferred, for two distinct reasons.

The first reason has to do with universality as such. Many studies comparing how effectively universal and targeted benefits schemes reach the poorest members of society point to the superiority, in this respect, of universal systems. In order to access benefits targeted at the poor, it is necessary to take steps that many eligible people run the risk of not taking or not completing, whether out of ignorance, shyness or shame. With means-tested schemes, the awareness campaign required to achieve the same take-up rate among net beneficiaries as with the corresponding universal scheme involves a considerable cost. Further, even with a scheme that uses nothing but low income as the relevant criterion, decisions to include or exclude leave a lot of room for arbitrariness and clientelism. With a basic income scheme, the automatic payment of benefits does not require any particular administrative steps. Society is no longer visibly divided between the needy and the others, and there is nothing humiliating about receiving a basic income granted to all. This does not only matter in itself for the dignity of the people involved. It also enhances effectiveness in terms of poverty alleviation. Thus, by avoiding complication and stigmatisation, a universal scheme can achieve a high rate of take up at a low information cost.

Universality as such also matters to the attempt to tackle unemployment. For the uncertainty people face once they are no longer entitled to benefits contributes to trapping the beneficiaries of social assistance. Access of the most disadvantaged to paid employment is made difficult by the very nature of many of the jobs they would qualify for: precarious contracts, unscrupulous employers, and unpredictable earnings. It can be risky for them to give up means-tested transfers, as they are often unsure about how much they will earn when they start working, or about how quickly they may lose their job and have to face complex administrative procedures in order to reestablish their entitlement to a benefit. Even when the probability of this happening is low, the prospect of triggering off a spiral of debt is likely to be perceived as a threat by people who are ill-equipped to know, understand, and *a fortiori* appeal to rules that can often be changing and opaque. By contrast, they can take a job or create their own job with less fear when they can be sure that their universal basic income will keep flowing no matter what.

This advantage of universality as regards access to employment is strongly reinforced by the effect of a second feature closely associated with it, but logically distinct: the fact that all earnings, however small, will increase people's net income. Why does this feature matter? In their attempt to be as efficient as possible, typical social assistance schemes use the available funds to make up the difference between the poor households' incomes from other sources and the level of income which the scheme aims to guarantee to all households of a particular type. This entails clawing back one unit of benefit for each unit earned by the poor through their own efforts. In other words, the concern not to waste any money on the non-poor amounts to implicitly imposing an effective marginal tax rate of 100 percent on any income they may get. This situation is commonly called a poverty trap or an unemployment trap: the earnings people receive for a low paid job are offset by the corresponding reduction or suppression of the means-tested benefit. A basic income, being universal, creates no such trap. It is not withdrawn or reduced but kept in full when people earn extra income. Whereas a conditional minimum income scheme provides a safety net in which people get trapped, a basic income provides a floor on which they can stand.

It is true, indeed self-evident, that this is achieved at a far higher level of public expenditure. Paying a given sum of money to all costs far more money than paying it only to the poor. But there is cost and cost. Much of the cost, in this case, consist in taking money with one hand and giving it back with the other hand to the same households. And the rest simply represents a redistribution of private spending between different categories of the population. This is quite different from a budgetary cost that involves the use of real resources, such as building infrastructure or employing civil servants, and thereby implies *ipso facto* an opportunity cost: there are other things that could have been done with the material and human resources on which public money is being spent. Abstracting from possible administrative gains and losses and from positive or negative behavioural responses, the shift from a means-tested to a universal scheme does not make the population as a whole either richer or poorer. It is, in this sense, costless.

An obligation-free income

A basic income is a cash income that is individual and universal. It further differs from social assistance (and social insurance) schemes in having no strings attached to it, in requiring no obligation for its beneficiaries to work or be available on the labor market, or, to use a more compact phrase, in being *obligation-free*. In social assistance and social insurance schemes, this duty typically entails denying the right to the benefit to those giving up a job at their own initiative, to those unable to prove that they are actively looking for a job, and to those not prepared to accept a job or other form of "integration" deemed suitable by the public assistance office. Basic income, by contrast, is paid without any such conditions. Homemakers, students and tramps are entitled to it no less than waged workers or the self-employed, those who decided to quit no less than those who were sacked. No one needs to check whether its beneficiaries are genuine job seekers or mere shirkers.

Thus, while universality is addressing the unemployment trap, obligation-freeness is addressing the employment trap. Without universality, obligation-freeness could easily prove a recipe for exclusion: the obligation-free mean-tested benefit would just be hush money for those hopelessly stuck in the unemployment trap. But without obligation-freeness, universality could prove a recipe for exploitation: work-conditional universal benefits would just be subsidies to employers. The latter could get away with paying lower wages to workers obliged to accept the job and to stick to it if they wanted to retain their benefit. By contrast, the universality of basic income admittedly constitutes a potential subsidy for jobs that are poorly productive (in an immediate sense), but its obligation-freeness prevents it from subsidizing those that are lousy or degrading. The conjunction of these two unconditionalities enables us to see why there is some truth to both the claim that a basic income would depress wages and to the opposite claim that it would boost them.

Universality facilitates saying *yes* to jobs that pay little, even so little or so unreliably that they do not yet exist. Average earnings, for this reason, may diminish. However, because of the benefit being obligation-free, the yes will only be forthcoming if the job is attractive enough in itself or through the useful training, gratifying contacts or promotion prospects it provides, irrespective of how little it is paid. For a duty-free income facilitates saying no to jobs that both pay little and are unattractive in themselves. Obviously, the higher the basic income, the greater this facilitation. But because the basic income is universal and can therefore be combined with earnings from attractive part-time or intermittent work, it can be much lower than what suffices in the long term for a decent life and can still produce this effect. If as a result of this enhanced freedom to say no lousy jobs fail to attract or retain enough incumbents, employers may choose to replace them by machines. If this is impossible or too expensive, the job will need to be made more attractive. And if this too proves impossible or too expensive, pay for these jobs will need to go up. Yes, those lousy, poorly paid jobs which you would not dream of doing will need to be paid better, perhaps even better than yours and ours. And this is good. Average earnings, therefore, may well go up.

The net effect of these opposing forces on the average level of labor compensation or on the overall employment rate cannot be predicted a priori. What it turns out to be will be affected by the balance of market forces but also by social norms and by such institutional factors as the regulation of part-time work and self-employment or the presence and scope of minimum wage arrangements. One thing is certain, however: the combination of the two unconditionalities gives more options and therefore greater bargaining power to those with least of it. A basic income will therefore empower those with most constraints, enable them to be choosier among possible occupations, taking full account of what they like to do and what they need to learn, who they get on with and where they wish to live. Both through existing jobs being improved and through non-existing jobs becoming viable, this is why the quality of the working part of people's lives can be expected to get a big boost, especially but not only for the most vulnerable among them.

A sane economy: beyond the quest for growth

Within the context of the present volume, it is important to stress that this improvement in the accessibility of a good life for many people goes hand in hand with a soft and efficient brake on growth that does not generate unemployment. For the conjunction of the same two unconditionalities – universality and duty-freeness – makes it also easier for anyone to work part time or to interrupt work altogether in order to acquire further skills, to look for a more suitable job, to engage in voluntary activities or simply to breathe when it is high time to do so. This reduces the risk of ending up with a labor force that is irreparably burned out or obsolete well before retirement age. Coupled with a redirection of the educational system towards lifelong learning, such a more flexible and relaxed labor market should be far better suited to the development of 21st-century human capital than one that involves a rigid division between young students and mature workers.

This positive impact concerns not only the human capital of the present working population, but also that of their children. Like other ways of making family income more secure, basic income can be expected to have a beneficial effect on children's health and education. By addressing the unemployment trap, it reduces the number of children who will end up on the dole as a result of their growing up in households without anyone employed. At the same time, by facilitating chosen part-time work and promoting a smoother conciliation of work and family life, it enables parents to devote more attention to their children when this is most needed.

The efficient working of our economy does not require maximizing the labor supply in shortsighted fashion. To make our economy more productive (sensibly interpreted) in sustainable fashion, one should not obsessively activate people and lock them in jobs they hate doing and from which they learn nothing. As the poet Kahlil Gibran (1923) put it, "if you cannot work with love but only with distaste, it is better that you should leave your work [. . .]. For if you bake bread with indifference, you bake a bitter bread that feeds but half man's hunger". Thus, it is not only fair but also clever to give all, not just the better endowed, greater freedom to move easily between paid work, education, caring and volunteering. A basic income scheme can therefore be viewed as desacralizing paid work: it is there to facilitate the search by each of us for something we like to do and do well, whether or not in the form of paid employment.

Involuntary unemployment is a major challenge. But activation and growth, routinely offered as self-evident remedies, are both unrealistic and undesirable. An unconditional basic income offers a way of addressing this challenge without relying on an insane rush for keeping pace with labor-saving technical change through the sustained growth of production and consumption. The time will come, Keynes (1930, 325, 328) famously wrote, when growth will no longer be the appropriate response, when "our discovery of means of economizing the use of labour" will be "outrunning the pace at which we can find new uses for labour". And then "we shall endeavour to spread the bread thin on the butter – to make what work there is still to be done to be as widely shared as possible".

A basic income is a smooth and smart way of moving in this direction. It does not impose a maximum limit on everyone's working time but it makes it easier for people to reduce their working time, both because it reduces what they lose if they do and because it gives them a firm income floor on which they can stand in all circumstances. It thereby helps attack the root cause of the trouble both for those who get sick by working too much and for those who get sick because they cannot find a job. It does not amount to giving up the objective of full employment sensibly interpreted. For full employment can mean two things: lifelong full-time paid work for the entire able-bodied part of the population of working age, and the real possibility of getting meaningful paid work for all those who want it. As an objective, the basic income strategy rejects the former while embracing the latter.

With a basic income, this objective is being pursued both by making it easier for people to choose to perform less paid work at any given point in their lives and by subsidizing paid work with low immediate productivity. At the expense of overall material consumption? In developed countries, certainly. And deliberately so. For our economy not only needs to be efficient. It must also be sane. And sanity requires us to find a way of organizing our economy that not only enables all members of the present generation to lead a good life but also that preserves this possibility for the generations to come. An unconditional basic income is far from being sufficient for either but it is a precondition for both.[4]

Notes

1 This contribution is largely based on part of chapter 1 of Van Parijs/Vanderborght (2017), A completely rewritten and greatly expanded and updated English version of Vanderborght/Van Parijs (2005).
2 This is the definition adopted by the Basic Income Earth Network, founded in 1986 as a European network and turned worldwide in 2004 (www.basicincome.org). Its affiliates now include over twenty-five national networks and a new EU-level network created in the aftermath of the European Citizens Initiative on basic income (http://basicincome-europe.org/ubie).
3 In 2014, this would mean about €700 per month for Germany, or about $1,100 per month for the United States.
4 From the beginning of the European discussion on basic income, the connection with the limits to growth was explicit. See for example Lionel Stoleru (1974, 308) in France: "By asking ourselves how to achieve such moderation [the moderation of growth in rich countries required by the solution of some of the contradictions of capitalism], we realized that this problem was fundamentally the same as the problem of putting into place a basic guarantee for every citizen".; Stephen Cook (1979, 6) in the United Kingdom:

"We need to encourage such responsible exploration of voluntary low-consumption life styles if we are to be able to adapt successfully to likely changes in world society, as the shortage of energy and other resources increasingly makes itself felt and as experience of 'affluence' leads to greater emphasis on personal fulfillment rather than material consumption".; and Wim Albeda (1984, 11) in the Netherlands: "From this perspective [of those who see permanent growth as a danger for our planet], a guaranteed annual income, which would weaken the incentive to work, would be welcome up to a point".

References

Albeda, W. (1984). *De Crisis van de Werkloosheid en de Verzorgingsstaat: Analyse en perspectief.* Kampen, NL: Kok.
Cook, S.L. (1979). *Can a Social Wage Solve Unemployment?* Working Paper 165. Birmingham: University of Aston Management Centre.
Gibran, K. (1923). *The Prophet.* New York: Knopf.
Keynes, J.M. (1930). Economic Possibilities for Our Grandchildren. In: *Essays in Persuasion: The Collected Writings* IX. The Royal Economic Society 1972, 321–332.
Stoleru, L. (1974). *Vaincre la Pauvreté dans les pays riches.* Paris: Flammarion.
Van Parijs, Ph./Y. Vanderborght. (2017). *Basic Income: A Radical Proposal for a Free Society and a Sane Economy.* Cambridge, MA: Harvard University Press.
Vanderborght, Y./Ph. Van Parijs. (2005 [2006]). *L'Allocation universelle.* Paris: La Découverte. Translated as *Ein Grundeinkommen für alle?* Frankfurt am Main: Campus; *La renta básica,* Barcelona: Paidos; *Il reddito minimo universale.* Milan: Bocconi; *Renda Básica de Cidadania,* Rio de Janeiro: Civilização Brazileira.

Part IV

Subjects beyond growth

Changing practices

13 Happiness, the common good, and volunteer work

Bettina Hollstein

In modern societies, happiness and the common good seem to be core concepts that influence our normative landscapes, our political discourses and our economic, legal and social institutions. On the one hand happiness is a key concept of liberal economic theories and serves as a justification for economic growth (Hollstein 2010). On the other hand economic growth often does *not* achieve happiness, but unhappiness – due to ecological crises, ever-expanding lifestyles without meaning, wasteful, and destructive technologies, and stress, burnout and depression (Scitovsky 1976; Lane 2001). Therefore, we need to develop alternative concepts of the good – maybe oriented towards concepts of the common good focussing on resonance (Rosa 2016), harmony with friends, family and nature; however, we must remain aware of the fact that these concepts of the common good are also susceptible to paternalism, particularism, esotericism and anti-emancipating strategies. The common good, including the named problems connected to it, stands at the heart of volunteer work, which – in addition to participating in the creation of the common good – also gives rise to an increased sense of civility and concern of others, as well as community bonds (Hollstein 2015).

In my contribution, I will concentrate on the experiences and practices of acting volunteers from a pragmatist perspective.[1] Samples collecting statements of volunteers show that volunteers very often state that volunteering makes them happy. At the same time the same persons see volunteering as something crucial for the public wealth of a community.[2] While in economic theory the search for happiness is the way to realise the common good (reduced to economic wealth) *behind the back* of the economic subjects, these concepts are not mutually exclusive ones in the mind of volunteers. They are not only motivated by the search for happiness but also by the aim to realise the common good in very different forms.

While an overview of the varying conceptualisations of happiness would be helpful to show that they can differ extremely (Thomä/Henning/Mitscherlich-Schönherr 2011), I will only point out the concept of happiness underlying mainstream economic theory here and contrast it with a notion of happiness focussing on meaningful activities as developed by Susan Wolf (1998). Concerning the common good – a concept that also changed over time – I will concentrate on communitarian arguments. I want to show that, by using a pragmatist action theoretical framework, happiness (in the sense of meaningful activities of the individual) and the common good are not only compatible, but are even dependent on each other.

Using the pragmatist approach, I methodologically focus on actions in specific (problematic) situations of volunteering. As Daniela Neumann points out, volunteering has become a core issue in societal and political discourse in Germany since the 1980s and has led to the emergence of the new policy field of volunteering policy (Neumann 2016). When existing routines are disturbed, the subjects have to reassess their aspirations for happiness along with their conceptions of the good and try to find the appropriate balance for acting in specific problematic situations in a creative way. By using the example of voluntary action I want to show how these theoretical considerations apply in practice and what conclusions we might draw for societal institutions that aim to improve happiness and the common good through volunteer work.

Concepts of happiness

In 2013, there was a popular song about happiness ("Happy", by Pharell Williams).

What did millions of people who heard this song learn? First, that "happiness is the truth", second that it is not self-evident what happiness represents for oneself (everyone needs to find out for themselves "what happiness is to you"), and finally that happiness might mean doing "what you wanna do".[3] Since the ambiguity of happiness is clearly revealed in these three aspects, the aforementioned insights made the people who sang this song true philosophers. But let us analyse this step by step.

When I ask my children what happiness is for them, then the most obvious meaning seems to be "doing what you want", namely playing computer games, watching TV, eating ice cream and so on. This explanation refers to our desires, and it seems clear that realising one's wishes must lead to happiness. That is also the main assumption behind economic theory: A *homo oeconomicus* is somebody maximizing his pleasure by realising his wishes. Happiness in society then is conceptualised as the maximisation of fulfilled desires of the greatest number of persons.[4] In modern societies consumption of goods and services is the predominant form of realising one's desires, because – given the right amount of money – we can buy almost everything we want, even tickets for concerts, dance lessons, services of sex workers and so on. In fact, happiness research reveals that not being able to consume or being poor is a major obstacle to happiness (Frey/ Stutzer 2002). Hence, having the choice to consume, consuming and realising wishes should be parts of the concept of happiness.[5] In the theory of resonance, developed by Hartmut Rosa, an important distinction is made in relation to consumption. The act of buying goods does not lead to resonance per se, but only the actions that become possible with these goods (Rosa 2016, 429f. and Rosa 2011). In this point this concept is very similar to Susan Wolf's model.

However, most of us would share the intuition that consuming is not really related to *true* happiness, truth being another aspect connected to happiness that is mentioned in the song. Since Plato, truth seems to be related to transcendental issues like the sacred, beauty or the good life. Yet, these things occupy a very different level then our wishes and consumer choices. To say, "I prefer black tea to herbal tea" may be a correct statement, but it does not relate to what in *truth* is really important for happiness. Asked in this way people might answer that what is truly important for happiness are good relationships with friends, family, and our partners, health, sane children, a fulfilling workplace, a good relationship with nature, etc. According to Martha Nussbaum or Amartya Sen these things can be called objective goods as outlined in their lists of capabilities necessary for a truly good life (Nussbaum 2001; Sen 1984; 1985). These lists can only provide a basis for determining the necessary conditions for a good life (Fenner 2007, 177). Between this 'objective' idea of goods and the 'subjective' concepts of desires we can locate the concept of 'informed desires'. This signifies that in the light of our true values, namely the things we truly appreciate in life (like peace, love, justice), we can evaluate our desires (Fenner 2007, 67 ff.; 123ff.). Along with Harry Frankfurt, Charles Taylor or Hans Joas, we can call these values second-order volitions, conception of the good or values, and they can help us evaluate our first order wishes or preferences (Joas 2000). "A value is not just a preference but is a preference which is felt and/or considered to be justified" (Kluckhohn 1962, 398). The wish to buy a sports car might be mitigated by the value of sustainable action. Happiness in this case would mean to live according to one's values and according to the norms we derive from these values. Empirical happiness research shows consistently that above a certain income level increased income and, thus, the opportunity to realise additional consumptive desires does not increase happiness (Scitovsky 1976; Easterlin 2004). Consumption and the possibility of living in a decent way in a given society are therefore important aspects of happiness (Fenner 2007, 105) but not by themselves sufficient to be truly happy. Additionally, we want to live according to our conceptions of the good and have the possibility to truly realise these values in our actions.

Our values can be universalistic (or: *claim* universal validity) in the sense that we can assert that they are shared by everyone and that the rights, which spring from them, should be granted to everybody. If, for example, I value a fulfilling workplace, the difference between a universalistic value and one that is not universalistic would be that in the first case I would claim that everybody should have a fulfilling workplace, while in the other I would be happy if I, and only I (as well as my friends and relatives), have a fulfilling workplace.

Finally, there is a third aspect mentioned in the song, namely that we often do not know what happiness is.[6] Consuming and living according to values often seem incompatible (I value vegetarianism but I wish to eat a Thuringian sausage.). We often do not act as rational as we would if we knew what happiness meant to us. Most of the time we act according to embodied routines and do not rank our wishes or preferences in a systematic way guided by values. Therefore, we must pay attention to our actions, practices, and bodily routines and not only to wishes and values to understand what makes us happy. This means that we have to connect happiness with our lived experiences in some way (Sumner 1996, 112).

The common good

In this book we are looking for new concepts of the good life. The notion of happiness as developed so far is such a concept because it includes wishes *and* values when we pay attention to embodiment and emotions. But we are particularly keen on finding concepts for a good life *beyond growth*. This aspect leads us away from the merely individualistic concepts of happiness to common issues such as growth, wealth and the common good. On the one hand, the common good includes aspects of material wealth allowing for a basic subsistence level for everybody, and on the other hand it also refers to the mutually respectful behaviour of citizens, their responsibility towards each other and their duty to take into account the concerns of others. Therefore, it involves also creating community bonds and solidarity.[7]

While the concept of happiness usually starts with individuals,[8] the concept of the common good often takes the community as its starting point (Bellah et al. 1985). While economists argue that the pursuit of individual happiness will indirectly lead to the common good (through the invisible hand of the market as first mentioned by Adam Smith), communitarians would prefer to address the common good directly without taking a detour by way of the individual preferences. This does not mean that one has to start with a totalitarian concept of one good for all. Instead it means acknowledging that all people are embedded in communities and depend on them. Thus, democratic deliberation about how we want to live together is essential for creating a good life for all (Fenner 2007, 152ff.). This impetus for democratic deliberation also lies at the core of well-known concepts for deliberation and discourse (Dewey, Habermas) but is also addressed by new movements, such as the 'economy of the common good' developed by Christian Felber (2015).[9]

Since growth is not just a problem on the individual but on the global level, the term 'common good' – much like the notion of happiness – potentially represents an important element of a model for the good life beyond growth. Economists would even say that happiness (in the narrower sense of maximizing utility) and the common good (in the sense of the wealth of nations) are closely connected. By maximizing our utility (or systems of preferences) we create wealth through the capitalistic market mechanisms. The pursuit of individual happiness is therefore a key concept of liberal economic theories and serves as a justification for economic growth.

Hence, improving individual happiness by creating more possibilities for consumption should automatically lead to a better situation for society. Unfortunately, in this economic conception happiness and common good are interpreted in a much too narrow way, and even the mechanisms leading to more wealth[10] are contested. Main critiques of this model are that the economic concept does not pay attention to values, civility, community bonds or bodily experiences. Above all, economic growth seems to eradicate the foundations of societies by destroying our natural environment and, therefore, the basis for human life. So, realising the common good through happiness in the sense of maximizing utility seems to be problematic at best. We need more precise conceptions what the common good could be. We have to define our conceptions in a more normative way by including questions like this: How do we want to live together? What could be a shared conception of the good life and the common good?

Sustainability

Theories of sustainability normatively assume that a universalistic conception of the good life should be valuable to all persons and should be granted to all human beings. It should care about the natural sources of life in a global way, including future generations. Sustainability, intending to combine global justice with intergenerational justice, seems to be such a value, and could therefore be helpful in order to realise a good life in a universalistic perspective (Ekardt 2010). It is a second-order volition that helps us to evaluate our first-order wishes. In this case, universality not only implies global justice for all our contemporaries, but also allows us to project this ideal into the past and the future by locating it on a wider temporal plane. The value of preserving natural resources can be supported by emotional experiences with nature, like a walk along the seaside or in a forest etc.[11] Of course, it needs space and time to have the possibility to experience nature. From a social perspective, sustainability also represents a specific interpretation of the common good for the citizens of the planet. We can derive societal norms from it and institutionalise these norms through juridical and organisational frameworks. We can, but we don't.

At this point practices come into play. In order to live in a sustainable way we often hear that we must change our consumption patterns – our wishes are subject to critique when they are not sustainable. For example: I should buy a car powered by electric energy instead of one powered by fuel. I should eat more vegetables and less meat etc. Unfortunately, we often observe that these sorts of discourses and recommendations based on values do not change much of our daily routines. Even if we embrace the universalistic value of sustainability on a normative level, this does not guarantee that we act in this way. In fact, empirical surveys show that people with a high environmental consciousness are not the people acting in the most sustainable way. In fact, lower income levels are a much more reliable indicator of sustainable behaviour than environmental consciousness (Baumgartner 2004; Neugebauer 2004). So what can we do?

Pragmatist theory of action

At this point I want to introduce the pragmatist theory of action. My intention is to show that the integration of some elements of neo-pragmatist action theory as developed by Hans Joas (1996) on the basis of the work of George Herbert Mead (1934) and John Dewey (1922) is a fruitful way to conceptualise an economic theory that is able to integrate both values and wishes, both individual and societal perspectives, and cognitive and embodied aspects of action. It does so by paying attention to the following issues:

- The embeddedness of human thinking in *human practices* means that we are constantly struggling with our natural and social environment. Ends are never fixed independently from action, but are developing and changing in a creative process while we are acting.

- The human subject is not an abstract thing, but a concrete, *embodied person* acting in the world.[12] This means that the abstract *homo oeconomicus* is eschewed in favour of individuals with a concrete corporeality living in concrete social structures and a specific lifeworld.
- Norms and ethical practices are not purely subjective or culturally relative. We cannot completely define and give reasons for our values. However, we can discuss them in a reasonable way with others because every action has an essentially *social character* opening up the possibility for mutual understanding.

Pragmatism presupposes that we normally act according to routines. We use the car today, like every morning; we eat at the university restaurant, like every day, and so on. It is only when this routine is disturbed and broken that we are obliged to reflect on it, to balance our wishes and our deeper aspirations and values. It is only then that we create a new way of acting which can become a new routine. My car is broken and I have to decide whether I buy a new one. Does my daughter insist on trying an electric car? Do my colleagues laugh at people coming to work by train? Are there cheap possibilities for using car sharing models or public transport? Do I feel uncomfortable in public transport? How much money can I spend? Do I consider myself a member of the world population? Do I feel solidarity with people far away or with future generations?

In such a situation we not only evaluate the pros and cons in an economic way but we also include more implicit normative aspects. When we decide in one way or the other and act accordingly, we may experience that this was not the right solution and we readjust our decision in order to find a new solution. When we feel comfortable with our decision, we install new routines and these experiences may enforce our values.

Volunteering

Let us now consider the field of voluntary action in order to provide some evidence of what this conceptualisation may imply for our discussion of the good life beyond growth. I define volunteering in the following way: volunteer works are (1) actions, (2) voluntary and not profit-oriented, (3) oriented toward the common good, (4) public and (5) generally practiced conjointly.[13] The third point is very important for my definition since the orientation towards the common good means an orientation towards objectively worthwhile actions accepted by an informed society longing for universalistic values. Non-profit acts based on particularistic or exclusive goals, which are not valued by society, yet are executed by organisations, are not part of this definition. This excludes for example the activities of neo-Nazi sports clubs.

Volunteers regularly state that voluntary action makes them happy because they are having fun; they feel important acting together with others; they participate in achieving important social goals, and they realise their values or deep intuitions of the good. It is clear that the narrow definition of happiness based on consumption[14] employed by economists does not fit here.[15]

Volunteers do rarely differentiate between wishes and values: in their voluntary action these aspects are confounded. In many cases, values are not the starting point for voluntary action. Instead, social contacts, a specific situation of need or spontaneous reactions to a perceived misery provides the motivation. While acting and expressing themselves in voluntary action, volunteers come to reflect on the mission of the organisation they work for, on the underlying values, and conceptions of the good. They have experiences of doing valuable things that they can be proud of. Volunteer work is therefore a field of action, in which individual wishes and social values are mostly in accordance.

Volunteers also can make the experience that voluntary action is recognised by society. The recognition and esteem given to voluntary action by others is an experience volunteers appreciate. However, besides this individual effect, public recognition of specific voluntary action articulates common societal convictions. It sheds light on the kind of society we want to live in. In this perspective, public recognition of volunteering is part of a society-wide reflection process.

Service learning on sustainability

Now let us look at a specific example: Each semester students of the University of Erfurt take part in a self-organised service-learning seminar[16] on sustainability. In this seminar they first get theoretical information about sustainability concepts, education for sustainable development and project work in groups. Then they start developing and performing micro projects in groups of about three to seven students, in collaboration with a cooperating partner from civil society, administration or business. These projects tend to contribute to the common good on the local level and address sustainability goals. At the end of the semester, the students have to reflect and evaluate their experiences in a report (Hollstein/ Tänzer/Thumfart 2013). Through this process, reflections on, and interpretation of, their own actions in the light of the values of sustainability are prompted and encouraged.

In these reports students often state that on the one hand designing and executing their project was fun, while on the other hand it helped to improve sustainability in the local context of Erfurt in a specific way. Most students argue that at the beginning of the seminar they came because other students had recommended it. Most of them did not know much about the subject matter beforehand. During the seminar they learned facts about sustainability but – more interestingly – we can read in their reports that they experienced their own self-efficacy through the projects by acquiring new skills of critical judgment, developing a capacity to cooperate, improving interpersonal and communicative skills and reflecting on their personal relationship to the value sustainability (Hollstein/Tänzer/Thumfart 2013, 100ff.).

In terms of pragmatist action theory the seminar interrupts the routine of "normal" seminars. The routinised attitude of students consuming theoretical facts and reproducing this information in a final examination is not applicable for this seminar. Rather, students had to change their regular habits and creatively develop a new way of acting. Since they do not only learn things in a theoretical way but also have to put it into practice, this provides *embodied* experiences. The interactions with the cooperation partner, the other students in the project, as well as the interactions with the wider public this project is aimed at are not only theoretical or "virtual", but they constitute real-life experiences. Such bodily experiences provoke intense emotions.

Yet the projects do not only affect the students but also affect the routines of the cooperation partners. Some of them explicitly want to invent and implement new procedures in their field in a more sustainable way. For example, the 'fox farm' – an institution for environmental education in a non-scholarly context[17] – asked for concepts for sustainable education addressing children from 6 to 10 years old. One group of students developed a forest-animal-day with puppets of four forest animals, thereby addressing sustainable education in a playful way. This concept was tested and evaluated with a group of children in collaboration with the professionals from the 'fox farm'. In the future this concept of a forest-animal-day developed by the students and the materials supplied by them (a quiz, memory games, walks in the forest, stories, costumes etc.), will be used by the 'fox farm' in sustainable education projects with children. Therefore, while this project changed the students' views on forests as an important resource for animals and humans, it also changed the routines of their partners and hopefully those of the children participating. Children learned a lot by playing and came to associate these experiences with positive emotions because they had fun with the 'forest animals' and with each other. Looking at bodily experiences and emotions helps to understand why and how cognitive knowledge guides action – and where it does not.

In sum, voluntary action offers an experimental space to enact values and conceptions of the good. It can be understood as a space where we can experience a meaningful life. According to Susan Wolf the projects and activities of agents ultimately make their life meaningful. However, this happens only when the projects and activities satisfy three conditions, two on the subjective side and one on the objective side. First, on the subjective side, one must be at least somewhat successful in carrying them out. This does not mean that one must fully complete one's projects and excel at the activities but, *ceteris paribus*, it implies that the more successful an individual is at completing his or her projects, the more he can contribute to the meaningfulness of his own life. Secondly, the projects and activities must be personally attractive to the individuals involved in them. People must experience subjective attraction towards the relevant projects and activities, and be gripped and excited by them. This implies that one must be passionate about the relevant projects and activities. When one is successfully engaged in projects and activities, one must experience some positive sensations – fulfilment, satisfaction, feeling good and happy and the like. Volunteer work in sustainability projects as experienced by the students often satisfies these subjective conditions: the students are successful with their projects most of the time; they have developed these schemes themselves, they are attractive to them and they feel satisfied when they realise them.

Third, on the objective side, one's projects and activities must be objectively worthwhile. For Susan Wolf objective values are not necessarily universalistic. When a member of a Mafia-clan gets recognition by his fellows for a murder, this activity may be objectively worthwhile for this particular group. However, in my view, such a particularistic value cannot be called 'objective'; it lacks the universality discussed above. Volunteering as I defined it relates to the common good in an objective *and* universalistic way – it receives recognition from all stakeholders and possibly by everybody. In the case of our students they gain recognition from the external cooperating partners who value their projects, from the people they encounter while engaged in the projects (like the children – the positive reactions of children are often quoted as highly motivating) and from the lecturer (myself) when I evaluate the final report along objective criteria communicated at the beginning of the seminar.

Conclusion

So, what did we learn from this? Happiness and the common good are not contradictory concepts but they are also not as straightforwardly related, as economists may believe. We can neither realise the common good by pursuing first-order wishes only – say by consuming this or that –, nor can a mere cognitive appreciation of the common good motivate us to act accordingly. By using a pragmatist framework we can integrate happiness and the common good as aspects shaping our actions in specific ways. Using the example of volunteering we can show that subjectively attractive and objectively worthwhile activities are central for a meaningful or a good life. Societies that aim to organise themselves in order to give people the opportunity to live a good and meaningful life should therefore create spaces where we can engage in such activities and make such experiences.

In another context some colleagues developed with me a draft for a framework providing time and space for experiences in sustainability. Especially local institutions[18] have the facility to offer up spaces for volunteering experiences, be it in community centres, public parks, communal rooms for associations, schools, universities, etc. (Baumgärtner et al. 2013, 192ff.). In the communal sphere these spaces are hybrid spaces because they are open to the general *public* and can be used for *private* joint activities of associations of the third sector. For example: last year residents of my neighbourhood organised a welcome picnic for refugees in the little public park near to the communal refugee homes. Such voluntary activities of appropriating the public space should be supported in order to enhance residents' resonance with the place they live in. These spaces are not restricted to the academic or civil sector but can also be created in businesses, administrations or within private spaces as families and friendship relations. Further research should be conducted to clarify the concrete requirements that have to be institutionalised in order to enhance *society* by providing spaces that fulfil good conditions for participatory and inclusive structures within volunteering organisations. However, even beyond the sphere of volunteering the pursuit of happiness through meaningful activities as described above might help us take a step toward a good life beyond growth.

Notes

1 I use the pragmatist approach as developed by Joas (1996).
2 I rely on the most complete sample for Germany, the 'Freiwilligensurvey' (Bundesministerium 2010, 2016).

3 See the lyrics at www.songtexte.com/songtext/pharrell-williams/happy-635c26fb.html (accessed 3rd August 2016).
4 This is the claim of utilitarian philosophy, as developed for example by Jeremy Bentham (1789).
5 L. W. Sumner for example presents a concept which connects welfare with happiness as life satisfaction (Sumner 1996).
6 As Kant states: "Unfortunately, however, the concept of happiness is so indefinite that, although each person wishes to attain it, he can never give a definite and self-consistent account of what it is that he wishes and wills under the heading of wanting happiness" (Kant 1785, 21).
7 Luigino Bruni shows how contemporary economic theory lost its connection with the terrain of "Civil Happiness" (Bruni 2006), but also that "genuine sociality matters in the economic domain probably more than current economic theory thinks" (Bruni 2006, 123). Relational goods depending on social interaction have a great influence on subjective well-being (Bruni 2006, 124; see Latouche in this volume).
8 One example for such a concept in philosophy is the concept of Sumner (1996).
9 This does not mean that the proposed solution developed by Felber is free of paternalistic or implausible assumptions and ideas, but this is not the place to discuss his concept here.
10 Not only the mechanism, but also the measure of wealth is contested. Main instruments to remedy this measurement problem were since the 1970s social indicators and later the measurement of subjective well-being leading to individualistic concepts (Sumner 1996, 150ff.).
11 Hartmut Rosa describes the possibility for such experiences along the axes of resonance that help us to hear the voice of nature (Rosa 2016, 453ff.).
12 See also Karl Marx: "But the essence of man is no abstraction inherent in each single individual. In reality, it is the ensemble of the social relations" (Marx/Engels 1969 [1888], 6). (I owe this reference to Christoph Henning.)
13 This definition is nearly identical with the definition of the Voluntaries survey of the federal government (Bundesministerium für Familie, Senioren, Frauen und Jugend 2005, 26). For a more extensive discussion of all these aspects related to volunteering see Hollstein (2015, 68ff.).
14 Very broad definitions of utility are not helpful since they tend to be tautological (Hollstein 2015, 68ff.).
15 Meier/Stutzer (2004) find, using the German Socio-Economic Paneel (SOEP) for the period between 1985 and 1999, robust evidence that volunteers are more satisfied with their life than non-volunteers (Bruni 2009, 123).
16 For a more complete description of the concept of service learning within the educational landscape for sustainability see Hollstein/Singer-Brodowski 2015, 152ff.
17 See the webpage of the "friends of the foxfarm" at www.fuchsfarm-erfurt.de (accessed 20th February 2017).
18 The ability to provide spaces for volunteering is not restricted to local organisations, especially when they are integrated into a global structure, but volunteering always takes place in a specific local context. For an example for research concerning organisational features see Feiler (2016).

References

Baumgartner, C. (2004). *Umweltethik – Umwelthandeln: Ein Beitrag zur Lösung des Motivationsproblems*. Paderborn: Mentis.
Baumgärtner, D./B. Hollstein/F. Heydel/J.Schmitt (2013). Mut zur Nachhaltigkeit – Zeit und Raum für Erfahrungen in nachhaltigen und entschleunigten Aktivitäten. In: H. Welzer/K. Wiegandt (eds.). *Wege aus der Wachstumsgesellschaft*. Forum für Verantwortung, Frankfurt am Main: Fischer, 181–199.

Bellah, R.B./R. Madsen/W. Sullivan/A. Swidler/S. Tipton (1985): *Habits of the Heart. Individualism and Commitment in American Life*. Oakland: University of California Press.

Bentham, J. (1789). *An Introduction to the Principles of Morals and Legislation*. London: Payne.

Bruni, L. (2006). *Civil Happiness: Economics and Human Flourishing in Historical Perspective*. London/New York: Routledge.

Bundesministerium für Familie, Senioren, Frauen und Jugend (2005). *Hauptbericht des Freiwilligensurveys 2004*. Ergebnisse der repräsentativen Trenderhebung zu Ehrenamt, Freiwilligenarbeit und Bürgerschaftlichem Engagement, vorgelegt von TNS Infratest Sozialforschung, München. Online at www.dza.de/forschung/fws/publikationen/berichte.html (accessed: 20th February 2017).

Bundesministerium für Familie, Senioren, Frauen und Jugend (2010). *Hauptbericht des Freiwilligensurveys 2009*. München. Online at www.dza.de/forschung/fws/publikationen/berichte.html (accessed: 20th February 2017).

Bundesministerium für Familie, Senioren, Frauen und Jugend (2016). *Freiwilliges Engagement in Deutschland: Der deutsche Freiwilligensurvey 2014*, ed. by J. Simonson/C. Vogel/C. Tesch-Römer. Berlin: Deutsches Zentrum für Altersfragen. Online at www.dza.de/forschung/fws/publikationen/berichte.html (accessed: 20th February 2017).

Dewey, J. (1922). *Human Nature and Conduct: An Introduction to Social Psychology*. New York: Henry Holt.

Easterlin, R.A. (2004). The economics of happiness. In: *Daedalus* (133.2), 26–33.

Ekardt, F. (2010). *Das Prinzip Nachhaltigkeit: Generationengerechtigkeit und globale Gerechtigkeit*. München: Beck.

Feiler, V. (2016). *Funktionslogiken organisierten freiwilligen Engagements: Eine Studie über das Kolpingwerk Deutschland*. Wiesbaden: Springer VS.

Felber, C. (2015). *Change Everything: Creating an Economy for the Common Good*. London: Zed Books.

Fenner, D. (2007). *Das gute Leben*. Berlin: DeGruyter.

Frey, B./A. Stutzer (2002). What Can Economists Learn from Happiness Research? In: *Journal of Economic Literature* (40.3), 402–435.

Hollstein, B. (2010). Glück und Gemeinsinn: Zwei ordnungspolitische Leitbegriffe in wirtschaftsethischer Perspektive. In: *Annual Review of Law and Ethics* 18, 59–77.

Hollstein, B. (2015). *Ehrenamt verstehen: Eine handlungstheoretische Analyse*. Frankfurt am Main/New York: Campus.

Hollstein, B./M. Singer-Brodowski (2015). Qualitätsentwicklung von BNE in der Erfurter Bildungslandschaft. In: R. Fischbach/N. Kolleck/G. de Haan (eds.). *Auf dem Weg zu nachhaltigen Bildungslandschaften: Lokale Netzwerke erforschen und gestalten*. Wiesbaden: Springer VS, 147–168.

Hollstein, B./S. Tänzer/A. Thumfart (eds., 2013). *InnoNet: Bildung für nachhaltige Entwicklung. Gemeinsam Nachhaltigkeit gestalten. Das Innovationsnetzwerk BNE und das Studium Fundamentale Nachhaltigkeit als Impulsgeber für vernetztes Handeln*. Erfurt: Universität Erfurt. Online at https://www.uni-erfurt.de/fileadmin/public-docs/InnovationsnetzwerkBNE/INB_eBook-1-1.pdf (accessed February 20th 2017).

Joas, H. (1996). *The Creativity of Action*. Chicago: University of Chicago Press.

Joas, H. (2000). *The Genesis of Values*. Chicago: University of Chicago Press.

Kant, I. (1785). *Groundwork for the Metaphysics of Morals*. Online at www.earlymoderntexts.com/assets/pdfs/kant1785.pdf.

Kluckhohn, C. (1962). Values and Value-Orientation in the Theory of Action: An Exploration in Definition and Classification. In: T. Parsons/E.A. Shils (eds.). *Towards a General Theory of Action*. New York: Harper & Row, 388–433.

Lane, R. (2001). *The Loss of Happiness in Market Democracies*. New Haven: Yale University Press.

Marx, K./F. Engels (1888 [1969]). Theses on Feuerbach. In: *Selected Works Vol. 1*. Moskau: Progress Publishers. Online at www.Marxist.org/archive/marx/works/1845/theses/theses.htm (accessed: 4th October 2016).

Mead, G.H. (1943 [1934]): *Mind, Self, and Society*. Chicago: University of Chicago Press.

Meier, S./A. Stutzer (2004). Is Volunteering Rewarding in Itself? *IZA Discussion Paper 1045*, Institute for the Study of Labor (IZA).

Neugebauer, B. (2004). Die Erfassung von Umweltbewusstsein und Umweltverhalten. In: *ZUMA-Methodenbericht Nr. 2004/07*. Mannheim. Online at http://www.gesis.org/filead min/upload/forschung/publikationen/gesis_reihen/gesis_methodenberichte/2004/0407_ Neugebauer.pdf (accessed 20th February 2017).

Neumann, D. (2016). *Das Ehrenamt nutzen: Zur Entstehung einer staatlichen Engagementpolitik in Deutschland*. Bielefeld: Transcript.

Nussbaum, M. (2001). *Gerechtigkeit oder Das gute Leben*. Frankfurt am Main/New York: Campus, 265–287.

Rosa, H. (2011). Über die Verwechslung von Kauf und Konsum: Paradoxien der spätmodernen Konsumkultur. In: L. Heidbrink/I. Schmidt/B. Ahaus (eds.). *Die Verantwortung des Konsumenten: Über das Verhältnis von Markt, Moral und Konsum*. Frankfurt am Main/New York: Campus, 115–132.

Rosa, H. (2016). *Resonanz. Eine Soziologie der Weltbeziehung*. Berlin: Suhrkamp.

Scitovsky, T. (1976). *The Joyless Economy: An Inquiry into Human Satisfaction and Consumer Dissatisfaction*. New York: Oxford University Press.

Sen, A. (1984). *Resources, Values and Development*. Oxford: Basil Blackwell.

Sen, A. (1985). *Commodities and Capabilities*. Amsterdam: North-Holland.

Sumner, L.W. (1996). *Welfare, Happiness, and Ethics*. Oxford: Oxford University Press.

Thomä, D./C. Henning/O. Mitscherlich-Schönherr, Olivia (eds., 2011). *Glück: Ein interdisziplinäres Handbuch*. Stuttgart: Metzler.

Wolf, S. (1998). Glück und Sinn: Zwei Aspekte des guten Lebens. In: H. Steinfath (ed.). *Was ist ein gutes Leben? Philosophische Reflexionen*. Frankfurt am Main: Suhrkamp, 167–195.

14 Is love still a part of the good life?

Eva Illouz

Aristotle has thought about love as an important part of Eudaimonia, the good life, but surprisingly enough it was Plato who provided us with the most significant elaboration for why love would be a part of the good life. In his famous *Symposium* Phaedrus opens the dialogue with the claim that Eros is the oldest of gods. The lover, says Phaedrus, wants to earn the admiration of the beloved, by showing bravery in war and in the battlefield, since nothing shames a man more than to be seen by his beloved committing an inglorious act. A handful of lovers being watched by their own beloved would be an invincible army and would defeat the whole world. Lovers find in themselves the most sublime impulse to sacrifice, for the sake of being admired by their beloved. (Achilles sacrificed himself for the revenge of his lover Patrocles, and Alcestis sacrificed and gave her own life to let her husband Admetus live). In short, and in the conclusion of Phaedrus's speech, love is the most honored and powerful god in helping man gaining honor and blessedness.

Phaedrus is also saying something additional (albeit obliquely): love is a very powerful source for social order, since armies are the most disciplined of all organisations. In a similar vein, Agathon, who speaks after Phaedrus, claims that love is reserved only for the young (this is a topic we will come back to) and it is a source of justice, moderation, courage and wisdom. So in Ancient philosophy, there is a theme that has quite disappeared from our culture: namely that love arises from or in turn elicits social order, moral virtues and good character. Diotima, Socrates' spokesperson goes one step further and claims that love has an aim, and that that aim is the perpetual possession of what is good and perfect. In short, in this text Plato exposes in a crystal clear way the ways in which love for many philosophers was conducive to goodness, to the good life, conceived here both as a social order and as a moral good known to all. Despite the different positions of the various speakers in the *Symposium*, what we can say very clearly is that love is in fact an objective fact conducive to virtues and to good society, and it enhances the individual self as such.

In the following I am going to talk only about love in modernity, and if I started with Plato's symposium it was to emphasise the fact that love has been connected to the discourse of virtues. So for all these reasons we can claim that love has been part of the good life, and that most modern theories of the good life cannot do without it (the good life is here understood in the Aristotelian sense of virtues that lead to the good life). And yet, this is where the company of philosophers and sociologists must part. This is exactly the point where I think that philosophical theories of the good life confuse the descriptive and the normative and do not build their normative theory through an empirical understanding of the good life as it is actually lived and practiced (but rather project the normative ideals into an idealised reality of antiquity). So instead of talking about love as a kind of normative project that should be part of the good life, I would actually like to examine whether modern love provides us really with a framework to build such normative theories. The question then that I would like to raise is whether romantic love as it has evolved in modernity still offers an adequate model of the good life. As a practice and model which emerged in pre-modernity, is it still a social form that can orient our normative models of the good life? This is the broad question that I beg to address in this lecture.

The most striking difference between modern and pre-modern love was the dis-entanglement of love from traditional moral virtues, from moral conceptions of the self and from a social cosmology. From the 16th to the 20th century, love underwent a number of transformations. It became individualised, privatised, and central to conceptions of selfhood that emphasised interiority and subjectivity as sources of experience and knowledge. It also became a secularised version of the love of god, transposing onto human beings the devotion and exclusivity which was dedicated to God. Paradoxically, love also played a fundamental role in conceptions of autonomy. Love – the quintessentially fusional emotion – ironically contains a fragment of the vast and complex history of autonomy and freedom, a history that has been told mostly in political terms. To take one example, the genre of the romantic comedy – which emerged with the Greek Menandre, continued with the Romans (the plays of Plautus or Terence) and flourished in the Renaissance – expressed the claim to freedom by young people against parents, tutors, and old men. While in India or China, love was told in stories shaped by religious values, was part and parcel of the life of gods, and did not oppose social authority, in Western Europe and in the United States, love progressively detached itself from the religious cosmology, was cultivated by aristocratic elites in search of a lifestyle, and contributed to the secularisation of the world by transposing to human beings the love previously destined to God.[1] This process was key to the formation of moral individualism, the view that persons are endowed with a value and interiority independent from their relationship to God and from social institutions.[2] Through many different cultural genres – in the theater, poetry and novels – love slowly affirmed itself against rules of endogamy, patriarchal or church authority and community control. In the 18th century, individualism and a new form of self-introspective interiority would coalesce in the cultural practice of romantic love, affirming the individual's right to his/her sentiments, and thus affirming the right to choose the object of his love and to marry according to one's will. Interiority, freedom, emotions and choice formed a single matrix. Will, in this new cultural and emotional order was not defined anymore as the capacity to regulate one's desires (as in Christian religiosity), but was defined precisely as the opposite capacity to act according to their injunction, and to choose an object that corresponded to individual emotions as emanating from one's will. In that respect, in the personal realm romantic love and emotions became the ground for moral claims to freedom and autonomy, as powerful as these would be in the public and male realm of politics, only that this Revolution did not have its public demonstrations, Parliament bills and physical struggles. It was an agent for the autonomy and for the autonomization of the individual, long before political theories put autonomy at the center of human action. By autonomy I mean the fact that people came to view themselves as the legitimate source of authority about their emotions, desires and goals and that they thought they should pursue only those activities that would neither jeopardise nor compromise such autonomy. So the claim of autonomy was mostly visible in the cultural claim that love should bypass the strictures of parents and community. That has been a very consistent theme for the past centuries in Western Europe to be found everywhere in theater, novels or later, movies. Love then was a central actor in the affirmation of emotional autonomy, and it is as such that it became central to the project of the modern individual, as a way to test out and exercise one's individuality.

At the end of the 19th century, and even more clearly in the 20th century, love underwent an additional change which is that it became associated and even central to a cardinal value of modern people, namely happiness, conceived as a utilitarian project to maximise one's pleasure. More precisely, love became the project of maximizing the pleasure of two people, which was not so much the case before and this has not been the case before, because love had been mostly associated with the formation of character and suffering. So, some could say that the association of love and happiness was merely a Hollywoodian invention, but I think that the Hollywood formula would not have been so successful if it had not resonated with a structure of needs and aspirations of modernity. The reason why love and happiness were so closely associated was because love really held the possibility of the promise of happiness.

This was so because of three main reasons that have to do with modernity. One is that love provided what Antony Giddens (1991) called an ontological security, when so much about modernity seemed to question the grounds for one's social identity and aspirations. In modernity, all values and norms are up for grabs, a point very well made by Ulrich Beck (eg., in Beck 1995). So, love provided in that way a kind of certainty about our identity. The second reason was that love provided the ultimate recognition for one's own individuality in a world that standardised individuality. In that sense love enabled to achieve quite easily a sense of singularity, and in that sense, it was crucial to individuation and individualisation processes. The third reason is that love provides intense intimacy in a world in which solidarity seemed to be lacking or at least became problematic. An intense bond then seemed to compensate for the fluidity, geographical, social, moral, etc. of the modern world. And that anchored the self in the reality of the intimacy of the couple.

Thus, for these reasons I think it is not surprising that love would have been associated with happiness. There were however cracks and fissures in that project of making love the centerpiece of modern happiness. And since I like to think with stories, I would like to use a story, a novel more exactly that brings home this point, the beginning of those cracks and fissures. If I had to choose an entry point to precisely examine these problematic relationship between love and happiness, I would choose Madame Bovary. Madame Bovary, as you know, is the story of a woman who is married to a provincial doctor who lacks ambitions, but who is respected by his fellow citizens. Charles, Emma's husband, is happy to come back home after a long day of work to eat the dinner that she has prepared, to read the newspaper, and to then fall asleep. He feels the contentment of people who do not dream of anything beyond what they have. Emma, however, although she has everything a provincial doctor's wife can have, longs for another life. Her dreams extend far beyond her husband and her social milieu. As she tells Léon, one of her disappointing lovers, in an act of unknowing self-definition: "if you only knew all the things I have dreamed of" (part III, ch. 1). So Madam Bovary wanted desperately to redefine her life as a good life, a life in which love would determine the main quality of her life. Instead of having a life determined by routine, by her public role as a wife and mother, by religion, she wants to have a life defined by a great love, by emotions, by her sense of autonomy, by a sense of self-realisation, by realizing, by being who she truly is, namely a great lover. What Emma wants really is a better life, she wants a good life. Certainly according to a simple hedonic principle, and certainly according to the view that by living more love she would realise her capacity to live a more self-determined life, she would realise a superior good that would give meaning to her meaningless life. But Flaubert, who is an extraordinary observer of France after the 1850s, the France after the 1848 failed revolution, has a much more ironic and acute gaze on the role that love has to play in the life of a provincial woman aspiring to modernise, that is to live both love and happiness.

For one, the novel shows extremely well how love-dreams of Emma are intertwined with the emerging consumer market of France. Madame Bovary was published in 1856 and *Le Bon Marché*, which was the first department store and the forefather of the Gallery La Fayette, was opened in 1852, four years before. A lot of studies of consumerism show how *Le Bon Marché* changed in a very serious way the ways in which women fantasied about the good life. Emma Bovary then dreams both of love and of a higher social status at one and the same time. She uses consumer culture and artifacts (like dresses, trinkets, etc.) to imagine and project herself into a different life. She imagines her life and love through consumer objects, the beautiful objects she purchases from Lheureux, the merchant who actually forces her at the end to commit suicide. Consumer culture then is another way of imagining her life, and like love, both are fundamental vectors of the good life as an imagined project. Thus the good life in modernity becomes an imagined project.

Flaubert's novel is all the more powerful that it shows that both projects, that is the consumer and the romantic project, turn out to be empty. They revolve around themselves in endless loops of longing, the subject desiring objects and the romantic subject both long for a receding line of emotional and material happiness, a goal, Flaubert suggests, that can never be satisfied or met. The novel is really the first that shows that a part of the good life is imagined, that the good life in modernity is intimately connected to the engine of capitalism and this in at least two ways. The first way in which romantic love and capitalism are connected in this novel is that through the mass market of books, romances and cheap mass culture that start to be produced in the 19th century, capitalism would at once and perversely so codify the realm of the family as a private sphere, that was central to the making of the bourgeois family, in which love and intimacy would prevail. And it did so by providing the heterosexual formula of love that was endlessly circulated through mass culture. The vision of the private sphere and the promise of love and intimacy became the new cultural commodities of mass culture. But that domestic sphere, with its strictures and unfulfilled promises, turned out to be a stifling place as Freud so magisterially showed only a few decades after Flaubert. The bourgeois family was after all quite banal. It was what Emma Bovary discovered it is; it is in fact an institution for the economic and biological reproduction of the bourgeois family. It also made love into an escape from that domestic sphere, from that stifling bourgeois domestic sphere; love being automatically almost adulterous as in the case of Emma Bovary. It is adulterous in the sense that it aims to transgress the domestic structure of the family, and to activate constant phantasies to overcome it.

So cultural capitalism, the invention of the novel, the circulation of a mass market of romances, the centrality of the family and love in the family, and love in the private sphere put then the heterosexual formula of love at the center of subjectivity. What it did then is that it strongly narrativised the self and gave it a narrative telos, a narrative and emotional telos all in one through love. And Madame Bovary is an exemplification of that narrativisation of the self, only that she cannot end the story as she wants or rather that she found out that the story that she wants to write is hollow from within, and this is what the novel in fact wants to convey.

The second way in which capitalism and love were intertwined, and this is a thread of the novel, is that love and sex were the main conveyor belts of the unending supply of consumer goods and for an unending desire for consumer goods, those creating slowly an autonomisation of sexual desire from the realm of religion, from the realm of morality, from domesticity and even from emotions themselves. For the first time I think, sexuality, sexual desire what became then sexiness, sexual attraction, etc. started having an inner logic, an autonomy that was carried forward by consumer and economic forces. Madame Bovary herself could not have been yet an actor of that full autonomisation of sexual desire, but she was certainly at the beginning of that process. And so Madame Bovary, had she been a woman of the 1990s, would have known to accumulate her lovers as sexual partners, and she would not have wanted to make them the kind of perspectival and unattainable point of the imagined and phantasised love stories that she tells herself. So, what is interesting for my point is that the autonomisation of sexual desire through consumer culture would slowly undermine the narrativisation of the self through love, and this is the stage I think that we are in now.

So I am moving now to the sexual revolution. All of this was really a way to foreground my main point, which is that the sexual revolution was in fact a reaction to the immense desiring machine liberated by the conjunction of love and consumer culture, and to the contradiction between the domestic family sphere and the consumer sphere in which desire was endlessly circulated. By sexual revolution I mean that movement of ideas which criticise patriarchy, gender relations and the social organisation of sexuality in order to create gender equality in sex. It was a movement aimed to achieve equality and autonomy, and the legitimation of sex and sexuality as such. So the sexual revolution is still so much a part of who we are, and it has achieved so many essential goods that we forget to look at its social effects. It had some powerful social effects I think, especially on romantic love itself.

Let me review these effects very quickly. The first is that the sexualisation of romantic or heterosexual relationships means that relationship between heterosexuals became entirely legitimate without the sanction of marriage. In that sense we are talking about the emergence of a new social relationship, which is the "sexual relationship". It has really its own form in the Simmelian sense of the word, in which what we are looking for is the performance and sexual pleasure. The other aspect of the sexualisation of relationships is that sexual pleasure and sexual attractiveness as such have become autonomous criteria in order to evaluate another person and a relationship. In sociological terms I would say that the sexualisation of relationships means also that it creates its own autonomous social fields. As social fields, that is, in which there are also fantastic economic interests invested. I t will be anything from discotheques to pornography, to the formidable industries that create sexual attraction like fashion, cosmetics, plastic surgeries, sport, all of these have as their purpose the purpose to create an attractive body that is constantly ready for a sexual relation. And we have to add to these the late comers of sexual internet dating sites which are mainly used by the youth (by the way in the changes and processes that I am taking about the youth play a significant role, it is the youth that set up the norms that are followed later by their elderly).

So the sexual field has become an autonomous field that activates an enormous economic machine. Take sex out of the economy and I believe that the entire world economy will collapse. So, my point here is that the sexualisation of relationships had the same effect on love that capitalism had on economic relations. That is, following the thesis of Karl Polanyi, the economic historian, it actually disembedded sexual or romantic relationships from moral and social networks; it de-regulated them. The result of this deregulation has been in fact to let capitalism entirely colonise the realm of love and to do to love what the market did to social relationships in general.

I am moving to the last point of my paper. I want to claim now that the analogy between the processes that happened in the realm of work and consumption and in the realm of love is quite striking. So, the first change that I noticed in love as the result of the sexualisation of relationships is the incredible enlargement of the samples from which people can choose their partners. After the sexual revolution these samples became huge. Before the sexual revolution, choices were more or less horizontal. In fact, there are even studies now in the US that show that very large numbers of marriages before the World War II happened between people living on the same blocks, so -this really shows very strong homogamy, people choosing people from their own group. But the sexual revolution had a revolutionary effect in that it lifted the taboos and the external constraints of class, religion, race, etc. on the choice of the partner. The former barriers of religion and class fell, therefore creating very large samples of people with whom we can have sexual relationships. The second effect is that it also created a new competition. If everybody now is available, people compete with each other along sometimes incompatible criteria. A beautiful woman competes with an intelligent women who competes with a rich woman, etc. Here I would like to quote another novelist: this is exactly the situation that Michel Houellebecq describes in his first novel *The Extension of the Domain of Struggle*. He said that economic liberalism is the extension of the domain of struggle; it is the extension to all ages of live, and to all classes of society. In the same way he said that sexual liberalism (I think he was the first to use this expression) is the extension of the domain of struggle, it is its extension to all ages.

So, let me say quickly how I think it may impact on the romantic relationship. The one is that the volume of interactions has considerably gone up. This is very different again from even the 19th century where a woman could hope to have three to four suitors maximum. Jane Austen herself, when she was proposed by Tom Lefroy and refused him, knew that she may not have another marriage offer, and this was indeed what happened: she never had another marriage offer. So the sheer volume of people with which we interact sexually and romantically has grown up extraordinarily. So we really can speak here of the volume of interactions, in the same way that we can speak on the volume of production. We can wonder if this effect does not affect the capacity to construct a story with a clear sharp beginning and with very clear characters; in other words, if we are still able to singularise others in the same way that we were able in the previous regime. This has, I think, led to new forms of polyamory, with a decline of norms of monogamy, which are a direct reflection of the sheer volume of interactions that people can now legitimately engage with in the sexual and romantic domain.

The second point is that speed itself became a characteristic of sexual and romantic relations. I concur with Rosa (2009) that this is one of the new characteristics of modernity and capitalism. If there is one thing that characterises it, it is the notion of speed. Adam Smith's famous pin factory or Fordism, which I think are the two most important technological and intellectual developments of capitalism, have to do all with speed. And we observe something very similar in the realm of love where we have a turnover of relationships that is extremely quick, and a constant invention of new forms, such as hooking up, one night stands, speed dating etc. Zygmunt Bauman (2003) has taken account of that change and called it "liquid love". He wants to speak also about the readiness to move to the next experiences or to the next relationships. But I think that the notion of liquid love misses the element of speed. And crucial also in speed is the element of accumulation. When we say "liquid love" or "liquid modernity", there is a sense of flow, of simple flow from one experience to another, where the new sexual subject that I am describing is about accumulating sexual experiences, so much so that I come up with the idea of sexual capital, when you accumulate sexual partners as it was in fact a capital (Illouz 2013, 56f; cf. Michael 2004).

All of this brings me to suggest that we find elements in romantic love that are very reminiscent to phenomena that we find in the work sphere and in the consumer sphere. Let me just enumerate a few. What Sennett (2006) described as being the characteristics of workers now is something that can be found in the modern, contemporary romantic era. One is a great instability and an anxiety to be "fired" from a relationship. Man or woman: it doesn't matter. There is a sense of people being constantly on the move and developing a personality adaptable to change, to develop the personality that will take into account the precariousness of relationships. In other words, precariousness is built in ahead of time as a given of the relationship, as well as a great need to manage the onslaught on self-esteem that frequent breakups in fact bring up.

The second change, and this has been talked about by sociologists such as Robert Bellah (I myself continued that in Illouz 1997 and 2013), is that people relate to each other as utility that is to be maximised, and that one is suspicious that one is the instrument only of another's desire.[3] In other words, there is an introduction of a consumer logic of disposing people, of disposable relationships, disposable sexual relationships. The logic of the consumer sphere is very much present.

And I would say that the third impact is that there is a greater difficulty to narrativise the self because one does not know in advance in which story one is. Is it a sexual story; is it just love; is it marriage? So there is a much greater difficulty to know simply in which story you are, which story you want to write. So confusion, ambivalence, lack of desire, and difficulty to project oneself in the future all point to the difficulty of knowing in which story one is located. And here, too, as Sennett (2006) said, one of the big changes that he noticed in workers today is that they have difficulties projecting themselves into the future. This is exactly what happens to young people who have difficulties imagining themselves in the future. This is an ironic counterpoint to Madam Bovary: Where she suffered and died from her overheated imagination, from her overheated capacity to imagine the future, I think that we are now at a stage where we have much less capacities to precisely imagine our future in a clear line story as was the case for her. Thus, what has changed profoundly is the historical connection that existed between the story or the novel, the capacity to narrativise the self, and the capacity to imagine the self as happy. It is this historical connection that has come undone, and which suggests that love is not any more the repository of the good life. And by this, I mean that it has become much more difficult to have the social conditions conducive to love. I am not saying that people are not happily in love or happily married, etc., I am saying that one needs to launch a kind of battle against the social conditions of sexuality and love in order for this to happen.

So, to answer my question whether love is a part of the good life, my answer is no. I would like to conclude with another novel that was in fact in close dialogue with Madame Bovary. This novel is Stoner, written by John Williams. This is a novel that is really a kind of re-write of Madame Bovary, only with a male character. Stoner entertains a very close intertextual dialogue with Madame Bovary, and it is even a mirror reflection of it. The similarity between the two novels are too striking to be fortuitous. Both novels have as their eponyms' title the name of the hero. Emma Bovary and William Stoner enter life both by discovering books, Emma as an adolescent and Stoner as a student in the university. Both married socially appropriate people; both live unhappy marriages; both have a single daughter who grows neglected by her mother. Both knew great love only outside marriage. Both consider living their marriage; both end up living lives of compromise and misery, by choice in Stoner's case and by necessity in Emma's case; both are ultimately crushed by a provincial and narrow environment; both have what we may call a failed life, a life without love. Yet, while Madame Bovary's life is not one we would characterise as worth living, Stoner's life is one that is worth living even though it is a faded life in many ways. Why? This is the question I would like to end with.

Stoner's interiority is not organised around a telos or by fixed images, or even by the desire for a better life. It is organised by what Charles Taylor would call "strong evaluations", that is; moral objects and categories that exist outside the self and orient it through meaning (Taylor 1989, see Taylor in this volume). These meanings are made known to the reader of the novel because Stoner has the opportunity every time to make choices, and he always forgoes the hedonic option. Stoner is the man who at every moment forgoes the comfortable hedonic choice. For example he could have been a land worker as his father had wanted him to be, but instead he chooses to go to academia and to be an English literature teacher. And so like for Emma Bovary, books are extremely important to him. But he uses them very differently, and it is this choice of being a scholar that orients the main events of his life. Such as for example having to forgo the great love he finds in Katherine Driscoll. He finds a women who is quite extraordinary, who falls in love with him. He has the actually very miserable marriage, and he chooses not to leave his marriage with Katherine Driscoll. What is the meaning of this anti-Emma Bovary choice? He forgo his love because he knows that in the very Puritan America of the 1960s, he would not find another university job. All his colleagues will shun him at all university departments. So I think it would be a mistake to conclude that Stoner made the male choice of forgoing love for his profession, or because of the pressure of his environment. In fact what determined his choice is his relationships to books and learning, because his relationship to his profession is in fact what Max Weber called a vocation (Beruf). And if there is a hero in the entire literature that symbolised what the Weberian idea of "Beruf" means, it is Stoner. Because his vocation, his love of books and his love of literature organises his self, it is the center of his being that in fact shapes the novel's action. In the thousands of literary characters Stoner stands out because he gives a narrative and moral significance to the idea of vocation. Books and scholarship reveal to him a world that is at once ungraspable and truly lived only through consciousness.

I am reminded here of a quote by Nietzsche in section 3 of the *Twilight of the Idols*, "how the true world became a fable". He said: "the true world – untenable, unprovable, unpromisable, but a cancelation and obligation and imperative merely be virtue of being thought". Emma's use of books can lead only to disappointment to an unseasonable disappointment, because the books she reads are full of promises, and because she reads in them her own need for promises. Stoner on the other hand, like in Nietzsche's quote, uses books to glimpse at the unattainable and ungraspable dimension of experience and existence. What makes Emma into a Bovarist hero is that she cannot develop a consciousness, that a dimension of life is unattainable and that it is only the world that is thought consoles us from the world that fails us. But Stoner, despite the fact that he has failed or lost most of what was precious in his life, is contrary to Emma, not bitter; he is never bitter. He actually espouses, endorses entirely his own life in the end of the novel. He is at once lucid and resigned the position that Max Weber precisely assigned to the scientist, in his unforgettable "Science as a vocation". It is indeed the heroic ethics of resignation that gives meaning to his choice to forgo the great love of his life and to choose his vocation as a teacher and scholar. What is resignation? I would define it as the morality of a specific intellectual quality; it is an intellectual morality. It is namely the capacity to except that the gap between the ought and the is, is unbridgeable, and it is the capacity to except that you have to forgo some goods for others. While this understanding can lead to either despair or to cynical capitulation, resignation is marked by the lucidness of the understanding that the world cannot be otherwise and places the dignity of existence in this knowledge itself. As Weber and Kierkegaard had seen it, the scholar might be the only one to stand for a heroic ethic of resignation against the empty subjectivist and consumerist promises of happiness of our time.

Notes

1 For this see Singer 1989, Lystra 1989, Seidman 1991 & Bloch 1992.
2 It was strangely omitted by Max Weber in his monumental study of the different cultural paths taken by the West and the East (Weber 1915).
3 See Bellah et al. 1985, Illouz 1997 and 2013.

References

Bauman, Z. (2003). *Liquid Love: On the Frailty of Human Bonds*. Cambridge: Polity Press.
Beck, U. (1985). *The Normal Chaos of Love*. Cambridge: Polity Press.
Bellah, R. et al. (1997). *Habits of the Heart: Individualism and Commitment in American Life*. Berkeley: University of California Press.
Bloch, H.R. (1992). *Medieval Misogyny and the Invention of Western Romantic Love*. Chicago: University of Chicago Press.
Giddens, A. (1991). *Modernity and Self-Identity: Self and Society in the Late Modern Age*. Cambridge: Polity Press.
Illouz, E. (1997). *Consuming the Romantic Utopia: Love and the Cultural Contradictions of Capitalism*. Berkeley: University of California Press.
Illouz, E. (2013). *Why Love Hurts: A Sociological Explanation*. Oxford: Wiley.
Lystra, K. (1989). *Searching the Heart: Women, Men, and Romantic Love in Nineteenth-Century America*. New York: Oxford University Press.
Michael, R.T. (2004). Sexual Capital: An Extension of Grossman's Concept of Health Capital. In: *Journal of Health Economics* 23.4, 643–652.
Nietzsche, F. (1990). *Twilight of the Idols & The Antichrist*. London: Penguin.
Rosa, H. (2009). *High Speed Society: Social Acceleration, Power, and Modernity*. University Park: Pennsylvania State University Press.
Seidman, S. (1991). *Romantic longings: Love in America, 1830–1980*. New York: Routledge.

Sennett, R. (2006). *The Culture of the New Capitalism*. New Haven: Yale University Press.

Singer, I. (1989). *The Nature of Love Vol. 3: The Modern World*. Chicago: University of Chicago Press.

Taylor, C. (1989). *Sources of the Self: The Making of the Modern Identity*. Cambridge, MA: Harvard University Press.

Weber, M. (1946 [1918]). Science as a Vocation. In: *Essays in Sociology* (ed./transl. H. Gerth/C. Wright Mills). New York: Oxford University Press, 129–156.

Weber, M. (1951 [1915]). *The Religion of China: Confucianism and Taoism* (ed./transl. Hans Gerth). New York: MacMillan.

15 Empowering ourselves in the transformation to a good life beyond growth

Felix Rauschmayer

A good life beyond growth, however it might look like, does not come by itself.[1] The individual as well as societal option to live such a life implies a deep and radical transformation of societies to create different structures, institutions, and organisations in order to respect the limits of ecosystems, which maintain and support human societies and economies; also societies that are conducive to more fairness among and between generations. Human agency is required to establish such transformed and transformative structures.

So far, existing individual agency has not been sufficient to initiate and maintain radical societal changes towards sustainability. Societal structures and power inequalities certainly are among the causal factors for this failure. But I assume that agency is not completely determined by societal structures, as there is space to freely choose actions as well as to reflect on this freedom and on the factors that are relevant for it. In this chapter, I will have a closer look at individual agency and at how we – as change agents – may empower ourselves in the societal transformation to a good life beyond growth.

The motivation behind such agency is important in this transformation process: Our idea of what is a good life, be it materialistically self-centred, *"buen vivir"*, happiness, sustainable living or anything else, influences the target of societal transformations, but also our ambition, resilience, and endurance on this way. At the same time, these transformations, especially when experienced at a personal level, may make us change our conceptions of a good life. By trying to achieve e.g. the limit of two tons CO_2 emissions per annum per capita, we gain an impression on why this is difficult, but also on what may be gained through a lifestyle that rather focuses on, e.g., local resonance (see Rosa in this volume) than on international travelling. Empowering ourselves in these personal transformations to a good life beyond growth also makes us reflect on the societal structures, institutions, and organisations that hinder us personally, and that may impede a transformation at a larger scale. This is also true for the opposite, the encouraging and enabling factors: we may get ideas on what kind of governance or societal structures can empower us (and others) in this transformation. It is clear that some processes of collective action are among these supporting factors.

For better understanding the interactions between individual and collective self-empowerment, it would be helpful to connect both processes to the same behavioural model. This model would have to comprise (1) an understanding of inner-individual processes showing the interdependency of different psychological variables, (2) an understanding of how these processes relate to behaviour, and (3) how cultural, social and other external variables interact with the internal processes and with behaviour change.

In what follows, I take the capability model of human freedom, which has been developed most prominently by Amartya Sen and Martha Nussbaum, as a basis and add aspects of inner change (second and third section) and collective action (fourth section). These two enlargements are most relevant for describing the potential transformation of individuals on their way to a good life beyond growth. These two elements are also well reflected in many current streams towards such life: The Global Ecovillage Network (GEESE 2012), the Transition Town movement as well as many parts of the Degrowth movement stress the necessity of inner individual change embedded in collective action and experimental living.

I spell this enlarged capability model out by current endeavours in transitions to a good life beyond growth. On the logic of internal transformation, I develop and exemplify the model through Non-Violent Communication (NVC), a method to develop and practice nonviolent attitudes towards oneself and others. NVC is popular among the Global Ecovillage Network, but also within degrowth and transition town initiatives. For collective action, I take the example of complementary currency initiatives that aim at more social inclusion, a lower environmental footprint and at the establishment of local alternatives to globalised markets, including financial markets.

I close the chapter by bringing both kinds of empowerment together. It is far beyond the scope of this chapter to develop a unified, let alone empirically tested model combining individual and collective self-empowerment. The sketch presented here, though, establishes links to a most prominent model of human development as well as to collective action and environmental psychology. Freedom to live a valuable life being the central goal of the Capability Approach points to the central issue of transformative policies: How to gain the freedom to live a good life beyond growth in a society that currently is geared towards the imperative of economic growth?

The capability approach enriched through environmental psychology

The Capability Approach (CA) claims that public policies should be designed so that they enlarge the factual freedom of people to live a valuable life, i.e. to enlarge their set of capabilities. As a partial theory of justice, the CA particularly focusses on the capabilities of poor people, i.e. the freedom to lead a dignified life. Evaluating states of policies along capabilities excludes to merely use resources, such as money or GDP, or feelings, such as content with one's life, as measuring rods. While resources, on the individual level, often are a necessary ingredient for freedom, happiness may be an outcome of it. But many resources cannot be converted into a factual freedom to lead a valuable life (e.g. a fifth pair of blue jeans in your wardrobe, a bike in winter in Murmansk, or a car without a male driver for a woman in Saudi Arabia), and happiness may arise despite of severe lack of freedom or it may not arise despite a considerable amount of freedom. Furthermore, capabilities are multidimensional: The ability to live a life in good health is clearly different from being able to live for and towards others, to cite two of Nussbaum's ten central human capabilities (Nussbaum 2000).[2] Alkire (2002: 186) specifies this as follows: "Dimensions of human development are nonhierarchical, irreducible, incommensurable and hence basic kinds of human ends". This makes the relation between resources, capabilities, and happiness complex.

Even though there is general agreement that capabilities are embedded in and dependent on societal institutions, there still is no general agreement on how this embeddedness could be modelled (Lessmann 2011).[3] Most resources in our modern lives emerge from social interactions, and the possibilities to use these resources also depend on social institutions, such as rights, morals or factual restrictions. In other words, we miss an understanding of the interaction between agency and structure in terms of the CA. Through such understanding, the CA would capture the creation of agency and capabilities to a fuller extent. Social interaction and collective action create collective agency (Davis 2015) which can initiate social change, such as a transformation to a good life beyond growth.

Furthermore, and in the context of these transformations most crucially, individual values that determine which life is perceived as valuable clearly depend on socialisation and public discourse. Values also co-determine how individuals use their factual freedom, i.e. which valuable doings and beings they realise. So far, CA scholars have neither focussed their attention on why people want to expand their capabilities, i.e. their motivations, nor their attention on how this translation between psychological factors, factual capabilities, and realised doings and beings happens and could be facilitated (but see Pick/Sirkin 2010, Pick/Hietanen 2015). The lack of looking at motivations is understandable as most CA literature focuses on poor or underprivileged people who are clearly motivated to expand their freedoms to finally live a dignified life. The question of motivations becomes more interesting, though, when people are motivated not by self-regarding values, but by considerations for other entities, be it other people, groups of people, or nature. Engagement for a good life beyond growth certainly is carried by such altruistic motivations to a large extent (see Steg/Vlek 2009 on motivations for pro-environmental behaviour).

For better understanding why people engage for a good life beyond growth through political action or through a conscious change of their own lifestyle, it certainly is helpful to better identify the important variables. Kaufmann-Hayoz et al. (2012) screen different theories for those factors that are considered most important for environmentally friendly behaviour. Named variables include: The personal environmental norm, social norms, awareness of problem and consequences, cost/ benefit expectations, ascription of responsibility, perceived behavioural control, and habits. Focussing on norms and values as a key variable, the norm-activation-model by Schwartz/Howard (1981) has been used as a standard approach in environmental psychology. It differentiates between different stages in decision-making, namely the attention, motivation, and evaluation stage, leading to a change in behaviour or the denial of its necessity or usefulness.

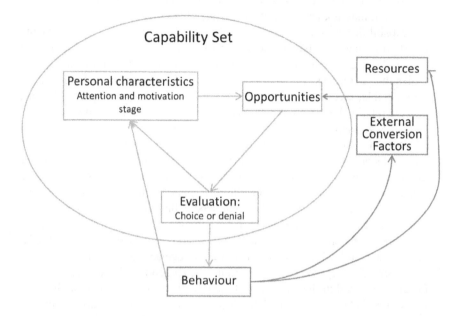

Figure 15.1 Simplified dynamic norm-activation-capability model

Combining these psychological considerations with the CA (see Figure 15.1) makes the capability-set be understood as the combination of personal characteristics (or personal conversion factors) and perceived external opportunities that arise in a combination of resources and social and environmental conversion factors (Pick/Sirkin 2010). The engagement for a good life beyond growth thus also depends on the relevant personal characteristics, such as skills, social norms and values, responsibility, self-efficacy, and awareness of the necessity to comply with these norms (Schäpke/Rauschmayer 2014). It is important, though, to notice that chosen behaviour feeds back on capabilities: Carrying out a chosen behaviour, or denying the need to carry it out, impacts the personal characteristics. Carrying it out also feeds back to the behavioural context and may change the behavioural opportunities. For instance, using the bicycle more often changes personal characteristics and also leads to higher traffic security for cyclists in general.

Nonviolent communication as individual self-empowerment

Many movements towards a good life beyond growth agree that societal transitions also require individual change, comprising of behaviour change and of change of world views, values, deep-rooted beliefs, etc., when conceived of as a self-empowerment to live a good life. For example, the curriculum designed by the Global Ecovillage Network considers worldview change as one of the "Four Keys to Sustainability Everywhere on the Planet" (GEESE 2012, 2). Nonviolent communication (NVC, Rosenberg 2001) can be understood as a tool for world-view change as well as for social change (a second key according to GEESE 2012). NVC aims to support individuals to adopt non-violence as a general attitude towards themselves as well as towards others.

We may now ask how practicing NVC can be understood as a self-empowerment for a transition to a good life beyond growth. Marcel Hunecke (2013) has identified six psychological resources for a transformation towards sustainable lifestyles: the capacity for pleasure, self-acceptance, self-efficacy, mindfulness, the construction of meaning, and solidarity. The first three "are resources that constitute the foundation for a strong personality, one which – as the humanistic view of human nature holds – is characterised by the pursuit and realisation of one's own needs and aims" (Hunecke 2013, 15). A confident person with a proper capacity for pleasure and high expectations of self-efficacy may also follow a very materially intensive lifestyle, though. It is the combination of the three directional resources of seeking meaning, solidarity towards others and mindfulness as a conscious perception of ones needs and feelings that increases the likelihood that confident persons transform their lifestyles and engage for a good life beyond growth. According to psychological studies on effects of NVC trainings (Little 2002; Altmann 2010), and to my own experiences after having trained people in NVC for ten years, it is plausible to assume that NVC has some positive effects on all six psychological resources. For some dimensions of these resources, studies have shown an effect or correlation.[4]

Conceiving of this in terms of the CA would yield something as follows (Figure 15.2): Individuals perceive opportunities to change their behaviour. These opportunities are externally constituted by resources and social and environmental conversion factors. It depends on their personal characteristics (including awareness, self-efficacy, self-acceptance) which of these opportunities are perceived as available and relevant, and the evaluation of these opportunities depends on the values and norms (such as solidarity). Meaning-construction can be understood as a motor of the dynamics looking for more meaningful capabilities. Mindfulness in a first stage links the evaluation of the opportunities (and of personal characteristics) to one's feelings and needs. In a second stage, and in combination with solidarity and meaning-construction, mindfulness facilitates the inclusion of others' needs and feelings as relevant factors for evaluating opportunities.

Tools of self-empowerment, such as NVC trainings that potentially have effects on all these psychological factors, herewith influence the capability-set besides any external changes relevant for the creation of opportunities. I want to mention four aspects of this: (1) NVC is depicted here as a skill intervening in the evaluation of opportunities, as it relates the assessment of opportunities to feelings and needs, herewith also increasing one's capacity for pleasure. (2) Personal characteristics determine whether and how NVC trainings are used, but self-efficacy and self-awareness are among the factors impacted by NVC trainings. (3) The increase in self-acceptance, as one of the three foundational resources mentioned by Hunecke, is one of the core targets of NVC trainings. (4) With its background in humanistic psychology where solidarity is recognised as a fundamental human need, and through its focus on the meaning of relationships, NVC contributes to

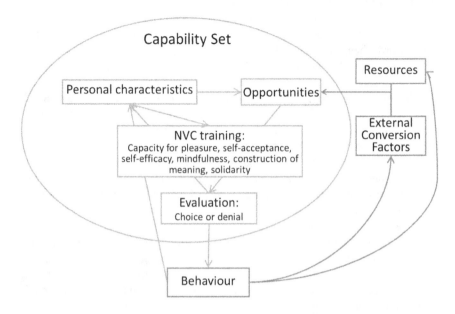

Figure 15.2 Dynamic norm-activation-capability model for sustainable lifestyles

expanding the normative source of evaluation from one's own well-being to that of others. It is this last point that relates the individual self-empowerment to the collective component.

Complementary currencies as collective self-empowerment

I take community currencies (CC), i.e. currency systems that supplement the national currency at a local level as a current example for collective self-empowerment. The most recurrent example for such CC are service credit time banks as a reciprocity-based trading system in which work hours are usually used as currency. Service credits often take the form of time banks and foster neighbourhood support, social care, and community activities. CC have gained popularity across the world, promising local answers to global challenges, such as the opacity of the standard financial system with its seeming tendency to redistribute wealth from the poor to the rich (Atkinson/ Piketty/Saez 2011). The aims of such complementary currencies include, inter alia, the creation or strengthening of a locally rooted resilient economy, giving value to skills and things not valued by the market, and creating social ties in neighbourhoods. Bernd Lietaer, a Belgian expert on finance and CC, is convinced of the strong impact that currencies and their characteristics have on society: "Money matters. The way money is created and administered in a given society makes a deep impression on values and relationships within that society. More specifically, the type of currency used in a society encourages – or discourages – specific emotions or behaviour patterns" (Lietaer 2001, 4).

Up to now, analyses of CC do not refer to a common and clear conceptual framework, but are strongly practice-oriented and case-study-based. Analysing CC through the lens of the Capability Approach has the potential to complement and enrich their current assessments. So far, CA scholars have focused on increasing the capability-set of individuals through politically-induced changes in resources and factors that enable the conversion of resources into freedoms. In terms of Figure 15.2, this can be represented as a claim to political systems to alter those resources and conversion factors in the widest box, i.e. in the realm of social institutions such as educational, tax, or health systems.

The closer study of self-help groups in a CA perspective has induced, though, a discussion on collective capabilities

> as the newly generated capabilities attained by virtue of their engagement in a collective action or their membership in a social network that helps them achieve the lives they value. They are not simply the sum (or average) of individual capabilities, but rather new capabilities that the individual alone would neither have nor be able to achieve, if he/she did not join a collectivity.
> (Ibrahim 2006, 404)

In fact, these "collective capabilities" should rather be understood as collective agency (Rauschmayer/Polzin/Omann submitted) in order not to create the misunderstanding that collective capabilities could or should be used as a normative basis for evaluating policies (Sen 2002). It is through collective action that adherents of a collective action group gain new agency to act within their environment. Figure 15.3 illustrates this through an intermediary, collective action box between the levels of the individual and wider societal institutions. The usual impact of behaviour on resources on individual and wider societal levels (grey dotted arrows in Figure 15.3 from Behaviour to Resources in all three boxes) can thus be complemented by the impact on resources through collective action: Using a CC influences members' resources directly, as they can buy and sell different goods and in a different exchange mode than without a CC (Seyfang 2006).

Volkert (2013) referred to direct agency as a direct control of decisions and actions. Within the financial system, which is an essential element of markets, direct individual agency is quasi non-existent. On a collective level, this looks different: whenever people create a CC in an act of collective action, they gain direct collective agency (see Figure 15.3) on the rules and implementation of the CC system. This collective agency adds influence on their resources and especially social conversion factors that would not have been available without. Figure 15.3 depicts these influences by three continuous arrows. Through setting the CC rules, i.e. through their collective agency, CC members influence their resources and external conversion factors, as resources and skills that may have been worthless in the traditional market economy become relevant for their factual freedom to lead a valuable life. Often, the impact on the resources and conversion factors of other members of the CC change (not depicted) are an intended rather than an unintended effect, as the motivation to reduce socio-economic inequality regularly is one of the main motivating factors for engaging for CC (Briceno/Stagl

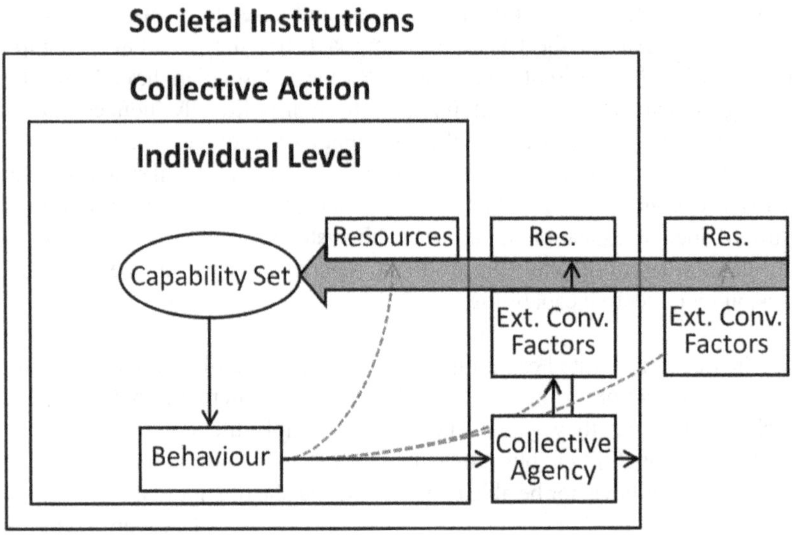

Societal Institutions

Figure 15.3 Collective agency and individual capabilities

2006). Finally, the CC members collectively co-determine the border between their collective action and the wider societal institutions that are beyond their control (arrow from Collective Agency to the border line between Collective Action and Societal Institutions).

All these aspects can be understood as different forms of collective self-empowerment: individuals gather in collective action to pursue a common interest (see Thompson in this volume) which increases their capabilities. The CA offers a normative standpoint (increase in capabilities foremost of the disadvantaged) that allows a justice-based assessment of such processes of collective empowerment.

Linking individual and collective self-empowerment

When inserting the capability-set from Figure 15.2 into Figure 15.3, i.e. when considering self-empowerment and collective empowerment jointly, we can see in Figure 15.4 how one form of empowerment can influence the other. The bold arrow between collective agency and training indicates two different issues: on the one hand, each engagement in collective agency is a training in itself. It has been shown for CC (Molnar 2011; Schwaiger 2006) that the process of setting up these systems creates group-efficacy, which can be a way out of inertia and laming feelings of helplessness. It has been shown as well (Seyfang 2004; Briceno/ Stagl 2006) that CC may also alter the values of its participants with regard to how economic processes should work. Learning how to interact, how to reach collective decisions, how to implement them, etc. is a learning process that has

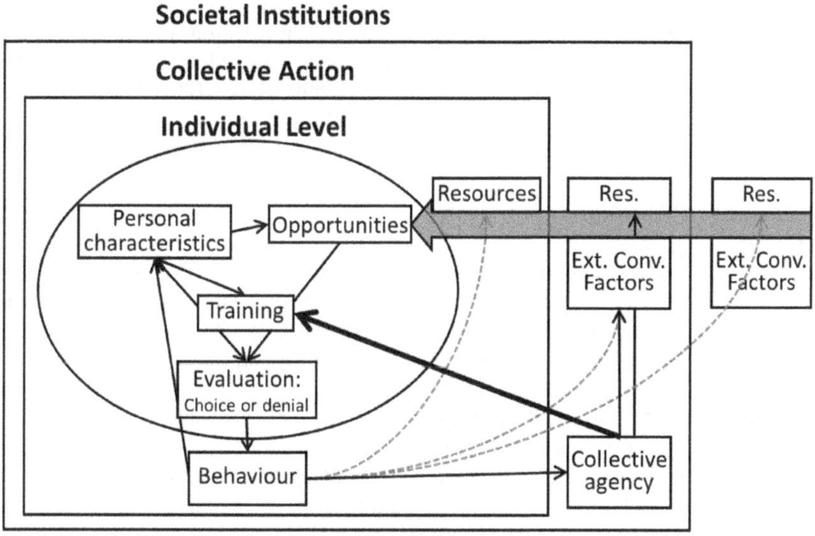

Societal Institutions

Figure 15.4 Collective agency impacting capabilities also internally

impacts on personal characteristics and thus alters the capability-set even without changing resources and external conversion factors. On the other hand, collective action can also comprise of formal training elements, and many initiatives have integrated this facet into their range of activities, such as the transition town initiatives or the Global Ecovillage Network.

Of course, not every learning process and training contributes to an increase in collective agency and to a good life beyond growth. The proposition by Hunecke (2013), mentioned above, can constitute an appropriate starting point for testing which trainings and learning processes can contribute to these psychological resources and which combination of what resources is necessary to gain the freedom to move towards a good life beyond growth.

Notes

1 Acknowledgement: I am grateful for the long collaboration with Ines Omann as well as for her constructive comments to this chapter.
2 Here, I do not discuss whether Nussbaum's central human functional capabilities are also those that are relevant in a frame of good life beyond growth. Despite some claims on the general match between the CA and issues of sustainability (Sen 2013), I maintain that the link between CA and sustainability is far from evident (Lessmann/Rauschmayer 2013).
3 The discussion on the embeddedness of capabilities in natural systems is still less developed (the most recent collection of papers on this issue can be found in Lessmann/Rauschmayer 2014). Even though one main rationale behind the aim to organize good life beyond growth on a societal level is the disrespect for the natural embeddedness of our societies worldwide, we cannot discuss this issue in this chapter.

4 It is neither the aim of this chapter to argue that the six mentioned psychological resources are necessary for individual self-empowerment for a transition to a good life beyond growth nor that NVC is conducive, let alone necessary for strengthening these resources. My argument merely builds on the plausibility of such relationships.

References

Alkire, S. (2002). Dimensions of Human Development. In: *World Development* 30, 181–205.

Altmann, T. (2010). *Evaluation der Gewaltfreien Kommunikation in Quer- und Längsschnittdaten.* Institut für Psychologie II. Universität Leipzig. Online at www.gewaltfrei-leipzig.de/ueber_gfk/Altmann_GfKEvaluation_Leipzig2010.pdf.

Atkinson, A./T. Piketty/E. Saez (2011). Top Incomes in the Long Run of History. In: *Journal of Economic Literature* 49, 3–71.

Briceno, T./S. Stagl (2006). The Role of Social Processes for Sustainable Consumption. In: *Journal of Cleaner Production* 14, 1541–1551.

Davis, J.B. (2015). Agency and the Process Aspect of Capability Ddevelopment: Individual Capabilities, Collective Capabilities, and Collective Intentions. In: *Filosofía de la Economía* 4, 5–24.

GEESE/Global Ecovillage Educators for a Sustainable Earth (2012). *Ecovillage Design Education,* Fifh edition. Gaiaeducation. Online at https://gaiaeducation.org/index.php/en/resources/publications.

Hunecke, M. (2013). *Psychological Resources for Sustainable Lifestyles.* Bonn: Denkwerk Zukunft.

Ibrahim, S.S. (2006). From Individual to Collective Capabilities: The Capability Approach as a Conceptual Framework for Self-help. In: *Journal of Human Development* 7, 397–416.

Kaufmann-Hayoz, R. et al. (2012). Theoretical Perspectives on Consumer Behaviour: Attempt at Establishing an Order to the Theories. In: R. Defila/A. Di Giulio/R. Kaufmann-Hayoz (eds.). *The Nature of Sustainable Consumption and How to Achieve it.* München: oekom, 81–112.

Lessmann, O./F. Rauschmayer (2013). Re-Conceptualising Sustainable Development on the Basis of the Capability Approach: A Model and Its Difficulties. In: *Journal of Human Development and Capabilities* 14, 95–114.

Lessmann, O./F. Rauschmayer (2014). *The Capability Approach and Sustainability.* London: Routledge.

Lessmann, O. (2011). Freedom of Choice and Poverty Alleviation. In: *Review of Social Economy* 69, 439–463, doi:10.1080/00346764.2011.577349

Lietaer, B. (2001). *The Future of Money: Creating New Wealth, Work and a Wiser World.* London: Century.

Little, M. (2002). *Total Honesty/Total Heart: Fostering Empathy Development and Conflict Resolution Skills. A Violence Prevention Strategy.* BA Linguistics. Victoria: University of Victoria.

Molnar, S. (2011). Time Is of the Essence: The Challenges and Achievements of a Swedish Time Banking Initiative. In: *International Journal of Community Currency Research* 15.D, 13–22.

Nussbaum, M. (2000). *Women and Human Development: The Capabilities Aapproach.* Cambridge: Cambridge University Press.

Pick, S./ A.-E. Hietanen (2015). Psychosocial Barriers as Impediments to the Expansion of Functionings and Capabilities: The Case of Mexico. In: *Journal of Human Development and Capabilities* 16, 15–32.

Pick, S./J. Sirkin (2010). Breaking the Poverty Cycle: The Human Basis for Sustainable Development. Oxford: Oxford University Press.

Rauschmayer, F./C. Polzin/I. Omann (submitted). Examining Collective Action Through the Capability Approach: The Example of Community Ccurrencies. In: *Journal of Human Development and Capabilities*.

Rosenberg, M. (2001). *Nonviolent Communication: A Language of Life*. Encinitas, CA: Puddle Dancer Press.

Schäpke, N./F. Rauschmayer (2014). Going Beyond Efficiency: Including Altruistic Motives in Behavioral Models for Sustainability Transitions to Address Sufficiency. In: *Sustainability: Science, Practice & Policy* 10, 29–44.

Schwaiger, K. (2006). Regionalgeld und Gemeinwesenarbeit. In: *ZfSÖ – Zeitschrift für Sozialökonomie* 43 149, 19–25.

Schwartz, S./J. Howard (1981). A Normative Decision-Making Model of Altruism. In: J. Rushton/R. Sorrentino (eds.). *Altruism and Helping Behavior*. Hillsdale, NY: Erlbaum, 189–211.

Sen, A. (2002). Response to Commentaries. In: *Studies in Comparative International Development* 37, 78–86.

Sen, A. (2013). The Ends and Means of Sustainability. In: *Journal of Human Development and Capabilities* 14, 6–20.

Seyfang. G. (2004). Time Banks: Rewarding Community Self-Help in the Inner City? In: *Community Development Journal* 39 1, 62–71.

Seyfang. G. (2006). Sustainable Consumption, the New Economics and Community Currencies: Developing New Institutions for Environmental Governance. In: *Regional Studies* 40 7, 781–791.

Steg, L./C. Vlek (2009). Encouraging Pro-Environmental Behaviour: An Integrative Review and Research Agenda. In: *Journal of Environmental Psychology* 29, 309–317.

Volkert, J. (2013). Concepts of Agency, Sustainable Human Development (SHD) and Collective Abilities. In: *Maitreyee: E-Bulletin of the Human Development and Capability Association* 22, 9–12.

16 Subjective limits to growth and the limits to a lifestyle oriented critique of growth

Stefanie Graefe

What does it mean to understand our contemporary society as a "growth society" which finds itself not only in a state of "multiple crisis" (Demirovic/ Dück/Becker/ Bader 2011),[1] but perhaps also on the threshold of a new social order? In summing up this "multiple crisis" in broadly accessible terms, the degrowth movement and related critiques of growth have performed a valuable service. In the official political discourse, the concept of growth – "for almost all parties a political motto and watchword" (Fischer 2014, 136) – remains inviolably linked with prosperity. The fact that "a trend of decreasing growth rates has been observed in all developed industrial countries in the last few decades" (Reuter 2010, 21) has done nothing to change this. The critique of growth is therefore at the same time a form of ideology critique, which demonstrates that the high living standards and the democratisation in those capitalist societies that saw early industrialisation were based upon (ideally) exponentially increasing productivity and material consumption, along with all the disastrous ecological and social consequences. In this way, the critique of growth aims to contribute to a fundamental social transformation, such that a "post-growth society" (however that may concretely be shaped) will ideally emerge from a socially just, democratically implemented, and yet still radical "shrinking" of the global economy (cf Schmelzer/Passadakis 2011, 65).

At this point in time, of course, we cannot say very much about the concrete form that a post-growth society might take. We can say, however, that it would be better for the transition to a post-growth society to take place by design than by disaster (Victor 2008; Paech 2012, 143), that is, through the "bottom up" implementation of alternative ways of living and economic models. If that is right, then the question of the transition to a post-growth society is bound up with the so-called "question of the subject" (Foucault 2013). In other words, it implies fundamental changes to our everyday ways of living and our normative models of subjectivity and modes of self-determination.

But what does "growth" mean when considered at the level of the subject? What notion of subjectivity captures the "particular kind of entanglement in which subjects find themselves within a growth society" (Lessenich 2014, 6)? This question plays an astonishingly small role in the relevant debates. In critical discussions of growth, the "question of the subject" is either not posed systematically or only posed in a restricted and thus problematic fashion (as an exception see Rauschmayer in this volume). It is often assumed, for instance, that the acceptance of ecologically destructive modes of production by consumers, and the absence of effective protest against political policies that trade the livelihoods of future generations for short-term electoral gains, can ultimately be attributed to a lack of information and elucidation. For the well-known growth critic Tim Jackson, for example, effective criticism of the " 'iron cage' of consumerism" (Jackson 2009, 87) is characterised by its departure from a dangerous "delusional strategy" (ibid, 188). As this thought goes, societies that have been led astray in this manner are drowning under a flood of information that does not provide any real elucidation (cf. Acosta in this volume).

Alongside and complementary to this argument, the notion of alienation plays a particularly prominent role in critiques of growth. What is contended here is that, ultimately, no-one wants or *can want* growth. Life in advanced capitalist societies, as Paech (2013, 205) puts it, is tantamount to a "mega-programme of individual degradation", inducing an "inner desertification" that, in tragic fashion, is then compensated for through further consumption. From this perspective, interrupting this vicious circle does not mean *losing* anything but rather (and even subjectively) *gaining* something. Indeed, our liberation from the pressure to consume and perform will allow us to return to the really important things in life, such as "human relationships, [. . .] justice, and solidarity" (Schmelzer/Passadakis 2011, 23).

In my view, however, the problem with both of these arguments is that they ultimately cannot explain why the ideology of growth is so widely and willingly accepted. Since subjects are integrated into the growth regime by means of "mental infrastructures" (Welzer 2011) of which they have only limited awareness, it cannot simply be a question of disseminating information or explaining to people that they are far more alienated than they realise. In the face of the "universalisation of patterns of production and consumption [among the middle and upper classes of the Global North, S.G.] that from a socio-ecological perspective are not universalisable" (Wissen 2014, 5), it is a question of nothing less than a fundamental *restructuring of subjectivities*, i.e. of day-to-day routines and ways of living, as well as the self-conceptions and desires of the majority of people in highly industrialised, capitalist societies, if not worldwide.

The present paper of course cannot answer the question of precisely how that might take place. It responds rather to a far more modest question, namely: how are "we" – understood here as an imaginary collective made up of the populations of those advanced industrial countries whose resource usage exceeds biological capacity by at least 50 percent (WWF 2014) – integrated into the day-to-day reproduction of growth regimes? In the following, I shall outline a response to this question in three stages: firstly, inspired by current debates on "post-democracy", I shall consider how models of growth, subjectivity, and consumption (as the central driver of growth) shape one another in contemporary societies. Secondly, I shall outline a shift within the relevant hegemonic subject-programs that seems to me crucial for the critique of growth, namely a shift from the "entrepreneurial self" to the "resilient self". Thirdly and finally, I shall draw a number of further conclusions.

Why "Mental Infrastructures" are so difficult to change

In relation to our problematic, Ulrich Brand and Markus Wissen have spoken of the "imperial way of life" of the Global North (Brand/Wissen 2013). The concept of a way of life is an analytical tool which brings together post-Fordist forms of regulation and everyday culture. The predominant way of life in our society is "imperial" because, particularly where consumption is concerned, it presupposes "theoretically unlimited access to foreign resources, space, workers, and waste disposal capacities" (ibid: 5). Of course, no-one consciously decides to live in an imperial manner. This way of life is rather mediated via "models of the good life which, in being integrated into business strategies and underwritten by the state, are then striven for and internalised" (ibid: 9).

Brand and Wissen thus emphasise the differentiated character of social structures and stress that the degree to which an "imperial" way of life is adopted depends on the social milieu occupied by a given individual. They note that it is precisely "people who are highly-educated, with relatively high incomes, and with high levels of environmental awareness" (ibid: 10) who exhibit the highest per-capita use of resources.

The imperial way of life goes together with an acceptance of increasing social inequality, not only at the global level, but also within one's own society. In this regard, Ingolfur Blühdorn speaks laconically of an "inclusion in the politics of exclusion, a co-opted participation in the politics of marginalisation, and the *democratisation* of the politics of increasing inequality" (Blühdorn 2013, 203, emphasis in original). On this view, the significance of the 'imperial way of life' is not limited to questions of global distribution and climate change, but also bears on the institutional bases of the Western liberal social order – on democracy.

This process has notably been described by Crouch (2004). For Crouch, democratic institutions continue to function today – and indeed do so in an impressively professional manner – yet at the same time, they are hollowed out from the inside: "A post-democratic society [. . .] is one that continues to have and to use all the institutions of democracy, but in which they increasingly become a formal shell".[2] Society increasingly comes to be guided from outside the democratic institutions that nevertheless continue to function formally. This guidance is entrusted to expert committees, which primarily serve the interests of politico-economic elites. In this regard, Rancière (2014) even speaks of a "hatred of democracy" that is incurred by anyone who calls into question the austerity programmes imposed by international creditors and implemented by unelected "institutions".

For Blühdorn, however, democracy is currently losing its attractiveness, particularly for the dwindling middle classes, "because the principles of equality and fraternity are coming into open conflict with the lifestyles and models of self-realisation at the limits of the growth paradigm" (2013, 155). Their nevertheless high demands with regard to their free time and possibilities for self-determination are delegated to societal and political service providers, who promise efficient solutions (145). For Blühdorn, this state of affairs results in a "simulative democracy", in which democratic norms are professionally staged rather than realised. This even seems to be adequate for the contradictory needs of post-democratic citizens and institutions (181). Here, then, we are not dealing with political apathy, but with an enthusiastic participation in a post-democratic lifestyle.

On the basis of the concept of an "imperial way of life" and the diagnosis of a state of "simulative democracy", we can now suggest three principal reasons for the highly stable acceptance of the postmodern "consumer culture" (Featherstone 1991) and the growth regime.

Firstly, most people experience the growth regime not as a form of compulsion or limitation but as an expansion of their possibilities. Most people see taking cheap flights to foreign cities, owning the latest iPhone or – if one can afford it – following the latest design trends not as forms of repression, but as attractive ways in which they can give expression to their individuality, their creativity – their "self". The broader the range of consumer goods, the more this is the case.

Secondly, consumption not only provides means of expressive self-realisation; it is also a – if not *the* – primary medium of social distinction. The restriction of one's options for consumption not only means that one has to do without certain everyday comforts, but also implies a reduction of one's capacity to performatively assert a social position. The fact that the search for one's "true self" through consumption rarely ends in success and instead gives rise to various frustrations changes little here. Even the decision to (partially) opt out of the consumer society is still bound up with the promise of discovering one's "authentic self" and, as Renata Salecl has shown, follows (e.g. in "simply your life" movements) the very logic that is to be overcome: "The trend to simplify one's life is [. . .] a reaction to overwhelming consumer choice replicating itself in another form of consumer choice" (ibid: 143).

The radical reduction of opportunities for consumption that would be necessary in a post-growth society does not only mean that certain everyday comforts would have to be foregone. It would also limit the possibility of performatively asserting one's social position within an "autonomous, highly self-referential system of signs and significations" (Hellmann/Schrage 2015, 14). Precisely because this practice is largely unconscious and does not obey the logic of rational choice (Salecl 2011, 7), transforming it cannot simply be a matter of elucidating it and giving an insight into the alienation it produces, but must rather involve the de-escalation of social struggles for status and the development of alternative, globally and ecologically more sustainable forms of self-presentation. In my view, however, there is thus far little to indicate that declining GDP levels are correlated with the disappearance of the individual need for distinction and self-expression.

Thirdly: Even the obvious costs of the demand for optimisation, increased output and more intense competition – costs which manifest themselves in ever higher rates of depression and burnout-related illnesses – have not led, as one might have expected, to the "degrowth" of the pressure on the subject to achieve and succeed. The demands placed on the subject have only come to take on increasingly subtle forms. I will consider this point in greater detail in the following section.

Resilience as a new normative model of subjectivity

According to governmentality studies and recent work in the sociology of work and the cultural sociology of the subject, we find ourselves today in the following historical situation: for the first time in history, social and economic power is not primarily exerted through the suppression, restriction, and normalisation of subjectivity. The subjective element, i.e. feelings, relationships, desires, corporeality, and individuality, no longer simply constitutes a necessary marginal condition of economic productivity and social acceptability. As Axel Honneth states, it rather has "become the ideology and productive force of the deregulated economic system" (Honneth 2010, 76).

Here we can invoke certain key terms, such as the subjectivation, delimitation, and flexibilisation of work, which transform the employee into the "entreployee" (Voß/Pongratz 1998), or the "entrepreneurial self" (Bröckling, 2016), who spends her life working to realise and optimise her own "potential". The "development of one's own 'human capital'" thus becomes the telos of every individual life (Reckwitz 2008, 131).

What is crucial here is that the ideal entreployee, who organises her whole life according to the maxim of marketisation, does so not only on orders from above, but also because she herself *wants* what she *ought* to want. Since it is a question here of a "double subjectivation" (Kleemann/Matuschek/Voss 2002) – where subjective expectations and organisational demands mirror one another – this inevitably implies the subject's hazardous employment of her own workforce and "lifeforce" (Jürgens 2006).

As a result, exhaustion rates are increasing. Burnout and depression, for example, have been described by Günter Voß and Cornelia Weiss as "the defining illnesses of flexible capitalism" (Voß/Weiss 2013). The idea of a "defining illness" (in German: Leiterkrankung) implies that it is not simply a question of work here, but of a fundamental socio-cultural transformation which is not limited to the world of work and employment, though the reorganisation of the latter is central to it.

In sum, if one pursues the relevant diagnoses, subjectivity itself is seen to have become a productive force today. This is historically new in this general picture. Statistically it is expressed in two complementary developments: On the one hand, productivity has greatly increased. Since 1991 productivity per working hour has risen by almost 35 percent. On the other hand, mental illness levels have increased year after year. Simply put: people are becoming more efficient – and more exhausted (for the link between productivity and structural violence, see Henning in this volume).

Nevertheless, the mass experience of exhaustion has not yet resulted in seriously questioning the demand for optimisation and efficiency. Instead, the range of options available to those suffering from exhaustion has simply expanded. Exhausted subjects can and should deal with their illness by means of specific interpretative scripts and treatment plans – here we think of the therapeutic approach to the social sphere (Gahntz/Graefe 2016).

It is precisely at this point that, in my view, we can observe an interesting shift. For while the entrepreneurial self, according to Ulrich Bröckling (2016), draws its practical knowledge primarily from the relevant self-management literature, today's exhaustion-prone subject is constitutively dependent on therapeutic expertise concerning the behavioural and biological bases of successful stress prevention.

In itself, this is not fundamentally new: the notion of stress was discussed by Walter Cannon as early as 1914. What is relatively new, however, is that the ability to deal with stress is seen as the essential element in what is currently a very popular "cultural script for a desirable personality" (Illouz 2004, 124). It is no coincidence that I recently encountered a particularly telling example of this "script" in a burnout manual. As a remedy for stress and strain, the manual recommends working on one's "resilience". It is not only healthy to have a "resilient personality"; it is also all that we could desire. As the authors put it:

> "This resilient personality is strong-willed and is engaged in a continual process of exchange with itself and the world. It makes conscious decisions and sets priorities; it is also confident enough to accept assistance when necessary. It is in touch with its feelings, with its body and its rhythms, and with its own needs. In a certain sense it is subversive in relation to the system, for it does not unconditionally submit to it – neither to the demands of the globalised world nor to the fears prevailing within a given society"
>
> (Unger/Kleinschmidt 2007, 148).

The resilient subject is thus not only successful; she is also in harmony with her body. She is not only geared toward competition, but also emotionally sensitive. She can accept help and knows her own limits and vulnerability. To be resilient is to have a psychological capacity for resistance, to be skilled in the art of overcoming problems, crises, and even traumata relatively quickly, so as to return to one's original, stable disposition. Resilience is a preventive and learnable universal remedy, not only for stress-prone entreployees, but also, for example, for soldiers in Afghanistan, Israeli schoolchildren, or those living in the coastal areas of Bangladesh (Gebauer 2015).

The figure of the resilient personality therefore does not *depart* from or *replace* that of the entrepreneurial self or the subjectivised entreployee, but constitutes an important psycho-biological enlargement of the latter. Nevertheless, the resilient personality is oriented more toward *restabilising* itself in accordance with the demands of the current context than toward its permanent self-*enhancement*. On the one hand, then, we might see the elevation of this economy of resilience to the status of an ideal personality-model as an indication of the stagnation of the growth dynamic.

On the other hand, however, it can be seen as contributing to the stabilisation and maintenance of the growth regime. The personality who is immune to crisis has no need to change the system. She only needs to permanently change herself. She is therefore subversive by herself and has no need of political organisation or social movements. If one is able to build up resilience into a form of capital in

Bourdieu's sense, one will not only be in a better position to deal with unstable social and economic situations; one will also be more successful – and perhaps even happier – than others. This brings me to my third and final point.

Conclusion: a new social contract?

My thesis is therefore that it is in the shape of resilient subjectivity that the growth regime and post-democracy – even and especially in their "imperial" dimension – not only become acceptable to individuals, but also come to be seen as attractive, at least by the health-conscious, consumption-oriented middle classes.

More precisely, we might say that resilience is the shape which subjectivity assumes in a simulative or consumer democracy. It proves to be highly effective at integrating the subject into the prevailing power relations, for three main reasons:

1 Because it links participation in society (via consumption, charitable engagements, and lifestyle communities) with individual well-being, or social recognition with self-realisation.
2 Because it takes the subject as a whole into account (her emotions, corporeality, relationships, and so on) and not only – like the entrepreneurial self – her rationality and efficiency.
3 Because if it is successfully acquired, resilience does not only raise one's chances of social success and subjective contentment; it also makes it easier to reduce social inequality to the different capacities people have to "be themselves", and thus to naturalise it.

This point might be pushed even further. Resilience as an ideal way of being is not simply a strategy for *dealing with* crises. Strictly speaking, it is rather *dependent* on crises. It is only in the face of unforeseeable challenges that the resilient subject can attain and affirm her identity and individuality.

As a psychological and pedagogical category, resilience has – as José Brunner (2014) has shown – close genealogical ties with the concept of trauma. Each term is the other's mirror image: while trauma revolves around vulnerability, resilience refers to the capacity of subjects and communities to resist crises, i.e. to prevent traumatisation. One might also say: resilience is the ideology that prepares subjects to survive in crisis-torn capitalist societies (which are ever more clearly confronted with endogenous limits to growth, Reuter 2010) by assuming responsibility for themselves amidst a lack of social support structures. Furthermore, the semantic and discursive extension of the concept of resilience can be interpreted as a displacement of the Western conception of politics. What is politically important is no longer the shaping of a better future, but rather the task of managing the essentially incalculable social and natural conditions of life. "Psychological resilience programs", Brunner writes, "can be seen as part of a shift in the Western conception of the social contract", a shift that is bound up with the date 9/11 (Brunner 2014, 244).[3] Since the concept of resilience transcends the spheres of subjectivity and psychology and is *"deeply connected to the security problematic"* (Neocleous 2015, 2, emphasis in original), it opens on to the link between subjectivity, the economy, and security that is so crucial for contemporary capitalist societies, and points toward a general "culture of preparedness" (ibid: 4) in which the proactive anticipation of potential crises becomes a general maxim of action.

Resilience thus not only provides a foundation for subjectively dealing with the uncertainty and instability of contemporary capitalist society but also constitutes a core competence in dealing with the social and ecological disasters produced through imperial ways of life. Conceiving the logic of subjective and politico-social action in terms of crisis management, however, is nothing less than a departure from the notion (so crucial to Western modernity) of collectively enhancing life conditions and social institutions, in favour of a psychologised expert-culture that transforms the demands of democracy into a need for counselling.

This specific ideological framework poses great difficulties for transformative critiques of growth.[4] Furthermore, growth is a highly abstract category, of which there is no immediate social or emotional experience. Yet, enlarged consumer markets and an ever-increasing range of therapeutic discourses and practices offer people the opportunity to work on their feelings and relationships in a very concrete manner. Whether it is a question of non-violent communication, mindfulness training or an Ayurvedic diet – all of these options promise a more attractive, because more enjoyable and multi-faceted life. And for certain social groups, this is not just a vague promise: a socially and ecologically sensitive life-style indeed implies the potential for more "well-being" (or at least for the pleasant feeling of being socially mature) – provided one's social privileges are not seriously challenged. A transformation of society in terms of post-growth and post-capitalism (in my view, you can't have the one without the other) will not be possible, however, unless the orientation to happiness, well-being or indeed resilience – which is widespread also in the post-growth movement – is itself called into question (Graefe 2016).

Actually, a lifestyle-oriented critique of growth not only tends to underestimate the *appeasing* function of resilience (as an indicator of a psycho-political paradigm shift that absorbs critical impulses). Resilience is at the same time promoted as a hopeful principle for accomplishing the transition to a post-growth society (Hopkins 2014). For visions inspired by a critique of growth, the concept of resilience has a certain appeal insofar as it does not aim at material enhancement but system preservation. As such, it seems to have a kind of built-in immunity to the exponential use of resources and the ideology of merit. But at the same time, resilience is also about the optimisation of (individual as well as collective) crisis response skills. Some actors will always be "more" resilient and others "less" so. Moreover, given its defining objective of flexible crisis response, resilience favours an alert life-style of permanent vigilance and readjustment of individual behaviour rather than contentment.

To be sure, boosting crisis response skills can make sense in concrete individual cases; as a defining principle of a democratic transformation of society, it is inappropriate if not outright dangerous: "The motto of resilience [. . .] no longer is: *Our Common Future* but *Our Common Fate*" (Exner 2013, emphasis in the original). Structures of power and domination are conceived of as a "general framework" that cannot be changed but only more or less understood and taken into account. Strictly speaking, therefore, resilience and structural transformation are mutually exclusive. Instead of a democratic dispute about positions and interests, the orientation is toward what is necessary or objectively advisable: "The focus is on the system adapting to the environment; the complementary option of adapting the environment to the requirements of the system is pushed to the background" (Bröckling 2013, 55). And this also means: resilience implies the assumption of a (more-or-less) closed system that is conceived of as constitutively vulnerable. As a result, the concept is in principle open to social, nationalist, or ethnic closures where the "system boundary" is assumed as a given. In the context of a critique of growth, this figure of thought is found whenever the return to local and rural communities is conceived of as an essential element of the transformation into a post-growth society.

In a nutshell: resilience is essentially an apolitical concept; it is hardly adequate for bringing about a (re-)politicisation of the growth issue. This, however, is imperative if the critique of growth seeks to be more than an academic niche topic and a (more-or-less) appealing life-style option. In other words: the "good life beyond growth" already begins once we refuse to be talked into believing that an exemplary life-style of self-proclaimed avant-gardes is capable of solving fundamental systemic problems.

In my view, then, the transition to a post-growth society is bound up with the significant challenge of elaborating alternatives to imperial ways of life – alternatives that not only significantly reduce our individual ecological footprints but also reverse the tendency toward the therapeutic depoliticisation of the social within stagnating growth democracies.

Notes

1 All quotations from German sources have been translated for the present text. The present paper is a revised, completed and translated version of Graefe (2016a).
2 Online at http://blogs.lse.ac.uk/politicsandpolicy/five-minutes-with-colin-crouch/ (accessed: 19th January 2016).
3 My thanks to Alexandra Rau for the reference to this stimulating line of thought, which is crucial for the argument outlined in the present paper.
4 This is especially true when resilience is adopted as an orienting framework for potential post-growth societies. Cf. e.g. http://globalchangenow.de/suffizienz-subsistenz (accessed: 19th January 2016).

References

Blühdorn, I. (2013). *Simulative Demokratie: Neue Politik nach der postdemokratischen Wende*. Berlin: Suhrkamp.

Brand, U./Wissen, M. (2013). *Sozial-ökologische Krise und imperiale Lebensweise: Zu Krise und Kontinuität kapitalistischer Naturverhältnisse*. Online at www.buko.info/fileadmin/user_upload/doc/reader/BUKO-Gesnat-Seminar-04-2013-Reader-V1.pdf, 3–16 (accessed: 19th January 2016).

Bröckling, U. (2013). Gut Angepasst? Belastbar? Widerstandsfähig? Resilienz und Geschlecht, In: *Freiburger Zeitschrift für Geschlechterstudien* 19.1, 49–66.

Bröckling, U. (2016). *The Entrepreneurial Self: Fabricating a New Type of Subject.* London: Sage.

Brunner, J. (2014). *Die Politik des Traumas: Gewalterfahrungen und psychisches Leid in den USA, in Deutschland und im Israel/Palästina-Konflikt.* Berlin: Suhrkamp.

Crouch, C. (2004). *Post-Democracy.* Cambridge: Polity Press.

Demirovic, A./Dück, J./Becker, F./Bader, P. (eds., 2011). *Vielfachkrise im finanzmarktdominierten Kapitalismus.* Hamburg: VSA.

Exner, A. (2013). Von der Nachhaltigkeit zur Resilienz? Mögliche Diskursveränderung in der Vielfachkrise. In: *Phase 2. Zeitschrift gegen die Realität,* 45, Online at http://phase-zwei.org/hefte/artikel/von-der-nachhaltigkeit-zur-resilienz-408/?druck=1   (accessed: 19th July 2016).

Featherstone, M. (1991). *Consumer Culture and Postmodernism.* London: Sage.

Fischer, L. (2014). Wachstum und Wachstumskritik – Renaturalisierung eines wirtschaftswissenschaftlichen Dogmas. In: F. Deus/A-L. Dießelmann/ L. Fischer/C. Knobloch (eds.). *Die Kultur des Neoevolutionismus: Zur diskursiven Renaturalisierung von Mensch und Gesellschaft.* Bielefeld: transcript, 135–167.

Foucault, M. (2013). Why Study Power: The Question of the Subject. In: H.L. Dreyfus/P. Rabinow (eds.), *Michel Focuault: Beyond Structuralism and Hermeneutics.* New York: Routledge, 208–216.

Gahntz, C./S. Graefe (2016). Burnout. Die widersprüchliche Logik der Therapeutisierung von Arbeitsstress. In: R. Anhorn/M. Balzereit (eds.). *Handbuch Therapeutisierung des Sozialen.* Wiesbaden: Springer VS, 367–389.

Gebauer, T. (2015). *Das Paradox der Resilienz.* Online at www.medico.de/blog/artikel/das-paradox-der-resilienz (accessed: 19th January 2016).

Graefe, S. (2016). Degrowth und die Frage des Subjekts. In: A.K. Postwachstum (eds.). *Wachstum – Krise und Kritik: Die Grenzen der kapitalistischen Lebensweise.* Frankfurt am Main/New York: Campus, 201–222.

Graefe, S. (2016a). Grenzen des Wachstums? Resiliente Subjektivität im Krisenkapitalismus. In: *Psychosozial* 143, 39–50.

Hellmann, K-U./D. Schrage (2015). Die Konsumgesellschaft von Jean Baudrillard. Zur Einführung. In: J. Baudrillard (ed.). *Die Konsumgesellschaft. Ihre Mythen, ihre Strukturen.* Wiesbaden: Springer VS, 9–33.

Honneth, A. (2010). Organized Self-Realisation: Some Paradoxes of Individualization. In: *European Journal of Social Theory* 7, 463–478.

Hopkins, R. (2014). *The Transition Handbook. From Oil Dependency to Local Resilience.* Cambridge: UIT Cambridge.

Illouz, E. (2004). *Gefühle in Zeiten des Kapitalismus.* Frankfurtam Main: Suhrkamp.

Jackson, T. (2009). *Prosperity Without Growth.* London: Routledge.

Jürgens, K. (2006). *Arbeits- und Lebenskraft. Reproduktion als eigensinnige Grenzziehung.* Wiesbaden: VS.

Kleemann, F./I. Matuschek/G.G. Voss (2002). Subjektivierung von Arbeit: Ein Überblick zum Stand der soziologischen Diskussion. In: M. Moldaschl/G.G. Voß (eds.). *Subjektivierung von Arbeit.* München/Mering: Hampp, 53–100.

Lessenich, S. (2014). Akteurszwang und Systemwissen: Das Elend der Wachstumsgesellschaft. *Working Paper 3/2014,* DFG-KollegforscherInnengruppe Postwachstumsgesellschaften Jena. Online at www.kolleg-postwachstum.de/sozwgmedia/dokumente/WorkingPaper/wp3_2014.pdf (accessed: 19th January 2016).

Neocleous, M. (2015). *Resisting Resilience: Against the Colonization of Political Imagination.* Online at www.medico.de/fileadmin/user_upload/media/Neocleous_Resisting_Resilience.pdf (accessed: 19th January 2016).

Paech, N. (2012). *Befreiung vom Überfluss: Auf dem Weg in die Postwachstumsökonomie.* München: oekom.

Paech, N. (2013). Wege aus der Wachstumsdiktatur. In: H. Welzer/K. Wiegand (eds.). *Wege aus der Wachstumsgesellschaft.* Frankfurt am Main: Fischer, 200–219.

Rancière, J. (2014). *Hatred of Democracy.* London/Brooklyn: Verso.

Reckwitz, A. (2008). *Subjekt.* Bielefeld: transcript.

Reuter, N. (2010). Stagnation im Trend – Leben mit gesättigten Märkten, stagnierenden Ökonomien und verkürzten Arbeitszeiten. In: *Zeitschrift für Sozialökonomie* 166/167, 21–32.

Salecl, R. (2011). *The Tyranny of Choice.* London: Profile Books.

Schmelzer, M./A. Passadakis (2011). *Postwachstum: Krise, ökologische Grenzen und soziale Rechte.* Hamburg: VSA.

Unger, H-P./C. Kleinschmidt (2007). *Bevor der Job krank macht: Wie uns die heutige Arbeitswelt in die seelische Erschöpfung treibt und was man dagegen tun kann.* München: Kösel-Verlag.

Victor, P.A. (2008). *Managing Without Growth. Slower by Design, Not Disaster.* Cheltenham/Northampton: Edward Elgar.

Voß, G.G./Pongratz, H.J. (1998). Der Arbeitskraftunternehmer. Eine neue Grundform der Ware Arbeitskraft? In: *Kölner Zeitschrift für Soziologie und Sozialpsychologie* 50, 131–158.

Voß, G.G./C. Weiss (2013). Burnout und Depression – Leiterkrankungen des subjektivierten Kapitalismus oder: Woran leidet der Arbeitskraftunternehmer? In: S. Neckel/G. Wagner (eds.). *Leistung und Erschöpfung: Burnout in der Wettbewerbsgesellschaft.* Berlin: Suhrkamp, 29–57.

Welzer, W. (2011). *Mentale Infrastrukturen: Wie das Wachstum in die Welt und in die Seelen kam.* ed by Heinrich-Böll-Stiftung Berlin. Online at www.boell.de/sites/default/files/Endf_Mentale_Infrastrukturen.pdf (accessed: 19th January 2016).

Wissen, M. (2014). *Auf dem Weg in einen grünen Kapitalismus? Die ökologische Modernisierung der imperialen Lebensweise.* Online at http://ifg.rosalux.de/files/2014/05/Imperiale-Lebensweise_2014-05-07.pdf (accessed: 19th January 2016).

WWF (World Wildlife Fund). (2014). *Living Planet Report 2014: Species and Spaces, Peoples and Places.* Online at www.wwf.de/fileadmin/fm-wwf/Publikationen-PDF/WWF-LPR2014-EN-LowRes.pdf (accessed: 19th January 2016).

Part V

One world without growth

Alternative conceptions of the political

17 The 'good life' of nations

A global perspective

Martin Fritz & Max Koch

Major socio-ecological issues such as climate change have a global character. For the atmosphere it does not matter from which point in the world greenhouse gases are emitted. The structural preconditions for any 'good life' likewise have global reach. In this chapter, we theorise and operationalise the individual, social and ecological dimensions for prosperity and the 'good life' at national level and empirically explore patterns of prosperity at the global scale. How are prosperity patterns structured in various parts of the world? Are there any country clusters that manage to develop (elements of) the 'good life' within ecological limits? And what are the future prospects for the different clusters and particularly for the Western world en route to achieving a surplus in prosperity?

Prosperity in a global perspective

Growth-critical scholars have begun to discuss the feasibility of providing welfare and prosperity in non-growing economies (Jackson 2009; Koch 2013; Soper/ Emmelin 2016). Related research addresses, for example, the 'good life' (Vega Camacho 2012), 'sustainable welfare' (Koch/Mont 2016) and '21st century socialism' (Alvarez Lozano 2012). These contributions stress those elements of human conviviality that require few, if any, material resources, allowing for a surplus in prosperity for one person or one generation while leaving room for the development of others. Yet the re-embedding of economy and society in the principles of environmental sustainability is not the only dimension of prosperity. Recent contributions from disciplines as different as inequality and consumption research, the psychology of well-being and needs theories suggest that prosperity should be understood by considering two additional dimensions: a social dimension covering aspects of inclusion and equity and an individual dimension which considers well-being and the quality of life (see, for a further elaboration on our concept of 'prosperity', Fritz/Koch 2014).

In relation to the social dimension of prosperity, previous studies provided the evidence that people in more equal and socially inclusive societies are better off and report greater amounts of subjective well-being than in more unequal ones where status competition is especially pronounced (Wilkinson/Pickett 2010). Consumption researchers argue that in rich countries buying things is not in the first place about the goods themselves but rather about the symbolic message that the act of purchase conveys (Soper 2016). What Hirsch (1976) called the competition for 'positional goods' is mediated through a social logic that Bourdieu (1984) referred to as 'distinction'. The more unequal societies are the greater the obligation to participate in the never-ending societal race to define the legitimate taste between avant-gardes and the mainstream.[1] The positional gains of this race are, by definition, short term, and do not contribute anything to human welfare in the long-term and contradict the principal reproductive needs of the Earth as an ecological system, since such competitive consumption practices are normally bound to matter and energy transformations and necessitate the burning of fossil fuels.

Concerning the individual dimension of prosperity scholars assume that human beings must have certain psychological needs satisfied in order to flourish and experience personal well-being. These needs include feeling safe and secure as well as competent and efficient. People also require love and intimacy and struggle under conditions of loneliness, rejection, and exclusion. Yet where "economic growth is a key goal of a nation" (Kasser 2011, 195), with its encouragement of self-enhancing, hierarchical, extrinsic and materialistic values, the fundamental needs required for human prosperity are undermined. The theme has also been taken up in theories of human needs (Gough 2015) and 'sustainable welfare' (Koch/Mont 2016). Following this literature, the satisfaction of essential needs would require relatively few material resources, allowing for a surplus in welfare and prosperity for one person or one generation without undermining the development of others. While due to planetary limits Western material welfare standards cannot be generalised to the rest of the world, the issue of whether more than basic human needs can be provided globally is an empirical one (Koch et al. 2017). Politically, this would be, in Gough's terminology, a matter of 'policy auditing', during which critical thresholds for the universal provision of human needs (and wants) would constantly be redefined in light of the best available scientific and practical knowledge.

Given the continuing lack of evidence for an absolute decoupling of GDP growth, material resource use and carbon emissions as well as the extraordinary small time periods within which climate change mitigation would need to become effective (IPCC 2014), any according institutional compromise would need to go beyond the national scale, on which post-war welfare arrangements were agreed, and encompass the entire globe. It is only at the global level that thresholds for matter and energy that countervail environmental challenges such as climate change can be defined. At the same time, these global bio-physical terms would delineate the leeway within which national and local economies and societies could evolve. For the degrowth-research community the emerging consensus is that degrowth should be understood as a process whose end goal is a global steady state economy (Martínez-Alier et al. 2010; Koch 2015), whereby the global North would need to embark on degrowth trajectories, while the global South would need to "follow a path of decelerating growth" (O'Neill 2012, 222). In other words, there would be space for different national and local paths to post-growth economies and societies that represent different traditions and institutional patterns and that could provide prosperity in different ways.

If the earth and its unequally developed parts are to embark on a social and ecological transformation path at the end of which the planet's economies and societies function and provide prosperity within ecological limits, the exploration of the ways and patterns that contemporary countries achieve prosperity is of interest because national transformation trajectories have to start from the status quo. In the following section, we therefore explore how the countries of the world perform in providing prosperity or the 'good life'. Are there groups of countries that share the same patterns? Do particular groups of countries in particular parts of the World succeed in their efforts of establishing a good quality of life and social inclusion within ecological limits (Swampa 2012)?

Data and method

The main objective of 'degrowth' is a "transition towards a just, participatory, and ecologically sustainable society". This is to be met by meeting "basic human needs" and ensuring a "high quality of life, while reducing the ecological impact of the global economy to a sustainable level, equitably distributed between nations". (Research/Degrowth 2010, 524). Basically, hence, there are three dimensions that are seen as universally relevant for a 'good life': ecological sustainability, social inclusion, and quality of life. These are multi-dimensional concepts themselves, that is, each contains a number of aspects. Here, we focus on the most general and important indicators available for a maximum of countries of the world. First, *ecological sustainability* is measured by three indicators related to two urgent environmental issues: On the one hand, the level of CO_2 emissions per capita reflects countries' contributions to global climate change. On the other hand, the size of ecological footprints of consumption and production indicates the quantity of natural resources that are used in a given country. Footprints take into account all material / natural resources and the space that humans use in production and consumption. By way of addressing the interconnectedness of all human activity with all other parts of ecosystems, it becomes clear that the mere size of human impact on ecosystems has potentially serious consequences – irrespective of whether it is a brown or green economy. There is as yet no empirical evidence that ecological footprints can decrease in growing economies (Jackson 2009).

Second, any 'good life' involves social conditions based on cooperation and trust. People must be able to live and act freely and help each other. We call this second dimension *social inclusion* and suggest a further distinction between two aspects: a) 'Social cohesion' or the degree to which people can safely live together without excluding or disadvantaging others. We operationalise this subdimension by using indicators for criminality (homicide rates) and inequality (Gini index for income inequality). In principle, the combination of social cohesion and ecological sustainability can be provided both by authoritarian and democratic political regimes. However, only the latter meets the Degrowth understanding of a good life: Individual freedom and autonomy are an essential part of the Degrowth declaration (Research/Degrowth 2010) and a major theme in human needs theory (Gough 2015). Thus, as a second aspect or subdimension of social inclusion b) 'Political freedom' accounts for the chances that citizens have in participating and

Table 17.1 Dimensions and indicators of the 'good life'

1. Ecological Sustainability
CO2 emissions in tons per capita
Ecological footprint of production in global ha per capita
Ecological footprint of consumption in global ha per capita
2. Social Cohesion
Gini Index for income inequality
Homicide rates per 100,000 persons
3. Political Freedom
Democracy Index
Freedom House Index
4. Quality of Life
Life Expectancy
Literacy Rates
Subjective Well-being

shaping their common political and social life by freely expressing their opinions and views. We measure political freedom by the Democracy and Freedom House indices, which both account for political rights and civil liberties. Recent research has shown that these both subdimensions of social inclusion are independent from each other empirically (Fritz/Koch 2016). Consequently, they are treated separately here as the two dimensions: *social cohesion* and *political freedom*.

Third, a 'good life' refers to individuals and their *objective* and *subjective quality of life*. For the objective aspect, we use life expectancy as an overall indicator for health, and we use literacy rates to measure the degree of education. Though literacy rates are a somewhat general indicator for education, they are nevertheless useful, since we compare a great number of countries including many developing countries with significant differences in literacy rates. We also consider self-reported well-being as an indicator for the subjective aspect of the individual quality of life. The debate around the Easterlin paradox (Easterlin 1974; Easterlin et al. 2010) and the question whether income has relative or absolute value indicates that the consideration of objective factors alone is not sufficient when evaluating the quality of life. The mechanism of the hedonic treadmill, social comparisons and psychological adaptation processes interfere with happiness gains in quality of life that are achieved through economic development (Hagarty/Veenhoven 2003). In the context of our cross-country study we cannot assess these adaption processes, but explore objective living conditions and subjective well-being simultaneously. In summary, we adjust our original three-dimensional approach to prosperity by using ten single indicators to apply a revised four-dimensional understanding for the conceptualisation of prosperity and the 'good life' (see table 17.1).

We compiled data for these dimensions and indicators from different sources including the Global Footprint Network, the World Bank and the OECD)[2] and for one year in the period 2008–2012 in order to minimise lacks through missing data. The resulting sample is comprised of 138 countries from all world regions. In order to explore which groups of countries share similar characteristics as described by our ten 'good life' indicators, we apply Hierarchical Clustering on Principal Components (HCPC). This method uses principal component analysis (PCA) "as a preprocessing step to denoise the data" (Husson/Josse/Pages 2010, 1) prior to agglomerative hierarchical clustering. PCA reveals the relations and associations between the indicators and summarises the information they contain by calculating few dimensions which capture the most important structures in the data. The countries' values on these dimensions are then used to perform a cluster analysis. The latter method is suited to identify typical classes of objects – here: countries – according to their similarities in the indicators. The following section discusses the results of both procedures in detail.

Results and interpretation: modernisation, extractivism, and anomie

The result of the preprocessing PCA is a three-dimensional solution with altogether 77 percent of explained variance. These three empirically resulting dimensions are different from our four theoretically derived dimensions: The first dimension, which represents half of the information contained in the entire dataset (50 percent explained variance), reflects socio-economic development in general. Here quality of life and political freedom are positively associated. However, the same applies to ecological degradation as indicated by the high positive correlations between CO2 emissions, ecological footprints and dimension 1 (see table 17.1). We label this dimension *modernisation*. This widely used term reflects the ambivalent meaning expressed in the associated empirical pattern: 'Modernisation' as technical, scientific and socio-economic development not only leads to a higher standard of living for many people but also involves uncontrollable risks for society and the environment. Increasing affluence in 'modernising' countries, for example, facilitates the use of means of private transport such as automobiles and airplanes and normally goes hand in hand with increases in carbon emissions, land use and the consumption of raw materials.

The second dimension captures 15 percent of the variance in the data and is mainly constituted by differences in 'social cohesion' as operationalised by inequality and criminality. Both indicators together make up for more than two thirds of the total inertia of this dimension. We call this dimension *anomie* since high values on this dimension mean low cohesion due to the negative polarity of the indicators. Despite this negative polarity, the empirical anomie dimension is identical with our theoretical social cohesion dimension. In practical terms the relation between inequality and criminality indicates that an unequal distribution of wealth and incomes undermines solidarity and facilitates the violation of social norms.

Finally, the third dimension is determined by the indicators Freedom (23.3 percent) and CO2 emissions (25.3 percent) which are here, in contrast to the first dimension, negatively associated to each other. Thus, high values on this dimension reflect unsustainable autocratic political systems as they are typical for many societies that strongly depend on resource extraction to generate wealth. Referring to Acosta (2013) we use the term *extractivism* to describe this dimension. Being originally related to the Latin America experience, this term identifies a global pattern of exploitation of natural resources. The latter are extracted and sold by ruling national elites, usually in partnership with multinational corporations, and largely without distributing or re-investing the resulting revenues within the country. The consequences include environmental degradation, stagnating qualities of life and increases in social problems such as criminality. Hence, while an extractivist regime may affect the economic performance of a country positively in the short-term, it is nevertheless also associated with a lack of investment in public infrastructures as well as with rudimentary democratic institutions such as the separation of powers (table 17.2).

In summary, the main relations between the ten 'good life' indicators can be described as interplay of three concepts: modernisation, anomie and extractivism. Unfortunately, there is currently no 'good life' pattern without negative side-effects: modernisation and extractivism are both ecologically harmful processes, while anomie is associated with low scores on the social dimension. Furthermore, the results indicate that the four theoretically derived dimensions of the 'good life' should be understood as analytical distinction and cannot, with the exception of 'social cohesion', be found purely, i.e. as separate phenomena, empirically. In fact, many aspects seem to be intrinsically tied to others as particularly indicated in the case of modernisation and extractivism.

To address the two further questions of typical constellations and combinations of these three concepts within countries and of which countries come closest to the degrowth understanding of a 'good life', we perform a Cluster Analysis. Hierarchical clustering using Euclidean distances and Ward's method groups the 138 countries of the dataset according to their similarities on the three dimensions extracted by the PCA. The resulting country clusters represent different ways or alternatives of how a 'good life' may look like. There are seven such clusters which are identified via HCPC (see table 17.3 and figure 17.1).

Cluster 1 is composed of the least developed countries of the world, for example African countries such as Angola and Cameroon. It is characterised by the worldwide lowest *modernisation* value. Accordingly, countries of this cluster cannot provide its citizens a good quality of life, neither in subjective nor in objective terms. Life expectancy is the lowest in the world at about 57 years (compared to a 70-years world average). While inequality is above average in the least developed countries, criminality remains at a medium level. Thus, *anomie* is not particularly high in these countries but neither are there visible signs to reduce it. Quite another story is political freedom. Although not the lowest, the mean values for the Freedom House and the Democracy Indices are well below the global average. The positive aspect is the excellent ecological performance: All three green indicators are on levels within planetary boundaries (Rockström et al. 2009). However, this good performance is largely caused by a lack of economic development and technological infrastructure. It is an unwanted status which people, in all likelihood, would change if they had the chance. All in all, and despite the positive

Table 17.2 Results of the principal component analysis

	Contributions (explained variance) in %			Factor loadings (correlations)		
	Dim 1 (50%)	Dim 2 (15%)	Dim 3 (12%)	Dim 1 (50%)	Dim 2 (15%)	Dim 3 (12%)
CO2 Emissions	9.0	3.5	25.3	0.7	−0.2	0.6
Ecol. F. of prod.	13.5	0.5	5.0	0.8	−0.1	0.2
Ecol. F. of consum.	15.1	1.7	3.6	0.9	−0.2	0.2
Inequality	3.4	30.6	9.4	−0.4	0.7	0.3
Criminality	1.4	38.1	12.5	−0.3	0.8	0.4
Democracy	10.9	11.5	17.2	0.7	0.4	−0.5
Freedom	9.0	9.7	23.3	0.7	0.4	−0.5
Life Expectancy	13.9	0.0	0.2	0.8	0.0	0.0
Literacy	10.5	1.1	1.1	0.7	0.1	0.1
Well-being	13.3	3.3	2.4	0.8	0.2	0.2

ecological performance, the citizens of the countries of this cluster are far from enjoying any type of a 'good life'.

At first glance *Cluster 2* looks similar to the previous one. However, there are significant differences. While *modernisation* is likewise very low in these mostly African and Asian countries such as Bangladesh, Ghana and India, social cohesion and political freedom scores are significantly higher than in the first cluster and match the global average. Since the ecological performance of *Cluster 2* is as good as in *Cluster 1*, and, hence, environmentally sustainable, the values for *extractivism* are clearly below the global mean. *Cluster 2* demonstrates that at least basic levels of political freedom and social cohesion can be achieved without compromising the natural preconditions of society. However, given that objective and subjective quality of life scores are extremely low, this cluster hardly represents a 'good life' in degrowth terms either.

Cluster 3 assembles Asian and Arab countries, among others China, Vietnam, Algeria and Iran, and represents another type of social organisation: These countries are able to provide a maximum of social cohesion (low anomie and Gini Index), but, apparently, at the prize of political oppression. Their values for freedom and democracy are even lower than in the least developed countries of *Cluster 1*. And how do these countries perform in providing a good quality of life for their people? Objectively, they succeed to some degree as life expectancy and literacy oscillate around the global averages, but subjective well-being is only marginally higher than in both preceding clusters and is still lower than the average of all countries. Finally, in terms of ecological sustainability *Cluster 3* features relatively low footprints of production and consumption, while CO2 emissions approach the global mean. Hence, *Cluster 3* countries likewise fail to provide key elements of the 'good life'.

Cluster 4 brings together elements of a 'good' but dangerous life. Many Caribbean and Latin American countries belong to this group but also Namibia and South Africa. Its most exceptional characteristic is the extremely high amount

Country clusters and dimensions

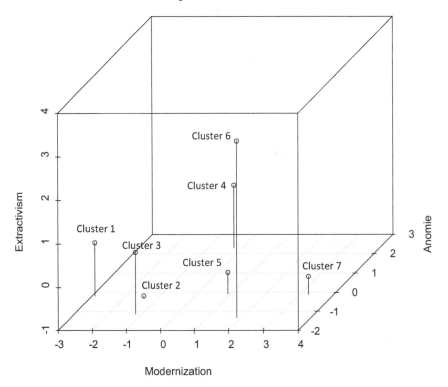

Figure 17.1 Country clusters and dimensions

of *anomie* in terms of skyrocketing inequality – the Gini coefficient exceeds a value of fifty – and very high homicide rates. However, expressed by democracy and subjective well-being values that are significantly higher than the world's average, *Cluster 4* countries are relatively free and its citizens are comparatively 'happy'. The remaining indicators for the objective quality of life and ecological sustainability are close to the global mean. In summary, this cluster meets the degrowth definition of a 'good life' to some extent but fails to provide basic social cohesion. The people who live in these countries are exposed to comparatively huge social risks.

The countries of *Cluster 5*, uniting mainly post-communist states but also countries such as Thailand and Malaysia, equally meet several 'good life' conditions. These countries achieve a very high objective quality of life with life expectancy and literacy clearly above average values. Since they provide a high degree of freedom and democracy for their citizens (albeit not as high as in Western countries), they perform better than most other countries in the world in political terms.

Another plus of this cluster is its low homicide rate so that life is rather safe. The downside is that ecological sustainability and subjective well-being scores do not deviate significantly from the respective world averages.

Cluster 6 is very small and comprised of eight countries only: Russia, United Arab Emirates, Saudi Arabia, Kuwait, Qatar, Trinidad and Tobago, Kazakhstan and Singapore. These countries are prime examples for *extractivism*, featuring the world's highest per capita values for CO_2 emissions and ecological footprints. At the same time, most of these countries suppress democracy, political participation and freedom of opinion more than other countries in order to secure social cohesion. Given the lack of freedoms, it is somewhat surprising that subjective well-being scores are well above average. A possible explanation, which could be explored in further research, is that people are relatively satisfied with their lives because these countries succeed in providing secure social conditions and a relatively good objective quality of life.

Cluster 7 assembles the socio-economically most developed countries. Western European countries constitute the most typical countries of this cluster, while the oversea Anglo-Saxon countries differ the most from all other clusters. In short, the situation in this cluster allows for leading a very good life but, unfortunately, at the cost of the natural environment. All ten indicators deviate significantly from the mean values of the World. *Cluster 7* combines social cohesion and political freedom with high objective and subjective quality of life. Yet, up until now and irrespective of welfare regime affiliation (Koch/Fritz 2014), the maintenance of this high living standard has not been decoupled from environmental damages as it requires large and unsustainable amounts of energy and resource throughput.

Conclusion

Taking a global perspective, we set out to comparatively analyze the structural preconditions for prosperity or a 'good life'. We were particularly interested in the issue as to whether there are clusters of countries that manage to develop the individual and social dimensions of prosperity within ecological limits. The main result is that there is no nation that would currently establish all four dimensions of the 'good life' at once. However, some groups of countries come closer to several of our ten good life indicators than others. The Western world, which continues to teach the rest of the world lessons in leading the 'right' way of life, has made significant progress in providing individual, political and social elements of the good life but has totally failed in doing so within ecological limits. The Western countries would need to reduce their environmental impact drastically to bring their economies and societies into the 'safe operating space' (Rockström et al. 2009). This enormous challenge is aggravated by the fact that objective quality of life indicators, CO_2 emissions and also ecological footprints have hitherto increased with GDP per capita, while these rich countries also feature the highest values of subjective well-being. To be realistic in this situation we would suggest focussing less on subjective well-being in post-growth research but more on how basic and 'objective' human needs can be met on a global scale (Koch/Mont 2016). Given that the currently richest countries would need to make the biggest contribution to achieve sustainability at global scale, we would not exclude by definition that subjective well-being scores – and corresponding ideas of the 'good life' – in the rich countries may (temporarily) go down. Policies aiming at, for example, the reduction of meat consumption, or the use of airplanes or electronic gadgets with a short life-span, have the potential of leading to decreases in subjective well-being scores, at least in the short-term. However, we would still argue that such initiatives are necessary because a business-as-usual scenario, where no measures towards the establishment of global sustainability are taken, would most likely be accompanied by continuous decreases in subjective well-being everywhere in the longer term due to the massive deterioration of living conditions in a 'broken world' characterised by climate change and other dimensions of the environmental crisis.

Table 17.3 Results of the cluster analysis

	Characteristics of indicators and dimensions		*countries*
		Mean in Cluster	*Overall Mean*	
Cluster 1 (n=21)	Inequality	44.21	39.14	*most typical:**
	CO2	0.33	4.86	Angola,
Least developed and	Ecolog. footprint production	1.14	3.01	Cameroon, Burundi,
ecologically sustainable	Ecolog. footprint consumpt.	1.18	3.06	Congo, Cote d'Ivoire
countries:	Freedom	1.88	3.58	
	Subj. well-being	4.18	5.41	*most specific:**
No good life regarding	Democracy	3.27	5.59	Central African Republic
social, political and	Literacy	59.68	84.42	Chad, Rwanda,
quality of life aspects	Life expectancy	56.90	70.40	Nigeria, Haiti
Cluster 2 (n=22)	Life expectancy	65.34	70.40	*most typical:*
	CO2	0.70	4.86	Bangladesh, Liberia, Sri
Weakly developed	Ecolog. footprint production	1.15	3.01	Lanka, Pakistan, Senegal
countries:	Subj. well-being	4.53	5.41	
Ecological sustainability	Ecolog. footprint consumpt.	1.42	3.06	*most specific:*
with some political	Literacy	67.15	84.42	Ghana, India, Benin,
freedom	Dim 1 (modernisation)	-1.46	0.00	Senegal, Bangladesh
	Dim 3 (extractivism)	-0.97	0.00	
Cluster 3 (n=20)	Subj. well-being	4.88	5.41	*most typical:*
	Inequality	35.06	39.14	Vietnam, Azerbaijan,
Weakly developed	Ecolog. footprint production	1.64	3.01	Algeria, Iraq, Jordan
countries:	Ecolog. footprint consumpt.	1.91	3.06	

(*Continued*)

Table 17.3 (Continued)

	Characteristics of indicators and dimensions			countries
		Mean in Cluster	*Overall Mean*	
Some social cohesion	Democracy	3.08	5.59	*most specific:*
combined with	Freedom	1.28	3.58	Iran, Belarus, Libya,
political	Dim 1 (modernisation)	-1.20	0.00	China, Uzbekistan
oppression	Dim 2 (anomy)	-1.14	0.00	
Cluster 4 (n=21)	Inequality	52.82	39.14	*most typical:*
	Homicides	25.29	8.15	Jamaica, Namibia,
Latin America and some	Subj. well-being	6.00	5.41	Colombia,
African countries	Democracy	6.59	5.59	Bolivia, El Salvador
	Dim 2 (anomy)	2.32	0.00	*most specific:*
A good and dangerous life				Honduras, Venezuela, South Africa, Guatemala, El Salvador
Cluster 5 (n=18)	Literacy	96.83	84.42	*most typical:*
	Life expectancy	75.21	70.40	Mongolia, Bulgaria,
	Freedom	4.47	3.58	Macedonia, Croatia,
More developed	Democracy	6.61	5.59	Thailand
countries, mainly	Homicides	3.11	8.15	*most specific:*
Post-communist	Dim 3 (extractivism)	-0.51	0.00	Mauritius, Malaysia,
A moderately good life				Bulgaria, Hungary, Romania
Cluster 6 (n=8)	CO2	23.08	4.86	*most typical:*
	Ecolog. footprint consumpt.	6.06	3.06	Kuwait, United Arab
Autocratic countries:	Ecolog. footprint production	6.35	3.01	Emirates, Saudi Arabia,
Rich, happy,	Subj. well-being	6.43	5.41	Kazakhstan, Russia
unfree and	Democracy	3.48	5.59	*most specific:*
unsustainable	Freedom	1.56	3.58	Qatar, United Arab
	Dim 3 (extractivism)	3.06	0.00	Emirates, Kuwait,
	Dim 1 (modernisation)	1.84	0.00	Trinidad and Tobago,
	Dim 2 (anomy)	-1.29	0.00	Saudi Arabia
Cluster 7 (n=28)	Democracy	8.41	5.59	
	Ecolog. footprint consumpt.	5.76	3.06	
The Western World	Freedom	5.91	3.58	*most typical:*
	Ecolog. footprint production	6.12	3.01	Ireland,
A very good life at the	Subj. well-being	6.79	5.41	Netherlands, Austria,

(*Continued*)

Table 17.3 (Continued)

		Characteristics of indicators and dimensions		countries
		Mean in Cluster	*Overall Mean*	
cost of the environment	Life expectancy	80.52	70.40	Germany, Czech Republic
	Literacy	98.94	84.42	
	CO2	9.23	4.86	*most specific:*
	Homicides	1.56	8.15	Canada,
	Inequality	30.78	39.14	Australia, Finland,
	Dim 1 (modernisation)	3.26	0.00	Norway, United States
	Dim 3 (extractivism)	-0.58	0.00	

* Most typical countries are those which are closest to the centre of the own cluster while the most specific countries are those which are furthest away from the centers of the other clusters

In relation to the less and least developed countries one can only hope that these manage to avoid imitating Western 'modernisation' trajectories but instead manage to combine a surplus in individual and social prosperity with ecological sustainability. To avoid global ecological collapse, much societal pressure and organisation is needed to convince Western policymakers to deprioritise economic growth, which is strongly linked to environmental damages such as climate change, as a core element of a wider socio-ecological transformation, but also to assist the developing countries in various technical, institutional and financial ways in their catch-up development. Societal mobilisation will also be necessary to initiate a transition from an economic model based on capital accumulation, unprecedented inequality and depletion of natural resources to a global steady-state economy based on preservation, stewardship and social equality.

To end this chapter on a slightly more positive note, we would like to highlight, in opposition to those who would like to see an 'eco-dictatorship' deal with the environmental crisis, that more democratic countries are at least not more environmentally harmful than less democratic ones. Hence, our analysis supports earlier studies of the 'commons' (Ostrom 1990) that open up for the possibility that democratic principles such as participation, power sharing and transparency may lead to more responsible and ecologically sustainable practices. So, if anything, democratic participation principles should be enlarged, rather than diminished, at all levels (global, national, local) en route to achieving sustainability and a possibly 'good life' for all people now and in the future.

Notes

1 And the greater the shame for those who cannot participate in this race due to their lack of economic, social and cultural capital.
2 The original data for all 138 countries is available online as supplementary material to Fritz/Koch (2016).

References

Acosta, A. (2013). Extractivism and Neoextractivism: Two Sides of the Same Curse. In: Permanent Working Group on Alternatives to Development (ed.). *Beyond Development: Alternative Visions from Latin America*. Amsterdam: Transnational Institute, 61–86.

Alvarez Lozano, L. (2012). Withdrawal From Growth: The Environmental Challenge for Twenty-First Century Socialism. In: *International Critical Thought* 2.1, 71–82.

Bourdieu, P. (1984). *Distinction: A Social Critique of the Judgement of Taste*. Harvard: Harvard University Press.

Easterlin, R.A. (1974). Does Economic Growth Improve the Human Lot? In: P.A. David/ M.W. Reder (eds.). *Nations and Households in Economic Growth: Essays in Honour of Moses Abramovitz*. New York: Academic Press, 89–125.

Easterlin, R.A. /L. Angelescu McVey/M. Switek/O. Sawangfa/J. Smith Zweig. (2010). The Happiness-Income Paradox Revisited. In: *Proceedings of the National Academy of Sciences* 107.52, 22463–22468.

Fritz, M./M. Koch (2014). Potentials for Prosperity Without Growth: Ecological Sustainability, Social Inclusion and the Quality of Life in 38 Countries. In: *Ecological Economics* 108, 191–199.

Fritz, M./M. Koch (2016). Economic Development and Prosperity Patterns Around the World: Structural Challenges for a Global Steady-State Economy. In: *Global Environmental Change* 38, 41–48.

Gough, I. (2015). Climate Change and Sustainable Welfare: An Argument for the Centrality of Human Needs. In: *Cambridge Journal of Economics* 39, 1191–1214.

Hagarty, M.R./R. Veenhoven (2003). Wealth and Happiness Revisited – Growing National Income Does Go with Greater Happiness. In: *Social Indicators Research* 64 (1), 1–27.

Hirsch, F. (1976). *The Social Limits to Growth*. Cambridge, MA: Harvard University Press.

Husson, F./J. Josse/J. Pagès (2010). Principal Component Methods – Hierarchical Clustering – Partitional Clustering: Why Would We Need to Choose for Visualizing Data? Technical Report – Agrocampus Ouest, Applied Mathematics Department. Online at http://factominer.free.fr/docs/HCPC_husson_josse.pdf.

IPCC/Intergovernmental Panel on Climate Change (2014). *Climate Change 2014: Synthesis Report: Summary for Policymakers*. Geneva. Online at www.ipcc.ch/pdf/assessment-report/ar5/syr/SYR_AR5_SPMcorr2.pdf.

Jackson, T. (2009). *Prosperity without Growth? The Transition to a Sustainable Economy*. London: Sustainable Development Commission.

Kasser, T. (2011). Capitalism and Autonomy. In: Chirkov, R./M. Ryan/ K. M. Sheldon (eds.). *Human Autonomy in Cross-Cultural Context*. New York: Springer, 191–206.

Koch, M. (2013). Welfare After Growth: Theoretical Discussion and Policy Implications. In: *International Journal of Social Quality* 3.1, 4–20.

Koch, M. (2015). Climate Change, Capitalism and Degrowth Trejectories to a Global Steady-State Economy. In: *International Critical Thought* 5.4, 439–452.

Koch, M./M. Fritz (2014). Building the Eco-Social State: Do Welfare Regimes Matter? In: *Journal of Social Policy* 43.4, 679–703.

Koch, M./O. Mont (eds., 2016). *Sustainability and the Political Economy of Welfare*. London: Routledge.

Koch, M./H. Buch-Hansen/M. Fritz (2017). Shifting Priorities in Degrowth Research: An Argument for the Centrality of Human Needs. In: *Ecological Economics* 138, 74–81.

Martínez-Alier, J. et al. (2010). Sustainable De-growth: Mapping the Context, Criticism and Future Prospects of an Emergent Paradigm. In: *Ecological Economics* 69, 1741–1747.

O'Neill, D.W. (2012). Measuring Progress in the Degrowth Transition to a Steady State Economy. In: *Ecological Economics* 84, 221–231.

Ostrom, E. (1990). Governing the Commons: The Evolution of Institutions for Collective Action. Cambridge: Cambridge University Press.

Research and Degrowth (2010). Degrowth Declaration of the Paris 2008 conference. In: *Journal of Cleaner Production* 18.6, 523–524.

Rockstöm, J., W. Steffen, K. Noone, Å. Persson, F. S. Chapin, III, E. Lambin, T. M. Lenton, M. Scheffer, C. Folke, H. Schellnhuber, B. Nykvist, C. A. De Wit, T. Hughes, S. van der Leeuw, H. Rodhe, S. Sörlin, P. K. Snyder, R. Costanza, U. Svedin, M. Falkenmark, L. Karlberg, R. W. Corell, V. J. Fabry, J. Hansen, B. Walker, D. Liverman, K. Richardson, P. Crutzen, and J. Foley.

(2009). Planetary Boundaries: Exploring the Safe Operating Space for Humanity. In: *Ecology and Society* 14.2, 32.

Soper, K. (2016). The Interaction of Policy and Experience: An 'Alternative Hedonist' Optic. In: M. Koch/O. Mont (eds.). *Sustainability and the Political Economy of Welfare*. London: Routledge, 186–200.

Soper, K./M. Emmelin (2016). Reconceptualising Prosperity: Some Reflections on the Impact of Globalisation on health and Welfare. In: M. Koch/O. Mont (eds.). *Sustainability and the Political Economy of Welfare*. London: Routledge, 44–58.

Svampa, M. (2012). Resource Extractivism and Alternatives: Latin American Perspectives on Development. *Austrian Journal of Development Studies* 28 3, 43–73.

Vega Camacho, O. (2012). Paths for Good Living: The Bolivian Constitutional Process. In: *Austrian Journal of Development Studies* 28.3, 95–117.

Wilkinson, R./K. Pickett (2010). The Spirit Level: Why Equality is Better for Everyone. London: Penguin.

18 Economics, relationality and the good life in Chiawa, Zambia

Sarah C. White[1]

For most local people in Chiawa, Zambia, life is hard. Located in a Game Management Area just outside the Lower Zambezi National Park, they live with the constant threat of damage to crops, personal injury, or even death, from the crocodiles, elephants, hippos and buffalo who roam freely through the territory. Houses are mainly self-built using home-made mud-bricks and thatch for roofing. Meals are cooked over wood or charcoal. Farming remains a mainstay of livelihoods, often in combination with other activities. Technology is limited; the main implement remains the hoe and mechanised irrigation is rare. Yields are low and subject to multiple hazards: not only damage from wild animals, but also drought from low rainfall and flash floods caused by opening the gates in the major dam upstream. Opportunities for other employment are scarce. For men, the main option is work in one of the safari lodges that flank the river. One in five of the men we surveyed was involved in this.[2] A similar proportion of women were involved in petty trading, mainly in extremely marginal enterprises. Other people do various kinds of casual labour and a small number (fewer than one in twenty people) do manual work on commercial farms.

Local amenities are basic: a primary health centre, an agricultural extension office, a community development office, four primary schools, two high schools and many churches. At the time of the research there was no metalled road and access to Chiawa was dependent on a ferry which ran from 6 am to 6 pm.[3] There was no public transport, so most people had to walk, cycle or rely on private pickups and small lorries which run along the main route providing transport to work or the ferry in the mornings and evenings. For most official business people have to cross the river to travel to the district capital of Kafue, and for hospital care to the nearest town of Chirundu.

In contexts like this, what does it mean to talk of 'the good life beyond growth'? This is the question which this chapter seeks to address. This introduction concludes with a brief description of the research on which it is based. Next presented are villagers' own perspectives on what a good life (or 'well-being') means. These emphasise the centrality of material sufficiency but locate this in a *relational* context: the importance of 'taking care' of others. The following section describes how the poverty of local livelihoods is only one part of the economy of Chiawa. It exists alongside, and is deeply intertwined with, a 'modern' development sector of high inputs and high profits. The chapter closes by describing what can be learned from the Chiawa case. Theoretically, it suggests the need to make relationality central to understandings of well-being. Substantively, it shows that Chiawa villagers do consider economic development to be a vital component of 'the good life', but that this needs to put relationships between people and the environment, not simply growth and profits, at the centre.

The field research on which this paper is based took place in two rounds of four months August-November, 2010 and 2012. A research officer led the fieldwork, working with a team of three local men and one nationally recruited Zambian researcher.[4] Focused on well-being, it considered both how people were doing in material terms (livelihoods and hunger, education and health) and how they were thinking and feeling about their lives. The main instrument was a survey, which combined objective (self-report) questions with questions about satisfaction and 'inner well-being', what people thought and felt themselves able to do and be (see White/ Gaines/Jha 2014). This was undertaken with 412 people in 2010 and 370 in 2012. When possible the same people were interviewed on both occasions to build up a sense of well-being over time.[5] In addition to the quantitative data we have fifty-four qualitative records of notes made during the survey interviews, fifty-two open-ended life history interviews and one focus group discussion. These were translated simultaneously and recorded and transcribed verbatim.[6]

Local perspectives on well-being in Chiawa

Given the harsh conditions and material scarcity of village life in Chiawa, it is not surprising that economic sufficiency is the first thing that people mention when you ask about well-being. The following comment from a married man is typical:

> Most essential thing I want to say is that one must be able to have sufficient food for him and also his family.

Many emphasised the importance of land and farming as the basis of their livelihood. For some this was everything. For others, though, farming was the basis around which other activities might take place. A school teacher talked about his hopes for retirement:

> Yes just buy a plot of a farm and just locate myself there. I can do some other things, but meanwhile I have the farm.

A married woman in her thirties whose husband had worked in a safari lodge, explained:

> I think that is not only the money that makes a better life because even when you are in the home you don't fight and we are able maybe to farm, get a good harvest, get enough food even without money that would still be a good life.

As these examples suggest, in the vast majority of cases people answered in a collective way, about their family's well-being. The following quotation expresses this clearly.

> For me a better life would start with the people that I live with in my household, they have to be able to have what they want – their basic needs, the things that they need should be there. And for me, I think I must have good employment, I must have money – not necessarily enough money but I must have money so that I am able to provide the necessary food that is needed, the necessary things that my people in my household need. Definitely then I would say my life is ok.

This introduces the second key issue that ran through most people's thinking on well-being – it involved *taking care* of others. The purpose of wealth was not to accumulate as an individual, but to provide for and share with others. Another man describes how his moral and social identity is built through his giving of care to his family:

> I am taking care of my wife; I am taking care of my son; and also I am taking care of my mother; my own brothers and sisters who are in the village. I buy my mum some clothes, some blankets, I also send some money there and even there in the village most people really seek to say that 'this mother's son is taking good care of her. He must be a loving and caring son'. So I do take care of my mother and my brothers and sisters and also of my wife and my own son. At least other people are able to tell themselves that this person is a 'father' to his family.

A woman whose husband had signally failed to provide for her or their children, similarly chose to emphasise a man's duties as the way things ought to be:

> What I can say for somebody to be living a good life is when one is in a marriage; first of all, your husband must stand up and say 'I have a wife whom I need to take care of.' Second also, one must be ready to bear responsibilities on his children. Also one must be ready to send his children to school so that if things fail you can say that things failed because of this reason, it's not that you neglected them.

As this quotation suggests, marriage – especially when 'in the home you don't fight' – is central to understandings of well-being in Chiawa. Here again the relationship is seen in active voice; it is not something inert or static but realised through the giving of care. This association of marriage with well-being has material dimensions – as a group, single women are doing worse than married people on virtually every economic indicator. In life history interviews, single women also talked a great deal about the social marginality that they felt, experiencing suspicion and hostility from married women and sexual predation from married men. Interestingly, the issue of 'taking care' was a strong theme in single women's explanations of both why they might, and why they would not, seek to marry again. While some hoped for a new husband who would look after themselves and their children, a larger number stated that they would not re-marry, in the belief that another man would never take care of their children as his own.

While caring for one's immediate family might be common across most if not all human societies, the web of care that people envisaged in Chiawa was particularly wide. As one man powerfully summed it up:

> Well, if one is to live a good life in our community . . . I think first of all one must have enough food for his family . . . for himself and his family. And must also have something to share with the community, because like you don't just say, 'No, this is for my family alone,' but you've also got some other relatives, some friends who can come and ask for things.

This echoes the broader ethnography of Africa. As the anthropologist James Ferguson (2006:72) states:

> "the production of wealth throughout wide areas of southern and central Africa is understood to be inseparable from the production of social relations. Production of wealth can be understood as pro-social, morally valuable 'work,' 'producing oneself by producing people, relations, and things' (Comaroff/Comaroff 1991,143). Alternatively it can be understood as anti-social, morally illegitimate appropriation that is exploitative and destructive of community".

While there are clearly distinct expectations of particular (gendered) roles, the overall context conjures a sense of generalised reciprocity – that what goes around, comes around, especially between kin. Within this the material and the relational are again closely intertwined. The following statement expresses this well:

> By helping both the sides I was not looking at my direct personal benefit because they being relatives, I felt maybe at one point that you never know who is going to help whom; because maybe if I helped my relatives maybe at some point they also help me or my children, or maybe their children who help my children. My wife's relatives also look at me as being a good person. Also, you never know who is going to be helped between my children and them.

Maintaining such an ethic in the face of material scarcity may not be straight-forward. Social pressure to express willingness to assist may compete with the knowledge that one's own resources are already over-stretched. More positively, the power of norms of reciprocity, coupled with the intricate interweaving of kin relationships in Chiawa, provides a strong argument for overcoming grievances, at least at the level of outward interaction. The following comment gives an example of this. Describing how he now goes drinking again with people who earlier caused him some major, deliberate harm, a man explains:

But he has openly come to me to ask forgiveness, forgiving for what I don't know. But I have said, 'oh, just forget, we are brothers', moreover he is my father's cousin, why should we continue remaining like this, let's forgive and forget about it.

This is, of course, the ideal. It may not express the whole truth, even of this particular exchange. What it does, however, suggest is that the relatively closed community of Chiawa, where so many people can trace a thread of common identity and belonging, results almost in enforced reciprocity – even if someone has done you great harm, you cannot avoid social interaction with him or her. A negative outcome of this is it seems to result in considerable levels of ambivalence and undercurrents of fear and mistrust, as people suspect that beneath the smiling faces there may be very different thoughts and intentions. One of the most common phrases was: 'You do not know what is in people's hearts', often used as a veiled hint of suspicions of witchcraft. As discussed later in the paper, this may also be a social indicator of the deep economic and political insecurity that is part of life in Chiawa.

This section has provided an introduction to the cultural construction of well-being in Chiawa, in which the material and relational are inextricably linked together. In the giving and receiving of material goods people affirm and confirm their identities and their personal and social relationships, extending through time and space. This may not be always how it is, but it is how people believe it should be.

The other economy

While the picture with which this chapter opened might conjure familiar associations of 'traditional' Africa, trapped in poverty, left behind by the modern world, in fact nothing could be further from the case. The marginal and precarious character of villagers' livelihoods is directly related to the 'modern development' that the area has seen. Connections between the two economies are evident at many levels. The Kariba dam upstream is a major source of electricity for both Zambia and Zimbabwe. Its construction in the 1950s reduced the natural rise and fall of the Zambezi river which had provided irrigation and renewed fertility to the land beside it (Lancaster 1981, 78). Such land has long been a popular, though risky, complement to the larger fields dependent on summer rains where the main subsistence crop is grown. When they flood now, however, it is sudden and disastrous, following the deliberate opening of spillways to relieve pressure on the dam. In 2011, the devastation this caused was so acute that it led Chieftainess Chiawa to announce a crisis of hunger and the need for food relief (Globe 2011).

As indicated above, it is the safari sector that provides local people with the best opportunities for employment. Nevertheless, the contrast in profits is striking. Chiawa lodges offer luxury accommodation options – a per person tariff of $500–600 per night is by no means unusual. Local staff salaries range from around $100 to $300 per *month*, although guides may make considerably more.[7]

While a job in the safari sector is very desirable for the mainly young men who can get them, the contribution of such jobs to the well-being of the community as a whole may be rather ambivalent. The main observable differences in Chiawa between 2010 and 2012 were more cars and more – and more fancy – bars. Such changes tally with what people say in the community – that the money from safari lodge work is mainly spent on conspicuous consumption, girlfriends or drink. This is supported by evidence from Harland (2008, 82) that lodge workers cheerfully discussed their 'girlfriends'. Harland also notes that in 2005 the Chiawa clinic officer reported that *all* pregnant wives of safari workers had tested positive for syphilis. In 2013, the clinic officer again confirmed that in most cases the sexual histories taken from people with sexually transmitted infections involved contact with a safari lodge worker. Older men also state that such work inverts the traditional patterns of dominance, as young men with more money no longer show them the respect they feel they deserve. By contrast, however, a number of the workers we spoke to suggested their safari wages were the means by which they could honour their responsibilities for 'taking care' of the extended family. No doubt the truth lies somewhere in between.

Land

Competing claims over land comprise the fundamental points of connection and contradiction between local livelihoods and the development sector. Historically, most of the land in Chiawa is customary land, held in trust by the Chieftainess. In 1995, however, the government, in compliance with donor conditionality, brought in a Land Act which allowed customary land to pass into private hands for the purposes of development. While in theory the Act makes it easier for ordinary villagers to gain title to the land they occupy, the need to gain the local chief's permission and the cost of the surveying and titling process are in practice prohibitive for all but the wealthy (Brown 2005, 90–91). Also, while no land should be alienated without full consultation with all stakeholders, including anyone living there, "this proviso is seldom adhered to" (Brown 2005, 92–93).

In areas like Chiawa, offering good potential for commercial agriculture and tourism, the process of land alienation has been rapid. Bond (1998, 148) notes that in 1996 there were only three outside investors with land-titles in Chiawa, but by 1999 there were twenty more.[8] By 2012, almost all the most desirable land along the river was in the hands of the safari lodges, except that retained by the chieftainess herself. Talk of a new bridge and road to be built sent the process of land alienation in Chiawa into rapid acceleration. In 2012, notices proclaiming 'private property' over an area of scrub-land were a common-place. In 2010 we saw few, if any.

The alienation of land to outside investors carries a nexus of worries for the community in Chiawa. The first is the loss of usufruct rights to the common property on which the fragile balance of their livelihoods depends. Whatever promises are made at the time of purchase, people fear that they will no longer be able to move freely. They will either be charged entry and exit fee or kept from going through the area at all. They will lose access to the river and grass and firewood.

The second concern is the indirect effects of the impact fenced off areas have on the movement of wild animals. The following quotation expresses this well.

> In the past, we didn't have these investments that we have now, animals were free to move longer distances, we have the elephant corridor, locally known as Kalungaile, this corridor is said to run from Mozambique up to the southern province and elephants used to go through that corridor and they had breeding places along the corridor, one of them is where Zambeef is, it was thick bush. But now that has been blocked, it is a fenced farm, where do the elephants go? . . . The points where they used to go and drink have been blocked by lodges, this has caused more human-animal conflict. Just here in Chiawa, between the chief's house and the high school, elephants used to pass there, now they are forced to pass through that narrow place. Already there is a fence coming they're saying that is private land. One day the owner will put a fence there, where will the elephant pass? It will pass through the village, and what will happen? Elephants will kill people. So those are things that need to be looked at if we want to develop Chiawa.

The third fear is the loss of their own homes and farms. In Chiawa, very few local people have titles to their land. While customarily those who have once been granted land have the right to remain on it, the ultimate fear is that people will be displaced from their land and their homes. Some have already been moved. Bawa Yamba (2006) reports evictions were already taking place in 1994. In our field-work, we encountered people who were currently being threatened with removal, their land staked out with beacons, and told that someone with a counter claim was going to occupy it. One large new area of land that has recently been allocated to investors extends to almost 16,000 hectares. Far from being consulted before the land was put on title, as the terms of the Land Act require, local people whose farms fall within the 16,000 hectares only found out about it two years after the transfer had gone through. It is in the competition for land that the potential conflict between economic development and local people's well-being becomes most acute.

Reflection

What do we take from the example of Chiawa for broader discussions of 'a good life beyond growth?' Theoretically, the chief contribution is to suggest the importance of relationality to well-being. This echoes the recognition in contemporary scholarship on happiness and psychological well-being that positive relationships with others are important to an individual's well-being (e.g. (e.g. Ryff 1989, Ryan/ Deci 2001, Saphire-Bernstein/Taylor 2013). But it also goes some way beyond this to put relationality, rather than the self, at the centre. For people in Chiawa, well-being shifts from being seen as an internal state that an individual has within him or herself to an energy, process or flow that happens in the interaction between people, especially between kin. A good life involves playing one's part well in enabling this flow to circle and increase. This in turn makes clear that a good life is not something abstract or merely subjective, but is materially grounded in a particular place and time. Taking care of others means meeting their material, not simply psychological or emotional, needs.

The materiality and relationality of well-being has another dimension also. This is that human well-being is intrinsically tied up with the processes of the natural world: the land, the river, the sunshine and rain, the animals. As with many similar communities, this mutual dependence used to be celebrated each year in collective rituals around harvest-time. The current Chieftainess Chiawa put a stop to these as a pagan practice not suitable for a Christian leader to follow. Nonetheless, the sense of that inter-dependence persists, as the last quotation above makes very clear. The elephants had their own trails, which local people knew and respected in locating their villages and negotiating access to water and other necessities. Ironically it was the safari lodges, for whose business the elephants play such an essential role, who failed to take this into account, and so disrupted the balance leaving both animals and villagers more vulnerable. The limitations of constructing human-environment relations in purely instrumental terms is beginning to be recognised in regards to the environmental cost of large intensive agri-business plantations. Further back in time the establishment of the Kariba dam can be seen to have caused a similar break-down in the accustomed mutuality of the rise and fall of the river level with the local agricultural system of river-side gardens.

To recognise such relationships is not to romanticise the past or to suggest 'the good life' lies in a return to 'tradition', whatever that might be. But it is to recognise the need to move forward together, the people and that part of the planet given to them. As Bikret (2012) suggests in a very different context, one dimension of this might be to re-kindle the sense of the sacred in the relations of the earth to its people. More prosaically, social institutions such as laws that configure rights to land, policies and market mechanisms that prioritise one form of investment (and investor) over others, or institutions of governance that designate chieftainship or democracy, clearly have a critical influence in mediating well-being. In thinking about well-being, or the good life, then, there is much to be said for taking a relational approach, which sees well-being as emerging through the interaction of personal processes (the interchange amongst kin and community), societal processes (laws, policies, cultural norms, governance institutions and market structures) and environmental processes (the rejuvenation, adaptation or degradation of natural systems). An image of this is presented in Figure 18.1.

In most of this chapter I have emphasised the 'good life' part of the book's title. In closing it is important to consider the 'beyond growth' dimension. In many ways Chiawa presents a hard case for this, because it seems clear that some degree of economic growth is required if people are to be able to live the lives they should be entitled to in the 21st century. There is certainly no doubt that local people have a tremendous appetite for development. The constant stress they placed on the education of their children as the hope for the future is evidence of that.

In considering the form that development might take, it is useful to apply the framework of relational well-being. Since farming remains the mainstay of livelihoods, there needs to be full investigation into the support required to make small-holder agriculture more viable. This should consider issues such as the

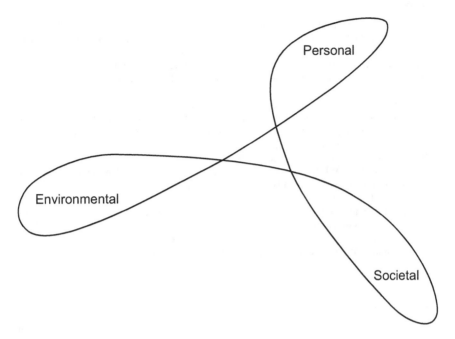

Figure 18.1 The Constitution of Relational Well-being as Process

appropriate crops; potential for irrigation; conservation practices to resist and reverse environmental degradation; fencing and other means to defend against predation from animals; scope for mechanisation; and facilities for the storage and marketing of produce.

While such measures may improve livelihoods, it seems clear that the safari industry comprises an important part of Chiawa's future. Models of co-ownership, such as the communal wildlife conservancies of Namibia, where local people are involved in the management of and share the profits from lodges in their area, need to be explored. Planned carefully, and with a readiness to re-locate some of the existing lodges, tourism profits could be produced far more efficiently, shared far more equitably with leave a far smaller environmental footprint.

This paper has shown that in many ways Chiawa already has the resources it needs for a positive future. It began by describing local understandings of well-being and their strong ethic of care and reciprocity which stretches across time and space, as people affirm and confirm their identities and their personal and social relationships through the giving and receiving of material goods. This is a powerful place to begin thinking about a new model of 'the good life', which is built on an ethic of mutual responsibility amongst people and between them and the natural world, rather than on the enrichment of some at the expense of others.

Notes

1 This work is supported by the Economic and Social Research Council/Department for International Development Joint Scheme for Research on International Development (Poverty Alleviation) grant number RES-167–25–0507 ES/H033769/1.
2 Details of this survey are given below. It was conducted in Chiawa ward, whereas the region of Chiawa also includes Kambale ward. As safari lodge employment was more common in Chiawa ward, our figure of 22% men working in lodges certainly over-estimates the prevalence of this employment in the region as a whole.
3 Since the research ended a new bridge has replaced the ferry (August 2014). Major work is also going on to build a new road through Chiawa from the Zambian capital Lusaka to the Zimbabwe border at Chirundu.
4 Similar research was led by the same research officer in a second site, in India. See e.g. Jha/White (2015). While we attempted to recruit women to the Zambia team we were unable to find any women locally who had good enough English.
5 358 respondents were interviewed in both rounds.
6 All quotations are from these interviews unless indicated otherwise. For further details see www.wellbeingpathways.org.
7 In 2012 prices.
8 This anomaly of dates (thesis completed in 1998 but figures given for 1999) is in the original.

References

Bawa Yamba, C. (2006). The Vindication of Chaka Zulu: Retreat into the Enchantment of the Past. In: T. Evens/D. Handelman (eds.). *The Manchester School: Practice and Ethnographic Praxis in Anthropology*. Oxford/New York: Berghahn Books, 253–271.

Bikret, F. (2012). *Sacred Ecology*. Third edition. New York/Abingdon: Routledge.

Bond, V. (1998). Household Capacity and 'Coping Up' in Rural Zambia: Dealing With AIDS, Other Illness and Adversity in Chiawa. Unpublished Ph.D. Thesis, University of Hull, UK.

Brown, T. (2005). Contestation, Confusion and Corruption: Market-based Land Reform in Zambia. In: S. Evers/M. Spierenburg/H. Wels (eds.). *Competing Jurisdictions: Settling Land Claims in Africa*. Amsterdam: Brill, 77–107.

Comaroff, J./J. Comaroff, J. (1991). Of Revelation and Revolution: Christianity, Colonialism and Consciousness in South Africa. Chicago: University of Chicago Press.

Ferguson, J. (2006). *Global Shadows. Africa in the Neoliberal World Order*. Durham/London: Duke University Press.

The Globe (2011). *Hunger Stalks Chieftainess Nkomesha's Chiefdom*. February 14. Online at http://theglobenewspaper.blogspot.co.uk/2011/02/hunger-stalks-chieftainess-nkome-shas.html.

Harland, C. (2008). Suffering Peacefully: Living With Adversity in Chiawa, Zambia. Unpublished PhD dissertation, University of Bath.

Jha, S./S.C. White (2015). "The Weight Falls on My Shoulders": Close Relationships and Women's Wellbeing in India. In: S.C. White/C. Blackmore (eds.). *Cultures of Wellbeing: Method, Place, Policy*. Basingstoke: Palgrave Macmillan, 144–171.

Lancaster, C.S. (1981) *The Goba of the Zambezi: Sex Roles, Economics and Change*. Norman: University of Oklahoma Press.

Ryan, R.M./E. Deci (2001). On Happiness and Human Potentials: A Review of Research on Hedonic and Eudaimonic Well Being. In: *Annual Review of Psychology* 52, 141–166.

Ryff, C.D. (1989). Happiness Is Everything, or Is It? Explorations on the Meaning of Psychological Well-Being. In: *Journal of Personality and Social Psychology* 57, 1069–1081.

Saphire-Bernstein, S./S.E. Taylor (2013). Close Relationships and Subjective Well-Being. In: I. Boniwell/S. David/A.C. Ayers (eds.). *Oxford Handbook of Happiness*. London: Oxford University Press, 821–833.

White, S.C./S.O. Gaines/S. Jha (2014). Inner Wellbeing: Concept and Validation of a New Approach to Subjective Perceptions of Wellbeing – India. In: *Social Indicators Research* 119.2, 723–746.

19 Europe, capitalist *Landnahme* and the economic-ecological double crisis

Prospects for a non-capitalist, post-growth society[1]

Klaus Dörre

The economic-ecological double crisis

Europe and indeed the entire Western world are in the midst of a crisis-ridden period of sweeping change, which some are comparing to the *Great Transformation* depicted by Polanyi in his book with the same title in 1944. Considering the complexity and diversity of social dislocations, the term 'multiple crisis' has been adopted by various publications on the subject. But is this terminology really a useful analytical tool? I would answer this question in the negative, because the term 'multiple crisis' implies that everything is 'somehow' in crisis. But using the term crisis in this way obscures more than it clarifies. I would argue that Europe is currently in the midst of an *economic-ecological double crisis* (Dörre 2015, 2016). The common market and the economic and monetary union were conceived as a common European response to globalisation, and were linked to promises of economic growth and prosperity. These promises can no longer be fulfilled, however, and the EU today finds itself in a state of secular stagnation. There are two main causes for this that I would emphasise:

Firstly, the EU in its current state represents an attempt at integration mainly via market mechanisms. Market-restricting institutions, trade unions, collective bargaining agreements, labour laws and collective security systems are all regarded, or at least tend to be regarded, as impediments to capital accumulation and growth that society must overcome. One consequence of this development is a growing inequality between and within the EU member states. The same is true for the core states of the EU empire. Germany is one of the most unequal countries in the industrialised world today, says liberal economist Marcel Fratzscher, president of the German Institute for Economic Research (DIW Berlin; Fratzscher 2016). According to recent studies, the top thousandth of the German population (or 0.1 percent) owns 17 percent of overall wealth, while the richest 10 percent own more than 64 percent. At the same time, half of all wage earners earn less today than they did 15 years ago. The German job miracle is based on an increase in precarious jobs performed to a large extent by women in the service sector. In other words: the fruits of economic growth are failing to benefit the majority of the population, even in affluent Germany.

And, *secondly*, in those few places where it is still possible to shore up economic growth on a fossilistic basis (based on oil or coal), this growth in turn leads to an exponential rise in ecological dangers. Measured against pre-industrial standards and the ecological 'tipping points' based on them, we have already crossed a Rubicon of damage as far as climate change, biodiversity and the nitrogen cycle are concerned. Acidification of the oceans, depletion of the ozone layer, fresh water consumption, land use and atmospheric aerosol loading are all rapidly approaching limits of planetary tolerance. The main polluters are the growth-driven capitalisms of the global North, although larger emerging economies such as China are quickly catching up in this race. Presently, a quarter of the earth's population – located primarily in the global North – consumes about three quarters of its resources and produces three quarters of waste and emissions. Europe for its part has only one solution to offer: 'De-growth by disaster'. Wherever the economy shrinks, such as in Greece, for example, emissions and resource consumption decline as well. The fact that some twenty-one countries managed to decouple their GDP growth from carbon emissions for the first time ever in 2015 (see table 19.1) changes little about the overall trend, at least for the time being, because globally we remain firmly tied to an ecologically destructive model of economic growth.

Table 19.1 Metrics of absolute decoupling[2]

Country	Change in CO_2 in % 2000–2014	Change in CO_2 Mt 2000–2014	Change in Real GDP 2000–2014	Change in Industry Share of GDP 2000–2013
Austria	–3%	–2	21%	–3%
Belgium	–12%	–20	21%	–6%
Bulgaria	–5%	–2	62%	2%
Czech Republic	–14%	–18	40%	–0.3%
Denmark	–30%	–17	8%	–5%
Finland	–18%	–11	18%	–9%
France	–19%	–83	16%	–4%
Germany	–12%	–106	16%	–1%
Hungary	–24%	–14	29%	–2%
Ireland	–16%	–7	47%	–9%
Netherlands	–8%	–19	15%	–3%
Portugal	–23%	–16	1%	–6%
Romania	–22%	–21	65%	–1%
Slovakia	–22%	–9	75%	–3%
Spain	–14%	–48	20%	–8%
Sweden	–8%	–5	31%	–4%
Switzerland	–10%	–4	28%	–0.3%
Ukraine	–29%	–99	49%	–10%
United Kingdom	–20%	–120	27%	–6%
United States	–6%	–382	28%	–3%
Uzbekistan	–2%	–2	28%	10%

Economic growth as the most important means for solving economic crises has itself become the driving force of ecological danger in contemporary capitalism.

The Greek example demonstrates what I call the *economic-ecological double crisis*. Modern capitalist societies are facing a growth dilemma: "in a growth-based economy, growth is functional for stability. The capitalist model has no easy route to a steady-state position. Its natural dynamics push it towards one of two states: expansion or collapse" (Jackson 2009, 64). Today, however, this growth dilemma is being uniquely intensified. Economic growth as the most important means of dealing with economic crises in its present fossilistic, carbonised form necessarily leads to an increase in environmental destruction. Growth becomes destructive growth, which has a negative impact on the lives of millions. In such a constellation, the early-industrialised capitalist countries ultimately have only two options: either they render economic growth socially sustainable, or societies emerge which must survive in the absence of permanent growth. Naturally, such post-growth societies cannot be capitalist.

In other words: Europe and the capitalist societies of the global North are entering into a major transformation; the outcome of which remains both unknown and – at least for the time being – open to both political and social influence. Natural scientists tend to keep silent on how exactly this transformation might look. For instance, German climate researcher Hans Joachim Schellnhuber (2015, 703) writes in his book *Selbstverbrennung* ('Self-immolation'): "Whether a 'social market economy' or a 'democratic socialism' is the best social model for the medium-term, or whether one even requires a social model in the first place, is not something I dare to pass judgement on". This is precisely where the opportunity for a sociology critical of capitalism emerges. It is the latter's task to develop concepts which a) allow for a better understanding of capitalist crisis dynamics and b) explore paths of democratically overcoming growth capitalism. The year 2015 also perhaps showed that a degree of latitude for reform and possibilities for a selective, social kind of growth do exist.

Landnahmen and their limits

Without denying the capacity for reform, however, it is nevertheless evident that the economic-ecological 'pincer-grip crisis' has systemic roots: namely, the expansive dynamic characteristic of all varieties of capitalism. There is no such thing as a pure, rational capitalism, as Marx's work, albeit at a certain level of abstraction, might suggest. Capitalism is incapable of reproducing itself exclusively from within. It relies on the ongoing conquest of 'new land'. This 'new land' should not be understood in a primarily geographical sense, but rather as the commodification of natural resources, territories, sectors, activities and lifestyles which were previously not, or not fully, commodified. Thus, capitalism is an expansive system that makes all of our lives, even those of the capitalists, dependent on market imperatives. Nonetheless, this commodification can never be complete, as Karl Polanyi has demonstrated. *Landnahme* (enclosure) is therefore always accompanied by specific forms of 'land surrender'. The valorisation of labour capacity in the form of wage labour would be impossible without the performance of largely unpaid care work. And if care work is to be commodified, then there must be a non-commodified 'exterior' to constitute the new market. The main reason for this was already established by Bourdieu in his early studies on Algeria. Entrepreneurial, market-conforming behaviour requires a consciousness of and orientation towards the future; but such consciousness can only emerge on the basis of long-term life planning, which itself is impossible without a certain degree of income and employment security. That means: capitalist markets require an exterior to guarantee their own security, allowing them to function and preserve what Polanyi calls fictitious commodities: money and financial markets, labour and its human 'container', and, not least, land and the extra-human natural world.

The nub of the matter is that the 'primitive accumulation' Marx describes in the first volume of Capital is periodically repeated. Each time the accumulation of capital encounters obstacles which cannot be surmounted within existing forms, special intervention is needed to get the process back on track. In such periods, political disciplining, repression, violence, over-exploitation and breaches of social norms are common. However, in contrast to Rosa Luxemburg's assumption, these continuous *Landnahmen* do not lead to the collapse of capitalism. A non-capitalist Other can be actively created. The welfare state represents a functional non-capitalist Other to capital.

This is the point from which a contemporary analysis of a *Landnahme* of the social proceeds. The new *Landnahme* strengthens private-capitalist ownership rights. It drives the re-commodification of areas of life previously withdrawn and thereby protected from the market. It rests on the subordination of economic activities to the rules of liberalised financial markets and restrictive fiscal policies. At its centre lies the weakening of wage-earners' power. Moreover, it amounts to restrictions on or even selective dispossession of publicly owned goods. Unless I am completely and utterly wrong, however, the crisis of 2008/2009 is an indicator that market-driven *Landnahmen* on a global scale are beginning to confront intrinsic, ineluctable limits. In other words, international financial market capitalism, as it has been consolidated in the capitalist centres since the 1970s, can no longer be maintained as a growth project without significant modifications.

The return of right-wing populism

We are currently at a decisive turning point. Capitalist market expansion, also known as globalisation, is destroying its own mechanisms of self-stabilisation, including credit, the system of innovation and the work-reproduction nexus. The political economy of labour, that is to say, trade unions, social democratic and socialist parties and welfare state institutions, have been weakened to a degree that even system-stabilising redistributive measures no longer fulfil their purpose. This is why globalisation and Europeanisation, both of which rely on ever more and accelerated *Landnahmen*, are reaching their limits, growing increasingly repulsive, and turning on their protagonists:

- in the form of a dramatic intensification of class inequalities, which have advanced to a point at which they function as growth impediments;

- in the form of migration movements triggered by war, climate change and social immiseration, the cusp of which even reached the Western centre, Germany included, in 2015;
- in the form of a de-democratisation linked to the state's management of these problems and afflicting the EU and its member states for a while now;
- and in the form of a new, multi-dimensional distributional struggle which pits not only the top and the bottom of society against one another, but also the poorer and the wealthier regions, the centre and the periphery.

Wage-earners may spontaneously exhibit exclusive solidarity, that is to say, an excluding solidarity, as the prospects for a democratic re-structuring of unjust relations of distribution grow more dim. They also become more susceptible to the lure of modern right-wing populism. The European right-wing populists are frequently workers' parties. In the most recent Austrian presidential elections, some 86 percent of workers voted for the Austrian Freedom Party. The AfD in Germany is the most popular party among workers and the unemployed. This is possible because the right-wing populists relate to forms of everyday consciousness which could be described as a form of nostalgia or longing for the bygone era of social capitalism. Some wage-earners deploy resentments against others as a targeted means of gaining an edge in the competitive struggle for limited resources and social status. They seek to retain the old social capitalist promise of security by limiting the number of those entitled to it along 'ethnic', 'national', or 'cultural' lines. Corresponding orientations include some elements of a workers' solidarity, the functioning of which, however, is threatened by ethnic or national heterogeneity.

What converges here is a rudimentary class instinct and a melange of malevolence and contempt, while those groups slightly above or slightly below one's own position on the social ladder are blamed for one's own misfortune. Even unionised workers in protected core workforces often differentiate themselves not only from the elites, but also from the unemployed and precariously employed below them, as well as from 'lazy Greeks' or 'useless' migrants. This makes them susceptible to the messages of a new Right which postulates a distributional struggle over the 'people's wealth', not between the top and the bottom of society, but instead between inside and outside, between the 'German people' and the supposed 'migrant invaders'. Right-wing populism has further reinforced the specific vulnerability of refugees with its deployment of such a semantics of aggression. It attributes migrants with a lower level of civilisational development and places them under general suspicion. Refugees are indiscriminately portrayed as potential violent criminals, terrorists and rapists. The answer to such a construed barbaric invasion, then, is the defence of the national citizenry, conceived as ethnically 'pure' and homogenous. Through such semantic operations, contemporary right-wing populism has managed to re-interpret migration movements, at least indirectly the result of market-driven globalisation, as an invasion of uncivilised barbarians. The most vulnerable social groups, of all people, are stigmatised as land grabbers committing genocide against the native population and as a quasi-naturalised national culture. In the context of distributional struggles reinterpreted as conflicts between weak and strong countries, or rather, cultures, the term *Land-nahme* serves as a linguistic weapon against society's weakest.

Four tasks for Europa

Wherever they take power – whether in Hungary, Poland, or, more recently, the US – *völkisch*, or ethno-nationalist populists demonstrate that the supposed inevitability of globalisation can in fact be reversed. Trump is forcing international corporations to relocate production to the US; Orban practices a nationalist-protectionist (or rather protective) economic policy; and one of the first measures enacted by the Polish PiS (Prawo i Sprawiedliwość, or *Right and Justice*-Party) was the introduction of an hourly minimum wage. While the right-populists have placed the issue of borders at the heart of their campaigns, thereby occupying the social question as their political terrain, the democratic Left lacks a plausible or convincing alternative vision of a non-capitalist future society in reaction to the economic-ecological double crisis. And this is very much a disaster, given that the new Great Transformation is already well underway – regardless of whether the Left likes it or not.

Essentially, what is valid for all other capitalisms applies to European capitalism as well: because the planet has become too small for capitalism, and because it is losing legitimacy in light of growing social inequality and uncertainty, I believe that contemporary growth capitalism may well come to an end in the next few decades. What I do not know is what will replace it. Change will most likely be driven forward by a mixture of external shocks (for instance, natural disasters), social movements against the compulsions of growth and competition, reforms from above, and alternatives to the dominant lifestyle already being practised today. However, these changes will not automatically make things better. At least for the time being, we can still influence this anticipated process of change through participation in democratic politics. It therefore makes sense to begin actively working towards the overcoming of capitalism today, despite what may seem like very slim chances for success, instead of passively resigning ourselves to this social formation's eventual demise.

We need a global debate on the contours of a democratic, egalitarian, non-capitalist, post-growth society. There are at least four coordinates which could serve as an adequate compass for such a debate. They include: the critique of growth, substantive equality, radical (economic) democracy, and global cooperation. These coordinates can then, as I suggest, be assigned to four core projects.

1   A *critique of growth* implies scientifically attacking systemic mechanisms which engender permanent destructive growth. We require modes of social regulation capable of rendering ecological and social destruction visible and counteracting the externalisation of its consequences. Furthermore, we need a global debate about ways of living that understand a rupture with superfluous consumerism and the ethical imperative of moderation as evidence of life quality.

2   *Substantive equality* is applicable, because ecological sustainability cannot be achieved without social sustainability. Projects of radical democratic re-distribution are urgently needed – from the North to the South, from the European centre to the European crisis countries, from top to bottom, from the strongest to the weakest – the 60 million refugees of whom only a small fraction actually reach the capitalist centres, for example. An initial step may be a tax policy that turns the right to possess wealth into a temporary one, that closes tax havens and taxes large assets in favour of investments in combating poverty, hunger, and ecological destruction worldwide (Piketty 2014).

3   No redistribution will occur without *radical, rebellious democracy*. Here, the expansion of democracy to the economic sphere is of critical importance. The project of a *new economic democracy* will have to be fought for in and against the 1,318 companies currently controlling four fifths of the global economy. These corporations are essentially social institutions; their decisions influence the lives of several billion people. It is therefore unacceptable for them to remain exclusively in private hands. Radical democracy means posing the ownership question. It means finding new forms of collective self-ownership (like employee-run companies, etc.) beyond private and state property, which socialise and democratise decisions regarding the 'what', 'how' and 'what for' of production.

4   Each of the projects mentioned here must take into account that a course towards democratic transformation today can only succeed on a global scale. Ecological threats, economic crises, refugee movements and wars demand a new 'global domestic policy' (Ulrich Beck). Achieving this will only be possible if differing interests and conflicts between different states and regions of the globe become cooperative. We must create – beginning in our respective national societies – a mode of *global cooperation*, without which the old sociologist's dream of a 'betterment of society' cannot be realised in a global order.

This is the task confronting us in Europe today. Instead of using access to the massive European common market as a tool to enforce social standards across the world economy, a supra-national disciplinary regime has emerged which increasingly relies on authoritarian means to ensure compliance. Austerity has engendered 'societies of contraction', such as in the case of Greece, which will require decades just to return to pre-crisis economic levels. Austerity reinforces the very debt economy it purports to overcome. Simultaneously, it promotes a post-democratic Europe which delegates 'the refugee crisis' to its outer borders. The crisis-stricken countries of the southern periphery are left to deal with an enormous additional burden, while human rights are sacrificed in a dirty deal with the Turkish state. The tragic outcome is the transformation of the Mediterranean Sea into a mass grave.

This kind of Europe has no legitimate right to exist. In order to advance an alternative, we must return to Walter Korpi's concept of *democratic class struggle* (Korpi 1983) and fill it with new life. This concept denotes a struggle that is

fought on the basis of wage-earniers' inalienable economic and social rights –
regardless of how intense these struggles become. The basic idea implies that conflict and dissent represent crucial elements of a functioning democracy, as opposed
to some kind of accidents or deviations. Europeanising and internationalising this
idea is a very daunting challenge indeed. Wage-earners in Germany must come
to understand that they have more in common with their French, Greek, Italian or
Polish counterparts than either of them have with their respective national economic elites. In short: What we need is a new, international as well as transnational, class-specific collective identity. Such an identity can only emerge out of
common struggle and experience. At the same time, it also requires the support of
political education and trade union cooperation at the grassroots level. Should this
task be left unattended, we may well see a European class society without positive
class identities among the dominated populations in the near future.

Conclusion

Is this a realistic perspective for social transformation, that is, does it stand a
chance at succeeding? To be frank, in my view there is little reason to believe so, at
least for the time being. The dystopia of authoritarian capitalism currently appears
far more real. But should or can sociologists accept this fact as given? Should
they quietly come to terms with a development in which presidential Tweets and
Breitbart-News threaten any form of critical discourse and anti-establishment
impulses? This in mind, let me rephrase the question: what can sociology do? At
this point we are seeing, at best, vague outlines of possible social alternatives. The
real challenge is developing these alternatives, particularly for a sociology that
aspires to be a public sociology (Burawoy 2015; Aulenbacher/Burawoy/Dörre/
Sittel 2017). These four suggestions should be understood in the sense of a democratic experimentalism. They obviously consist of questions more than anything
else, many of which are also for sociology: are these core projects adequate? Do
they have to be amended or expanded? How can they be specified in detail? With
whom could they be successfully carried out? And, not least: what should a new
and better society be called? Like Erik Olin Wright (2012), I have no difficulty
working on a compass that describes the coordinates for a transformation towards
neo-socialist post-growth societies. But that is just an individual preference. My
suggestion to sociologists is this: let us begin a debate about a better society
beyond capitalism, beyond growth, and develop viable alternatives in dialogue
with civil society – globally, through constructive controversy, immediately.

   What is crucial, however, is that it does not remain a debate by sociologists
solely for sociologists. What is needed is a bridge to the everyday critique and
action of civil society. The desire for a better society may begin from a critique of
destructive lifestyles just as well as from conflicts over wages or practical assistance to refugees from the global South. It is possible in opposition as well as
from the government bench. What is crucial is that each intervention is pursued
as part of a transformative politics. Behind the demands for higher pay by, say,
striking German child care workers, lies the desire for appreciation and social recognition of reproductive activities. This desire ultimately aspires to a fundamental

reshaping of society, its reproductive sector and the funding thereof. To realise this goal is not only important for the women and migrants working in this sector, but is also in the interests of the parents and children involved. Should adequate corresponding measures be implemented, they would gradually replace the tendency to increase productivity by displacing living labour. The growth drivers could at least be weakened, leading to an outcome of selective, social growth. To point out these connections means engaging in transformative progressive politics. And it is certainly better to practise such a politics than to go down without a fight in the face of a system that seems to promise the majority little more than a miserable life.

Notes

1 Paper presented at the 3rd ISA Forum of Sociology, July 10–14, 2016, Vienna, Austria – Plenary Session: Facing the Multiple Crisis in Europe and Beyond, Session organized by Brigitte Aulenbacher, Johannes Keppler Universität Linz.
2 Table by the *World Resources Institute*, available online at www.wri.org/blog/2016/04/roads-decoupling-21-countries-are-reducing-carbon-emissions-while-growing-gdp (accessed on August 11, 2016), the data used there comes from *BP Statistical Review of World Energy* 2015 & *World Bank World Development Indicators*.

References

Aulenbacher B./M. Burawoy/K. Dörre/J. Sittel (2017). *Öffentliche Soziologie: Wissenschaft im Dialog mit der Gesellschaft*. Frankfurt am Main: Campus.

Burawoy, M. (2015). *Public Sociology: Öffentliche Soziologie gegen Marktfundamentalismus und globale Ungleichheit*. Weinheim: Juventus.

Dörre, K. (2015). Social Capitalism and Crisis: from the Internal to the External Landnahme. In: K. Dörre/S. Lessenich/H. Rosa (eds.). *Sociology, Capitalism, Critique*. London: Verso, 247–279.

Dörre, K. (2016). Limits to Landnahme: Growth Dilemma as Challenge. In: J. Dellheim/F.O. Wolf (eds.). *Rosa Luxemburg: A Permanent Challenge for Political Economy*. Basingstoke: Palgrave Macmillan, 219–261.

Fratzscher, M. (2016). *Verteilungskampf: Warum Deutschland immer ungleicher wird*. München: Hanser.

Jackson, T. (2009). *Prosperity without Growth: Economics for a Finite Planet*. London: Earthscan.

Korpi, W. (1983). *The Democratic Class-Struggle*. London: Routledge.

Pickety, T. (2014). *Capital in the 21st Century*. Cambridge, MA: Belknap Press.

Schellnhuber, J. (2015). *Selbstverbrennung: Die fatale Dreiecksbeziehung zwischen Klima, Mensch und Kohlenstoff*. München: C. Bertelsmann.

Wright, E.O. (2012). Transforming Capitalism through Real Utopias. In: *American Sociological Review* 78.1, 1–25.

20 Towards radical alternatives to development

Ashish Kothari

The crisis of maldevelopment

Our current model of development is straining the resilience of the biosphere and producing glaring economic inequalities.[1] Levels of poverty, deprivation, and exploitation remain unacceptable, as do conflicts over access to natural resources, food, and water. The roots of these crises lie in structural problems within the economy, society, and humanity's relationship with nature. All of this calls for a fundamental rethinking of the human project in the 21st century.

India is a good example of what is going wrong, especially now that it projects itself as one of the world's fastest growing economies. Four decades of state-dominated "development" after Independence in 1947, followed by nearly three decades of corporate-dominated economic globalisation, have led India down the path of unsustainability: it now has the world's third largest ecological footprint (Shrivastava/Kothari 2013). While some forms of poverty have been reduced, others persist. 60 million people have been forcibly evicted by "development" projects. Roughly three out of four Indians suffer from deprivation of at least one of the following basic needs: adequate and nutritious food, safe drinking water, sanitation, energy, gainful and dignified employment, education, health care, and adequate shelter. India continues to fare poorly in most global surveys of human indicators. Net job growth in the formal sector has benefited less than 5 percent of the population over the last twenty years, condemning tens of millions to exploitative conditions in the informal sector. Economic inequality is abysmally high and getting worse, as the richest 1 percent own over half of the country's private wealth (Credit Suisse 2014; Rukmini 2014; Singh et al. 2008; Kalpavriksh 2013).

Unfortunately, the lure of "growth" as an engine of well-being still holds sway, even within the new paradigms of 'green economy' and 'sustainable development'. Economic growth is central to the Sustainable Development Goals (SDGs), adopted at a special United Nations General Assembly in late 2015. With its seventeen goals to be achieved by 2030, the SDGs are undoubtedly a significant improvement over their predecessor, the Millennium Development Goals (MDGs) in putting sustainability and equality as core concerns. However, the SDGs retain several crucial flaws of the conventional model, including the focus on economic growth despite overwhelming evidence of its unsustainability and the inequalities inherent in it, the inability to move towards direct democracy in which people rather than nation-states have decision-making power, the lack of articulation of fundamental ethical values that should underpin human endeavour, and others (Rijnhout et al. 2014; Kothari 2015a). As pointed out by a large number of academics and activists recently, the SDG approach will take 200 years to alleviate the plight of the 2 billion people currently classified as poor (leaving aside for the moment the problems with such classification), and will require a twelve-fold increase in the size of the economy to do so, which is clearly unsustainable in a situation where humanity is already over-using the earth's resources.[2] Therefore the need to explore radically different approaches, of which I will focus on one here while referring to others (Kothari/Demaria/Acosta 2014).

Another paradigm

We can find elements of an alternative pathway in the thousands of grassroots initiatives, resistance struggles, and movements for social transformation around the world that point to a very different vision of the future. This emerging framework – referred to here as *radical ecological democracy* – puts collectives and communities at the center of governance and the economy. It offers a systemic approach to social transformation, resting on political, economic, socio-cultural, and ecological pillars, which we shall consider in turn.

The political pillar

In central India, the indigenous Gond community of the village Mendha-Lekha has a saying: *Dilli Mumbai mawa sarkar, Mawa nate mate sarkar* ("It is our government in Mumbai and Delhi, but *we* are the government in our village"). The village *gram sabha* (assembly of all residents) meets regularly to make key decisions by consensus and insists that any decision regarding the use of land or resources within its territorial jurisdiction can only take place with the *sabha*'s consent. It has set up subsidiary bodies like *abhyas gats* (study circles) to provide the necessary information to guide its decisions. Outside of regular meetings, any villager can call for the *sabha* to convene if an urgent matter arises. In Venezuela, neighborhood assemblies arose in the 1980s around the notion "we don't want to be a government, we want to govern". Recent far-reaching changes in governance include the devolution of power to *consejos comunales* (communal councils), with about 44,000 established by 2013 (Azzelini 2013).

These examples of direct democracy challenge the notion that the heart of democracy lies in elections for representative bodies. They have sprung up not only in villages, but in cities as well. City-based communal councils in Venezuela contain between 150 and 400 families each. In India, urban wards are considerably larger and more unwieldy, stimulating discussions both within government and in civil society networks about decentralizing them into smaller units (such as *mohalla sabhas*, or neighborhood assemblies).

Grassroots democratic units, however, cannot work in isolation, since some decisions need to be taken at larger scales, from regional landscapes to the planet itself. Village and city assemblies or communal councils need to be embedded within larger institutions of governance (what Gandhi called "oceanic circles") with elected representatives from the local bodies. The challenge is to ensure that such institutions do not become power centers that dominate the grassroots. Promising policies for countering such domination include the right to recall, regular election of representatives, rotation of officeholders, mandatory consultation with constituents, and full transparency in decision-making. For example, the northeastern Indian state of Nagaland has enacted legislation empowering village councils with substantial decision-making powers, including some control over the allocation of government funds for education, health, and power (Pathak Broome 2014). The new Aam Aadmi Party in India, which arose out of a popular anti-corruption struggle, has incorporated *swaraj* (self-rule) and support for mechanisms like the right to recall into its election manifesto, though some of its radical appeal has been lost due to the authoritarian streak of its charismatic leader Arvind Kejriwal, prompting break-away members to form a Swaraj Abhiyan or self-rule campaign with a mass base (Kothari 2014b; www.swarajabhiyan.org).

How will such direct democracy translate into national governance (assuming that nation-states persist)? Neither capitalist nor state-centered socialist countries have been willing or able to cede power to the grassroots or to be fully responsive to local self-governance. The concept of the "communal" or "plurinational" state that has emerged in several Latin American countries holds interesting possibilities. Such a state, in theory, accommodates channels of communication and delegation that enable empowered grassroots communities to influence provincial and national decisions, and it respects the identity and voice of a plurality of cultures and peoples within the country. However, in practice, officials remain extremely reluctant to relinquish their centralised power, which is inextricably linked to the continued reliance on large-scale resource extraction (Acosta 2013; Prada 2013). Notwithstanding such limitations, such efforts provide valuable lessons and principles for envisioning a more democratic state. Switzerland's decentralised political governance system, with considerable autonomous powers to counties, a system of referendums involving all citizens for major decision, and an annually rotating presidentship, is also worth learning from.[3]

Of course, even in a decentralised world of radical ecological democracy, the state (represented by a government) would still have a legitimate role, at least for the foreseeable future. These include the protection of the marginalised, both human and non-human, and the guarantee of fundamental rights. The state would also be important for generating financial resources for public services, enforcing environment regulation, and ensuring personal and collective security – but all in the spirit of service to the public rather than accumulation of power.

In the new vision, political boundaries would become sensitive to ecological and cultural contiguity and diversity. In western India, seventy-two riverine villages formed the Arvari River Parliament, which for a decade met regularly to make ecological, economic, and social decisions; it then ran into problems, but provides crucial lessons in landscape level governance (Hasnat 2005). In Venezuela, communal councils used social, cultural, and economic relations to define geographical boundaries. In Australia, the Great Eastern Ranges Initiative is attempting an ambitious linkage of landscapes over 3,600 kilometers (Pulsford et al. 2013). Each of these is attempting to combine some form of localisation with larger-scale, bioregional decision-making.

Eventually, such an approach may lead people to question nation-state boundaries and jurisdictions. The fragmentation of bioregions and communities by political boundaries has caused considerable ecological, social, and economic distress. Through history, such boundaries have been continually questioned and often changed. Treating bifurcated regions – like the high Himalaya (currently separated between India and Pakistan on one side and India and China on the other) or the world's largest mangrove stretch (divided between India's and Bangladesh's Sundarbans) – as an ecological unit governed democratically by local communities and larger, accountable institutions that span countries could provide lasting peace and shared benefits.

Bioregions would not be the only determinants of political boundaries; cultural and economic factors would be influential as well. One's identity and relations need not be limited to a single territory; there could be fluid, diverse, and overlapping identities. A young fisherperson could belong to the Sundarbans ecoregion, to a larger cultural community of Bengalis, and to a virtual global community of youth using new communications technologies to supplement local methods of knowledge generation and information dissemination.

In our increasingly interdependent world, the great challenge of global governance comes to the fore. While the United Nations is currently organised around nation-states, the creation of peoples' assemblies at global and sub-global levels could offer a more democratic alternative.[4] A path forward might only emerge as direct democracy at the grassroots level grows and merges with new forms of participatory communication and networking. There is space for a diversity of solutions, as long as they rest on shared principles of irreducibility, subsidiarity, and heterogeneity: a minimal set of matters are properly assigned to the global level, decision-making should go to the most local level feasible, and diverse local approaches to meeting collective goals are accepted and encouraged (Raskin 2012).

The economic pillar

Recent economic crises have led many to question the centrality of growth and globalisation in economic decision-making and to explore possibilities for greater localisation that embed production and consumption patterns within communities. Dozens of self-governed companies and cooperatives in India, for instance, are enabling farmers, craftspersons, fishers, pastoralists, and industrial manufacturers to have increased control of the entire chain from raw materials to marketing.[5] Although achieving widespread capability for high-tech production will likely take some time, decentralised, community-based production of solar products has already begun. With the democratisation of knowledge, science, and technology, this can happen for other high-tech products that society considers necessary.

Even where centralised or large-scale production and services may remain necessary, the radical democratisation of the workplace is possible. Innovations in Argentina, Venezuela, and other countries demonstrate the feasibility of non-hierarchical, worker-led production processes. Consumer cooperatives are beginning to bring greater attention to ecological and social concerns in products and production practices. Worker-owned production, retail, and banking – as well as author-owned publication houses – are appearing in various parts of the world. Examples include the Self-Employed Women's Association of India, the Seikatsu Consumers' Club Co-op of Japan, and the Mondragon Cooperation Corporation of Spain (Bakshi 2009; Kelly 2012). At the same time, direct producer-consumer linkages are in many instances eliminating the exploitative middleman or corporation, especially where governmental or civil society facilitates the process. There is greater demand to reclaim the central role of the "real" economy from the "virtual" one at the heart of recent economic crashes (Korten 2013).

Efforts to decentralise control over natural resources are an important feature of localisation efforts. Such control rests on the principle of subsidiarity, in which those living closest to ecosystems and resources have the greatest stake in and at least some of the essential knowledge for managing them. Of course, the obstacles and limitations to localizing control are significant. In India, two centuries of centralised policymaking have crippled community institutional capacity and eroded customary rules. Moreover, localised economies do not necessarily imply local democracy: local elites can dominate decision-making or contribute to divisive partisanship. Moving toward more localised natural resource management will require sensitivity to these pitfalls and proactive steps to avoid them. Some efforts at reclaiming forest commons under the Forest Rights Act 2006, and managing them for conservation and sustainable livelihoods, are pointing to such localisation (Tatpati 2015).

Economic democracy also entails the right to dignified, secure livelihoods, what the International Labour Organization (ILO) and United Nations Environment Programme (UNEP) call "decent work". There are enormous opportunities to generate such livelihoods through organic farming, renewable energy development, efficient resource use, public transport, small-scale manufacture, and recycling projects (UNEP 2008). Jharcraft, an initiative of the eastern Indian state of Jharkhand, has enhanced the livelihoods of over 300,000 families by providing credit, technological assistance, recognition of producer cooperatives, and marketing opportunities to an array of craftspeople.[6] Several villages in India have reversed the trend towards outmigration by revitalizing local economies and reducing social inequities, through watershed management, enhancing agricultural productivity, investing in health and educational facilities, small-scale industrial manufacture and dialogue-based resolution of caste tensions.

Finally, we require new economic theory and frameworks for ways to assign value (including the intangible and unquantifiable) and to achieve sustainability and equity through steady-state economies, as well as practical applications of new indicators and measures of well-being going beyond GDP. It means the embrace of local currencies and non-monetised forms of exchange like time banking, and it demands that we rethink the nature of larger-scale trade to make it harmonious with local self-reliance and environmental stewardship (Alexander 2014; New Economics Foundation 2009; Tebtebba Foundation 2008; Bakshi 2009).

The socio-cultural pillar

Hierarchies and exploitative relations along axes of gender, ethnicity, race, and status, inherited from the past or emerging anew, must be addressed tenaciously. While movements explicitly challenging inequities and divisions based on birth will remain crucial, we can also tackle such disparities through collective action that bridges such divides. In India, the initiatives of *dalits* (the so-called "outcasts" of Hindu society) and *adivasis* (indigenous people) for forest conservation, agricultural sustainability, and manufacturing-based livelihoods, and against destructive "development" projects, have increasingly pushed dominant castes or classes to accept their equal status, though the move to eradicate caste per se continues to flounder. Equally important, the strong role of women in the leadership of these movements has brought about greater gender equity. At the same time, youth-led initiatives have gained the respect of elders, reducing rigid age-related hierarchies and inequities. For example, at the village Nayakheda in western India, youth mobilizing around reclaiming rights to forests and generating livelihoods based on forest produce have brought together elders of two ethnic communities who earlier did not see eye to eye (Mutha/Pathak 2014). In the northeastern Indian state of Nagaland, student associations have contributed to village decision-making through their initiatives on conservation, hygiene, education, and health.

The loss of cultural diversity has accompanied the dominant market-based, growth-driven development paradigm, especially through the globalisation and commercialisation of mass media. Radical ecological democracy seeks to reverse these trends by sustaining the earth's cultural diversity, including its threatened languages. In India, the NGO Bhasha is attempting to do just that by documenting extant languages and providing schools and other learning materials to promote their revival or sustenance (Kothari 2015b).[7] This type of effort helps maintain the knowledge, wisdom, and worldviews that provide resilience in the face of growing ecological, social, and political uncertainty.

Encouraging the synergy of various kinds of knowledge is equally vital. The global Indigenous Peoples' Climate Change Assessment combines the observations and information of indigenous peoples with those of modern climate scientists to understand the many dimensions and impacts of climate change and to generate adaptive mechanisms (IPCCA, 2014; Nickels 2005). Similarly, public health initiatives in India have empowered communities by combining traditional and modern systems that strengthen the links between safe food and water, nutrition, preventive health measures, and curative care, and by advocating for fundamental rights to health services (a prime example being the Jan Swasthya Abhiyan, http://phmindia.org). Indigenous peoples groups have also been active in international conventions and forums on creating indicators for sustainability, justice, and other goals (Tebtebba Foundation 2008).

Public involvement in scientific and technological innovation and development is also important in dismantling the monopolisation of knowledge. Debates around GMOs, geoengineering, climate change, and other issues have underscored the failures of a knowledge-generation model dominated by corporations and the state, where intellectual property regimes and bureaucratic red tape restrict access. While not flawless, alternative models of public innovation and research, such as those seen in the agricultural sector in Cuba and southern India, point to possibilities for democratizing knowledge.[8] The explosion of open source technologies, copyright-free material, public generation, and peer review of material (e.g., Wikipedia) has helped bring knowledge into the commons.

Finally, the arena of the self will be central to the socio-cultural pillar for a new society. The relationship between the individual and society has often been contested as traditional collectivism gave way to the extreme individualism of modernity. Resolving this tension requires exploring new ways to balance and find harmony between the individual and the collective, including through engagements in spiritual quests and in social movements (Kapoor 2007).

The ecological pillar

Achievements in the political, economic, and socio-cultural arenas will be illusory and fleeting unless we are able to safeguard the fundamental environmental conditions that make life on earth possible. This requires understanding and recognizing ecological limits, restoring degraded landscapes, conserving what remains of ecosystems, respecting the right of the rest of nature to thrive, and finding synergies between ecological resilience and human well-being.

The meaning of "conservation" is a cultural construct imbued with and shaped by dominant worldviews. This is evident in the struggle over protected areas, where exclusionary approaches have led to conflict with marginalised peoples, and often backfired on conservation itself (Adams et al. 2004; Brockington 2002; Dowie 2009; Worboys et al. 2014). Fortunately, conservation paradigms have begun to shift in the last decade, emphasizing the need for such principles as respect for rights, participation, accountability, and transparency. This also includes recognition of sites for conservation that are governed by indigenous peoples and communities.[9]

At a broader level, sustainability needs to be pursued across the entire landscape and seascape and in both rural and urban areas. We can learn from the experience of indigenous peoples in combining democratic, spiritual, social, and economic dimensions to sustaining ecosystems for generations. We also learn from the rest of nature, which works in circular and complex systems involving biochemical cycles, recycling, and reuse. Several initiatives for food, water, and energy sovereignty and security are seeking to mimic these "virtuous cycles" and sustain or enhance resilience (Jones/Pimbert/Jiggins 2011).

Achieving sustainability also requires the "official" recognition of an ethical position that faiths and communities around the world have long held: the inherent rights of nature and its species. Bolivia's Law of the Rights of Mother Earth, Ecuador's inclusion of the rights of nature in its constitution, and New Zealand's recognition of a river having a legal voice are steps towards such recognition, even if implementation is not necessarily ideal.[10]

Challenges and pathways

The transformation towards a sustainable and equitable world will be resisted by the votaries and beneficiaries of the dominant system. We can see this in the enormous clout of private corporations and the military complex, and more subtly by the reinvention of capitalism in the form of "green growth", corporate social responsibility, and techno-fixes. At the same time, the inadequacy of knowledge and information subverts efforts to manage complex webs of ecological problems.

As stubborn as the hurdles are, the growing number and reach of peoples' initiatives to resist the system and create alternatives offer hope. Peoples' movements and civil society organisations (including progressive workers' unions) will continue to be the primary agents of change for radical ecological democracy. At times, sections and individuals within government, political parties, spiritual and academic institutions have taken the lead or assisted communities and civil society organisations, and we must continue to push such institutions to play a stronger and more effective role. The powerful statements of Pope Francis and a number of Islamic clerics, in the run-up to the climate summit in 2015, are also important influences (Kothari 2015c). Over time, political parties will feel greater pressure from their constituencies to reorient their focus to issues of well-being based on sustainability and equity.

Businesses will make adjustments in the face of consumer pressure; in the long run, though, the capitalist corporate sector will have to yield to forms of community enterprise that share the means of production and distribution, a public sector managed by the state (under full democratic control), and the emerging "social enterprise" sector, where it is genuinely public-oriented. International agencies, under pressure from peoples' movements, have an important role to strengthen environmental and human rights treaties. Ultimately, the state itself must be transformed to play its critical role as guarantor of rights, facilitator of communities, and regulator of industry, at least until such a role is no longer needed.

Local-to-global movements

In this era, we are witness to an important historical conjunction between the local and the global. At one extreme are the localisation movements that have been the center of attention of this essay. At the other is the growing mobilisation around global issues, such as climate change, the global financial system, and the hegemony of multinational corporations. The conditions of the contemporary world including large-scale disasters are fostering mutually-reinforcing local and global mindsets.

Transforming this potential for linking the local and the global (the 'glocal') into cohesive action is one of the biggest challenges we face. This requires building platforms where practitioners, workers, thinkers, visionaries, politicians, and artists (these are not exclusive categories, of course!) can gather, searching for synergy even as they retain their diversity of perspectives and ideologies. Sharing a common enemy (the "system") will not be sufficient for sustaining motivation and cohesion: that will take a common framework of values and principles and a shared vision of the world that we want. Articulating common values and visions of well-being from indigenous peoples, local communities, and civil society can enrich the transcultural mobilisations now proliferating. In India, a process called Vikalp Sangam (Alternatives Confluence) is attempting to provide such a platform.[11]

Local movements will have to push harder for participation at formal national, regional and global forums to make them less state-centric and more people-centric.[12] They will be critical to ensuring that environmental and human rights agreements have teeth and that economic and trade agreements are subservient to them. The actions of the WTO, the IMF, and the World Bank will have to be resisted if such organisations cannot be fundamentally restructured to elevate human and ecological well-being over profit. Peoples' assemblies, bound together through national, regional, and global federations, will be important to counterbalance or even replace the current nation-state-dominated United Nations.

Grassroots mobilisation for radical ecological democracy will be fundamental to this broader movement. The challenge is to scale up these small, scattered initiatives without losing their site-specificity, to cultivate synergies, and to link them to form a broader global network to advance the radical ecological democracy agenda. The essentials of what made a successful initiative thrive or a failed one collapse, as well as the values and principles that underlie them, can be transferred from one place to another.

A consensus of such values is emerging, including ecological integrity, equity and inclusiveness, diversity and pluralism, governance based on subsidiarity and direct participation, collective work and reciprocity, solidarity and the commons, resilience, simplicity and frugality, and the rights of nature. These and others are common to many alternative worldviews such as *buen vivir* and sumac kawsay in Latin America, commons and solidarity movements in industrialised countries, degrowth in Europe, ubuntu-related movements in parts of Africa, and swaraj or radical ecological democracy in India (Kothari/Demaria/Acosta 2014).[13] These ancient and new worldviews can be shown as viable alternatives to both conventional development and the green economy and growth-centered sustainable development models, and serve as a rallying point for cultural and behavioural change, coming as much through the heart as the head.

Notes

1 This chapter is based on Kothari 2014a.
2 See the petition at http://therules.org/petition/sdg-open-letter.
3 See http://direct-democracy.geschichte-schweiz.ch; https://en.wikipedia.org/wiki/Swiss_Federal_Council.
4 An interesting version of this idea is proposed in Falk/Strauss (2000).
5 For an example, see Kothari 2014.
6 See Jharkhand Silk Textil & Handicraft Development Corporation: Creating Opportunity, Changing life, online at www.jharkhand.in (10/7/2017).
7 On People's Linguistic Survey of India, http://peopleslinguisticsurvey.org/Default.aspx; on Bhasha, www.bhasharesearch.org/.
8 See the webpage of the Deccan Development Society at www.ddsindia.com, accessed 20 February 2014; see also Levins 2008.

9 See the outcomes of the World Parks Congress in 2003, the 7th Conference of the Parties to the Convention on Biological Diversity in 2004, and World Conservation Congresses in 2008 and 2012; see also www.iccaconsortium.org for material on Indigenous Peoples and Local Community Conserved Territories and Areas (ICCAs).
10 For a few examples, see http://celdf.org/rights-of-nature-background.
11 See the "Alternatives Knowledge Center" at the website of Kalvaparish, online at http://kalpavriksh.org/index.php/alternatives/alternatives-knowledge-center/353-vikalp-sangam-coverage.
12 Note that here and subsequently, "national" is not necessarily equated to the "nation-state" but extends to peoples considering themselves nations, such as Canada's indigenous peoples or the ethnic communities in "plurinational" Bolivia.
13 See a list of such values in the Peoples' Sustainability Treaty on Radical Ecological Democracy, available at http://radicalecologicaldemocracy.wordpress.com; and an evolving list as part of a framework note emerging from the Vikalp Sangam (Alternatives Confluence) process, available at www.vikalpsangam.org/about/the-search-for-alternatives-key-aspects-and-principles-4th-draft.

References

Acosta, A. (2013). Extractivism and Neoextractivism: Two Sides of the Same Curse. In: M. Lang/D. Mokrani (eds.). *Beyond Development: Alternative Visions from Latin America*. Quito: Rosa Luxemburg Foundation/Amsterdam: Transnational Institute, 61–86.

Adams, W.M. /R. Aveling/D. Brockington/B. Dickson/J. Elliott/J. Hutton/D. Roe/B. Vira/W. Wolme. (2004). Biodiversity Conservation and the Eradication of Poverty. In: *Science* 306.5699, 1146–1149.

Alexander, S. (2014). Post-Growth Economics: A Paradigm Shift in Progress. *Post-carbon Pathways Working Paper Series* 2/14. Melbourne: Melbourne Sustainable Society Group, University of Melbourne. Online at www.postcarbonpathways.net.au/2014/02/07/post-growth-economics-a-paradigm-shift-in-progress.

Azzelini, D. (2013). The Communal State: Communal Councils, Communes, and Workplace Democracy. *NACLA Report on the Americas* (46.2), 25–30.

Bakshi, R. (2009). *Bazaars, Conversations and Freedom: For a Market Culture Beyond Greed and Fear*. New Delhi: Penguin.

Brockington, D. (2002). *Fortress Conservation: The Preservation of the Mkomazi Game Reserve*. Bloomington: Indiana University Press.

Credit Suisse's Global Wealth Databook (2014). Online at http://economics.uwo.ca/people/davies_docs/global-wealth-databook-2014-v2.pdf.

Dowie, M. (2009). *Conservation Refugees: The Hundred-Year Conflict between Global Conservation and Native Peoples*. Cambridge, MA: MIT Press.

Falk, R/A. Strauss (2000). On the Creation of a Global Peoples Assembly: Legitimacy and the Power of Popular Sovereignty. In: *Stanford Journal of International Law* 36.2 (Summer), 191–220.

Hasnat, S. (2005). Arvari Sansad: The Farmers' Parliament. In: *LEISA Magazine*, December. Online at www.agriculturesnetwork.org/magazines/global/practice-and-policy/arvari-sansad.

IPCCA/Indigenous Peoples Climate Change Assessment (2014). *United Nations University*. Online at http://archive.unu.edu/climate/activities/ipcca.html.

Jones, A./M. Pimbert/J. Jiggins (2011). *Virtuous Cycles: Valus, Systems and Sustainability*. London: IIED/IUCN CEESP.

Kalpavriksh (2013). *Globalisation in India: Impacts and Alternatives*. Pune: Kalpavriksh. Online at www.kalpavriksh.org/images/CLN/Globalisation%20Brochure.pdf.

Kapoor, R. (2007). Transforming Self and Society: Plural Paths to Human Emancipation. In: *Futures* 39, 475–486.

Kelly, M. (2012). *Owning Our Future: The Emerging Ownership Revolution*. San Francisco: Berrett-Koehler Publishers.

Korten, D.C. (2013). *Agenda for a New Economy: From Phantom Wealth to Real Wealth*. San Francisco: Berrett-Koehler.

Kothari, A. (2014). *Timbaktu: Very Much on the Map*. Pune/New Delhi: Kalpavriksh. Online at http://kalpavriksh.org/images/alternatives/TimbaktuCollectiveCasestudyreport2014_Apr2015.pdf.

Kothari, A. (2014a). Radical Ecological Democracy: A Path Forward for India and Beyond. In: *Great Transition Initiative*. Online at www.greattransition.org/publication/radical-ecological-democracy-a-path-forward-for-india-and-beyond.

Kothari, A. (2014b). Decoding Manifestos: What They Say About the Things that Really Matter. In: *India Together*, April 16. Online at http://indiatogether.org/comparison-of-congress-bjp-aap-manifestos-government.

Kothari, A. (2015a). A Flawed Agenda for Development. In: *The Hindu Business Line*, September 26.

Kothari, A. (2015b). The Language of Diversity. In: *India Together*, December. Online at www.vikalpsangam.org/article/the-language-of-diversity/#.VnpOlFR941I.

Kothari, A. (2015c). Pope's Encyclical: Is This the Push the World Needed? In: *India Together*, August. Online at http://indiatogether.org/articles/pope-s-2015-encyclical-op-ed.

Kothari, A./F. Demaria/A. Acosta (2014). Buen Vivir, Degrowth and Ecological Swaraj: Alternatives to Sustainable Development and the Green Economy. In: *Development* 57.3/4, 362–375.

Levins, R. (2008). *Talking About Trees: Science, Ecology and Agriculture in Cuba*. New Delhi: LeftWord.

Mutha, S./N. Pathak (2014). *Ecological Regeneration and Livelihood Security Through Forest Rights: Nayakheda, Maharashtra*. Pune/New Delhi: Kalpavriksh, Online at http://kalpavriksh.org/images/alternatives/CaseStudies/Nayakheda%20village_30April2014.pdf.

New Economics Foundation (2009). *National Accounts of Well-Being: Bringing Real Wealth onto the Balance sheet*. London: New Economics Foundation. Online at www.nationalaccountsofwellbeing.org.

Nickels, S./Furgal, C./The Communities of Ivujivik, Puvirnituq and Kangiqsujuaq/Kativik Regional Government – Environment Department. (2005). *Unikkaaqatigiit – Putting the Human Face on Climate Change: Perspectives from Nunavik*. Ottawa: Inuit Tapiriit Kanatami, Nasivvik Centre for Inuit Health and Changing Environments at Université Laval and the Ajunnginiq Centre at the National Aboriginal Health Organization.

Pathak Broome, N. (2014). Communitisation of Public Services in Nagaland – A Step Towards Creating Alternative Model of Delivering Public Services? Case Study Report for the Project. In: *Alternative Practices and Visions in India: Documentation, Networking, and Advocacy*. Pune/New Delhi: Kalpavriksh. Online at www.kalpavriksh.org/index.php/alternatives/alternatives-knowledge-center/351-sangam-case-studies.

Prada, R. (2013). Buen Vivir as a Model for State and Economy. In: M. Lang/D. Mokrani (eds.). *Beyond Development: Alternative Visions From Latin America*. Quito: Rosa Luxemburg Foundation/Amsterdam: Transnational Institute, 145–158.

Pulsford, I./G. Howling/R. Dunn/R. Crane. (2013). Great Eastern Ranges Initiative: A Continental-Scale Lifeline Connecting People and Nature. In: J. Fitzsimmons/I. Pulsford/G. Wescott (eds). *Linking Australian Landscapes: Lessons and Opportunities from Large-scale Conservation Networks*. Collingwood: CSIRO, 123–134.

262 *Ashish Kothari*

Raskin, P. (2012). Scenes from the Great Transition. In: *Solutions* 3.4, 11–17. Online at www.thesolutionsjournal.com/node/1140.

Rijnhout, L. U. de Zoysa/A. Kothari/H. Healy. (2014). *Towards a Global Agenda of Sustainability and Equity: Civil Society Engagement for the Future We Want.* Kenia: Unep Perspectives, Issue 12.

Rukmini, S. (2014). India's Staggering Wealth Gap in Five Charts. In: *The Hindu*, December 8. Online at www.thehindu.com/data/indias-staggering-wealth-gap-in-five-charts/article6672115.ece.

Shrivastava, A./A. Kothari (2013). *Churning the Earth: The Making of Global India.* New Delhi: Penguin.

Singh, S./F. Krausmann/S. Gingrich/H. Haberl/K.H. Erb/P. Lanz/J. Martinez-Alier/L. Temper. (2008). India's Biophysical Economy, 1961–2008: Sustainability in a National and Global Context. In: *Ecological Economics* 76, 60–69.

Tatpati, M. (ed., 2015). *Citizens' Report 2015: Community Forest Rights Under the Foret Rights Act.* Pune/New Delhi: Kalpavriksh, and Bhubaneshwar: Vasundhara, in collaboration with Oxfam India on behalf of Community Forest Rights Learning and Advocacy Process, online at: fra.org.in/document/CITIZENS' REPORT 2015 COMMUNITY FOREST RIGHTS UNDER THE FOREST RIGHTS ACT.pdf.

TEBTEBBA Foundation (2008). *Indicators Relevant for Indigenous Peoples: A Resource Book* Baguio, Philippines: TEBTEBBA Foundation. Online at http://ilcasia.files.wordpress.com/2010/09/indicators-resource-book1.pdf.

UNEP/ILO (2008). *Green Jobs: Towards Decent Work in a Sustainable, Low Carbon World.* Nairobi: United National Environment Programme and International Labour Office. Online at www.ilo.org/wcmsp5/groups/public/@ed_emp/@emp_ent/documents/publication/wcms_158727.pdf.

Worboys, G. et al. (2014). *Protected Area Governance and Management.* Canberra: ANU Press.

Index

Note: Page numbers in *italic* indicate a figure and page numbers in **bold** indicate a table on the corresponding page.

economic-ecological double crisis 241, 243

economic growth: direct producer-consumer linkages 255; employment relations and 132–134; finite world and 30; "good work" as impediment to 134–135; happiness and 165; India and 251. *See also* degrowth; growth

economic inequality 251

economics: diverse 79–80; ecological 78–79; employment and 159; of liberty 85; life and 77–80; morality and 88–89, 108–109; neoclassical 78; private property and 86–88; safari sector 233–234; sex and 181–182; steady-state economy 111–112; sustainability of 110–114; tied to ethics 88–89

economy of the common good 168

Ecuador 32–33

Ellul, Jacques 18–19

employment trap 158

engagement, for good life beyond growth 191–192

Enlightenment movement 17–18

Enlightenment naturalism 60–61

entreployee 205

entrepreneurial self 206

environmental psychology 190–192

ethical pluralism 40–41

ethics of resignation 186

existential resonance 49–50

experimentalism, democratic 248

Extension of the Domain of Struggle, The (Houellebecq) 183

extractivism 220–221, 223

Fable of the Bees (Mandeville) 21

fear 51

Felber, Christian 168

félicité 18

felicity 23–24

felicity index 23

Ferguson, James 232

Fichte, Johann Gottlieb 61

financialisation 102

flexibilisation 136, 138

flexible capitalism 101–103

flexible working hours 136–137

Fordism 183

Fordist growth society 99–101

forest-animal-day 172

freedom, distinguishing from animals 61–62

free wage workers 97–98

frugal abundance 22

functional dimension of dividualisation 102

Gadrey, J. 22

Galindo, Alberto Flores 36

gender equality 182

Genesis 58

Genovesi, Antonio 24

genuine progress indicator 22–23

German Trade Union Confederation 139n3

Giddens, Antony 179

global capitalism 86

Global Ecovillage Network 192

Goethe 56

Goodin, R. 142

good life/good living: books as central axes of 45; country cluster and dimensions *222*, **225–227**; creating emancipatory project 37; definition of 29; dimensions and indicators of **218**, 219; fundamental axes of 33–34; indicators 220–221; multi-scale implications of 35–36; music as central axes of 45; non-capitalist communal roots of 34; in the plural 32; preconditions for 41; principal component analysis **221**; realised utopia 31–33; recovery of utopias and 36–37; resonance conception of 46–50; social inclusion 217; as way of life 33. *See also* prosperity; well-being

"good work": as challenge for union strategies 137–138; economic growth and 132–134; as historical exception to economic growth 134–135; identifying normative criteria 137; as impediment to economic recovery 134–135; liberal consensus and 134

grassroots democratic units 252–253

grassroots mobilisation for radical ecological democracy 258–259

Great Chain of Being 59

Great Eastern Ranges Initiative 253–254

Great Transformation 246

Green, T.H. 124

green growth 110–111, 142, 258

grey labour market 137–138

gross domestic product 142, 143–144

gross national happiness (GNH) 148–150

growth: argument against 141–145; Aristotle and 84; capitalist paradigm of 119; climate change and 141–142; decommodification and 143–144; in GDP 142; global justice and inequality